Teaching Tourism

ELGAR GUIDES TO TEACHING

The Elgar Guides to Teaching series provides a variety of resources for instructors looking for new ways to engage students. Each volume provides a unique set of materials and insights that will help both new and seasoned teachers expand their toolbox in order to teach more effectively. Titles include selections of methods, exercises, games and teaching philosophies suitable for the particular subject featured. Each volume is authored or edited by a seasoned professor. Edited volumes comprise contributions from both established instructors and newer faculty who offer fresh takes on their fields of study.

Titles in the series include:

Teaching Cultural Economics
Edited by Trine Bille, Anna Mignosa and Ruth Towse

Teaching Nonprofit Management
Edited by Karabi C. Bezboruah and Heather Carpenter

Teaching the Essentials of Law and Economics
Antony W. Dnes

Teaching Strategic Management
A Hands-on Guide to Teaching Success
Sabine Baumann

Teaching Urban and Regional Planning
Innovative Pedagogies in Practice
Edited by Andrea I. Frank and Artur da Rosa Pires

Teaching Entrepreneurship, Volume Two
A Practice-Based Approach
Edited by Heidi M. Neck, Candida G. Brush and Patricia G. Greene

Teaching Environmental Impact Assessment
Angus Morrison-Saunders and Jenny Pope

Teaching Research Methods in Political Science
Edited by Jeffrey L. Bernstein

Teaching International Relations
Edited by James M. Scott, Ralph G. Carter, Brandy Jolliff Scott and Jeffrey S. Lantis

Teaching Marketing
Edited by Ross Brennan and Lynn Vos

Teaching Tourism
Innovative, Values-based Learning Experiences for Transformative Practices
Edited by Johan Edelheim, Marion Joppe and Joan Flaherty

Teaching Tourism

Innovative, Values-based Learning Experiences for
Transformative Practices

Edited by

Johan Edelheim

*PhD, Professor, Graduate School of International Media, Communication
and Tourism Studies, Hokkaido University, Japan*

Marion Joppe

*PhD, Professor, School of Hospitality, Food and Tourism Management,
University of Guelph, Canada*

Joan Flaherty

*MA, MSc, Associate Professor Emerita, School of Hospitality, Food and
Tourism Management, University of Guelph, Canada*

ELGAR GUIDES TO TEACHING

Cheltenham, UK • Northampton, MA, USA

Cover image: Photo by Jamie Ginsberg on Unsplash.
Illustrations by Minori Morioka.

Published by
Edward Elgar Publishing Limited
The Lypiatts
15 Lansdown Road
Cheltenham
Glos GL50 2JA
UK

Edward Elgar Publishing, Inc.
William Pratt House
9 Dewey Court
Northampton
Massachusetts 01060
USA

Paperback edition 2022

A catalogue record for this book
is available from the British Library

Library of Congress Control Number: 2022931137

This book is available electronically in the **Elgar**online
Geography, Planning and Tourism subject collection
http://dx.doi.org/10.4337/9781800374560

ISBN 978 1 80037 455 3 (cased)
ISBN 978 1 80037 456 0 (eBook)
ISBN 978 1 0353 0182 9 (paperback)
Printed and bound by CPI Group (UK) Ltd, Croydon, CR0 4YY

This book is dedicated to all those from whom we have learned throughout our lives and who have shaped our values and worldview. Many of them would never have seen themselves as teachers; indeed, many of them sat in our classrooms as our students. But their words and actions have influenced who we are today. They are the reason we are concerned about the state of the world, not so much for our own sake but rather for the sake of the younger generations and those yet to come. Our children and grandchildren will be left with the results of what our generation, and those before us, have created. Therefore, when writing about alternative worlds and worldviews, we hope that this critical consciousness can act as an organism in a compost, breaking down the waste from before and helping to recreate it for an enriched future that nurtures all life, both human and non-human.

Johan Edelheim, Marion Joppe and Joan Flaherty

Contents

Figures

Contributors

Mette Simonsen Abildgaard: My research often involves auditory technologies as they are used in everyday life and in teaching. I like to incorporate elements of auditory learning, either through sound examples or as exercises with sound material. Switching from primarily visual texts and slides to sounds can help students change to another mode of sensing – from a more distributed attention to concentrated listening. In fact, listening to a foreign environment or a disarming tone of voice often carries with it surprises that can completely change a classroom's atmosphere.

Barkathunnisha Abu Bakar: The COVID-19 pandemic has presented the space and pace in my teaching and learning to reflect on the impact tourism has on our planet and its potential as a world-making force. The spiritual pedagogical approach that I use guides my conversations with my students. We have meaningful dialogues on the mutual interdependency of tourism and the environment, the importance of values and ethics in our industry post COVID and the need to nurture a deep sense of compassion, personal responsibility and an inner consciousness in all of us for the reconciliation of the ecological and social worlds.

Linda Armano: As an anthropologist and Marie Curie Fellow, my research spans from the anthropology of mining to luxury branding to the interdisciplinary analysis between anthropology and management of intangible property (folk traditions, use of places) useful to develop tourism proposals. Collaborating with international colleagues, most notably Prof. Eric Zvaniga, I provide support for the collection of qualitative data of ethnographic matrixes, which can be used in our courses, allowing students to design future tourism scenarios. Student creativity is my favourite grade item as it is also useful to create ad hoc data collection methodologies for each project.

Stefanie Benjamin: Exposing students to new experiences, epistemologies and intellectual frameworks is one of the most valuable functions of education. A resulting awareness of different views ultimately provides students with a greater understanding of the world's complex web of humanity and, hopefully, inspires a quest for determining their own place in it. I embrace humour to show that sometimes we must laugh at ourselves to understand our underlying communalities. We learn to use laughter as a powerful tool to help lighten sensitive subjects, learn to be empathetic and present, and realise we are not alone – potentially sharing similar challenges and barriers.

Karla A. Boluk: I am a kinesthetic learner. As such, I prefer engaging as many of my senses as possible to participate in and support my learning. Learning outside of the conventional classroom is typically my preference. Any skill I have acquired over the years, from skiing and cycling to critical thinking, has been a consequence of practice, reflection and engaging with others.

Elin Bommenel: Learning is expanding not only your knowledge but also expanding who you are. I like constructing knowledge with my students. When they take the lead, they are powerful builders of new understandings. I like giving students clear boundaries of the direction we need to expand our knowledge in. I like laying out the tools and trying them together. I like presenting them with real problems I struggle with. The best days of my teaching are the ones where the students construct new landscapes within the boundaries, give the tools new uses and solve problems in ways I would never have thought of. On days like that I go home not only more knowledgeable but also a slightly different person.

Samantha Bouwer: Born in the UK, I have over 25 years' experience in the field of leisure, tourism and hospitality education and skills development, both in the UK and in South Africa. My doctoral studies centred upon developing a values-based ecotourism management curriculum. I am currently a Tourism Management lecturer at the Tshwane University of Technology. My philosophy on learning is simple: "Involve me and I learn" (Benjamin Franklin). I embrace a holistic approach to learning, which includes the fostering of appropriate behaviours and values in learners. My experience has taught me the importance of creating a learning environment that promotes learner individuality and creativity.

Blanca A. Camargo: I am a Full Professor of Tourism in the Business School at Universidad de Monterrey, Mexico. Originally from Colombia, I received my doctoral degree from Texas A&M University, and my research is oriented towards sustainable tourism with a focus on ethics and justice in tourism development, marketing and management. My teaching philosophy is one of student engagement, critical analysis and knowledge co-creation for sustainability in hospitality and tourism. I will learn from you as you will learn from me, I will support your research ideas and we both will seek to have an impact on our surroundings.

Helene Balslev Clausen: As an anthropologist I am passionate about understanding the relations of power that constitute and restructure our world. It is not enough just to describe or map connections. Essential to my research and teaching is a critical approach to sustainability transitions and the intertwining with technologies. So how do we confront the economic, social, political and institutional challenges that drive necessary change? My engagement is to generate new knowledge on ways in which master's students experience and learn, grappling with real-world societal challenges. I draw upon a range of methods across humanities and social and political sciences, such as study trips, innovative and participatory processes, and activism.

Alexandra Coghlan: I am an Associate Professor in Sustainable Tourism at Griffith University, with a particular focus on sustainable behaviour change through building eco-literacy. Rather than developing broad, content-filled courses, my approach to teaching is to focus on depth of understanding and fostering students' ability to identify and work with concepts in practice, always asking the question "What does that look like?" A maximum of three ethically related threshold concepts that stay with students in the long term is far more beneficial to the world as a whole than a curriculum full of theoretical content.

Émilie Crossley: In my role with Capable NZ in New Zealand, I mentored postgraduate professional practice learners from diverse backgrounds and professional fields. Working closely with these learners showed me the transformative potential of learning that is ascribed personal meaning, draws on life experience and is framed as a catalyst for strengthening professional identity. I have found that there are enormous benefits to engaging with higher education later in life, in which learning is informed and enriched by a wealth of professional experience.

Jonathon Day: I am an Associate Professor in Purdue's School of Hospitality and Tourism Management with over 25 years' experience in tourism management. An award-winning marketer, I have worked with destinations marketing organisations in Australia, New Zealand and the Americas. In recent years, my work has focused on sustainable tourism, responsible travel and how tourism can be used to not only enrich travellers but support destination communities. Some of my favourite teaching experiences take place on study-abroad programmes where students can immerse themselves in new cultures and new experiences. I particularly enjoy helping students to be mindful during their travels and reflect on the meaning of their experiences. Whether in a village in Nepal, the outback of Australia or the classroom, I like to help students "connect the dots" between theory and the real world.

Johan Edelheim: I am curious by nature, always excited to learn more about fields new to me. These moves into new fields have shown me how learning is a constant cycle, going from unconscious incompetence via conscious incompetence and conscious competence to an unconscious competence before I again do not know what I do not know. I learn, I think, as much from my students as they from me. We explore and discuss topics together, and it is often through off-hand and unexpected questions about familiar concepts that my greatest revelations happen. Japan, my current home, is the eighth country I have lived in. These moves have taught me how culturally specific all values are, a realisation I try to remember every time I come across a practice or custom I cannot understand.

Deborah Edwards: I am an Associate Professor with the Business School, University of Technology Sydney. I have an industry background and have published inter alia on sustainability in tourism, business events and visitor experiences. As an active and visual learner, I need to be involved in the learning activity or process – I can get very excited. Talk to me for too long and I might go to sleep. I like to have individual discussions with students because this enables me to understand their knowledge gaps. Students have taught me that they can have a boundless capacity for innovation and creativity.

Richard Ek: Learning is an existential endeavour, and thus all about our understanding of the world, our understanding of our knowledge about the world and our moral and ethical standpoints in that world. Pedagogic is its institutional expression, but its content is philosophical. As a geographer, for me learning as existential endeavour is always already spatio-temporal and thus a constant but spatially dispersed process. I learn the most from students in the spaces-in-between; for instance, in a break when I talked about spicy noodles with an Estonian student. You get a just-a-few-seconds-long insight into their existence when you least expect it.

Stephen Fairbrass: With an academic background in Economics and Development Studies, I worked in education in the UK for some 30 years, as a teacher in schools, as a project co-ordinator for an educational non-governmental organisation and finally as a teacher educator, preparing postgraduate students for a teaching career. My ambition was always to encourage students to consider how decisions are made in global society, and to reflect on how, through their own agency as consumer, producer and citizen, they could impact the decision-making process, hopefully for the better. In my twilight years I have taken up a new career, and I now work as a Ranger in the UK's Broads National Park, taking care of the park and its tourist visitors.

Joan Flaherty: Here are three lessons I have learned from my students. Every student has something to contribute, although their contribution might not come in the form that I had expected. It is best not to grip too tightly onto "the right answer"; the world is complicated, full of unexpected nuance that might completely justify a change of position. And the most successful teaching/learning experiences happen when I walk alongside the students as a learner rather than always positioning myself at the head of the line as their "teacher". In other words, my students have taught me some key lessons contained in *Teaching Tourism* about the value of diversity, open-mindedness and humility.

Joanne Paulette Gellatly: My 30 years of international managerial experience in hospitality and tourism in every one of its major sectors allows me to draw on many concrete examples to highlight various aspects of theory and practice. These examples bring material to life, clarifying it for my internationally diverse students. Real-world examples and a commitment to teamwork that allows students to construct ideas by negotiating meaning with others are the hallmarks of my teaching approach. Critical thinking and problem-solving for common goals are my personal mantras to live by.

Brynhild Granås: I work as an Associate Professor in the Department of Tourism and Northern Studies, UiT The Arctic University of Norway. I think of teaching as a nexus in my life as a learning human being. After many years of teaching international student groups, I have come to see the students as mentors who connect me to wider geographies and histories of tourism worlds and human livelihoods.

Jaume Guia: I like experiential learning through fieldwork, where the students are given and take autonomy and responsibility for their own learning paths and perform observation, inquiry, reflection, discussion and diffraction. This pedagogical approach is preceded by extensive search of information about the visited field and relevant academic articles, and is followed by teamwork discussions and assignments, and one-to-one tutorials. Here, in a safe environment, students learn to be creative and produce difference, instead of repeating sameness; to be collaborative instead of competitive; to be attuned to unperceived injustices; and to understand what political responsibility means and how to put it into practice.

Sisko Häikiö: Multicultural groups of tourism students are the source of my creativity and motivation in teaching. I have been teaching Finnish and German languages and Intercultural Communication to international students at Lapland University of Applied Sciences for over ten years. My mission is to guide the students to see the world through different eyes; to look for similarity and respect diversity. The students' intercultural experiences, shared and reflected in class discussions, empower both individuals and the whole group. Learning situations outdoors sparkle the learning atmosphere, fostering mutual connections and student engagement. Hence, my most memorable learning situations have been outdoors with international students.

Emily Höckert: During the past years, I have explored the idea of hospitable pedagogies, wondering how different kinds of hosts and guests share and receive knowledge in tourism settings. My journey has been guided by Emmanuel Levinas' writings on ethical subjectivity that underline our responsibility to welcome and care for otherness and the other. This means, in line with critical pedagogy, embracing the possibilities of mutual (un)learning where the roles of storytellers, teachers and learners are constantly changing.

Maria Huhmarniemi: I am a curious person who loves new experiments, nature and culture. I study and learn by making socially engaged art, crafting and dialogical interventions. Interested in enhancing sustainability through creativity, interculturalism and education, I make political art and develop arts-based methods for tourism, environmental education and social work. My focus is the Arctic region, where I work as an artist and a lecturer at the University of Lapland, Faculty of Art and Design.

Tazim Jamal: I am Professor in the Department of Recreation, Park and Tourism Sciences at Texas A&M University. Over the years, my students and I have grappled with the notion of "sustainability" in tourism and how to study this phenomenon richly and critically. Together, we are striving to understand important principles of justice and ethics (including equity, diversity, recognition and democracy) that can help inform just and responsible tourism practice. My most recent book, *Justice and Ethics in Tourism* (Routledge, 2019), contains cases written by my current and former students as well as other researchers from around the world.

Gunnar Thór Jóhannesson: Working as a Professor in Tourism at the University of Iceland Faculty of Life and Environmental Sciences, I like listening to and learning from stories and dialogues. In my research I seek to trace different kinds of storylines, spanning the human and more-than-human with various success; and, in that sense, it is the most joyful kind of a learning process.

Marion Joppe: As a Tourism Professor at the University of Guelph, I often draw on my extensive private and public sector experience in financial institutions, tour operations, consulting groups and government to help students understand our complex and dynamic tourism system. I aim to engage my students to think about global geopolitics and political ideologies, and how these shape every aspect of this sector and determine government responses to wicked problems. Understanding the interrelatedness of all these factors with tourism allows students to become more open-minded global citizens and prepares them to become "leaders for a sustainable world", reinforcing our business school's motto.

Ece Kaya: I am an Education Focused Lecturer with an interdisciplinary background at the University of Technology Sydney Business School's Management Department. My research interests involve digital applications in teaching and learning practices, improvement of student engagement in the online teaching and learning space, urban tourism, placemaking and creative space, industrial heritage and revitalisation of industrial spaces. I am an active learner who enjoys collaboration, hands-on and creative activities, and discussions involving exchanges of thoughts and ideas with the purpose of developing opinions and understanding concepts. I am passionate about making my classes engaging and interactive so my students can also become active learners.

Outi Kugapi: I have been focusing on autoethnographic methodologies, researching handicraft tourism. Researching the tourist experience by being a handicraft tourist and enthusiast myself, I find the best way of creating knowledge is through examining my own and other participants' experiences. In terms of my teaching/learning approach, I am a more tactile and kinetic learner. In other words, I learn best if I am doing something else at the same time. Most of the time, that "something" is knitting, but sometimes even holding a pen works. This is something I try to include in my teaching as well. Handicrafts are part of who I am – as a researcher, a teacher and a person.

Tanja Lešnik Štuhec: Working with students can offer teachers an unencumbered perspective on issues, which they often only roughly address with tourism industry employees. Gaining a fresh perspective on challenges distances us from professional deformation and provides a broader insight into the problem. Consequently, working in parallel with students and the tourism industry on rural development through tourism becomes all the more interesting and effective. It facilitates raising awareness of the importance of short supply chains and collective brands as tools for rural development in recognised green tourist destinations, which are also my profession and life mission.

Monika Lüthje: My preferred learning style is conducting research. As a social constructionist interested in materiality, participatory approaches and practices, I see learning and knowledge as socio-material. In general, the aim of my courses is that, by various means, the students learn not only from me but from each other – and I learn from them.

Xavier Michel: In my teaching approach, I focus on the learners' own memories and opinions to illustrate theories. This method allows learners to become familiar with academic ideas, and also empowers them to speak and consider the value of their remarks. I find outdoor settings work well here, as we can take advantage of the surrounding landscape to communicate either in one large group or in paired discussions. The "outdoor classroom" also provides an appropriate setting for personal reflection.

Maggie C. Miller: Student-centred, I work hard to maintain an inclusive, dialogical and immersive tourism classroom at Swansea University. As an adventurer, immersion has always been important to me. When your mind and body are engaged, you learn – you apprehend knowledge differently. In adventure pursuits this may be more obvious as one traverses a slick granite slab while climbing. Yet learning is also about navigating multiple terrains, facilitated by equipment and techniques collected along the way. It is in these immersive instances where I feel we learn the most about our disciplines, the world and ourselves.

Minori Morioka: My doctoral studies in the Faculty of Education at Hokkaido University focused on Japanese language education and support for people living and working in the community. As a student, I did internships in several foreign countries to become a language teacher. Now I teach Japanese to international students and technical intern trainees in Japan. For me, the most striking immersion education scene occurred in the United States, where I learned how practically everything can be taught in various ways, such as through singing, dancing, painting, manga and gesturing. Now I make great use of these methods in my own teaching.

Nick Naumov: My teaching and learning approach is student-centred and knowledge-focused. I believe that learners should be able to construct their own knowledge, challenge their way of thinking and find new approaches to learning. In that sense, our focus as educators is to provide more meaningful ways to learn and facilitate an environment that enables them to be active, critical and engaged. I am passionate about new and more participatory forms of teaching, such as problem-based learning and active-blended learning, as they reflect the changing nature of our learners and their transition from passive learners to more active, creative and critical individuals.

Brendan Paddison: I teach across a range of tourism-related subjects, including responsible tourism, destination management, and social and political perspectives in tourism. I am a visual and auditory learner, with my preferred learning style a combination of visual media, conversation and listening. My students continue to inspire me and have taught me to become more reflexive. I am motivated and enthused by their growing activism, strong sense of social justice and political engagement. They continue to challenge the status quo and refuse to accept irresponsible economic, social and political practices and behaviours.

Miranda Peterson: In my experience with facilitating climate action, I have found that solely focusing on global issues through a problem-based approach does not provide students with problem-solving experience or even the hope that these issues can be solved. When we do not take time to foster hope and allow students to imagine a better world, it is no wonder that they are left tired, hopeless and apathetic. In the end, we leave them with just enough knowledge and energy to be aware of a dark reality but unable to do anything about it.

Giang T. Phi: My teaching approach is strongly connected to my research areas in the field of innovation, sustainability and social entrepreneurship. I have developed a framework for teaching, which seeks to develop three major areas of attributes and competencies for students: the "professional core", the "entrepreneurial core" and the "social core". My role as a teacher is thus to assist students in discovering how they can contribute to make this world a better place through their chosen profession. This has been achieved by applying a wide range of active learning pedagogies (for example, problem-based learning, game-based learning, design-based learning, experiential learning and values-based learning), which encourage students to interact with the learning materials and with the teacher and industry partners both inside and outside the classroom.

Outi Rantala: As Associate Professor of Responsible Arctic Tourism at the University of Lapland, I enjoy listening to lectures where the lecturer develops carefully a critical idea, step by step, engaging the audience into the thinking process – and I can lean back in my seat, relax and write notes in my notebook. However, I prefer to learn by doing, by spending time in the field – engaging with the rhythms of nature.

Stuart Reid: I think learning is part of living, so we learn all the time. The great thing about learning is that it is transformative – it changes us and what we do. To me, teaching is about nurturing learning. My favourite thing about teaching is when learning happens, those "ah ha" moments when new vistas emerge. It is like a new energy is created – an energy of new possibilities! I often learn from my students, and I think that is one of the best things about teaching. So the most important lesson I have learned from my students is that we all learn together!

Carina Ren: Working within the theoretical realm of relational materialism, I think of the way that we know and learn about tourism as a collaborative achievement enacted through the ongoing work of the human as well as the non-human actors that make up tourism. In order to experiment with alternative ways of knowing tourism, I am dedicated to exploring it in "the midst of things" and together with others: students, fellow researchers, practitioners and all of the more-than-human actors in and around tourism.

Bradley Rink: I enjoy teaching because I love to learn. The most rewarding teaching and learning experiences for me are when I gain new insights from my students. Teaching allows me to bridge the theory–practice divide, to challenge my theoretical "expertise" and to build knowledge from a range of tourism experiences, perspectives and subjectivities. The most important lesson learned from my students is to always consider multiple perspectives on any tourism (or other) phenomenon. Engaging students in the process of collecting, analysing and sharing knowledge thus yields new insights for the entire class – myself included.

Sarah Ripper: I am a social animator working within the intersection of arts, community development, education, well-being and business. My work is varied (for example, from the United Nations in East Timor to the largest citizen journalism project in Asia, India: Unheard) yet always grounded in the intention of connection and innovation. My educational approach is underpinned by learning and teaching as a process of embodiment, enthusiasm and new possibilities. I view education as a growth journey with the potential to encapsulate the mind, heart and entire being to explore and experience diversity and embrace the threads of connection that unite all of life.

Kathleen Rodenburg: I am passionate about deep-dive learning. Nothing beats the feeling and sense of accomplishment that comes from solving a challenging real-world problem. These challenges provide wonderful catalysts for transformational learning moments. My years of business and industry experience in senior management positions at a Tier I organisation inform me of how critical it is to give students the opportunity to apply the central concepts and models from theory to a real business environment. Not only for their success, but for our success in building leaders for a sustainable future. For me, it is Experiential Learning Theory all the way!

Sudipta Kiran Sarkar: I am a Senior Lecturer in Tourism Management at Anglia Ruskin University, Cambridge, UK. I have tried to cultivate soft and experiential skills among students by exposing them to situations and cases both in classroom and outdoor settings. While teaching areas of tourism professional activity, I have endeavoured to inculcate environmental learning skills and create pedagogical value by engaging students in nature-based study trips of moderate difficulty levels. I have often noticed in my teaching that students, if provided with fewer structured and predetermined objectives, tend to move the critical and conceptual aspects relating to a topic in an interesting direction.

Chiaki Shimoyasuba: I am a former professor at the Center for Advanced Tourism Studies, Hokkaido University. My specialties are ecotourism, human ecological planning and cultural anthropology in Africa. Born in 1956 in Osaka, Japan, I earned my PhD in Arts and Culture. I have studied by not only reading books but also by carrying out fieldwork. Specifically, I learned about biodiversity and cultural and social commonality through the field-survey of Indigenous culture in Cameroon in Central Africa. I am now a director of a non-profit-organisation that promotes walking tourism as one tool of social and regional sustainable development.

Kaarina Tervo-Kankare: I am a Senior Lecturer in Tourism Geography at the University of Oulu. I believe that for learning to happen, there needs to be interaction, and that we constantly learn from our surrounding environments, both natural and human. My favourite methods of learning are by doing and by observing. The most rewarding moments are when theory and practice complement each other and produce something completely new.

Maja Turnšek: As an educator, I believe strongly in the power of mentoring: we learn the most when we are lucky enough to be given a demanding but encouraging mentor. In a world that will require our students to show an extreme degree of flexibility and passion, we as mentors must also step up to the challenge. Here I come to follow Robinson (*The Element: How Finding Your Passion Changes Everything*, Penguin, 2003), who helped me to understand that we are true mentors only when we aid students in identifying their passions, encourage their interests, smooth their paths and push them to make the most of their capabilities.

Minna Väyrynen: In my work as a teacher of languages and Intercultural Communication, I have the privilege of encountering students from various cultural backgrounds and using Finnish, English and Swedish in my daily communication with them. While observing cultural variety in both behaviour and communication is interesting, still the most valuable lesson I have learned from my students is the understanding of the universal human qualities we all share.

Preface

Johan Edelheim, Marion Joppe and Joan Flaherty

As a hallmark activity of the postmodern world, tourism plays a significant role in shaping our world and the people who live in it. At the time of writing *Teaching Tourism*, the COVID-19 pandemic is raging, and while it has brought the world of travel to a near standstill globally, this hiatus also presents a unique opportunity for all tourism stakeholders, and especially educators, to think critically about the dominant tourism discourses and structures and to recalibrate the role of tourism as a world-making transformative force (Sheldon, 2020). This transformation requires that we guide our students, who are our future practitioners, in their engagement with the human and non-human world from an ethical, values-based perspective and – more importantly – with a solid moral conscience (Caton, 2012). An awakening of lived values and consciousness (Edelheim, 2020; Sheldon, 2020) is needed for tourism and tourism education to be transformative. What is relevant in this period is an educational paradigm that integrates ethics, values and an inner consciousness in learners. In the cautionary words of Jamal and Camargo (2018, p. 207):

> Lest we forget our own values and positionality in the politics of tourism research, metrics and promotions interests, an ethical responsibility lies upon us here too. What we as researchers believe about tourism, its goals, operations and intended outcomes, how it ought to be governed, our personal and political values, and the way these shape our research also need to be critically analyzed, made explicit and open to be challenged. What do we choose to include/exclude in our (always partial) research lens and methodologies, based on our theoretical influences, sociocultural and political values?

In writing this book we address the teaching of tourism at different levels of the educational path and for all fields of science that tourism is taught within and through. Teaching tourism, therefore, is an ambitious undertaking, made more so by the fact that tourism is not a "thing" or "field" easily delineated, with neatly defined borders. Consequently, depending on the particular teacher or classroom, tourism might be compared to modernity in action, connected to internationalisation, discussed in terms of globalisation as well as (neo)-colonialism or examined from an impossibly wide range of scientific angles. In other words, the approaches to teaching tourism are as diverse as the societies that produce and host it.

For an educator, being able to choose from, and navigate through, these diverse approaches is intellectually exhilarating. However, it can also be overwhelming. And, more importantly, it can leave both teacher and student feeling lost in a landscape of unlimited learning possibilities without a compass to guide them.

At the risk of sounding presumptuous, this book is our attempt to provide that compass. It focuses on teaching *values-based* tourism, an approach that acknowledges and examines the integral role of values in all aspects of tourism. The reason for this focus is straightforward: since values shape our beliefs and guide our behaviours, they also determine our tourism policies, their implementation and their impacts. Because tourism is worldwide, this process – which starts with a value-shaped thought – affects lives in every corner of the world. We need to pay attention to values. In a world dominated by corporatist economic interests that prioritise efficiency, growth and profit, the task before us is not an easy one. And the first step begins in the classroom: regardless of the specific subject matter, we believe that our courses must reflect, implicitly or explicitly, a worldview that values biocentricism and community well-being above individualism.

It has been clear for some time that we are destroying the Earth through our actions and lifestyles, and despite our well-intentioned efforts to be environmentally responsible, most of us have contributed further to the problem by deepening our carbon footprint. Initially because we did not know about our carbon footprint, and later because we tried to silence our conscious mind (Gössling et al., 2019). This book and our work as value-conscious academics are efforts to give voice to that silence, ensuring that past patterns and mistakes not be repeated.

We recognise, however, that the value of humans has been elevated to such a degree in today's world that biocentricism can be controversial in practice, if not in theory. Unless we extend inherent value to all living things and appreciate more systematically the importance of non-living elements of the environment, the future of humans of this planet of ours risks being quite dismal. This has long been core to Indigenous worldviews but is only now slowly being understood by mainstream academia and society. As Indigenous populations assert their rights to their culture and recognition of ancient names – be it Uluru (Ayers Rock) in Australia, Sagarmatha (Mt Everest) in Nepal or Aotearoa (New Zealand) – dominant cultures are being forced to re-evaluate their approaches and assumptions about the world and the reality they have created.

The applied chapters in this book examine ten forms of values that have a bearing on how tourism learning is facilitated, or how the values could be facilitated in different settings. The first five are what we have called lived values. These are values that shape the way society rationalises actions and visions on a daily basis. The departments, schools, colleges and universities each of us work at/for are organised according to these lived values. This organisation is either overtly based on scientific positionality, or somewhat covertly through funding models, metrics, tenure or work casualisation, performance indicators, prescribed curricula, advisory boards, and the like. We call the five latter values aspirational, in that they reflect universal values aimed at transforming tourism into a force for good.

It is important to emphasise that we do not use the term "values" as a synonym for "ethics" in this book. Ethics is one aspect of values, but *Teaching Tourism* highlights how there are always certain lived values as well as aspirational ones that shape the way tourism is imagined and the different ways in which it is taught.

A book on teaching tourism could easily fall into one of several different categories of the Scholarship of Teaching and Learning (SoTL) books available: a "cookbook" serving up recipes of different teaching/learning strategies and techniques; a "factbook" identifying what needs to be taught according to different schools of thought and their proponents; a "travel guidebook" explaining various teaching approaches, depending on the place or the setting; or a "policy report" providing a meta-perspective of teaching, related theories and the importance of higher education in addressing "real-world" needs and demands.

Each of these options is valuable in its own right, but this book extends to a further level by posing one central question: what is our purpose as tourism educators? Identifying that purpose is important, because it is the driving force of our becoming reflective teachers who are interested in all that informs our teaching, including our research and our service to our communities. By always asking "why" as we figure out how to develop and deliver values-based teaching in tourism, we are also reminded of our purpose.

It is always challenging to critically analyse the premises one works by. This kind of analysis carries with it the danger of undermining one's message, credibility and rationale – which is probably why reflexivity is not self-evident in all academic literature. However, when examining "lived values" (for example, Chapters 3–7 on the political, ecological, social, cultural and economic premises of values), we must also reflect in a metacognitive way on the values this book is built on. For example, the latter part of the book refers to what we have called "aspirational values".

It should be acknowledged that these aspirational values were originally identified by a relatively small and culturally homogenous group of people (Padurean and Maggi, 2011). Apart from being thought leaders and respected tourism academics, most were also Caucasian, well-educated, middle-class, Anglophone individuals. The authors of this book also fall within this culturally homogenous group of people, and indeed were part of the development of the aspirational values at different stages. However, by inviting a large number of diverse scholars from different parts of the world to contribute to these pages, we have attempted to broaden our lens and ensure relevancy across cultures and development stages.

The process of creating the aspirational values was a dynamic group effort over several years, with publications and meetings leading to the final result (Sheldon et al., 2011). The aspirational values are not proven to be incorrect by any research, but therein lies the challenge. Epistemology is negotiated in groups of experts that often inhabit the same paradigm and, more importantly, share ontological conceptions of reality. This is the reason we start this book by overtly creating both a didactic and an axiological foundation: we try to be conscious of the values we live by, and we try to include a multitude of views and voices in illustrating how these values might take shape.

But why turn to philosophy and to a complex philosophical concept like axiology when writing a book on teaching and tourism? Both matters are concrete and practical, embodied and applied, part of the reality we inhabit and our daily lives, so does philosophy not just make all of this terribly theoretical and convoluted? Well, perhaps, if we would see either teaching or tourism as simply actions devoid of other meanings than their own being. But we are sure that you will agree this is not the case. Therefore, we would like to use philosophy in its original meaning: *philo sophia*, "the love for wisdom". Philosophy is thus a practical matter, something all of us, as thinking individuals, are striving for – wisdom in the sense of "getting it right", whatever "it" is and however "getting" is performed.

This is where we see the need to question the status quo: many of the contributions in this book exemplify inequalities or structural hurdles of the tourism phenomenon, and they show how learners are given tools to unravel lived values and empathise with alternatives. Part of this comes from the humility we as learning facilitators need to have, to accept that we are no longer in a position where all knowledge stems from us. Rather, we are mentors, guides and learners alongside our students on this educational path, raising questions and providing support that help our students find their own answers. By equipping students with strategies that allow them to stay multiliterate in a changing society, we are also giving them keys to be the agents of transformation that they all have the opportunity to be and, as educated global citizens, should be assuming.

The full name of this book, *Teaching Tourism: Innovative, Values-based Learning Experiences for Transformative Practices*, is chosen with care as each word in the title contains clues of what the book aims to deliver. Teaching tourism is the premise we start from, and we acknowledge above that this can take a myriad of forms through a multitude of paradigms. "Innovative" is a fashionable word, and it is happily used by authors who want to highlight that their texts are new – but innovation is not just about novelty. It is equally about radical developments that enhance practices (Brooker and Joppe, 2014). The first innovative aspect of this book is that it emphasises the importance of moving beyond the classroom, into the broader community and into the learners' hearts as well as their minds. All chapters and contributions are therefore aimed at the transformational capacities inherent in learning. The innovative aspect of the book continues in grounding this practice in axiology as its philosophical underpinning to put the emphasis on values (see Chapter 2). That we consider everything to be values-based is a recurring theme throughout the book.

All the chapters, and many of the contributions, are co-authored. This was a deliberate decision as all texts have been developed in an iterative and incremental fashion between different contributors. We are all shaped by the values we live through, and we are often blind to both their roots and their consequences, unless we reflect on them in the light of other people's values. But to open oneself up to comments and critique by others is always hard because it might prove that something we have believed in might not be supported by a strong foundation. As Irshad Manji says in a conversation with Nam Kiwanuka: "We take disagreement as a source to be offended. [However, to] hear, you must first be willing to listen" (Kiwanuka, 2019). It has therefore been a great privilege to work with all the contributors of this book, as each person has been sent drafts of all chapters connected to their own contributions and been invited to comment on them.

We acknowledge that many blind spots were found in this process, and many important nuances have been added to the chapters as a result. All chapters have therefore both authors and contributors, with acknowledgements made to those among the latter whose insights helped directly shape the chapter's text. Some have provided several paragraphs, others several sentences, and others their insights on words used and assumptions made. This ethos of mutuality and respect is reflected throughout the different chapters. We also respect the fact that there will be colleagues who have radically different views on how tourism "should" be taught, or what "should" be included, but we are again guided by Irshad Manji's words: "Ask not how to change the other person's mind, ask what you are missing from the other person's argument" (Kiwanuka, 2019). Because therein lies the core of respect, the willingness to listen to others and to reflect on the values that underpin their arguments and rationale. As teachers, we need to keep Manji's advice close to our hearts when we interact with different tourism and education stakeholders. We are not always right, and by having enough humility to accept this we empower others to teach us – and we empower ourselves to learn from those teachings.

Teaching Tourism's chapters are built around the diverse contributions from all participating colleagues. Some of these contributions are short conversation starters, others are individual or group activities, others again complex assignments or full units involving field trips. All the different contributions have small icons illustrating the type of learning experience involved.

These icons, and many of the other illustrations in the book, were created by Minori Morioka, whose field is lifelong learning pedagogy and whose visual commentary on and in the chapters adds some welcome humour to the text. At the end of the book there are two contributions quite different in format and content from the rest. The first is Sam Bouwer's TEFI (Tourism Education Futures Initiative) Values Survey, which can act as a way for teachers to introduce students to aspirational values and give them a way to reflect on their own values' positionalities. The second is a role play called "The Tourism Game" created by Stephen Fairbrass. It includes a brief background and different community roles.

In sum, *Teaching Tourism* aims high: to provide you with a transformative reading experience. Its chapters, theories, reflections, contributions, practices and instructions are all designed to give you many ideas on why teaching tourism matters – to all of us, to our students and, indeed, to our world.

Finally, why does it matter? Well, we are placed in a privileged position where we can influence the way future tourism professionals and fellow human beings in our communities learn about values that underpin our realities. To quote a Buddhist thought about this matter:

The thought manifests as the word,
The word manifests as the deed,
The deed develops into habit,
And the habit hardens into character.
So, watch the thought,
And its way with care,
And let it spring from love,
Born out of respect for all beings. (Miller, 2019, p. 206)

Matrix[1]

Activity	Authors	Topic	Preface	1	3	4	5	6	7	8	9	10	11	12
Conversation starters														
31	Boluk	Introducing critical topics to transform our practice					X							
19	Day	Cultural awareness						X						
28	Flaherty	The power of values to effect positive change 1								X				
29	Flaherty	Industry ethics								X		X		
48	Flaherty	The power of values to effect positive change 2												X
33	Joppe	Calculating a carbon footprint				X					X			
25	Naumov	Tourism and World Heritage Sites 1							X					
21	Naumov	Tourism and intangible heritage					X	X						
49	Rodenburg	Solving wicked world problems												X
16	Shimoyasuba	Access rights to the Commons					X							
9	Shimoyasuba	Iomante rituals: ecological and economic values meet cultural values				X								
Individual activities														
18	Armano	Deep Cultural Interpretation Model: a tool to understand the tourists' culture						X						
40	Abu Bakar	Tourism teaching and learning using spiritual pedagogy											X	
22	Gellatly	The unfolding of SARS-CoV-2							X					
26	Naumov	Tourism and World Heritage Sites 2							X					
50	Tervo-Kankare et al.	Value-reflexive engagement and dialogue											X	

Activity	Authors	Topic	Chapters											
			Preface	1	3	4	5	6	7	8	9	10	11	12
Group activities														
2	Benjamin	Yes-and: how to create a brave space by incorporating improvisational theatre games			X						X			
32	Boluk	Using systems thinking and the UN's SDG framework as an opportunity for fostering critical dialogue				X					X			
20	Huhmarniemi and Kugapi	Co-designing creative tourism activities for preserving and promoting local cultural traditions						X					X	
6	Jamal and Peterson	Climate action for a climate-friendly educational destination				X					X			
12	Edelheim	The Tourism Game 1					X		X			X	X	
27	Edelheim	The dilemma of protecting workers in the face of entrepreneurship									X			
4	Joppe	Unintended consequences of policy implementation			X									
34	Joppe	The limits to biocapacity				X					X			
51	Turnšek	Emotional labour and the future of automation												X
39	Turnšek	Combating negative prejudice against young people			X							X		
Assignments														
41	Boluk	Fostering critical thinking utilising Brookfield's Critical Incident Questionnaire											X	
1	Bommenel, Ek and Reid	Meta-pedagogical meliorism 1: didactics	X											X
10	Bommenel, Ek and Reid	Meta-pedagogical meliorism 2: social values						X						
42	Bommenel, Ek and Reid	Meta-pedagogical meliorism 3: knowledge											X	
36	Camargo	Promoting mutuality through service-learning: La Santa Catarina restaurant										X		X
47	Crossley	Professional practice review of learning												X
13	Edelheim	Film and tourism: constructing social realities						X						
23	Gellatly	Tourism resiliency post COVID-19								X				
37	Häikiö and Väyrynen	Video project "Enjoy Lapland Safely"							X					
24	Kaya and Edwards	Authentic assessment: activating purposeful learning for a diverse student cohort									X			
38	Lešnik Štuhec	Cooperation between students and the tourism industry to solve project challenges in sustainable rural destinations										X		
7	Michel	Mobilising learners' tourist memories towards a deeper, more authentic understanding and practice of tourism					X			X				
14	Paddison	Values-based learning and storytelling					X							

Activity	Authors	Topic	Preface	1	3	4	5	6	7	8	9	10	11	12
			Chapters											
44	Phi	Design-based learning and design thinking for innovation education											X	
45	Rink	Seeing tourism landscapes: teaching tourism at the confluence of theory and practice				X					X		X	
30	Rodenburg	Solving ethical dilemmas in the tourism industry								X				
15	Sarkar	Experiential learning in gastronomy tourism					X							
Field trips														
46	Clausen and Miller	The value of the unintended in tourism education: Mexico											X	X
11	Clausen and Miller	The value of the unintended in tourism education: Nepal					X							
5	Coghlan and Ripper	Reflecting on sustainable behaviour				X					X			
43	Flaherty	Field trip findings presented through a photo essay											X	X
3	Guia	Tourism to promote political responsibility			X									
35	Rantala et al.	Stewardship: an in-field dialogue model									X			
8	Sarkar	Experiential learning in nature-based recreational settings				X								
Complex activity/resource														
17	Abildgaard et al.	Enhancing culturally sensitive tourism in an online learning environment						X				X		
52	Bouwer	The TEFI Values Survey	X											
53	Fairbrass	The Tourism Game 2	X				X		X			X		

NOTE

1.   Shaded cells indicate where the teaching case is primarily used.

1. Tourism didactics

Johan Edelheim; **Marion Joppe**; **Joan Flaherty**;
Barkathunnisha Abu Bakar; **Elin Bommenel**; **Richard
Ek**; **Stuart Reid**; Mette Simonsen Abildgaard; Karla
A. Boluk; Joanne Paulette Gellatly; Jaume Guia; Emily
Höckert; Tazim Jamal; Ece Kaya; Monika Lüthje; Miranda
Peterson

INTRODUCTION

To teach is always a privilege. Teaching, after all, offers the potential to help a person transform themselves and, in doing so, transform their environment, both present and future. Transformations are also, as Freire teaches, mutual. Learning together means that all parties can transform in the process. Understanding and applying the responsibility that comes with this privilege is a key theme of *Teaching Tourism*.

This chapter introduces that theme by outlining the book's didactic philosophy and by acting as a touchstone for the applied chapters, which focus on different values. It also prepares the reader for Chapter 2's discussion of axiological thinking in teaching practices. This approach is our quest to expand beyond ontological matters of being and meaning of teaching in higher education, and to also expand beyond epistemological issues related to truth claims, or pure knowledge production for its own sake, of which higher education is too often accused.

It has been said that an idea that is thought can never be unthought, and we teachers are continuously aiming at conveying ideas to our students. The most effective way we can do that is through conscious values where we take ownership of ideas that empower students to realise their potential in the world around them.

This is why a teacher should be so much more than just a medium transferring information, and instead be a coach, a mentor, a guide and/or a role model. We could even imagine ourselves as partners and co-creators of knowledge, particularly if we see knowledge as situational, and therefore as being "made" anew with every new interaction and thought (Braidotti, 2018).

THE IMPORTANCE OF THINKING ABOUT LEARNING BEFORE TEACHING

This book is part of an Edward Elgar Publishing series featuring "teaching" in each title, hence the title of the book you are holding in your hand or reading on your screen: *Teaching Tourism: Innovative, Values-based Learning Experiences for Transformative Practices.*

Teaching is often paired with the word "learning", and it tends to be the first part of that duo. Scholarship of Teaching and Learning (SoTL) offers one example of this ranked pairing, as do the names of many higher education development departments in postsecondary institutions across the world. Perhaps we have become so accustomed to focusing on teaching before learning simply because it is comfortable to do so. After all, "teaching" is within our power. We can direct it, alter it and control it – attributes which describe, and perhaps account for the longevity of, the "sage on the stage" envisioning of the teacher's role.

However, we want to start by reversing this order. Teaching on its own has very little inherent value, unless seen as a means of learning. Thus, the act of teaching is secondary to personal learning. If lots of teaching takes place, but very little learning results, then it is time to question the rationale for that teaching. By thinking first about learning, we are prioritising what is important: achieving our learning outcomes. Better teaching will then inevitably follow.

Therefore, we present this book from the perspective of "learning" as the verb to be focused on. All of us engaged in this project are interested in being facilitators of successful learning and becoming better at it – a process which requires being learners ourselves along the way. This book could have been called *Facilitating Learning for Values-based Tourism*, but that would not have fit into the series of books by the publisher, and it might not have been found by prospective readers because the profession still tends to focus on "teaching" as the major term. Let us therefore move on to how successful values-based learning can be facilitated, the premises and the pedagogical philosophies presented in the following chapters.

CREATING FOUNDATIONS FOR SUCCESSFUL LEARNING

Teaching and its related terms are often perceived as some form of transmission of information from one person to others. This transmission can be done in person or by proxy – such as through written work. To do research and to publish that research is therefore also viewed as teaching. But herein lies a problem: when teaching is restricted to the sense of transferring, then learning becomes a mere effect of a cause. If teaching is purely imagined as a transfer of information and is seen in the same light as publishing academic work, then we are in trouble, because that is where neo-liberal management methods are driving the sector. Pre-recorded online lectures, Massive Open Online Courses (MOOCs) and giant auditoriums where somebody stands and reads out text have one thing in common: they are efficient and cost-effective at reaching a large audience. But whether they facilitate learning is another matter. That is not to say that nobody would learn anything from these forms of teaching. They can indeed be well presented and inspirational for motivated learners, and there lies the clue: different learners have different preferences, and massification of teaching is seldom able to cater to many diverse learning preferences.

Successful learning takes place in an open system that has some stable components, and lots of external inputs and outputs that influence the system (Figure 1.1). The stable components are as follows: a teaching context domain, the learner(s), a process of learning and some predetermined objectives of learning. What is important in this open system is that the different components are considered as a whole, rather than as pieces, and therefore they need to be aligned with one another (Biggs and Tang, 2011).

With facilitation of successful learning as the premise, we have adapted the model originally introduced by Biggs in 1999 to this values-based tourism context. In the centre of the model

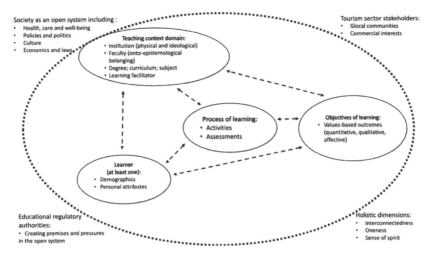

Source: Chapter authors, adapted from Biggs (2003, p. 19)

Figure 1.1   *Values-based learning in tourism*

stands the process of learning, with activities and assessments. (Note that, here, the latter are not purely measures that evaluate success. They are also modes of learning.) The process of learning is directly related to the three other stable components: learner demographics, personal attributes and motivations, such as dreams about a future career; the teaching context domain; and the objectives of learning, or learning outcomes. The learning is also indirectly affected by the macro drivers of the open system; that is, the society in which learning takes place with its internal idiosyncrasies. Included within that society are the educational regulatory authorities, which create the premises for the learning by defining the learning context and by funding the learning or setting boundaries for how the funding can be operationalised.

The open system is also indirectly, and in some cases directly, influenced by stakeholders in the larger tourism sector. These stakeholders can be local communities with an interest in tourism, but more often they are commercial interests connected to tourism who see higher education in tourism as a source of employees, and who therefore attempt to influence the system for their own interests. The final, crucial – and overlooked – influence of this open system is a holistic dimension that does not separate the learner from their contexts, but rather emphasises the learner's connection to a greater non-human whole. Viewed from this holistic perspective, humans are but one component of this greater whole, where all parts interconnect. Therefore, for example, nature is not a separate entity, a place to be visited from time to time, but rather an intrinsic part of who we are. Thus, the well-being of one is inseparable from that of the other. (More about this below, and in Chapter 4 on ecological values.)

A key factor of successful learning is an alignment of the stable components in the system, as well as an active awareness and acknowledgement of the external factors of the system. Biggs and Tang (2011) point out that we often overemphasise the roles of the teacher or the learner when trying to analyse successful teaching and learning. For example, a common complaint we have all probably heard – and voiced – is about the quality of students, accompanied by a lament for earlier years, which always miraculously seem to have yielded brighter, more engaged students, regardless of the timeline. Putting the onus squarely on students for the success of learning is an easy way to escape responsibility for the hard work of being an effective facilitator of learning. Students, with their different motivations for attending class and their different abilities, clearly have an impact on the process, but it does not end there.

The learners whom we have the privilege to work with are just as good as we give them an opportunity to be, and the other parts of the system need to align with that too. "Alignment" in Biggs and Tang's vocabulary refers to ensuring that each piece of the learning system contributes to the whole. For example, a multiple-choice test on speech terms in a communications class would be rather tenuous if the aim was to get students to communicate effectively. Theories about deep-learning and surface-learning also often grossly generalise populations of students, or assign roles onto individuals, without investigating if the teaching and assessment methods in reality have created the outcome. If, for example, class activities and assessments mostly relate to memorisation or piecemeal learning rather than contextualised understanding, then it is natural that students "surface" learn; it is what the situation has demanded of them. If, on the other hand, class activities and assessments require students to actively reflect on concepts presented, on their past awareness of similar matters, and on connections to cases in practice, then the foundations for "deeper" learning are more solid.

Another common mistake is to imagine that the teacher is the star who will save the show and magically make learning effective. Again, there are naturally engaging and knowledgeable colleagues with wit and charisma who keep their audiences enthralled, but those qualities by themselves are not what makes learning successful. We are, as teachers, often too confident that students will see the material in the same way we do, starting from the theme of the unit, to the objectives, the assessments and finally the delivery of the material. For their part, students often focus initially on the topic and then on the assessments, strategising what they need to do to receive an acceptable grade. Thereafter, students figure out how to manage their time to best address what they hope to achieve in the course – and in all their other concurrent commitments. And maybe, as a final matter, they look at the objectives of the unit (Biggs and Tang, 2011). This is where the alignment of the components needs to take place: the learning activities and assessments need to be chosen carefully, depending on the context, the learners and the objectives.

TRANSFORMATIONAL LEARNING

"Students entering the uncertain world of the future and, in particular, the vulnerable tourism sector, need different skills, aptitudes and knowledge to succeed" (Sheldon et al., 2011, p. 3).

"Uncertain" and "vulnerable" set the context for our task, as COVID-19 has reshaped travel and tourism in a way that no one – not even those who made the above statement – could have envisioned. The pandemic has forced us to radically rethink why and how societies engage with tourism and, consequently, why and how tourism should be taught. A crucial part of this equation is to articulate how we define effective learning, especially within tourism's changing landscape of uncertainty and vulnerability.

Certainly, there is no shortage of conventional definitions or measures of what constitute successful learning. However, in the context of this book we have values as our focus, and the capacity to transform as our goal.

Here, we borrow heavily from the academic network Tourism Education Futures Initiative (TEFI), which focuses on tourism as a force for good, on individual, communal, societal and ecological levels. The ultimate objective, therefore, for values-based teaching is for students to make the world a better place and thereby transform themselves. The individual transformations take place on various levels: cognitive, intellectual and ethical/moral. The means by which this improvement occurs involves meta-pedagogical discussions, contemplation and reflection. It also involves the awareness that, insofar as power and knowledge are intertwined, learning always contains a political dimension – and, thus, an ethical and moral dimension as well.

Whilst the above might sound hopelessly idealistic to some readers, it is only through fostering hope and presenting utopias to strive for that we can help our students, and our colleagues, imagine a better way of being and doing (Pritchard et al., 2011). Neither hope nor utopias should be misconstrued as passive daydreaming, but viewed rather as active and engaged commitments that can take a multitude of forms, as evidenced by all the valuable contributions in this book.

CONVERSATION STARTER

 Elin Bommenel, Richard Ek and Stuart Reid have created a multilevel introductory week called "Meta-pedagogical meliorism" for their new students (see Activities 1, 10 and 42). We introduce a few of their conversation starters in this chapter and in a few other chapters.

Discuss "communities of practice" – see Bommenel et al. for a definition of the term – you might find outside academia, such as chess clubs, surfer collectives, gaming communities, online and offline interest groups, and so on.

How can you most easily join a community of practice? How can you help others who want to join? Ask the students to share with one another and discuss how they joined a community of practice on an earlier occasion.

Share an occasion when you wanted to join a community of practice. What did you *do*? Watch? Imitate? Decode? Assimilate? What were the fears and what were the rewards? What made you feel like entering? What made you decide to stay? What made you want to contribute? Was the community stable over time or did it change/evolve? Was it stratified, hierarchical, or was it open and welcoming, democratic?

Following Miller's (2019) work on the holistic curriculum, we propose that teaching can be seen as representing three separate positions: *transmission*, *transaction* and *transformation*, each of which is tied to its own value sets and characteristics. The three positions are explained below through the metaphor of baking bread.

Teaching as Transmission

In the teaching-as-transmission mode, the teacher is akin to a baker who carefully measures out and places all the ingredients into a bowl – either with or without the expectation that those ingredients will turn themselves into a loaf of bread. Thus, the teacher's role in this mode is limited to gathering and presenting all the relevant facts, figures, theories and concepts to their students – either with or without the expectation that the students will do something with that information.

Teaching as Transaction

In the teaching-as-transaction mode, the teacher is akin to a baker who places the carefully measured ingredients into a bread-maker that automatically mixes, kneads, times and bakes a loaf of bread. Thus, a teacher in the transaction mode extends beyond simply transmitting the material by following a rational series of steps – and by depending on technology – to achieve the desired result.

Teaching as Transformation

In the teaching-as-transformation mode, the teacher is akin to a baker who takes the same carefully measured ingredients, but this time places the yeast, some of the flour and water into a separate bowl. This mixture is given time to develop and mature at the right temperature overnight before adding the final ingredients and kneading the dough and then finally baking it in an oven (see Figure 1.2). In contrast to the transaction-baker scenario above, this loaf of bread has a softer texture, a more complex flavour – and it stays fresh longer. Thus, the teacher in this mode uses, but moves beyond, transmission and transaction. The process is more time-consuming and complex, but it yields more nuanced and long-lasting results.

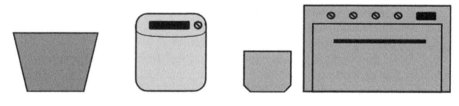

Source: Chapter authors

Figure 1.2   Transformational bread-making metaphor

Each mode has a necessary part to play, depending on the setting. Therefore, transmission is not to be dismissed as ineffectual: as illustrated in the bread-baking metaphor above, an aspect of transmission is always contained within the transaction and transformation modes. Similarly, aspects of transaction exist in the transformation mode. The problem occurs when teaching does not go beyond transmission, or, at best, transaction. Miller (2019) describes the transmission mode as reminiscent of laissez-faire economics: a teaching/learning environment restricted to this mode is characterised by individualism, competition, standardised tests, conservatism and a short-term perspective. The transaction mode is related to rational planning and interpretations, use of the scientific method and a strong belief in a "technofix", whereby current problems will be overcome sometime in the future through a wished-for breakthrough in technology and research.

In contrast, one of the transformation mode's central aims is to create a learning environment that acknowledges and honours the interdependency and interconnectedness of all beings. Therefore, key characteristics associated with this mode include openness to multiple perspectives, knowledge and dimensionality; and the need for individual scale, one which recognises, for example, that tourism spaces are public spaces, inhabited by local peoples and shared with a large number of other species, all of which create a tourism ecosystem. Recognising that none of this can be achieved overnight and that all of it requires collaboration, the transformation mode connects to the slow movement and incorporates non-violence. In short, the transformation mode of teaching is values-based teaching.

There is a need to move tourism teaching away from a laissez-faire economics that continues to reproduce an egotistical and short-term view of reality. Conservative and hierarchical teaching methods that emphasise the transmission of fixed epistemological positions should be used sparingly if at all, and only as a means of introducing a common paradigm for a field. Learning and teaching should instead be built around transactions and sparring between learners, and also between learners and learning facilitators, to investigate and question the status quo of the field. An ultimate aim of learning experiences is to create a safe and caring environment that allows individuals to situate themselves, their personal values and their aspirations in the field of tourism. It is when students learn to question their values and worldview as well as reflect on their own learning and on the ambitions that they have for their studies that actual transformations can take place.

Values-based tourism teaching and learning is, therefore, not just an epistemological endeavour that suggests certain topics be added to a curriculum in order to create a preferred truth. Neither is it a purely ontological enterprise where techniques and mechanics of teaching would lead to the right kind of meanings. Rather, it is very much an axiological undertaking that underpins each and every aspect of the learning experience: the values lived by are made visible, and the values aspired to are verbalised and operationalised in order for transformation to take place.

HOLISTIC TRANSFORMATIONS THROUGH SPIRITUALLY ORIENTED LEARNING

A core dimension of the transformations highlighted above is holistic education, which includes an awareness and acknowledgement of the learner's spirituality. Spirituality is often viewed in a restricted sense, as pertaining only to religious matters or to mysticism – an oversimplification which might reflect the education systems and epistemological foundations one is brought up within. There is, however, a strong lineage of thinkers who propose a much broader, all-encompassing view of spirituality, such as Thoreau, Montessori and Roszak. In this wider perspective, spirituality is about the interconnectedness of all living beings on earth, and the awe any one of us can feel when we stop for a moment to ponder on the wonder that nature actually is. The integration of spirituality in tourism education is proposed to direct students toward their inner selves, enable them to expand their consciousness and see their lives as part of the universal human experience (Barkathunnisha et al., 2018). Thus, an educational approach that integrates spirituality aims to develop students' sense of interdependency and interrelationships with all aspects of life and centres on nurturing a deep sense of *sympoiesis* and unity. The educational experience is focused on a movement toward a *metanoia*, a holistic intellectual, affective and spiritual shift from alienation into a deeper awareness of one's meaning, interrelatedness and purpose (Vella, 2000). One aspect of this holistic thinking in our field might be reciprocal tourism endeavours that cultivate community well-being as part of the tourism experience.

"Spirituality" refers to a way of being and meaning-making in the world that influences how we engage *inwardly*, within ourselves, and *outwardly* with the human and non-human environment around us. Three key themes characterise spirituality: (i) spirituality as a state of transcendence where one is involved in meaning-making and in a quest for the purpose in life; (ii) spirituality as a process that involves achieving self-awareness, being authentic to one's future self and connecting to something larger than one's ego; and (iii) spirituality as a sense of wholeness, the ability to experience meaningful connection to one's core self and a mutual interdependency with other humans and the biosphere (Canda and Furman, 2010; Estanek, 2006; Lindholm and Astin, 2008).

Miller (2019) highlights that one of the challenges faced by modern educational systems is the compartmentalisation of knowledge into separate subjects. This approach makes learners' connections to data abstract, and distances the subject being taught from the larger community. Examples of how to overcome this compartmentalisation in the tourism literature can be seen in integrated curriculum developments (for example, Boluk et al., 2019c). Epistemologically, the spiritually oriented educational experience acknowledges and embraces different forms of knowledge, resulting in a holistic learning experience: *sensibilia* (knowing through sensations and perceptions), *intelligibilia* (knowing though concepts and thoughts) and *transcendelia* (knowing through the experience of the spirit or gnosis, or spiritual knowledge) (Wilber, 2000, p. 38).

Multiple ways of knowing that include mind, intuition, emotion, body, interconnections of human and non-human, the seen and the experienced are embraced in the classroom. This development of the cognitive, affective and spiritual domains is regarded to be complementary in the holistic educational process. Thus, for example, the affective domain, which influences reactions, feelings and emotions, helps learners make sense and meaning of what is learned through the intellect. Palmer (1998, p. 4) alludes to the vital interplay amongst all three domains when he writes, "reduce teaching to intellect and it becomes a cold abstraction; reduce it to emotions and it becomes narcissistic; reduce it to the spiritual and it loses its anchor to the world". Intellect, emotion and spirit are inherently interconnected. A connection with subjective knowing and experiences can facilitate a deeper understanding of a subject matter (Shapiro et al., 2011). Ontologically, a spiritually oriented approach adopts the perspective that education occurs in a community where multiple realities exist; and these realities are acknowledged, honoured and shared in the teaching and learning environment.

MULTILITERACIES IN TOURISM EDUCATION

We state in the Preface that we need to equip students with strategies that allow them to stay multiliterate, but what does that mean in practice? Literacy used to be simplistically viewed as having the skills and knowledge of reading, writing and arithmetic that were needed to function satisfactorily in a defined group or community (UNESCO, 1962, cited in Anstey and Bull, 2018). Part of this view was built on the assumption that there existed a finite set of knowledge that any one individual could need. The definition reflects the time that it was created in, before global electronic multimedia totally reorganised the way societies work, people think and realities are constituted. To be literate in the 21st century is very different compared to even a short time ago, just as it will change also in the future. Many learning facilitators today were brought up with that old definition of literacy, but we are tasked to create learning opportunities for those born in a different and constantly evolving world.

Factors such as language, culture, class, economic standing or technological access create diverse contexts where different kinds of text production and consumption take place. "Text" refers here to any meaning-making entity available, including written (linguistic), spoken or sung (audio), painted or photographed (visual), performed as pantomime or with a wink of the eye (gestural) or laid out as components in space, with their proximity, angle and position creating meanings (spatial). These five meaning-making entities are referred to as modes, and multiliteracy incorporates all of these multimodal components (Anstey and Bull, 2018). Reading and writing text in a specified language, according to conventions within one group, such as international tourism academics, is often as far as literacy is taught in tourism courses. But the question is, does this really prepare learners for becoming the transformative world-makers they all have the opportunity to be?

Workplaces are no longer static, neither in the sense that employees stay for very long due to casualisation and mobility, nor in the sense that the workplace itself follows the same set of rules for very long. Higher education is an excellent example, having undergone substantial changes over the past two decades. Often, these changes have been a source of bewilderment for the postsecondary institution (for example, curricula that is curtailed by regulatory authorities' demands for quality assurance and uniformity; neo-liberal demands of productivity and efficiency; industry stakeholders' demands for work-readiness to solve problems of yesterday and today). The sense of confusion brought on by these changes is exacerbated by the fact that many instructors began their teaching careers in a time when budgets were done with paper and pencil, and reports were prepared in their mother tongue, not in an internationally prescribed language or other communicative modalities. Dredge et al. (2012) describe a "force field" in which curricula are created, a space that is in almost constant flux, depending on the forces with which different stakeholders at any one stage can influence the composition of the field. Addressing these challenges requires strong leadership, a vision and an insight into the multiple modes in which "text" is created and the kinds of values underpinning them. It is therefore essential that education consciously creates a pathway that makes learners multiliterate.

Learners who are born into a world where text is multimodal are by no means inherently multiliterate. This is, however, a common and unfortunate misconception amongst teachers, and consequently the education system is not paying adequate attention to multiliteracy or multimodal learning experiences. The amount of information that exists is overwhelming, and being a teacher is no longer a task of offering up a definitive and full account of any one matter, but rather of exposing learners to important questions that are jointly examined. Students enter the learning arena with a wealth of knowledge, data and many preconceived ideas of the states of being as well as conflicting worldviews and values. Therefore, students should be given opportunities to reflect in different ways on what they have all learned about the world, and what they have been taught about the world through different learning regimes, executed through different pedagogies, heuristic approaches and didactic performativities. This meta-pedagogical interactive contemplation further makes it easier for international students to realise that their new programme of higher education is based on a specific, contextual way of teaching and learning, and that they need to master this new regime – not just to receive a passing grade, but to transform themselves and the world around them.

ACTIVITY

Elin Bommenel, Richard Ek and Stuart Reid's contribution continues with a seminar activity. In it, students are given an opportunity to read a thesis written by a graduate from the same programme, and then jointly analyse, discuss and develop one another's input to create a constructive co-learning environment. See the theoretical background to it in "Meta-pedagogic me-liorism 1: didactics", Activity 1.

MULTIMODALITY IN TOURISM EDUCATION

These realities need to be taken into account when learning activities are designed. A precon-ception may not be incorrect in an epistemological sense, but it might be based on an illog-ical thought chain or even a minority worldview. Learning is therefore to design functional connections between strands of information. Neither the information nor the connections should be seen as fixed positions. The metaphor is not to build bridges between islands, but rather to operate ferries between pontoons. Indeed, as teachers it is our duty to help students self-reflect on their worldview and values to invite new possibilities for knowing the world, not impose our understandings on them. Tertiary education takes place in change, and to be part of narrowly creating work-ready graduates who know "all there is to know" today is the same as condemning them to being utterly irrelevant in a different future. Being multiliterate means that the individual is continuously metacognitive and has created strategies of how to efficiently produce and consume meaning across all semiotic modes of text (Anstey and Bull, 2018).

Tourism, and society at large, have gone through tremendous changes in recent years, and there is no indication of this evolution stopping now, with effects of climate change being ever more visible. The world as we know it continues to evolve – stability is rather an illusion. Naturally, COVID-19 has created a new dimension to the world of tourism, and it will probably have ramifications on the field for years to come, but it will not stop change from happening. Medical, political, societal, ecological, cultural, technological and economic changes alter the way we reflect, think, act and imagine the future. The systemic values that all these changes mirror become muddled in a world where news reporting can be instantaneous on a global scale, but simultaneously biased by commercial interests, political ambitions and channels used and/or trusted, to name only some dimensions. A gullible insistence that the topic one is teaching, or the persona one is inhabiting, can be value-free is truly a blinkered view on reality. All text is ultimately the outcome of the values it is designed, produced and consumed in, just like the book you are holding in your hands right now, and the way you interpret the meaning of it.

ACTIVITY

 Elin Bommenel, Richard Ek and Stuart Reid's contribution ends with an activity that turns the table of how assessments are normally viewed in classroom settings (see Activity 1). Rather than just being a mystery to students, this activity makes the assessments into part of the learning activities.

Let the students themselves design an examination aimed to encourage a deep approach to learning. Let them then try out each other's examinations, grade the examinations, write a motivation for the grade and then inform the student group how it felt to design and grade the test.

The students should take turns at each task; that is, being someone who takes a test as well as someone who designs and grades a test.

2. Axiology, value and values

Johan Edelheim; **Marion Joppe**; **Joan Flaherty**; **Emily Höckert**; Karla A. Boluk; Jaume Guia; Miranda Peterson

Values are neither 'subjective' nor 'objective' in a radical axiology, as such a dichotomy is axiologically false. 'Subjects' in the actual world are reflective of historical values, not a fictional world of subjects detached from the world. Radical axiology as radical involves the rejection of such a Cartesian problematic and framework at the root. A radical philosophy of values would abandon this subject-object dichotomy as inadequate for, alien to, and a distortion of value. An appropriation of value that uses a model of value that is not itself axiological, based on value problematics, cannot do justice to value. [...] To ask, 'what are values' in any form reduces questions of value to ontology (or in a later version, consciousness or concepts: substance as a subject). [...] To raise the question of the 'ontological status' of values, or whether they are 'subjective or objective', or 'what we mean' by the 'concept of value' [...] concedes the value of another paradigm: the legitimacy of treating value in its terms. (McDonald, 2004, p. xxi)

INTRODUCTION

The purpose of this chapter is to explain the philosophical foundation for *Teaching Tourism* by examining values, particularly in the context of tourism and teaching. Admittedly, taking on this topic is daunting. So much already has been said, and so many influential thinkers have spent their lives producing profound thoughts about values. (See, for example, works by Plato, Aristotle or Hume on goodness and good life which encapsulate values at their core.) For this reason, we acknowledge from the outset that our goal is straightforward: to explore some dimensions of the topic and some ways in which it has been understood – which seems like a logical enough endeavour, given that this book revolves around values-based teaching.

More specifically, this chapter presents different forms of *axiology*, which is the foundational philosophy focused on "value" (in the same fashion that *ontology* is foundational for "being" and "meaning", and *epistemology* is foundational for "knowledge" and "truth"). Values and values-based tourism research and education have been investigated comprehensibly from the perspective of two other foundational philosophies. See, for example, Pritchard et al. (2011) on tourism values from an ontological perspective, and Caton (2012 and 2015) on values-based tourism from an epistemological perspective. Macbeth's (2005) development of a sixth "ethical platform" in tourism research is also a precursor to this chapter as he specifically states that the ethics platform represents value-full rather than value-free tourism scholarship. This chapter follows therefore the aforementioned colleagues' thorough work from an axiological perspective by investigating different axioms of value, some common axiological fallacies and finally a hierarchy of values, showing how we can axiologically steer away from value relativism in our teaching of tourism.

AXIOLOGY

The quotation that starts this chapter is radical indeed, as it aims at placing axiology in the centre, ahead of the two other traditions more commonly found in academia that either emphasise epistemology or ontology as their base. Thus far, axiology has received scarce attention in the field of tourism studies, even less than epistemology or ontology (Edelheim, 2020). The two latter traditions are often discussed in reference to research. As such, research students are frequently directed to outline their paradigms, as well as their ontological and epistemological stance, in reference to their thesis. Methodological chapters of dissertations generally start with attempts at outlining these, more often resembling the individual students' sense of what the words might mean, rather than actually outlining the stance that the students take. The truth is, of course, that all these foundational philosophies are complex. To truly understand them requires a great deal of effort.

The effort is well worth it, however – particularly in the case of axiology. In the fourth edition of their leading handbook on qualitative research, Denzin and Lincoln (2011) offer this reconsideration of an earlier view: "If we had to do it all again, we would make values or, more correctly axiology, … a part of the basic foundational philosophical dimensions of paradigm proposal" (p. 116). Similarly, Killion and Fisher (2018) have included axiology in their chapter on qualitative methodologies of tourism research as one of the key components (together with epistemology, ontology and methodology) that form a researcher's paradigm. Recently Guia and Jamal have also offered posthumanism as "a new axiological perspective to current debates around travel, mobilities and (post)modernist conceptualizations of tourism" (2020, p. 2). Therefore, there is a rising awareness among researchers, including those in the field of tourism, of what axiology is and why it is important.

Much of this importance lies in the fact that values are always active. They are the result of constant evaluation, which is something all of us do every day, every moment of our lives: we evaluate how to act, what to do, what to believe in and what not. We live through values, we live axiologically. The sentences you just read, and now might re-read in order to think deeply about them, are your axiology in action. However, axiology itself, according to Hartman (2019), is not about determinations of what is good or bad in a moral sense. Instead, it is about "the principle of value" (p. 23) or, more precisely, "a method of thinking which one is free to use and, consequently, develop one's own sense of value" (p. 53). Thus, writing a book on teaching values-based tourism is the authors' axiology in action. And we are aware of the obvious risk: falling into the trap of presuming some sense of moral superiority by claiming that we have found the ultimate universal values, which all others should embrace. We seek to avoid that risk through axiologically examining values that societies live by as well as some that they aspire to live by. We suggest the latter, the so-called aspirational or universal values, are appropriate and meaningful values that "ought", in the sense that Moore (1903) used the word, to be incorporated into tourism education. An axiological approach allows us, as the chapter's starting quotation stated, to go beyond subjectivities and epistemological truth claims, or objectivities and ontological meaning-making attempts.

Agreeing on what values can be deemed universal is challenging, but even more so is the fact that people might agree on the idea of a value but disagree on the means suitable to achieve that value. For example, if the value that one aims to achieve is peacefulness, would any means to reach peace be allowed? This conundrum leads people to adopt different approaches: some argue for non-violent action while others suggest that violence is acceptable if it leads to less violence and ultimately to peace.

These questions relate to individual hierarchies of values or, in common parlance, our value choices. Those choices and where they rank in the hierarchy of values may vary depending on the individual and the setting. At this point, positivists and researchers with a keen sense of the supremacy of epistemology as a foundational philosophy sigh and presume that values are relative, constantly moving targets that elude the researcher's grasp, and therefore nothing productive comes of contemplating them. However, this argument misses the point that epistemology, and so-called facts that stand as the core of it, is based on value determinations. As McDonald (2004, p. xx) states,

> values have been treated from a non-axiological and often hostile, sceptical perspective that has been arbitrarily hoisted upon them, precisely because they are based on first philosophies that were not first philosophies of value, including the 'metaphysical basis' of value [epistemology], the 'ontology' of value, or the 'experience' of value.

Thus, to state that values are relative is to perceive them through epistemology and an all-consuming belief in "truths" or "facts", something we will return to in Chapter 11 on knowledge. At the focus of axiology stands value, and at the core of value stands that which is "good". Therefore, in order to determine what is good, axiology has developed axioms of value.

AXIOMS OF VALUE AND "THE GOOD"

At first glance, the meaning of "value" seems to be self-evident, but when we slow down to think about it, we realise that it is a rather complicated term. Value relates to what is good – and naturally what is good is context-dependent. However, this does not mean that value is purely relative: in many senses it is what makes up the complex realities we live in and the sense we make of our lives.

When we ask, "Does X have value?", we are ultimately asking, "Is X good for … (whatever we are after)?" For example, if we ask, "Does an umbrella have value?", one person might respond, "Yes it does, because it is good for keeping us dry in the pouring rain." Another may say, "Yes, it does because it provides shade on a hot and sunny day." And yet another's answer might be, "Yes, it does because it is worth 2000¥." These responses and a multitude of other possible answers are correct because they look at value from different perspectives. Throughout our lives we assign value to people, experiences, events, things or ideas, and we base this value on the *good* they provide; in other words, what they are *good for*.

Valuation studies are often focused on dynamics of markets, and value is therefore often tied to monetary values, but not exclusively. For insight into valuation studies, and the study of good, one can turn to Heuts and Mol (2013), who investigate what a good tomato is.

Their wonderful examination of a mundane, or at least non-controversial, matter investigates the value of tomatoes by interviewing different users, all referred to as experts in their own right. They find that different experts invoke different "registers" of what makes a tomato good to them (monetary, embodied, temporal, natural, sensual), all of which have different priorities. But rather than simply taking a relativist standpoint, they draw four conclusions:

1. Value resists simplification because different aspects of "good" take prominence.
2. Valuing is performative – what is made into good goes hand in hand with actions.
3. Good-making actions do not offer full control as different materialities and practicalities inform and co-shape value.
4. Goodness is ultimately determined through consumption, in this case by eating a tomato.

 Ren et al. (2015) have applied valuation studies to tourism and showed that the two dominant schools of thought, managerialism on the one hand and critical studies on the other, both invoke value as a factor of importance, but that value has different attributes in the different paradigms. They refer to how value is a case of "mattering" or of what matters, and how mattering functions as a way for scholars in the different schools of thought to validate their own premises. However, this conclusion still leaves values as a relative concept, caught between epistemological and onto-logical arguments, so a clearer axiom of value is needed.

One of the first modern philosophers who examined what "good" means, and whose name is often referred to when values are discussed, was G.E. Moore, starting with his *Principia Ethica* (1903). Moore's focus in that book was ethics, and he criticised other philosophers who discussed ethics without initially defining its core, namely, "What is good?" His formulation of so-called intrinsic and extrinsic values came from the book's central questions: "What kind of things ought to exist for their own sakes?" and "What kind of actions ought we to perform?" (p. viii). As Caton (2012) suggests, epistemological trends that focus on truths rather than consequences make it difficult to talk and reflect about values that guide tourism education. Nevertheless, critical (Pritchard et al., 2011) and collaborative (Jóhannesson et al., 2015) tourism inquiries have explicitly welcomed us to gather around the values of partnership and ethics in tourism education, research, policy and practice.

The questions posed by Moore (1903) are still influential in values philosophy and valuation studies. Intrinsic values are those that are good in themselves, such as our health. Extrinsic values are those that are good for what they contribute to intrinsic values, such as food we eat that promotes our health. Moore's rejection of earlier philosophers who equated good with different properties of what is good or valid is discussed in the next section, about axiological fallacies. His formulation that good is undefinable, and that values consist only of intrinsic and extrinsic dimensions, has marred much research that has followed this line of thought. However, Hartman (2019) proposed in 1967 both a more fully fledged axiom of value by building on Moore and one additional level of values – more about this in the final section of this chapter, relating to axiological hierarchies.

Hartman referred to the dimensions of good as "properties" and stated in his axiom of value that "A thing is good if, and only if, it fulfils the set intensional properties of its concept" (p. 67). That is, a thing, matter, thought, and so on, is good when it fulfils all the expectations and intentions one has of it. A criticism of this view from radical axiologists is that it resembles (a neo-Platonian take on) ideal forms. However, Hartman and his followers, who adhere to formal axiology, have rejected this claim. They state that the axiom does not require an imaginative ideal form but can rather be applied by thinking in terms of "good-making properties" and "bad-making properties", each of which adds to or decreases the property fulfilment of the value (Edwards, 2010, p. 13).

A later variant of the axiom of value comes from McMurtry (2009–10) in his work on life-value onto-axiology. He grounds the need for an axiom on the same premises as Moore and Hartman above, on the necessity to answer the questions of what good is and how we are to live. His axiom bears a resemblance to Hartman's good- and bad-making properties; however, rather than defining good on its own, McMurtry focuses on value in his axiom. In what he calls the "Primary Axiom of Value", he states,

> *x is value if and only if, and to the extent that, x consists in or enables a more coherently inclusive range of thought/feeling/action than without it*
> Where these three ultimate fields of value are defined as:
> *thought = internal image and concept* (T)
> *feeling = the felt side of being* (F)
> /senses, desires, emotions, moods
> *action = animate movement* (A)
> *across species and organizations*
> Conversely:
> *x is disvalue if and only if, and to the extent that, x reduces/disables any range of thought/experience/ action.* (p. 213; emphasis original)

Thus, value in McMurtry's axiom is that which the earth is better off having than not having. Or, in practical terms: all thoughts, feelings and actions that improve the quality of life on earth have value, and the more they improve the quality, the more valuable they are. He goes on convincingly to prove that quality of life is a concern not only for human beings but for all living beings, as it is the whole of earth that is creating life-value. This is a perspective that we follow because life-value creates the foundation of new-materialist and posthumanist paradigms (Baruchello, 2018). More importantly, he explains that quality of life should not solely be equated with an economic dimension of human life, since the latter might in reality be a disvalue for life on earth.

VALUES AND AXIOLOGICAL FALLACIES

Values are typically defined as deeply held beliefs. Now, "beliefs" is the easy part of that definition: I believe my shirt is stylish; I believe my cat is hungry, because he is meowing; I believe a good winter day in Sapporo has lots of snow. All of these are beliefs and are close to being simply my opinions. They are states of mind, but rather inconsequential for anybody apart from myself (and perhaps my cat, who still believes he is hungry). However, a deeply held belief – and hence, value – is not simply a really strong opinion. Rather, it stands as the basis for all opinions that we create in our minds and the decisions and actions that we ultimately live by.

McMurtry (2013) writes,

> One way or another a society lives in accordance with a value system – an underlying set of rules of how to live. These are taken for granted more deeply than the rules inside a game and govern speech

and thought like a grammar. Philosophy can excavate them in their ultimately regulating principles, evaluate their truth and value, and seek their more enabling form. (p. 1)

If the values of the societies that we live in are never openly acknowledged, then they can never be questioned or evaluated. This lack of examination, in turn, would lead to a myopic view of reality without alternatives, which is a scary thought in a time when societies around the globe are dealing with the consequences of the COVID-19 pandemic. Instead of actively creating life-enhancing practices that are good for all life on earth, many, if not all, societies around the globe are desperately clinging to that which has been valued before. Hence, more and more money is pumped into businesses and industries, workplaces and other tax-paying institutions to rescue and restore practices ultimately leading to disvalues for the greater good, without asking for anything in their operations to change for the future. Examples of this relevant for tourism are aircraft manufacturers, airlines and other transport companies, but also fossil fuel exploration and food producers. This is examined in more detail in later chapters dealing with economic values, but also political, ecological and social values. Hartman (2019, pp. 15–16) proposed that the examination of values roughly falls within four positions:

1. An ontological position – examining the meaning of values
2. A psychological position – examining values as attributes of attitudes of like and dislike
3. A sociological or anthropological position – where values are functions of situations
4. As non-referential statements, like mathematics, values refer to nothing but apply to everything

Teaching Tourism generally follows the final position on this list – a choice governed by the fact that tourism is interdisciplinary. Those who teach and study tourism are from a wide variety of fields. Accordingly, many different kinds of tourism-related values are discussed – an approach which also increases the likelihood of encountering conflict among those values (that is, what is good for one matter may be bad for another).

One way to solve some of the conflicts between different value dimensions is to look at so-called axiological fallacies, which are mistakes made by incorrectly mixing different frames of reference and sets of phenomena.

The first one, called a "metaphysical fallacy", is to confuse values and axiology with a frame of reference from a different field, one which is built on different ontological and epistemological assumptions. This fallacy comes about when somebody is trying to reach conclusions about values purely based on one frame of reference, overlooking the fact that other frames of reference always exist. This error, however, is exactly what happens when, for example, a multinational company suggests that its investments are more valuable than the living space or archaeological remains that an Indigenous population wants to protect.

The second fallacy is referred to as a "naturalistic fallacy": confusing different axiological sciences or natural sciences with one another, such as confusing ethics and psychology by equating good with pleasure, or confusing ethics and theology by suggesting that doing good is the will of a god. Much of classic philosophy, up until Moore at the beginning of the 20th century, was marred by this fallacy as the concept of what is good was not analysed on its own, but rather confused with that which is good.

The third fallacy is a "moral fallacy", which is confusing something that is good in general with something that is morally good. For example, a person might be a good thief, whereas stealing is morally bad. Just because an act is immoral does not mean that the person could not be good at performing that act. The moral fallacy is related to the naturalistic fallacy, but it is more directly confusing the concept of good with just one type of goodness, regardless of how worthy that type might be regarded as. The reason it is mentioned separately here is that values often are connected to ethics and morals, as if they were the same matter. An example of this can be seen on many corporate websites that devote a page to their values. To a very large extent, that page will simply list different moral values – even when the company's core value is to make money and to earn profits. There is nothing wrong with wanting to earn profits, but a company that openly lists profit-making as its core value, or even as one of its core values, risks gaining a reputation for greed, purely due to the moral fallacy.

The fourth fallacy is called an "empirical fallacy", which is to confuse science in general with natural science. This fallacy presumes that certain properties of a subject matter are properties of all sciences, a common fallacy committed when natural scientists consider their methods and procedures to represent all sciences, thus discounting social sciences, humanities and the arts. An extension of this fallacy occurs when qualitative methodologies are interpreted based on quantitative measurements of relevance. An example would be criticising small sample sizes or questioning "validity" in studies that analyse discourses based on the argument that quantitative measures represent the "scientific way" to carry out research (Hartman, 2019, p. 30–36; Moore, 1903, p. 10).

To clarify values from an axiological perspective and move away from relativity and confusions of frames, the final section of this chapter investigates value hierarchies.

VALUE HIERARCHY

Are values commensurable? In other words, can values be compared based on the same sets of reference, allowing us to rank them in a hierarchy of values? Richardson states that

> the commensurability issue lurks as a reef upon which hopes for rational deliberation of ends seems likely to be wrecked: If values are commensurable in the relevant sense then maximizing good consequences, according to some end taken for granted, is the order of the day; whereas if values are not commensurable in this sense, then rational deliberation seems often impossible. (1994, p. 89)

He then goes on to show that values are incommensurable, based on classic and modern works of philosophy. However, there is a bedrock upon which the argument can be built, and that is found in McMurtry's concept of "life-value onto-axiology":

> [A] universal life-ground of value is already proven – in humanity's universal preferences to breathe clean rather than polluted air, eat and drink non-poisons, have commodious shelter rather than not, relate to others as human not beasts, and have life-meaningful tasks to fulfil rather than meaningless ones. Whether they are relativists, postmodernists, nihilists, cynics, market self-maximizers, tea-partiers or just go-along folks, these objective life-goods are undeniable in reality. For whatever the self's desires, deprivation of any of these life goods leads to loss of life-capacity towards dehumanization and physical death. Yet which life-good and its provider is not in increasing peril for a growing majority of the world in our global value and rule system? (2013, p. 1)

Therefore, values can be compared or ranked based on the extent to which they help foster these "objective life-goods". We can build on this ethos by borrowing a holistic hierarchy from another axiological field and by referencing the work of Hartman, and later Edwards, from formal axiology. Stepping into this field is like navigating a minefield as different schools of thought can be divisive and insular. At the same time, it can also be fascinating: notwithstanding their lack of cross-referencing, many of these thoughts are quite complementary, sometimes using the same rationale to arrive at the same goals.

Formal axiology has created a helpful – albeit slightly complicated – three-layered hierarchy. This hierarchy is helpful because it moves values away from an emphasis on "ought" as in Moore's philosophy, and focuses on the "good" as the centre of values. The first two layers of this hierarchy were introduced earlier in this chapter: intrinsic (internal, affective or singular) and extrinsic (behavioural or external) values. The third layer is systemic (conceptual or synthetic) values (alternatively, just "ideas"). This third layer is important because it signals a rejection of abstractions as a central component. An idea can be limitlessly worthy and good, but it can never think itself. It has to be thought by a living entity. One might query whether artificial intelligence (AI) refutes this argument, but we counter that AI, at least so far, cannot recreate itself. It does not have an inherent life-value that contributes to a holistic natural balance. This could, however, be objected to by posthumanist approaches, where the "more-than-human" substitute the "human" of modernism, particularly if one takes object-oriented ontology's tenets as ontological reference (Harman, 2018).

In this hierarchy, intrinsic values are good for their own sake, namely living things. Edwards (2010) states that intrinsic values are based on the entity's consciousness and self-awareness, its creativity and capacity to value, an end *to*, *in* and *for* itself. Some philosophers include in this category only human beings, others expand it to all conscious beings (Hartman, 2019) and some refer also to animals (Edwards, 2010), with the widest inclusion taking into account plants (McMurtry, 2009–10). Without delving into animism, we see McMurtry's argument about life-value, quoted above, as the reason to take a holistic perspective when including all living beings into intrinsic values.

Extrinsic values are, in Edwards' (2010) terms, useful or potentially useful objects, processes or activities. He states, "Extrinsic properties are spatiotemporal properties existing in our common perceptual environment, our shared everyday world of space-time as given to us in ordinary sense experience" (p. 60). Emphasising that extrinsic values are spatiotemporal again highlights that mere ideas, ideologies and other abstract thought processes are systemic and not extrinsic, as they are often referred to in articles and books that do not have this three-layered hierarchy.

If we therefore apply this hierarchy to *Teaching Tourism*, we find that the thoughts and ideas presented here all count as systemic values. The actual book, and we in our roles as researchers and teachers, are counted as extrinsic values. The only intrinsic values are the unique and distinct individuals that each of us are in our own rights, reading this and thinking about these matters within our own contexts.

The following chapters thus build on this foundation, adapting and illustrating the hierarchy of values in action. There are chapters with examples of systemic values that we live in accordance to, such as ideas and ideologies that relate to politics, societies, ecologies, economics, growth and development. However, if incorrectly implemented, these same values become disvalues holistically for the earth. There are also chapters that highlight another type of systemic value – aspirational values that aim at enhancing axiological life-values. And among all values (intrinsic, extrinsic and systemic) in the value hierarchy, there is also an internal hierarchy that relates to their good- or bad-making properties, so that some are more preferred, and others less.

In sum, by learning how to value matters axiologically, and by considering this approach as a first philosophy, *Teaching Tourism* aims to move beyond the object–subject dichotomy of ontological and epistemological investigations and present a truly values-based teaching of tourism.

3. Political values

Johan Edelheim; Marion Joppe; Joan Flaherty; Jaume Guia; Stefanie Benjamin; Maja Turnšek

OBJECTIVES

This chapter provides readers with insights and engagement activities to help students:

1. Determine why people could be called *Homo politicus* rather than *Homo sapiens*
2. Discuss the connection between democracy and political correctness, and the advantages and disadvantages of the latter in a democracy
3. Appraise why populism is gaining momentum in modern societies, and why it does not offer substantive promise for the future
4. Examine connections among nationalism, colonialism and tourism
5. Understand how worldviews influence political values

INTRODUCTION

Political values might sound like something solely restricted to politics and politicians, but all of us are political beings in our daily lives and actions. Sometimes our political values are explicitly expressed, such as through memberships in political parties or engagement for or against certain causes. But sometimes these values are expressed more subtly, such as through clicking the *Like* button in social media to express support or participating in boycotts of certain products or services to express disagreement with what they represent. Teaching and research are inherently political, because they reflect our decisions on what to include and what to exclude from the material we present to students in our classes and to colleagues across the world reading our peer-reviewed articles. Naturally, we strive for impartiality, aiming to be as objective as our topic requires us to be. A moment's reflection on our teaching and research might reveal that we are applying this objective approach to promoting specific political agendas in our classes and in our publications – thus confirming that we are, indeed, political beings (*Homo politicus*). Being aware of this aspect of our identity can make us stronger teachers and researchers, which is one reason PhD candidates are asked about the epistemological and ontological positioning of their dissertations – questions, we feel, that should also be directed to their axiological positioning.

This chapter looks at how political values at all levels (local, regional, national and global) are strongly connected to tourism flows, trends and developments. Politicians have a role here: to promote the place they represent, while enhancing the lives of the people they represent (or, at least, that is their role in theory). We therefore investigate how some bases of democracy, liberalism, party politics, populism and nationalism have an impact on how we teach and learn tourism. We also query the impact of political correctness on political values and on what we choose to say (or not say) to our students, both in and outside the classroom.

HOMO POLITICUS

Human beings are *political beings*, a fact made evident through our *explicit* and *implicit* actions, as described above. And underlying those actions are political values. When we go about our daily lives, selecting products and services to consume, we are constantly valuing; and the choice not to consume something is as much a value-directed action as to consume something. Boycotts are well-defined examples of this. We learn why a company or an entire nation is "bad" according to somebody we respect or trust, and we follow their lead in not consuming products and services from that entity. However, we have also the responsibility to be aware of what we *do* consume because every act of consumption is simultaneously a political act of accepting the premises by which that consumption is made possible.

Let us take a simple example: we go shopping to buy a new shirt. We find a shirt we like at a fast-fashion shop. It is stylish and cheap, so we buy it. Now, we have in this act accepted *everything* that is related to how that shirt is produced, transported and marketed. The fibres to make the shirt might come from fossil fuels, the primary contributor to climate change; the dyes to make the colours might be environmental toxins, killing local nature where it is produced; the workers who make the shirt might be underpaid, or they might even be forced to do the work as prisoners or refugees; and the profit made from the sale of the shirt might end up in a tax shelter, no part of it contributing to the greater good of the community. We cited fast-fashion here, but it is simply an example – and not an exceptional one, at that. We could have used any brand of any product or any service to illustrate our point, including those in the tourism industry. Indeed, selecting to go on holiday somewhere is just as much a political act as all other forms of consumption. We are not just *Homo sapiens* – thinking beings – but equally *Homo politicus* – political beings.

The idea of *Homo politicus* is therefore an extension of *social reality*, which is examined in Chapter 5 on social values. Both themes examine how actions reflect *norms* in our societies. Consequently, buying a cheap shirt or going on holiday to a nation led by a military leader who throws opposition politicians and union leaders in prison might be perfectly normal behaviour. Judging by our spending habits and vacation preferences, we are no different from our friends and relatives; quite the contrary. Insofar as we follow the norms in our societies, we function well in the given roles of our social realities.

However, that does not take away our responsibility as political beings.

Although some might not be comfortable with our earlier assertion, it bears repeating: each academic is, in essence, a political being. Therefore, each act we commit is a political act insofar as it accepts or rejects a range of other acts. This statement sets the foundation for Greenwood's (previously Gruenewald) ethos of critical pedagogy, where he quotes Giroux (1988): "educators and students should become 'transformative intellectuals' [...] capable of identifying and redressing the world's injustices" (Gruenewald, 2003, p. 4). To do otherwise – that is, to know about an injustice and decide not to address it – makes us, in essence, complicit to the injustice.

CONVERSATION STARTER

Your students might disagree that we are all political beings, so in order to test the premises of this argument, ask them to give examples of any open and public act they may make (that is, an act that carries no social or legal censure) that in no way whatsoever forces them to accept norms in society or has a political dimension to it. As your students soon will discover, this is almost an impossibility.

Discussing whether certain destinations should be boycotted because of human rights or animal welfare abuses can make for a lively debate about the pros and cons of such action and exposes students at the same time to countries with which they might be less familiar. The discussion might also expose students to a perspective they may not have previously considered: their own complicity, potential or real, in perpetuating these abuses. Human rights and animal welfare violations can stem not just from the destination itself, but also from the behaviour of tourists visiting the destination. In this case, the discussion might also revolve around the right of certain destinations to impose stricter control over tourists' behaviour. Good candidates for the discussion could be Muslim countries where tourists dress and behave in a manner blatantly disrespectful of their host communities' beliefs and customs; destinations considered sacred by the local population that are desecrated by tourists whose behaviour is openly irreverent (for example, swearing, using loud voices, photographing people at prayer); colonial settler countries where Indigenous populations are expected to conform to Western sensibilities around animal hunts; and Morocco and its occupation of the Western Sahara, which has forced many of the Sahrawi people into refugee camps and is the focus of the activity below. Students can also be asked to make their own list of countries with offensive practices they are aware of – and come to their own conclusions about whether their home countries should be included on that list. This discussion would also bring in ethical values and a reflection on the economic pain imposed on the destination's population.

ACTIVITY

In his teaching case "Tourism to promote political responsibility", Jaume Guia takes the notion of tourism as a political act to an extreme (see Activity 3). The case presents a course involving a field trip to an actual refugee camp where students are challenged to rethink the consideration and care for host communities, which is often romanticised and, at most, moralistic but not political. He suggests that, as a consequence, even with the best "moral" intentions, tourism loses its potential for curbing structural injustices, and visitors return home happy to have improved their skills, thus reinforcing the neo-liberal system at the base of the structural injustices.

The Internet also abounds with pictures and videos of holidaymakers on the beach completely unfazed by refugees and migrants making their way ashore after an arduous and hazardous journey to escape horrific conditions. Do an online search of videos that present the above scenario. YouTube is a good source. Could this be an alternative exercise to get students thinking about the incongruency of pleasure versus desperation – and the political values underlying this juxtaposition?

POLITICAL CORRECTNESS

Political correctness is embedded with values that teachers must openly address. Democracy is often seen as the preferred political system in nations that respect universal values and human rights. Like so many other words, "democracy" is related to politics in Western languages, borrowed from the original Greek words *demos* (people) and *kratos* (to rule). Those two words give us an insight into what democracy is meant to be. If we live in a democracy, we live in a nation where the people (of that nation) rule over how the nation should be governed (or that is, at least, the intention).

A democratic nation should give all its citizen equal and fair opportunities to be and become whatever they choose to. Free speech is one part of democracy, ensuring that people's opinions are not censored, even if those opinions do not appease the people in power. As always, freedom comes with responsibility: to be free to express one's opinions, one should simultaneously make sure that these opinions are in the interest of the overall good. Freedom is by nature axiological, and the three layers of the axiological hierarchy can be seen where talks and ideologies that are proclaimed belong to systemic values. The actions taken to enhance people's living are extrinsic values, and the actual effect on living beings relates to intrinsic values. If somebody is using their right to free speech to hurt others, then it is a disvalue and should be stopped. This intervention is not a limitation of free speech in an axiological meaning, but rather the fulfilment of common good.

Another part of living in a democracy, related to the disvalue of misusing free speech, is that one should not be afraid of being discriminated against because one belongs to a less powerful or minority group. No ideology, action or speech can justify discrimination of less powerful individuals or groups, based on political opinion, age, physical or mental state, ethnicity, social standing, religion, sex, gender, sexual orientation or any other possible non-mainstream grouping.

The wish not to express, intentionally or unintentionally, discriminatory views toward a minority leads to another issue: political correctness.

Political correctness, sometimes abbreviated as PC, is an openly stated goal at most educational institutions, reflected in, for example, anti-harassment measures or ethics approvals of research projects. However, it is also a covert social norm that anyone should know how to navigate within the context in which they act. The overt measures are helpful for all involved as they clearly describe social expectations that aim to create a fair and democratic environment where no one has anything to fear from others' actions. Politically correct statements are, or at least should be, respectful. They should not take for granted any one group's privilege, but rather act inclusively to incorporate all. It is thereby politically correct to not make sexist remarks, joke about stereotypes or show disrespect toward any individual or group that in any way might be regarded as not having the same privileges as the speaker.

At the same time, political correctness is not unproblematic (Ely et al., 2006). It is often accompanied by an assumed moralistic superiority on the part of those upholding political correctness toward those they perceive as trespassing set rules (Fox, 2018). An excellent parody of the downsides of political correctness can be seen in the American animated TV series *South Park* from season 19 onwards, when the new principal of the elementary school  is introduced, PC Principal, followed by the vice-principal, Strong Woman, and their children, referred to as PC Babies. The writers use these characters as ironic portrayals of the hypocrisy that can lurk beneath the surface of political correctness. The PC Babies, for example, cry at the most minute reference that can be (mis)interpreted as politically incorrect. Their extreme sensitivity and expectation of being treated with "kid gloves" is used to poke fun at the so called "snowflake generation" (Abrahams and Brooks, 2019). More seriously, it is also used to warn about the folly of political correctness taken to extremes.

This lesson takes us back to teaching tourism in our present classrooms. On the one hand, we have the responsibility to raise socially, culturally and politically uncomfortable matters; on the other hand, we also have the responsibility to not offend our students. Fox (2018) makes excellent arguments for how universities are part of the problem in creating rules aimed at curbing "hate speech". These rules, however well intentioned, impose layers of censorship that reduce students' ability to listen to diverse viewpoints. (This topic is examined further in this chapter, under *Populism, political platforms and ideologies*.)

In sum, free speech, political correctness, anti-discrimination measures and democratic processes all have an axiological communal good at heart, yet their mutations and misuse are clear examples of disvalues. In many instances, this dichotomy is illustrated in a struggle between generations. For example, in an effort to support the values associated with political correctness, younger generations may too easily dismiss or even mock what they perceive as the overly conservative views of their elders. Other examples of this dichotomy result from a kind of communal amnesia brought on by ever faster cycles of information spread that might not be epistemological in nature, but rather based on emotion. Concepts like "cancel culture", "intersectionality" or "trigger warnings" (Wyatt, 2016) relate to this debate. All have been used, in many cases incorrectly, by social elites and conservative forces to challenge justified critiques of their positions and practices. The first one, "cancel culture", is described by Clark (2020) as "an expression of agency, a choice to withdraw one's attention from someone or something whose values, (in)action, or speech are so offensive, one no longer wishes to grace them with their presence, time, and money" (Clark, 2020, p. 88). Now, "cancelling" or withdrawing one's attention to a person, cause or business may be a rational and justified course of action – but not when it is prompted by a mob mentality. Fox (2018) uses the example of a Labour-supporting drag queen, Vanity von Glow, who after performing at an event also attended by right-wing speakers found herself "cancelled" by her own community, and declared "guilty by association" (Fox, 2018, p. 4). Thus, what Vanity said at the event was not taken in consideration, but rather that she performed at an event alongside people with different opinions to her and her community.

Thus, even with the best intentions, any rules and norms that are "imposed" can always prompt counter arguments by those positioned on the other side. The result is then a conversational combat, where rational arguments often cannot compete with emotional positions. In other words, the dominant logic is dialectics. Posthumanist positions, drawn from Deleuze's philosophy and made explicit by Braidotti (2018), break away from dialectics and embrace an affirmative ethics of difference and production of the new – instead of the negative ethics of sameness and the defence of the old, the original (which does not exist because of the implicit infinite regress).

Therefore, censure is a problem here, and political correctness is essential, but perhaps it does not have to be "normative" in a universalistic sense. Perhaps political correctness could be an individual and situated responsibility (that is, a responsibility of all individuals), which would require a capacity for attentiveness and attunement that the current pedagogies definitely do not develop.

The point we want to make here is that it is important to be aware of these pitfalls and to actively consider them in one's own teaching practice. It is worthwhile not only to follow the debates on pertinent issues through media and discussion groups, but also to create one's own axiological position, for a clearer understanding of where one's values reside in these matters. It is easy to laugh at silly antics in satires such as *South Park*, but it is also very important to locate one's own privileged position and make sure that one does not moralise away valid statements of grief by people in less powerful positions.

CONVERSATION STARTER

Fox (2018) quotes research that states that 74 per cent of respondents who are 16–26 years old feel that they are psychologically damaged by being referred to as "snowflakes". Ask half the class to take a position supporting this notion and the other half to take a position against it.

This exercise could also be linked to Maja Turnšek's "Combating negative prejudice against young people" (see Activity 39).

ACTIVITY

In her teaching case "Yes-and: how to create a brave space by incorporating improvisational theatre games", Stefanie Benjamin presents improvisation (improv) as a way of getting beyond locked positions and parties who do not want to hear opposing views (see Activity 2). Improv is a communal art form that requires spontaneity, offers generous mutual support and forces participants to get out of their heads and access deeper parts of themselves to help them manage change. Stefanie shows us how we can use improv to take the focus off ourselves and suspend personal judgement.

POPULISM, POLITICAL PLATFORMS AND IDEOLOGIES

In a growing number of nations, people with limited political experience – and, in some cases, no experience at all in party politics – are holding high-level political positions. The rise of "non-political politicians" can be traced to media and to changes in our societies. As discussed in Chapter 5 on social values, these changes have been gradual, but are now accelerating, which leaves people in a state of uncertainty as they struggle to navigate their changed societal structures.

Our societies have held onto remnants of earlier societal structures that have no reason for being maintained. Some of these are now targeted for a rapid change. For example, being present at a physical location called "work" for eight hours per day is a remnant of earlier times that is often unnecessary. If a person's job is to process information on a computer, on their own, then why would that person have to perform the work in a certain place at a certain time? As long as a task gets done within the required time, then it should not really matter precisely when or where it is performed. Or does it? Right now, as we are writing this book, COVID-19 is bringing these questions to the forefront, prompting changes to the old conventions. Consequently, many employers are allowing non-contact employees to work from home, which leads to speculation on whether this practice will continue post pandemic. Microsoft, Google and Twitter, among others, have already announced that remote work will be a long-term business strategy for them – a strategy that imposes a radical change into people's lives.

The connection between these kinds of changes and populism, political platforms and ideologies may be subtle, but it is real.

In times of change and uncertainty, such as in the above example, people worry about how their lives will be affected. And one reaction to worry is anger. After all, the changes might threaten an individual's chosen and familiar way of life. In fact, the changes might not include that individual at all, obscuring the clear future they had planned for themselves. One way to escape all this worry and anger is to embrace an affirmative ethics, which brings hope for the perpetual return to the different (instead of the same). However, humanist and modernist politics (also the liberal democracies that we live in), with their rootedness on norms, essences and foundationalism, fail to advance this. Consequently, the fear and anger persist. If a politician, or an opinion-leader, at this stage suggests that the reason for the threatening change is easily eradicated and thus the status quo restored, then it might be tempting to believe that person. Judging by recent history, these opinion-leaders do not even need a reasonable plan to implement their proposed changes. They simply have to focus on the changes and on the uncertainty, worry and anger that these changes have created.

As part of that strategy, ultra-conservative politicians and populists often target political correctness and its different dimensions, such as anti-discrimination policies and "trigger warnings", which attempt to change unfair structural positions. Instead of taking the critique to heart, the populist movement distorts the critique into an assault on common values, whereby they present themselves as defenders of the common good – all while rejecting attempts at larger equality.

When political leaders position themselves as representing "ordinary people" who are seen as "good" in juxtaposition to "the elite" who are somehow corrupt or self-serving, they are appealing to those citizens who see themselves as ignored in the midst of societal change or even victimised by the change. These leaders speak to their fears and general opposition to liberal pluralism. In additional, populists often see themselves as true patriots and tend to hold fundamentalist religious beliefs that they wish to see imposed on all aspects of society.

Populism has also led to a time of "post-truth", where arguments are not supported with data and reason, but rather with emotions. For instance, we saw much anger expressed during the pandemic at having to wear masks, ostensibly because it infringes on the freedom of individuals. Indeed, these emotively backed arguments are often presented as conservative values, but are actually their opposite. Here the systemic value of freedom is put against the extrinsic value of care for others. Populist politics do not strive for clearly defined goals as values do. Rather, they act as anti-opinions, being against anything that does not serve their restrictive agenda.

A tremendous responsibility lies with us, as educators, to introduce our students to politics and political values. The goal here is not to subjectively push our students to accept only our opinions, but rather to explain how different political platforms function, and to encourage students to examine what the different political parties in their societies stand for. Tourism is often seen as a relatively apolitical act and sector – especially so by the business communities that want to highlight travel and leisure as "breaks" from regular society. However, as discussed above, acts are always political, and it is of essence for students to understand what role they themselves play in the larger picture.

As also discussed in Chapter 8 on ethics, trust in politicians is very low all over the world – a sad fact since many of us personally know people who engage in politics for the good of their communities. Their integrity and belief in their abilities to make a positive difference is admirable, and it is therefore very concerning that the common picture of somebody engaged in politics is, in many cases, quite negative. Media has a role in this: storylines are often more enticing when they highlight political failure and deception rather than success and promises kept. Although most professional journalists aim to be objective and factually accurate, all media are biased. However, some media channels are more openly supportive of certain positions and more blatantly dismissive of the opposition. Each individual also bears a responsibility for this bias. We tend to seek out in the media those opinions and values that we agree with, while opposing opinions are rejected or silenced in one's mind.

The importance of staying neutral as teachers and allowing for differences to be aired and debated in our classrooms is critical. It would be easy to invite only politicians that we agree with into our classrooms, but by doing so we would, in essence, be contributing to the distrust in politics at large. Instead, by giving students the power to interrogate ideologies behind different political views, we help transform students into independent thinkers. Certainly, this would be an excellent opportunity to teach affirmative ethics (and politics), instead of perpetuating the failed dialectical logic that dominates and completely permeates our current ideologies (when it comes to party politics, liberal democracies and populism alike). Only the concept of radical democracy opens a way toward affirmative ethics and toward a real "political" responsibility of each individual. At most, the current ideologies will foster "moralisms" and therefore will reinforce depoliticisation and dialectics.

Ideologies are, in Harari's phrasing, "the stories we choose to believe and tell one another" (Harari, 2014, p. 27), and that each listener or reader either accepts or rejects. Dominant ideologies seem logical to all who accept them. Otherwise, they would not be commonly accepted. But no ideology is more than a systemic value. It expresses ideas and wishes for a common good, but it is never more than the words and ideas that it entails. The actions that come out of different ideologies are extrinsic values. Extrinsic values, such as environmental or social activism, are the ones we should give our students an opportunity to question, so that they understand how the actions resulting from those values affect so many living things.

CONVERSATION STARTER

 The story of Canada's worst ever outbreak of E. coli contamination in a small rural town and the attempt by the government to restore people's faith in the quality of the drinking water had the unintended consequence of shutting down many small businesses that were engaged in tourism activities to supplement their main source of income. This story is captured in Marion Joppe's "Unintended consequences of policy implementation" (see Activity 4).

ACTIVITY

 Ahead of a local or national election in the region where you are active, invite representatives from different political parties to present the impact of their policies on, for example, inbound and outbound tourism, or any other issue being dealt with in your courses. Give clear guidelines for how long you want each representative to talk and what issues you want them to focus on.

It is generally good to discuss these matters in class before having the guests, so that students come prepared to ask questions and actively probe the different representatives on how their positions will differently affect the students' future lives and careers.

NATIONALISM AND OTHER STORIES WE TELL OURSELVES

The subject of the above subheading is deeply engrained in our collective imagination and strongly entangled with tourism. Our reference to "collective imagination" is borrowed from Benedict Anderson's (1991) work on nationalism. He shows that all modern nation states have relatively short histories, but all share a common feature: they lay claim to historical antecedents that are jointly presented as a logical entity called the "nation". Tangible elements (for example, flags, stamps, currency) or intangible features (for example, anthems, landscapes, art) are jointly presented as representing a unity. Nationalism is a result of nation-building, an exaggeration of certain features claimed to be distinct and specific, much in the same way tourist destinations present themselves to potential tourists. (The problem with this is presented below.) Nations around the world all have their own myths and stories that collectively function as the "glue" for large communities to feel a sense of harmony and cohesiveness, but also a certain superiority to other nations. Politicians are naturally strong proponents of the idea of a nation, and many are proudly nationalistic.

Through their shared pride, people are happy to work for the common good, sacrificing small parts of their well-being and, in emergencies, perhaps even their own lives, to protect their nation's ideals and values. There is, however, another side to nationalism. A sense of unity does not allow for discord, and people of alternative viewpoints can therefore be shunned. Nationalism might be used unscrupulously by some people who advance their own interests under the guise of being nationalistic.

Tourism can have a negative role to play in this as well. Tourism branding is used by countries as a strategy for their nationalistic strength, and most travellers fall into that trap (or they are fine with it in the first place), thus reinforcing the perpetuation of "the same". This is particularly seen in the romanticising forces that some visitors put into the visited societies, which like all others are in constant change, but have to remain (or pretend to remain) as tourism likes it, so that the tourists can be satisfied. A lot of community tourism is based on this argument and as a result culture is commodified, which is problematic. Even more problematic, however, is that the commodification of culture reinforces depoliticisation.

National and Indigenous minorities are relevant here because through tourism they may have some recognition, which in centralistic and conservative states is a good thing. (Otherwise, they would be silenced and, to borrow from a term used earlier, cancelled out.) But this recognition also "folklorises" the national minority, which at most gets locked as a "differential folklore" within the "sacred" unity of the nation state, thus violating blatantly the right of minorities for self-determination. Most constitutions do not allow for the self-determination of minorities and are thus violating human rights. But nobody cares. The rule of law seems to be regarded as a superior (divine?) value. Everybody (including the vast majority of travellers, who are not attentive to these matters) seems to accept it. Why else, for instance, do tourists not use the name of the minority nation region or land when they refer to their destination, instead of using the ubiquitous "legal" names of the current nation states? Many scholars committed to ethics in tourism also fail to be attentive to this. By reproducing the words of the dominant framework, we are also acting politically and reinforcing the institutional injustices of the status quo.

A nationalist from any nation would probably strongly oppose these views, and claim that they, in their specific nation, represent something special, which we (as outsiders to their unity) cannot understand.

The point of bringing nationalism as a political value into this chapter is to highlight that it is a construct just as society and ideologies are constructs. Nationalistic values are always hard to argue against. The moment a person attempts to unravel a claim, they can be accused of being unpatriotic and, therefore, an enemy of the nation. The same is true for religions and any other communal beliefs that people adhere to. Finally, nationalism is connected to both colonialism and post-colonialism. According to Anderson (1991), the latter even accounts for the emergence of nationalism. The basic idea of colonialism, that any one nation should have the right to impose, for its own benefit, its rule, values and power on another nation, and at the cost of that ruled nation, comes from the ideas of culture and its accompanying sense of superiority that are examined in Chapter 6. Tourism could essentially be considered a continuation of the same, though now cloaked in the guise of leisure and pleasure. For an extension of this argument, see Edelheim (2015).

CONVERSATION STARTER

Think of two specific national features of a nation that you feel affinity with. How do those features define you, and how are they so specific to your nation that no outsider would be able to understand them?

4. Ecological values

Johan Edelheim; **Marion Joppe**; **Joan Flaherty**; Karla A.
Boluk; Alexandra Coghlan; Tazim Jamal; Xavier Michel;
Miranda Peterson; Bradley Rink; Sarah Ripper; Sudipta
Kiran Sarkar; Chiaki Shimoyasuba; Maja Turnšek

OBJECTIVES

This chapter provides readers with insights and engagement activities to help students:

1. Characterise the different dimensions of *nature* that humans understand and relate to
2. Explain what it means to live in the Anthropocene
3. Provide a calculation to determine a person's fair share of the total carbon consumption on
   Earth in a year
4. Discuss the role various industries of the tourism sector play with respect to climate change

INTRODUCTION

Eco-centred values are more than a recurring theme throughout this book. In many ways, they
are the reason for the book. In our introductory chapters on holistic education and axiological
life values, we emphasise the need to move beyond thinking about nature and, instead, to think
through nature. The distinction is important as this latter concept refers to the lenses through
which we consider nature based on how we have looked at environmental history until now
and the challenges the future holds for our survival on the planet. This is something we can do
by supporting "students in developing approaches that are based on more sensitive entangle-
ments between the Earth systems and humanity" (Höckert et al., 2020, p. 170).

Ecological values are often the first casualty when different kinds of changes, developments
and investments are proposed. For example, supporters of a holiday resort typically focus on
the potential employment and tax benefits of the development. However, prioritising these
economic and social values may come at a cost: reduced available land for animals, plants
and general liveability; a polluted water supply, which means local fresh water has to be
supplied from elsewhere; and so on. It is a simple example, but it shows clearly the vulnerability of ecological values when pitted against other kinds of values, particularly economic.
Tourism research in the late 1970s and 1980s, most notably epitomised in Jafari's "Cautionary
Platform" (Jafari, 1990), warned us about this vulnerability and its consequences. In doing so,
it presented us with the first wave of the ecological values discussed here.

This chapter discusses different kinds of ecological values and presents an argument for incorporating them in almost all subjects taught in a tourism degree. An unfortunate development in tourism curricula (and, indeed, in higher education generally) is the practice of assigning "ownership" of a specific theme to a particular course or programme. Concepts with broad relevance, such as nature, the Anthropocene, greenwashing and ecotourism, get sequestered in their own academic unit of study. Therefore, other subjects or degrees are implicitly "released" from their responsibility to think through the same issues, even though these issues may be intimately connected with the subject or degree at hand. The contextual dimensions within which all knowledge exists are thus lost, and higher education moves increasingly closer to a focus on transmission of information rather than transformation of its learners.

The ethos engrained in ecological values and, more largely, in a holistic values mindset has taken different shapes and ebbed and flowed over the past decades. More recently, research has focused on terms such as "ecotourism", "sustainable tourism", "responsible tourism" and "regenerative tourism" that have, like waves, washed over the tourism research and education landscape, slowly but not fully awakening us to a holistic perspective. For example, the tourism sector still cynically – and ironically – cherry-picks sections of the holistic movement to further its own selected interests. This practice has given rise to a multitude of new definitions and demarcations, such as ecotourism versus sustainable tourism, or sustainable tourism versus responsible tourism, each with its own proponents. All the while, tourism's greater impact – climate change – has been largely ignored.

To understand how tourism can be supportive of the good for ecology and the ecosystems it functions in, we need to clearly see it from a holistic perspective. We need to incorporate messy issues such as people's fair share of carbon consumption, peak oil and the Anthropocene beyond courses and degrees with names like "Environmental tourism" into the full curriculum. It is the separation of subjects in our degrees that encourages insular, blinkered thinking in both ourselves, as educators, and in our students. Therefore, this chapter investigates dimensions of ecological values and proposes teaching contexts to address these values.

CONVERSATION STARTER

It is always challenging to forge new thought paths. The ones where our mind has already wandered feel familiar and safe. However, our task as educators is to encourage students to explore new paths, perhaps by asking them to examine distinct cases of congregated value sets that might alter the way they consider similar situations elsewhere. Chiaki Shimoyasuba's con- tribution "Iomante rituals: ecological and economic values meet cultural values" illustrates how an Indigenous tradition involving the ritual killing of a bear cub, which was banned for decades in the name of "civilisation", has been re-established as it exemplifies the convergence of culture, human and more-than-human coexistence (see Activity 9).

ACTIVITY

Tourist authenticity not only connects with objects and places of visit, but more widely with one's way of living in the world. Xavier Michel's "Mobilising learners' tourist memories towards a deeper, more authentic understanding and practice of tourism" aims to make tourists aware of the authentic tourist experiences through (1) the tourists' mindfulness of their presence in the world and (2) the tourists' environmental ethics (see Activity 7).

ECOLOGY: NATURE

Ecological values relate to the natural systems of Earth, those that exist and function without need of human input and the emphasis humans put on these systems. We often combine the terms "ecology" and "nature", usually in contrast to "culture" or "civilisation" – a theme touched on in Chapter 6 on cultural values. "Nature" is again a tricky word: at once self-evident, it is also very complex, which is why we have decided to talk about *ecological values* rather than *natural values* in this book. A simplistic view might suggest that everything that is not created by humans is "natural", and everything made by humans is "man-made" and therefore "unnatural". However, humans have existed on Earth for millions of years, and many things we consider natural nowadays were actually created in the past by other humans. Most, if not all, of the plants we cultivate, animals we domesticate and even landscapes we inhabit have to a large degree been shaped by human actions over the course of history. Even the word "natural", which we use so *naturally*, exists only as a definition within cultures. If this culturally imposed definition did not exist, then nothing and/or everything would be natural.

Suopajärvi (2001), in her research on local land use, developed a model describing diverse ways nature was perceived by different stakeholders. Her model was based on a tripartite interpretation of how nature was referred to: from a pre-modern perspective, nature as a living space containing traditional livelihoods; from a modernist perspective, nature as full of natural resources to be extracted; or finally from a postmodern perspective, nature as a stage to be experienced. This model is one of the best explanations of why a group of stakeholders from around the world might well run into conflict when they discuss nature with each other: three different ways of understanding what nature means to different groups of people sets the stage for potential misunderstandings and disagreements.

At the risk of adding fuel to the fire, we add a fourth perspective to this model: human beings as not separate from nature, but rather one with nature or, conversely, nature as a person in its own right according to the law (see Figure 4.1). This perspective could represent an Indigenous holistic reading of nature following cases in Ecuador, Colombia, New Zealand and India, where rivers and forests have been granted legal status as persons (FSDS, 2015; Funes, 2018; Hollingsworth, 2020).

The way we perceive nature and the natural, the ecosystem and ecological matters, is also tied up with the languages we speak because languages shape the way we think. Boroditsky, an American psycholinguist, has proven how different linguistic patterns make people think differently (2011). She tested her subjects' perceptions on topics such as order, time, metaphors, agency and sex to determine if a relationship existed between their perceptions and the

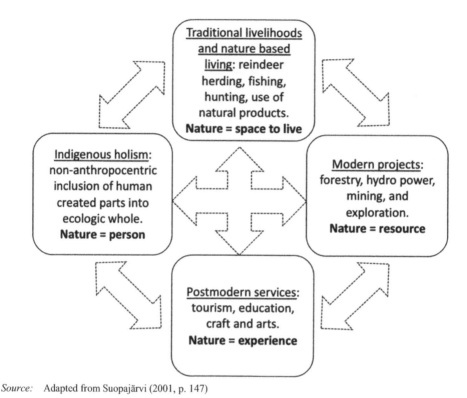

Source: Adapted from Suopajärvi (2001, p. 147)

Figure 4.1   Four dimensions of nature

language in which they were tested. Her results confirmed that linguistically diverse groups think differently about the same groups of objects or geographical features.

"Ecology" might therefore be a better word to characterise the values presented in this chapter. Ecology is closely connected to biology, geology and other natural sciences. Thus, it is related to the "real world" that exists "out there", outside of our books and papers, computers and buildings, but naturally it is also a part of the air we breathe and the ambient climate we inhabit. Ecological values are also in focus whenever people think of the impact of human actions on Earth. In order to survive on Earth, we depend on its ecosystems functioning as they did for billions of years – before human actions caused its resources to become exploited and entire species to become extinct.

CONVERSATION STARTERS

Ask your students to brainstorm food products regularly consumed in your society that are entirely "natural". In other words, these foods have not been modified, moved to new geographical areas or changed by human action ever. Regardless of where in the world you start this conversation, you will find that the list is short, and that many of its entries are signs of a modern globalised society. This discussion links what we see as natural with what we see as traditional, national or authentic, all of which are value dimensions touched on in other chapters.

Connected to how language shapes our realities, as mentioned above, view Lera Boroditsky's TED talk on "How language shapes thought".[1] It is a short and thought-provoking investigation of how people perceive similar situations differently, depending on their mother tongue.

ACTIVITY

 Karla Boluk describes "Using systems thinking and the UN's SDG framework as an opportunity for fostering critical dialogue" as a way to teach interdisciplinary topics related to both lived values and aspirational values (see Activity 32). She highlights how this is of essence to tourism teaching due to the trans- and intra-disciplinary sciences the field depends on, where the status quo can be challenged only by active critical thinking, reflection and dialogue.

THE ANTHROPOCENE

The Anthropocene is a new concept slowly gaining prominence in tourism research. One way to understand the Anthropocene is to refer to the geological epochs of Earth and to examine the time we live in right now, on an Earth shaped by human actions. In contrast, earlier epochs were characterised by, and classified based on, environmental factors predominant at those times, such as temperature and rainfall. Some of the factors were beneficial for organisms and some were detrimental.

While not all scientists agree that the Anthropocene should be considered a separate geological epoch, the term refers to a period of significant human impact on Earth's geology, ecosystems and atmosphere, starting in 1950. Of course, human activity had impacted Earth before this. Agriculture left traces in the rocks as long ago as AD 900, and the Industrial Revolution's environmental effects began in the early 1800s. However, environmentalists in particular point to the start of the atomic age in the 1950s as the time when humans became fully aware of their actions' planet-scale influence, but chose to continue down that path nonetheless. The choice was predicated on humans' perception of themselves as being beyond or outside nature, rather than being a part of nature. All the extractive modernist projects that see nature as a resource for the human race to utilise belong in their rationale to Anthropocene values.

These values have led to the sixth mass extinction – or the Anthropocene extinction – which refers to the extinction of numerous plant and animal species because of human actions. Tourism contributes significantly to this ongoing ecological disaster as many resorts and other leisure facilities are still being built close to water. In the process, we drain swamps and cut down mangrove forests, both of which filter waste, stabilise soil and provide spawning and nursery territories for many species. We harden the edges of rivers, lakes and oceanfront, destroying various grass species on the sand dunes that prevent erosion and protect nesting animals. We even build entire islands to maximise development of highly prized waterfront property. For example, the construction of Dubai's megaprojects Palm Islands and The World has caused massive damage to the marine habitat by burying coral reefs and oyster and sea grass beds, leading to a substantial loss of biodiversity.

ACTIVITY

To distinguish ecological values from other values, students need to develop their ecological literacy. This thinking builds on a multiliteracies perspective that extends the idea of what it means to be literate beyond simple reading and writing, but also incorporates critical literacy. Tazim Jamal and Miranda Peterson present "Climate action for a climate-friendly educational destination", where they show the need for students to be climate literate to become climate active (see Activity 6).

CARBON FOOTPRINT: FAIR SHARE

Life on Earth is structured around carbon and oxygen, in different forms. That is, in order for most plants and animals to exist they need to receive and to release carbon and oxygen. One compound created from the two is carbon dioxide (CO_2), which is essential for plant growth but becomes lethal in too large concentrations. A calculation that shows if an action increases or decreases the amount of CO_2 in the surrounding environment gives us that action's carbon footprint. All activities and events on Earth have some kind of carbon footprint. In other words, everything that happens either increases or decreases Earth's CO_2. Researchers estimate how many activities can take place in any one area without damaging its ecology. This estimate is referred to as "carrying capacity". In order to maintain a balance in the ecology, and not overuse resources, different carbon footprint calculators have been developed. These calculators help us estimate what effect the consumption of any one service or product has on the ecology as a whole.

Right now, consumption in privileged countries far outstrips the actual resources available on Earth. This overconsumption is annually highlighted through Earth Day, which identifies the day of the year by which resources that Earth can reproduce in one year have already been used up. This day is different in different countries. Generally, however, Earth Day falls on an earlier date each year due to the general increase in consumption in most societies. Reversing this trend means that each society must limit itself to its fair share of environmental resources (McMullin et al., 2020). Fair share is calculated by dividing Earth's carrying capacity to absorb and utilise the CO_2 produced in a year by the number of humans living on Earth right now. Satterthwaite (2011) cites the Stern report[2] (2009) when he states that in order "to bring down global emissions by 2050 sufficiently to avoid dangerous climate change, it needs a global average of around 2 tonnes of CO2e per person" (p. 1769). The resulting figure tells us how much each person could consume as a fair share of the whole, if everyone would consume within or below the carrying capacity. To maintain our planet's health, the simple rule is that non-renewable resources should not be exploited faster than substitute, renewable resources are developed.

ACTIVITY

Ask students to search the Internet for carbon footprint calculators and, based on their own personal details, calculate their carbon footprint. What is their carbon footprint per year? Is this footprint above or below the average? Is it a "fair share"? Assuming they maintain the same consumption for the rest of their lives and assuming an average life span of 75 years, at what age would they have used up the fair share for any person on Earth? (See also Marion Joppe's "Calculating a carbon footprint" and "The limits to biocapacity", Activities 33 and 34, respectively.)

CLIMATE CHANGE AND PEAK OIL

The biggest common issue we have to consider in our lives is arguably climate change. A major driver of climate change is global warming, which refers to the increase in temperature on Earth, largely caused by human-induced activity such as the burning of fossil fuels, deforestation and farming. While some people still deny that human action is the cause of the many changes in Earth's climate, the facts do not support their argument. From one perspective, though, their support of an untenable position can be understood: acknowledging the truth and acting on it threaten the kind of lives many of us are privileged to live right now. It threatens the values many of us have prioritised: economic. And it threatens the outcome of those values that many of us chase after: unfettered growth.

Ecological values are founded on the principle that Earth's ecological systems are valuable in their own right, for the environments that they provide to all organisms on Earth. That is, nature is good for its own sake. It does not need to be assigned a monetary value to be considered so. However, the economic values of growth and trade have always formed a strong incentive for humans to monetise ecological resources for their own benefit. Humans first relied on long living organisms and other renewable resources to sustain themselves. After discovering metals, they also started mining and using more refined tools. Still, it was not until the Industrial Revolution that non-renewable energy sources started becoming a strong driver of change. At the risk of stating the obvious, there is a finite amount of anything that is non-renewable, such as coal and oil. After these resources have been depleted, they cannot be renewed, at least not for millions of years.

These facts represent the challenges facing, and the urgency for, ecological values. Becken (2015) writes about our addiction to oil with this analogy: every drop of oil needed to carry out an activity is equivalent to 10,000 calories a human would need to consume to carry out that activity or a similar one. By thinking about oil and other non-renewable resources in these concrete terms, we start to realise how mindlessly we consume them – and therefore how much we devalue them or take them for granted. "Peak oil" refers to a time when oil consumption reaches a peak that cannot be sustained by production anymore, after which extraction declines and the oil resources are gradually used up totally. These types of research aim at raising both awareness of our actions, but also lead to a transformation of values that are currently dominating societies around the world.

Another important consideration in sustainability is the planet's sink function; that is, the absorption and recycling of waste produced from human activity. Waste disposal should be relative to the ecosystem's capacity to assimilate it, but industrialisation, urbanisation, population growth and consumerism are all contributing to pollution of the air, land and water that far exceeds the planetary boundaries in this regard. Furthermore, the materials that human ingenuity has created, such as the ubiquitous plastics, take hundreds of years to decompose and be absorbed.

CONVERSATION STARTER

Ask your students to investigate online sources relating to peak oil, and then debate whether Earth has already reached the peak of oil availability, or if it is still off in the future. Discuss what implications either of these alternatives have on global tourism as we know it today.

ACTIVITY

Open up the website www.flightradar24.com, which shows live air traffic all around the world. The number of flights that are in the air at any one time is really amazing, even in the midst of the COVID-19 pandemic, which stopped much so-called "non-essential travel", the category to which tourism belongs. The number of flights is even more amazing in light of the fact that only a quarter of Earth's population owns a passport that allows them to cross borders (for example, 75 per cent of Australians and Canadians, approximately 50 per cent of Germans, 42 per cent of US citizens, 24 per cent of Japanese people, 10 per cent of Chinese people and 5.5 per cent of Indians have a passport; in most countries belonging to the Global South the number is below 1 per cent of the population). Now, ask your students to estimate what the flight-tracking site would look like if even half Earth's population had a passport.

SUSTAINABLE TOURISM AND SUSTAINABILITY

In the 1980s, terms such as "sustainable tourism" and "ecotourism" were introduced. The idea of causing no harm to regions visited, but instead preserving those areas for coming generations is an appealing concept. We sustain something to keep it unchanged, but also to make sure it thrives. Smith et al. (2010) offer the following straightforward definition of sustainable tourism as "striv[ing] towards tourism that has the least possible impact on host communities and the environment, while maintaining economic viability" (p. 169). And of ecotourism: "Ecotourism takes place in unspoiled natural areas and is a form of tourism that strives to conserve the environment, enhance the lives of local communities and educate the visitor" (p. 49).

The reality, unfortunately, is not as straightforward as the definitions. The words "sustainable" and "ecotourism" are often used more for their marketing appeal than for their meaning. Their appearance on marketing websites and brochures is no guarantee that a business is operating in a manner that protects rather than destroys. The duplicity is not always evident, camouflaged behind small, superficial actions that give the appearance of honouring sustainability and ecotourism. This tactic is called "greenwashing". Examples abound in the tourist industry: tourists flying to destinations far away but staying in accommodation marketed as "eco-friendly" because of its power-saving lights, and sheets that are washed every third night.

Both the lights and laundry are good and important, but they do not compensate for the journey's carbon footprint. In 2014, the industries that made up tourism were already consuming 12 per cent of all energy on Earth. This consumption is estimated to rise to 25 per cent by 2025 and to almost 50 per cent by 2040, if tourism continues growing unhindered (Becken, 2015). The respite in travel growth caused by the COVID-19 pandemic will potentially alter these estimates. However, the talk about a "bounce back" in demand of travel as soon as humanity has learned to live with COVID-19 makes it unlikely that the pandemic will lead to any major ecological transformations. Tourism might not look like a factory that is spewing out pollution, but its relatively benign façade perhaps makes it an even more dangerous threat to Earth. Despite appearances to the contrary, tourism is a major contributor to climate change.

ACTIVITIES

In "Reflecting on sustainable behaviour", Alexandra Coghlan and Sarah Ripper define sustainability as our relationships with the natural environment, the resources we depend on, our employees, our investors, our families, our community and the governance structures that support our societies (see Activity 5). The purpose of the activities is to help students understand this intrinsic link between relationships and sustainability.

Sudipta Kiran Sarkar describes in "Experiential learning in nature-based recreational settings" how students can learn about ecological and social values by immersing themselves in an experiential learning activity and how this experience can develop their own professional expertise (see Activity 8).

SCAFFOLDED PHOTOGRAPHIC ESSAY

If the personal experience of being a tourist is uncommon for a given cohort of students, Bradley Rink's "Seeing tourism landscapes: teaching tourism at the confluence of theory and practice" provides a semester-long, scaffolded assessment task that allows students to "see" tourism in the everyday, while also critically reflecting on tourism's positive and negative impacts (see Activity 45).

NOTES

1. www.youtube.com/watch?v=RKK7wGAYP6k.
2. Stern, N. (2009). *A Blueprint for a Safer Planet*. Bodley Head.

5. Social values

Johan Edelheim; **Marion Joppe**; **Joan Flaherty**; Karla A.
Boluk; Elin Bommenel; Helene Balslev Clausen; Richard
Ek; Stephen Fairbrass; Maggie C. Miller; Nick Naumov;
Brendan Paddison; Stuart Reid; Sudipta Kiran Sarkar;
Chiaki Shimoyasuba

OBJECTIVES

This chapter provides readers with insights and engagement activities to help students:

1. Explain what a society is and identify the different societal stages that have dominated Earth during human existence
2. Demonstrate what social reality is made up of, how social positioning works and how rights and obligations are always counterposed by the other
3. Distinguish why social class is still a matter that needs to be addressed, and how it is linked to societal inequality
4. Appraise what actual needs a society has that can be called social needs, and how tourism should be considered in this context

INTRODUCTION

"Social" and "cultural" are often treated as the same thing – or as so closely related that one is rarely discussed independently of the other. To a certain extent, the same applies to "social" and "economics". These interlinkages are reflected in so many discussions you have no doubt encountered about "sociocultural" or "socio-economic" issues.

This chapter, however, separates these concepts.

"Culture" is broadly defined here as the manner in which material and non-material customs are performed in selected communities. In contrast, "social" is more narrowly interpreted: it directly relates to the people living in those same communities and their social interactions among themselves and others. And "economics" refers to interpreting and acting on the world through a lens of monetary transactions and exchange values. Of course, the definition of culture overlaps with the other two. In the end, though, fussing over the difference between, say, "customs" and "interactions" is hair-splitting. In truth, all three definitions are substantial simplifications of what a cultural studies scholar, a sociologist or an economist would accept. The point here, however, is to disentangle the concepts of "sociocultural" or "socio-economic" into three distinct entities. This might seem contradictory to our criticism of compartmentalisation in Chapter 1 on didactics, but the reason is here to highlight how lived values have distinct influences on our lives and understandings of realities. We do not forget other dimensions while examining any one of them, thus the frequent references to other chapters. We attempt instead to highlight features of all lived values that might go unnoticed had they been treated as one.

Social values refer to accepted criteria shared by a majority of a society. The values aim for "ideal" ways of acting and behaving, and for regulating and organising daily life, with the underlying assumption that the result is a better society (Türkkahraman, 2014). Education plays an integral role in conveying these values through means such as nationally set curricula and syllabi, funding models for different fields of studies and standardised testing across cohorts of students. All are examples of social values shaping education in different ways, with the goal of socialising individuals into becoming functioning members of society.

It is, when we think of it, quite amazing how human beings can agree on so many things in the complicated societies we live in, and how those agreements form the possibility for societies to function in the first place. Our countries and borders, passports and visas, laws and rules are all human-made agreements, maintained and defended by police and defence forces, lawyers and bureaucrats. This whole reality is simply based upon people figuring out ways to live together in these determined societies (Lawson, 2019). This chapter, therefore, touches on issues such as society and its different formations throughout history, social reality, class and equality, and social needs.

SOCIETY

Society as a concept relates to how people interact in groups. Historically, humankind has undergone four large shifts in terms of how we cooperate to enhance our community life. Each shift has unfolded more rapidly and within a shorter time period than the one before. The first shift was characterised by a societal structure in which humans banded together in small hunter and gatherer groups. They shared the tasks needed to survive. The second societal structure was prompted by the shift to an agricultural society where life centred around farming and animal husbandry. The third shift centred around an industrial society, where manufacturing of goods became the mainstay for humankind. The fourth shift led to the society we live in today: an information society where most people – at least in the more advanced economies – work in professions related to information processing and sharing. According to some futurists, we are now on the cusp of yet another shift, a move into Society 5.0. Indeed, Japan has already adopted this "human-centered society that balances economic advancement with the resolution of social problems by a system that highly integrates cyberspace and physical space" as part of its economic strategy (Cabinet Office Government of Japan, 2020). Some, however, disagree that the convergence between cyberspace and physical space will lead to a human-centred society. Those sceptical of developments such as Society 5.0 warn instead that various forms of self-learning and deep learning technologies associated with this shift will result in the manipulation of humans for what is falsely perceived as "the good of society" (Harari, 2016).

We can find evidence of all these societal structures existing at the same time if we look at society as it is right now. One societal structure does not fully extinguish the previous, but rather gradually replaces it as the mainstay of how humankind in general makes its living.

For example, Finland has a highly educated population, most of which (85 per cent) lives in urban areas. Yet that same population still has a strong tradition of foraging wild berries and mushrooms in late summer and into autumn. A Finnish freezer in a regular home is typically filled with frozen berries and mushrooms to be eaten throughout winter and spring, awaiting the next season to be replenished. However, the fact that this practice has been retained from an earlier societal structure does not make this highly educated, urbanised population a society of hunter-gatherers.

As societies transition from one societal structure to another, different types of competencies, knowledge and skills are required. To compete successfully, ever higher levels of education are a prerequisite. The pandemic brought the resulting inequalities into the fore: in December 2020, the average unemployment rate in the United States was 8.1 per cent for those with only a high school diploma versus 4.2 per cent for those with an undergraduate degree or higher (Sacks, 2021). Many societies nowadays rely on the knowledge economy to create value, meaning work that involves collecting, processing, storing and sharing information. With the phase-out of other societal structures, certain social values that were once taken for granted no longer hold true. As mentioned earlier, one need only examine the changing curricula of educational institutions over time to see these changes. For example, courses that were once mainstays of secondary education, such as typing or home economics, have been replaced by studies in technology or family relationships.

But that shift in values does not come without a cost. The fear and frustration among people who feel that there is no longer any need for their skills is palpable. For example, in the United States many workers in the manufacturing sector have helplessly witnessed their jobs disappear due to globalisation, and in India millions of farmers have protested the new agricultural laws out of fear that their way of life will be lost to the corporatisation of agriculture. It is never easy for anybody to simply start doing something else, and all shifts in society come with periods of unrest in different shapes.

CONVERSATION STARTER

Topical issues in many of the world's developed nations are their ageing populations, mechanisation and urbanisation. These societal changes are accompanied by challenges that will be passed on for our students to address in the future. Chiaki Shimoyasuba's "Access rights to the Commons" illustrates a case where different community stakeholders' interests need to be
balanced (see Activity 16). For example, to what extent should tourists be allowed access to sites of interest located on private property? The case illustrates how access to private and public land is negotiated in different societies.

STORYTELLING

"Values-based learning and storytelling" presents the connection between social values and our changing vacation patterns (see Activity 14). Brendan Paddison's case also illustrates how storytelling can help us examine social values over time. Students listen to stories about holidays in earlier times and what people valued about them, and then reflect on the social patterns those stories reveal about tourism as it existed then – and now.

SOCIAL REALITY

We are all inhabiting reality, are we not? We are all living beings who sleep, wake up, attend to work and studies, process information in different ways, eat, engage in leisure activities, spend time with friends or alone, and go back to sleep at some stage. All of that is reality. And when we study societies, we study that reality, especially the interactions between people in those societies. But what if we want to investigate how social realities really function? What do we need to do then?

Lawson addresses these questions in *The Nature of Social Reality: Issues in Social Ontology* (2019). Here, he discusses the concept of social positioning, which arises through two key elements that exist within all societies: positions, and occupants of positions. Each position carries certain expectations or norms that have been set by its society or community. The people who occupy these positions and follow their expectations are thus reinforcing the norms through their role performance.

This social positioning is a stable yet continuously changing set of roles that all members of society are socialised to follow. For example, a person who assumes the role of teacher is given certain rights and obligations in regard to other stakeholders in society (for example, students, parents, employers). However, that person is not always performing the role of teacher. They also shoulder a multitude of other roles, such as consumer, commuter, local politician, parent to their own children, child to their own parents, and so on.

An important element of Lawson's theory is that all positions and their occupants have set rights as well as obligations to other position occupants. A teacher has the right to set the class-room agenda. A student has an obligation to follow the teacher's instructions and to complete assignments. The teacher has thereafter an obligation to students to mark assignments according to fair rules and to provide their students with feedback and grades, and so on. However, tourism educators in particular need to remember another dimension of this: the same role in one society might entail totally new rights and obligations in another society. Certain actions as well as reactions might therefore be seriously misunderstood when performed in another society's reality. These misunderstandings can occur in interactions between tourists and locals, and between instructors and international students – or anytime academics are working in an international context.

CONVERSATION STARTER

Based on Lawson's thoughts above, ask your students to consider the teaching situations in which they meet (be it in virtual or face-to-face classrooms) and the various people involved (for example, the students, the instructors and the staff that make up their reality). Ask them to outline what positions exist; and who occupies these positions. Further, give examples of rights and obligations that at least three different position occupants have in regard to other position occupants.

ROLEPLAYING GAME

One of our longer contributions in the applied section of *Teaching Tourism* is a roleplay game called "The Tourism Game" by Stephen Fairbrass (with a set-up contribution by Johan Edelheim; see Activities 12 and 53). This is a simple set-up, but the potential learning outcomes are wonderfully complex because the game truly highlights different values in action. We refer to the game in a few places throughout our chapters and suggest how you can engage your students in applied roleplay games by letting them take on, and negotiate with, different roles. From the perspective of social reality, and class and inequality (see below), let your students play a first half round of the game. The second half is referred to in Chapter 7 on economic values.

ACTIVITY

We return here to the idea of "learning regimes" introduced by Elin Bommenel, Richard Ek and Stuart Reid in Chapter 1 on didactics. The re- flexivity required of both teachers and students to conceptualise what they "do" when they are learning is intimately linked with social realities, rights, obligations and positions. This metacognition is essential for one's learning. In Phase One of the introductory week of meta-pedagogical thinking on teaching and learning regimes, students are asked to reflect not only on the vocabulary of their teachers but also on their own vocabulary and experiences (see Activity 10).

CLASS AND INEQUALITY

As much as we would like to believe that a classless society can exist, humans have always found a way to distinguish between classes. Whether seen in Marxist terms of two classes (bourgeoisie and proletariat) or the more common perception of three classes (upper, middle and working), humans compete for status. We create hierarchies based on factors such as wealth, income, education, culture, race, fame or social network. According to Lawson's (2019) concept of social realities with positions and occupants, societies have always "assigned" people to their class roles depending on a range of complicated factors. A debate centres around the way in which these roles are assigned. Is it simply a matter of the so-called "classes sustaining themselves", perhaps for generations (that is, once we find ourselves within a class role, we are likely to stay in that role)? Or are class roles more fluid, assigned based on each individual's abilities? Both arguments have their proponents.

The former – class roles sustain themselves – is often tied to a conservative ideology. The argument here is that one's position within, for example, an upper-class role has been acquired due to hard work either by the individual or by their family members from previous generations. To a certain extent, this argument is based on meritocracy. "To a certain extent" is the operative phrase: the argument typically stops short of being extended to racialised people and other minorities. The latter position – class roles depend on people's abilities – is more closely associated with a liberal ideology, one that argues for reforms to foster equality and to overcome systemic barriers largely due to socio-economic status and racialisation. The result would be new entitlements and expectations for these marginalised groups in society. A look at the accusation against Harvard University over discrimination of Asian Americans, referenced in Chapter 10 on mutuality, would be topical here, as it clearly illustrates both arguments.

The COVID-19 pandemic shone a light on the structure of societies and the systemic inequalities within and among them. During the pandemic, for example, global access to vaccines was based on wealth: rich countries, constituting only 14 per cent of the world's population, reserved more than 50 per cent of all available vaccines (Twohey et al., 2020). Within individual countries, the wealthy and those in positions of privilege (often denoted by their skin colour) were often able to acquire vaccinations ahead of priority groups (Mazzei, 2021; Morales, 2021).

The pandemic also widened the digital divide between those with access to broadband and those without. The former could work from home, safeguarding their income and their health, perhaps even their lives. The latter could not and therefore found themselves in a much more vulnerable position than their privileged counterparts. This aspect of the pandemic was particularly devastating for students. Limited access to computers and the Internet meant limited access to schooling and to safe socialisation opportunities, which put these students at risk of falling behind their more privileged classmates, increasing class divisions (Anonymous, 2021b).

A broader concern revolves around the risk of vaccinations creating a society divided between those who are vaccinated and those who are not. Israel's introduction of a "green badge", which denotes that an individual has been vaccinated, generated a heated debate about personal rights versus the greater good. Although employers cannot force anyone to get vaccinated, some have the right to dismiss those who are unvaccinated, including hotel workers and educators (Kershner, 2021). As "vaccination passports" similar to Israel's approach gain momentum, they could lead to barriers for employment, especially in tourism, and for leisure and other social activities.

Rawls considered justice to be "the first virtue of social institutions" (1971, p. 3) both in how individuals are treated and in how resources are allocated to different categories of citizens. Any societal response to sweeping, significant events like a pandemic must be measured against its potential to inadvertently upend this vision of justice.

CONVERSATION STARTER

Ask your students to list what kind of values they think are hidden in different "classes" of society? Do all people, regardless of the class they inhabit, value the same things, in the same way, or are there differences? Let them also consider the extent to which their answers have been shaped by stereotypes (see Chapter 10 on mutuality). Compare these differences and let them suggest how inequalities could be reduced.

ACTIVITY

In Karla A. Boluk's teaching case "Introducing critical topics to transform our practice", students learn how the tourism sector might function as a conduit to think about responsibility, equity, agency and sustainability (see Activity 31). Many of these topics, such as mutuality and stewardship, are discussed in further detail in later chapters, but this teaching case shows how these aspirational values are possible to achieve only by unravelling the social values within which they were initially created.

SOCIAL NEEDS

Humans are social animals. The need for love and belonging that social contact can provide corresponds to Maslow's third level of social needs. During the pandemic, when face-to-face contact was both risky and restricted, online platforms rapidly expanded to facilitate virtual contact with family, friends, colleagues and collaborators. However, such connections are forged in an immaterial dimension and, no matter how helpful, they do not take into account the fact that touch is the only sense crucial to our survival. Touch also helps us deepen bonds and build trust with others, essential in both our personal and business lives (Anonymous, 2021a).

The travel restrictions imposed in many countries to combat the pandemic reminded us of how important travel is, and will continue to be, in both regards. Our desire to be with family and friends drives our desire to travel, especially since families today are often spread out in geographically distant parts of the world. Our desire to conduct business also drives our desire to travel, especially since we live in a globalised business community. It is much easier to build trust with business associates from other parts of the world – people who are essentially strangers – when there is common ground to share, which is usually discovered in social settings, like dining together, rather than in boardrooms. In fact, in many Asian cultures, business is guided by social relationships. In China, *guanxi* refers to a web of relationships among family, friends and business acquaintances that has been built over time through favours and many social encounters. Therefore, establishing rapport and building trust, especially between international partners, often requires travelling to each other's communities and countries. Virtual encounters are a poor substitute.

Tourism can also play a role in addressing the higher-level needs on Maslow's hierarchy: esteem and self-actualisation. Apart from travelling to connect with others for personal and business reasons, people also travel to connect with themselves. Whether it is travelling to "exotic" destinations, to escape weather conditions or to explore the local culture, the myriad personal reasons people travel all share a common element: they allow opportunities to experience different ways of being and, consequently, to raise one's consciousness about their own way of being. Travelling for pleasure offers that opportunity.

Therefore, people have good reasons to travel. And increasingly they have the means to do so as the middle classes have rapidly expanded in advanced economies. These factors have led to exponential growth in travel both domestically and internationally – the travel disruptions due to the pandemic notwithstanding. Globally in 2019, 1.5 billion international tourist arrivals were recorded, to which at least 12 billion domestic trips need to be added (UNWTO,

2020). In short, people travel frequently and for many reasons – to the point where they have come to see travel as a right. When prevented from travelling, as in the pandemic, we have seen people become angry and aggrieved about the restrictions on their freedom. In Chapter 4 on ecological values we comment on the environmental costs of travel and on a "fair share" of carbon consumption. Tourism and modern consumerism are thus deepening our carbon footprint to satisfy the wants of a privileged group.

While most tourism is undertaken for leisure purposes and therefore should be considered a want, not a need, there is no doubt that the sheer mass of people moving around the globe is an important social phenomenon.

CONVERSATION STARTER

 Let your students identify social needs that your particular society cannot be without. When you have created a list of these needs, think about what professions society could not be without. Next, have the students conduct a quick Internet search of average salaries for different kinds of work in society. Do these salaries align with the list of society's high-priority needs and professions? If not, why not? What values are emphasised?

ACTIVITY

 Johan Edelheim's Film and Tourism: Constructing Social Realities is a master's-level course where students learn to reflect on how tourism is imagined and constructed in films (see Activity 13). The purpose of the activity is to give students tools to unravel why individuals, when they take on the positions as tourists, embody socially created expectations and consume socially described/prescribed needs.

COMMUNITY WELL-BEING

This important social phenomenon – the movement in time and space of billions of people – has given rise to a highly complex tourism system that, pre-pandemic, contributed over 10 per cent to the global gross domestic product and accounted for one in 10 jobs (WTTC, 2020). But tourism has also profoundly affected residents of destinations and their overall sense of well-being. The positive economic impact that tourists bring to a community or region often receives the most attention, especially from politicians. However, tourists also compete with residents for common resources, thereby undermining the residents' perceived quality of community life. Fortunately, in the last two decades, an understanding of these negative impacts has gained momentum. Research has shifted from tracking objective, largely economic, indicators of tourism's impact to subjective indicators, such as need satisfaction, life satisfaction, sense of well-being and happiness – all of which provide a much broader understanding of the concept of quality of life, especially in a national or international context. Resident satisfaction with tourism and tourism visitor rates are two domains that were added to the Happiness Index (Musikanski et al., 2019), one of a number of indices that track community well-being.

Empowering local populations to help shape tourism development has gained attention in the last few years, fuelled in large part by increasing concerns and complaints about "overtourism" and its ecological, cultural and social impacts. At the same time, the number of destinations that suffered from "undertourism" as a result of pandemic travel restrictions spotlighted the consequences for local livelihoods of an overdependence on foreign visitors. But most decisions about large infrastructure projects (airports, cruise terminals, rail and road access, and so on) are made at a much higher regional and/or national level in the name of economic growth. In these cases, the financial costs are borne by the populace at large, while the environmental and social impacts are largely felt at the local destination level.

From an Indigenous perspective, community well-being goes even further than these sustainability considerations. For example, at the heart of the Māori worldview lies relational well-being that connects people with the spirit of the land and aims for an equitable distribution of benefits (Ransfield and Reichenberger, 2021). These holistic and relationship-based values that espouse both intergenerational and intragenerational equity are often at odds with capitalist and neo-liberal systems which focus on economic profit. Here, in contrast, business success is measured not just in financial terms but to what extent it can provide holistic value to internal and external stakeholders, including the environment (Ransfield and Reichenberger, 2021).

CONVERSATION STARTERS

Many excellent documentaries focus on popular tourism destinations, their development over time and the challenges they face as the local population struggles to cope with the influx of visitors. Some examples are *The Goose with the Golden Eggs: Tourism on Costa Rica's Pacific Coast, Iceland's Tourism Revolution*, and *Life and Debt* (Jamaica). Such films are thought-provoking about the positive and negative impacts on societies, the types of tourism development that support sustainability considerations, and the obstacles that local communities face in having their voices heard, even in terms of infrastructure development.

Nick Naumov's conversation starter on tourism and intangible heritage as a driver for positive/negative sociocultural changes to society and heritage commercialisation is a good introduction to Sudipta Kiran Sarkar's teaching activity below (see Activity 21).

ACTIVITIES

Field trips, particularly to lesser developed countries, can be eye-opening for students as the infrastructure that supports tourism and local residents in their daily lives is often wanting. These are considerations that students do not necessarily think about when asked to develop strategies for the development of tourism, and the "teachable moments" that occur during such trips give rise to animated discussions in reflective briefings. Helene Balslev Clausen and Maggie C. Miller bring this to life in "The value of the unintended in tourism education: Nepal" (see Activity 11).

Local food has become increasingly important in creating highly valued tourism experiences and is allowing gastronomy to be used to support local food traditions as well as create competitive distinctions among destinations within countries. The field visits presented in "Experiential learning in gastronomy tourism" by Sudipta Kiran Sarkar help students understand how these gastronomic creations can not only establish highly successful restaurants and other food venues, but also help to preserve a community's cultural heritage (see Activity 15).

6. Cultural values

Johan Edelheim; **Marion Joppe**; **Joan Flaherty**;
Linda Armano; **Emily Höckert**; **Monika Lüthje**; Mette
Simonsen Abildgaard; Jonathon Day; Sisko Häikiö; Maria
Huhmarniemi; Outi Kugapi; Nick Naumov; Carina Ren;
Minna Väyrynen

OBJECTIVES

This chapter provides readers with insights and engagement activities to help students:

1. Distinguish four different meanings of "culture" and consider how cultural values are connected to these meanings
2. Explain how traditions and heritage have developed and why they are maintained in cultures
3. Illustrate how languages are a mirror of the cultures within which they are created
4. Compare art and festivals from different times and places to distinguish how they embody individual cultural values
5. Visualise how modernity is in flux, and never stable

INTRODUCTION

When we teach cultural values, it is often in connection to intercultural management, communication or perhaps marketing, but culture and cultural values are deeply imbedded in tourism practices and therefore highly relevant to tourism education. After all, many different motives prompt us to travel, such as the desire to escape to a warmer climate or to experience a change of scenery, but each motive is tied to a common theme: exposure to a culture different from our own. This exposure offers the potential to foster our growth as human beings, because travel can help us uncover insights about ourselves. The funny habits and quirks we had always taken for granted and accepted as natural might be seen in a different light when we are in a different setting. This self-realisation, however, is not an automatic outcome of being exposed to a new culture. It requires humility to accept that the customs, assumptions and traditions one has grown up with and perhaps never questioned may not be universally shared and are, in fact, rooted in one's own cultural values.

"Culture" is a complicated word that means many things. Cultural values often refer to the fabric of how different groups of people make sense of their own being through material and non-material means. Education is a culturally scripted embodiment of values, necessities and aspirations. This can be seen through the different forms that education takes – or maybe, rather, the different forms that education took before colonialism and later globalisation homogenised our ideas of what education "should" be like. Built into the ways that we as educators view our roles, deep beyond our conscious training as educators and/or tourism professionals, our cultural values reside. Much of modern education is built on Western ideals that emphasise individualism, rational thought and compartmentalisation. (This theme and its implications, especially regarding the need for holistic education, are also discussed in Chapter 1 on tourism didactics.)

The challenge to even consider, let alone develop and implement, alternatives to our teaching, learning and educational process is rooted in our own cultural values, which have shaped our views of good teaching and successful learning. There are a growing number of researchers who challenge the blinkered view of general university education and highlight how that prioritised perspective simultaneously silences other ways of learning and knowing. For examples of alternative cultural education perspectives, see the following: in an African context, Asante (2020); in an African American context, Emdin (2020); in an Asian context, Miike (2019); on epistemological racism, Kubota (2020); and from an Indigenous perspective, Kuokkanen (2007).

Language is one of the most prominent differences between cultures, and connected to language are different kinds of texts and communication styles. Granted, some different cultural groups speak the same language, often as a result of emigration or colonialism. However, even within these groups certain words and expressions take on different meanings, specific to the particular group's values. Note, for example, that in Chapter 1, which deals with different learning and teaching philosophies, we emphasise that the book is structured around didactics, rather than pedagogy. This emphasis stems from a linguistic perspective. Borrowing from the Germanic/Nordic tradition, Künzli (1988) defines didactics as "the embodiment of knowledge about instruction" (as cited in Keiding and Qvortrup, 2014). In contrast, pedagogy is "the art and science of teaching" (Bangura, 2005, p. 13). However, pedagogy is also seen to refer more directly to the teaching of children, whereas andragogy is "the art and science of helping adults learn" (Bangura, 2005, p. 13). Bangura further shows how the science of teaching has been divided into "ergonagy (the art and science of helping people learn to work), and heutagogy (the study of self-determined learning)" (2005, p. 13). However, he points out that all of these teaching paradigms are built on Western values and may not, then, be appropriate for teaching in non-Western cultures. For example, ubuntugogy, based on traditional African cultural values, subsumes all of the other paradigms, and is more suitable for teaching in an African context (Bangura, 2005). Thus, language communicates not just meaning, but also cultural values inherent in meanings, and it is of essence to locate one's own assumptions before transmitting these to others.

This chapter introduces culture as a complicated concept, including traditions and heritage as manifestations of cultural values. Tourism heavily depends on cultural values and the differences between these: cultural values are part of the attraction in tourism, and they also form the basis for the hospitality that is provided to guests through informal and formal means. The chapter provides teaching examples and discussion starters that are related to cross-cultural features and art and craft in an attempt to make cultural values tangible to tourism students.

"CULTURE": A COMPLICATED WORD

"Culture" is a complicated word because it can mean many things, depending on the context and because it includes everything from fashion to sports. In order to understand cultural values, we borrow here a categorisation where Edelheim (2005), based on Jenks (1993), divided culture into four categories (see Figure 6.1).

In Jenks' framework, Box A represents a definition that is somewhat old-fashioned but nonetheless relevant to tourism: culture as a cognitive category or a state of mind. This is the culture that the Romantic authors referred to when they wrote of an ideal that may not exist in the here and now, but that ignites the imagination as a lofty goal to strive for, as it encapsulates the essence of "being cultured". This definition is relevant to tourism for two reasons. First, it harks back to the history of tourism around the world, where artists and wealthy people set out on grand tours to become cultured (Löfgren, 2002). Second, it relates to the problematic legacy of stereotyping groups of individuals by creating simplistic generalisations. For instance, imaginaries of Indigenous groups re-construct misconceived stereotypes of exotic, traditional cultures as though they existed outside of time and space (Gardiner, 2021; Olsen et al., 2019).

Box B defines culture from an empiricist perspective. Starting with Darwin, anthropological authors have claimed that the development of the human race leads to the current civilisation – or the current culture. Colonial and neocolonial ideas of one's own culture's superiority are visible here (Simmons, 2004). The current status is at all times imagined as the highest achievement of humankind. All "less developed" people of the world are therefore to be "cultivated"; that is, taught the cultural values of the so-called civilised world. This definition of culture is still seen in travel brochures where tourists are invited to experience the "authentic" culture of some distant region (Morgan and Pritchard, 1998). It is also seen in educational export, where degree programmes are taught in partnership, or as franchised entities in different locations. Full programmes are situated in a different culture without the right to change many parts of the content, as it is deemed to be "correct" based on imported cultural values (Phan, 2017). This is a conservative view of culture that places different traditions and different cultures in a perceptual hierarchy.

| A) **Culture** as a cerebral, or certainly cognitive category; culture becomes intelligible as a general state of mind. It carries with it the idea of perfection, a goal or an aspiration of individual human achievement or emancipation. | B) **Culture** as a more embodied and collective category: culture evokes a state of intellectual and/or moral development in society. This is a position linking culture with the idea of civilisation and one that is informed by the evolutionary theories of Darwin. | C) **Culture** as a descriptive and concrete category: culture viewed as a collective body of arts and intellectual work within any one society. This is very much an everyday language usage of the term 'culture' and carries along with it senses of particularity, exclusivity, elitism, specialist knowledge and training. | D) **Culture** as a social category: culture regarded as the whole way of life of a people. This is the pluralist and potentially democratic sense of the concept that sociology and anthropology and lately cultural studies tend to use. |

Source: Edelheim (2005, p. 249), based on Jenks (1993)

Figure 6.1   Four definitions of culture

Box C defines culture in its most common use – "high culture" but also "pop culture". High culture is associated with various "cultural" events and exhibitions, such as theatre, opera, classical concerts, museums and art exhibitions. However, it is becoming common to also include popular culture here. Examples can be seen in the Japanese pop culture of anime, manga, cosplay, games, music and fashion. There has always been a clash between high culture and pop culture. Some people see the latter as diminishing a cultural heritage that they consider worth keeping. Consequently, they resist the intrusion of culture which the populace is consuming (popular culture), disapproving, for example, of sports being included in culture (Dobson, 2006). History has shown that this elite stance often has substantial power and is therefore able to uphold some of the cultural heritage, while parts of the pop culture are transformed into that same heritage as new popular trends emerge. The instances where the definition of culture from Box C apply to tourism can be seen in cultural tourism, where tourists visit museums, historic homes and ruins; or attend different festivals, art, music or sporting events, or performances.

Lastly, Box D defines culture as a social category, a way of life of a certain group of people. A modern notion about cross-cultural knowledge highlights this definition. People are aware of their own way of life, but they have to be educated to recognise differences that appear in other societies and cultures. How people are raised and what they value and acknowledge as valuable all reflect their society's dominant culture and, therefore, cultural values. When tourists are motivated to travel by the desire to experience different cultures, then this definition of culture is mostly driving their decision. A crucial difference between Box D and boxes A and (especially) B is that Box D views culture as a neutral, not hierarchical, value concept.

CONVERSATION STARTER

 Let your students investigate online what type of "cultural tourism" is on offer in a place they are familiar with. Make sure that they investigate both incoming and outbound tourism, as these two tend to be rather different. Ask them to determine what kind of culture, based on the definitions above, most of these examples represent. What cultural values are tied to these uses of culture in different categories by tourism stakeholders?

Armano (2018) describes how cultural values can be understood, and illustrates how they can be used in tourism practice and in classes (see Activity 18). She is the author of the Deep Cultural Interpretation Model (DCIM; Figure 6.2), which, starting from the bottom, is made up of Cultural Models that could be explained through the concept of "world vision". These models guide people to classify the world they live in based on specific defining traits (such as cultural values and norms). Cultural Values are ideals towards which people in a particular culture tend and which influence behaviour. Cultural Rules are norms, such as procedures, which explain the right behaviour to ensure cultural values are upheld. Unconscious Habits are the implicit behaviours (understood as *habitus*) that group members regularly express without necessarily being able to articulate why. Finally, Communication is the explicit behaviours that manifest, with words or deeds, people's thoughts and feelings. Notably, these two latter categories distinguish information emerging from actions and spoken language to achieve a deeper understanding of the complexities that appear through personal stories.

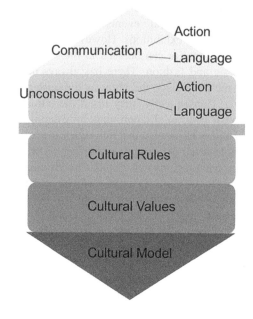

Source: Armano (2018)

Figure 6.2   *Deep Cultural Interpretation Model*

ACTIVITY

Getting students to work in culturally sensitive ways with local cultures, making tourism thus more culturally sustainable, is the goal of the online course Cultural Sensitivity in Arctic Tourism. The platform covers five countries (Finland, Sweden, Norway, Greenland and Canada) and uses a variety of learning environments, including videos, inspirational presentations, academic articles and blog posts. Mette Simonsen Abildgaard, Emily Höckert, Outi Kugapi, Monika Lüthje and Carina Ren describe this in "Enhancing culturally sensitive tourism in an online learning environment" (see Activity 17).

VIDEO PROJECT

To develop cultural awareness and mutual understanding and respect, students are asked to create a safety video for a certain cultural target group of tourists. This project, carried out in multicultural teams, develops awareness of one's own culture, the cultures of the other team members, the tourism target cultures and the local culture of the operating environment. Through exposure to cultural diversity in this way, the students gain a greater understanding of how cultural values affect one's behaviour and attitudes. Sisko Häikiö and Minna Väyrynen share this approach in "Video project: 'Enjoy Lapland Safely'" (see Activity 37).

TRADITION AND HERITAGE

The concepts of tradition and heritage are strongly connected to cultural values. A tradition can be imagined as a certain way of doing or performing an act or event. Every tradition has a temporal lineage that can be traced back in its culture. Some traditions are old, others relatively young. Some traditions started based on seasonal factors connected to natural phenomena, others on hygiene, politics or religions. Studying traditions in different cultures can be incredibly informative as they can explain historical transitions and shed light on values that still exist today in modern society. One tradition strongly connected to tourism is hospitality, which can be viewed as one of humanity's most important features: the care of others. Hospitality exists in all cultures, taking different forms, stronger and weaker, based on many historical factors and on the importance placed on "us" versus "them". To varying extents, hospitality lives on in traditions in people's homes, in the social and in the commercial domain (Lashley, 2018).

CONVERSATION STARTER

Ask your students to identify three traditions that their parents or other older people have passed on to them, and then ask them to explain what those traditions might be based upon and why their culture still values them.

Heritage is synonymous with tradition, but it is also a category of history that has been objectified and memorised in a particular way. If we define history as a description of everything that has happened in the past (albeit recognising that our definition is not complete as history relies on generalisations and is shaped by the biased perspective of who creates it and when), then heritage is a selected part of history that is given a value above and beyond other histories. This value can be seen when nations, and even the global community, select certain places, traditions and events to be protected because they represent heritage. That is, they are determined to be worthy of saving for future generations. UNESCO's World Heritage Sites provide prominent examples of "heritage", which also commonly become prominent tourist attractions.

CONVERSATION STARTER

Tourism can be a powerful force that brings a number of cultural changes to society. Nick Naumov's "Tourism and intangible heritage" uses this context as it is ideally suited to stimulate a critical and engaging discussion on the extent to which tourism revitalises cultural values and tradition while, at the same time, contributing to their exploitation for commercial purposes (see Activity 21).

LANGUAGE

Language, a means of communication distinct to a particular group of people, is an important representative of cultural values. Several thousand languages are estimated to be in use around the globe today – a number considerably smaller than what existed in earlier times, when people were less mobile. And small language groups continue to disappear. We need to pay attention to the loss inherent within this trend.

Languages were always developed to communicate meaning in a set context, and different features within that context therefore require different words. When the number of languages decreases, the ability to communicate nuanced meanings relevant to the culture associated with that language is similarly decreased. In the modern world, nation states typically designate certain languages – or perhaps only one language – as "official". But being restricted to the official language means we are communicating at a more general, restricted level. Or, stated more plainly, a poorer level. Regional features that are essential in certain areas might continue existing in dialects, but the official vocabulary has eliminated them, because those features are not necessary to be understood in another area. An example of this is the different words describing features of ice in northern Finland, all relevant and with different practical implications for travellers within that context, but less known in southern Finland, which does not have the same climate, and therefore does not need to distinguish among a similar range of ice formations.

CONVERSATION STARTER

Language evolves. New words are invented to describe new features in society while some words are borrowed from other languages. Ask your students to identify three "new" words that have been created or borrowed within the last decade, for use in the language they are most familiar with. Why could an old word not be used for these phenomena, and what values do the new words entail?

Translation between languages is always a delicate endeavour because the same word can have multiple related, yet still different, meanings. These varied meanings are captured within the term's denotation and connotation. "Denotation" refers to the

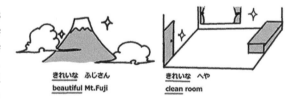

きれいな ふじさん
beautiful Mt.Fuji

きれいな へや
clean room

word's definition or its literal meaning; "connotation" refers to connections in meaning that the word contains – that is, the meaning suggested or evoked by the word. One example of how language can illustrate cultural values is by thinking of the Japanese word きれい[な], as it simultaneously can be translated as "beautiful" and "clean" in English, thereby showing a connection that anybody coming from outside Japan experiences very tangibly in society, and that Japanese travellers experience when travelling out of the country. The connotation is often thus a reflection of the cultural values. To truly understand and communicate with someone on a meaningful, nuanced level we need to understand the connotation, which can only happen if we understand their cultural values.

Another aspect of communication that is deeply rooted in cultural values is non-verbal language. It is not just the words that we use, and the level of comprehension of those words, that are of importance, but also the way the words are expressed, and the facial expressions and body language that accompany them. People of different cultural backgrounds have different preferences for how communication is carried out. Some want the conversations to be animated and competitive. Others prefer calm and harmonious interactions. For example, perceived levels of trust and engagement with people, and the messages they transmit, are strongly related to the manner (excited vs calm) and the facial expressions (broad smile vs no smile) that the receiver prefers (Sims et al., 2018). This is one of the reasons we, as professional communicators, should always remind ourselves to form our messages so that they are suitable for the audience in front of us, whether that audience consists of one person or a thousand.

ACTIVITY

Jonathon Day presents a two-part exercise in "Cultural awareness" to increase cultural awareness and build a shared understanding of the meaning of respect. The activity can be done in pairs or in small groups (see Activity 19).

ARTS AND FESTIVALS

Arts and festivals express something about cultural values. They are born within cultures, and they often manifest values that symbolise those cultures. Now, arts and festivals are very diverse and take a multitude of shapes, so the preceding statements are broad generalisations. Consider, for example, the word "art". It shares the same root as "artificial", something that has been created. Some art has been created to express the artist's opposition to a society's dominant cultural values. Paradoxically, however, even that expression of opposition might be a reflection of the culture. The artist reacts to the existing cultural values by protesting against them. Picasso's famous painting *Guernica* is a well-known example of this.

CONVERSATION STARTER

Ask your students to brainstorm examples of what they consider to be "good" art and "bad" art. Record the suggestions on the board, a flipchart or a screen, so the entire class can see them. After you have received enough examples, ask the students, working in pairs, to identify common elements or themes that link some – or all – of the examples (that is, what are the defining characteristics of good art or bad art?). Roam the room and check if they agree on the categories. Ask them to consider how their perceptions of good and bad art might differ from other people's perceptions, both within and outside of your community. Initiate a class discussion where you ask students to reflect on what they think these differences tell us about cultural values.

As earlier stated, art is commonly situated in Box C of culture, a descriptive or concrete form of culture. However, it can also fall within Box B, as a reflection of a culture's state of development, which is particularly highlighted when different cultures are compared. Different nations have national galleries where the art perceived to best represent their values is collected. Art and aesthetic expressions are very closely linked to values, and people who imagine that the world is totally rational and explained through natural sciences often equate artistic values with relativism. We disagree. Granted, art is not "knowable" in the same way as mathematics, but neither is it purely relative. Art is meant as an embodiment of culture. Its point, therefore, is not necessarily to create meaning, but instead to create feelings. That is where its value lies.

ACTIVITY

In their teaching case on cultural sustainability Maria Huhmarniemi and Outi Kugapi have developed a workshop, "Co-designing creative tourism activities for preserving and promoting local cultural traditions" (see Activity 20). It includes art and craft-based activities that have, at their best, the potential to enhance cultural revitalisation and act as mediators of traditions, cultural values and discussions. These activities increase the appreciation of local traditions and crafts as well as Indigenous and similarly situated knowledge. They also transfer heritage and cultural capital in general in a way that respects cultural continuity and cultural identities and promotes social inclusion. It can be said that creative tourism breathes new life into cultural traditions and fosters appreciation for handicraft skills and designs. In this group activity, art and tourism entrepreneurs and students collaborate to co-design craft-based services with an aim to preserve and promote local, place-based business practices.

ACTIVITY

A very visual feature of modernity in action is advertisements, and students can learn a lot about what is considered modern at any one time by looking at advertisements from different years and decades. Ask students to search out some classic advertisements from one field (travel, make-up, homeware, whatever they fancy) from the 1930s, 1950s and 1970s, and describe what values were dominant at those times. After this, ask them to look at some contemporary advertisements and discuss what values are emphasised today.

7. Economic values

Johan Edelheim; **Marion Joppe**; **Joan Flaherty**; Deborah Edwards; Joanne Paulette Gellatly; Ece Kaya; Xavier Michel; Nick Naumov; Kathleen Rodenburg

OBJECTIVES

This chapter provides readers with insights and engagement activities to help students:

1. Explain the importance of assumptions to economic sciences
2. Elaborate on and query economic values as they form lived realities
3. Give examples of different stories that create trust in abstract entities such as money and national economies
4. Infer the presumed causes and effects of taxes, debts and employment on different nations' wealth and, by extension, on values
5. Predict what would happen in a society if there were no more investments and no more growth

INTRODUCTION

The past years have witnessed many upheavals for the tourism industry, but one fact is particularly telling: at the start of 2020, COVID-19 entered the public consciousness at the same time as the term "overtourism" peaked in Google searches. These two factors, whilst by no means directly correlated, provide a snapshot of our current society because their indirect correlator is economic values. For decades the mantra repeated by political leaders of almost every party has been some variation of these themes: growth, gross domestic product (GDP), investment, inflation, wealth and, often connected to these, employment.

Economic values are so ubiquitous in daily parlance that we seldom question how they have come about or even what they actually mean. Are they exempt from this scrutiny because we have long accepted them as the most important values for human beings? Put more bluntly, is money the most important thing to us? The answer to the latter is likely to be less straightforward than the question itself: any person who can afford to say "No, money is not the most important thing" has probably quite enough money to sustain themselves comfortably. However, money and sustenance are not the same as economic values, and, as we examine in this chapter, many economic values are actually disvalues, taking more out of the system than they give.

In other words, the term "economic values" carries meaning beyond the typical associations of monetary transactions, salaries paid for work done, prices paid for goods and services, taxes paid (or avoided by some means), investments, currencies, foreign exchange fluctuations, and so on.

This chapter delves into that meaning, its assumptions and implications. The core of the chapter examines the role of economic values in modern societies, particularly in light of the problems these values have created; and presents possible solutions to these problems. It touches on the fact that economic existence builds on shared stories that aim to bring trust to interactions between large groups of people. Intriguingly, this trust is at some levels engrained in properties that almost take on features of faith.

Finally, we discuss the disconnect between economic value and societal values through the move away from objective economics to subjective economics, the separation of money from physical realities, the so-called "gold standard" and the belief in never-ending growth as a physical possibility.

ECONOMY: EXCHANGE VALUES AND ASSUMPTIONS

At its roots, an economy refers to exchange values. People have traded throughout history in order to get that which they do not have themselves. This basic trading function stands as an historical core to modern economics, but much has changed in the past five decades. Let us therefore start with a short story to illustrate something about economic thinking in modern times:

Three university students, majoring in biology, engineering and economics, respectively, set off on an overnight camping trip in a wilderness area. They brought all they needed for the trip: sturdy shoes, spare sets of clothes, durable tents and sleeping bags, and plenty of food. However, as they set camp after a long day of hiking, far from other people and civilisation, with their tents made up and a fire burning brightly, they realised that they had forgotten to bring a can opener. All their canned food in front of them, but not one opener, not even a utility-tool opener.

After an initial round of blaming each other for not bringing a can opener, they agreed that they should be able to solve the problem through science. As good students in their own fields, each set out to solve the challenge – and, in doing so, to also prove their field's superiority over the others. After ten minutes they gathered, and each explained the solution they had arrived at, based on their scientific field. The biologist had examined  *lichen and mosses around the site, collected those with good bacteria, and placed these on top of the cans. This material would weaken the can's metal and eventually open the can (in two months' time, the biologist added under their breath). The engineer pulled out a calculation showing how the can should be thrown off a nearby cliff with a distinct angle and rotation, and how the lid would be sawed off upon impact with the stones at the bottom of the cliff (and the food to be scooped off nearby bushes and stones, the engineer added under their breath). The economist, who had been sitting by the fire the whole time smiled broadly and said, "Yet again, economics shows its superiority. We assume that we have an opener, and the problem is solved."*

With apologies to any economist who thinks that the story unfairly pokes fun at their field of study, let us unravel a few relevant themes. The story highlights one of the basics of economic theories, modelling and thinking: they are built on assumptions, and any so-called knowledge of the field is only as good as the assumptions made. The assumption is never an answer on its own, as the students in the short story above soon realise, with the cans remaining securely sealed, but that fact is rarely acknowledged by any economist. The assumptions are simply inferences of possibilities of the future, neither more nor less. Thus, all economic modelling, impact calculations and benefit analyses are at their core hinged on the same factor: assumptions of what will happen in the future – based, often incorrectly, on the past repeating itself in a statistically measured way in the future.

Tourism economics is an applied field of economics connected to how tourism creates value in society. It is a complicated field, as tourism is so multilayered and enmeshed in diverse functions of all societies. Tourism economics exists in tourist-generating regions, for example, in the forms of travel agent activities, in economic leakages through outbound tourists and in all the infrastructure created for the industries connected to tourism. It can be applied to the flow of travellers through and past any transit hub and region. And, most commonly, tourism economics is applied to tourist destination regions when local inhabitants, entrepreneurs, community organisations and politicians respond to the complex effects, positive and negative, that large inbound groups of travellers have on their communities. Fearmongering and boosterism, where certain impacts are emphasised over and above others, are essentially always tied to different assumptions, and rational economic modelling is then presented as a neutral answer to solve these issues. Once again, however, those models are, at their core, assumptions. Granted, these assumptions are more accountable than baseless rumours, as they take into account more options. But they are still unable to predict all eventualities, something the COVID-19 pandemic has proven beyond any doubt.

Booking system based in Netherlands
Brand franchisor based in Ireland
Real estate developer from Singapore
Financing by bank in Luxemburg
Owned by investment fund registered in Virgin Islands
Staff from the Philippines
Management from Switzerland
Computer network from South Korea
Electronic locks from Sweden
Hotel Management System from USA
Wines from South Africa
Seafood from Chile and Vietnam
Lamb from New Zealand
Beef from Argentina
Maple syrup from Canada
Furniture from Indonesia
Linen from Bangladesh
Elevators from Finland
Air Cons from Japan

For example:
A group of Chinese tourists order and pay for their all-inclusive holidays to a travel company in China. They fly to the destination with a Chinese carrier on an airplane made in France. Their tour guides and bus drivers are also Chinese, and so are the designated souvenir shops they are taken to.

Who profits most?

CONVERSATION STARTER

The "foreign exchange" illustration is a good starting point for a discussion in class about foreign exchange, income multipliers and leakages. What kind of countries might earn lots of foreign exchange from tourism? What countries earn money from tourism based on leakages? What countries can maximise economic multiplier effects? What countries might lose money due to foreign exchange?

ACTIVITY

In "Authentic assessment: activating purposeful learning for a diverse student cohort", Ece Kaya and Deborah Edwards present a holistic set-up for
a graduate cohort to reflect on the information and apply the skills they have
gained through their studies (see Activity 24). The authentic assessment not
only has practical dimensions aimed at the industry sectors that graduates are intending to
join, but also offers theoretical and reflective dimensions as students need to justify values
and synthesise what they experience and find in practice.

ECONOMIC VALUE

Before we examine the different components of economic values in our societies, let us pause
for a moment and investigate what actually constitutes value in economic terms. The economist Mariana Mazzucato (2019) provides in her brilliant TED talk three historical definitions
of how economic value can be understood. Up until the 1700s, during the time when societies
depended on agriculture for their livelihoods, only those actively working the land were
creating "value". They were the Productive class. In contrast, merchants, artisans and traders
were referred to as the Sterile class, and landowners were called Proprietors. These latter two
groups were not seen as creating any value, but as simply extracting wealth for themselves.
This view changed with the Industrial Revolution, where value took on an objective role,
measuring, for example, industrial labour. During this time, value became a negotiating chip
where unions could bargain for better wages based on the value of work performed. The third
definition of value is that of neoclassical economics based on consumers' preferences; more
about this below.

The high regard that economics enjoys as its own discipline is a recent phenomenon. This
might be hard to fathom today, considering the attention economics garners in the media, the
trust placed on economic advice, and the repeated emphasis on economics by political leaders
around the world. But the discipline's high profile was not always the case – as illustrated by
the following story.

In 1896, the Swedish inventor and scientist Alfred Nobel died, leaving behind a highly
contested will. The source of dissent, mostly disgruntled relatives, came from the fact that
he bequeathed his wealth to a fund that was to award people who had "conferred the greatest
benefit to humankind" in different fields once a year:

> one part to the person who made the most important discovery or invention in the field of physics;
> one part to the person who made the most important chemical discovery or improvement; one part to
> the person who made the most important discovery within the domain of physiology or medicine; one
> part to the person who, in the field of literature, produced the most outstanding work in an idealistic
> direction; and one part to the person who has done the most or best to advance fellowship among
> nations, the abolition or reduction of standing armies, and the establishment and promotion of peace
> congresses. (NobelPrize.org, 2021)

Intentionally or not, Alfred Nobel's will exemplified the dominant values leading to the good
of humankind and, perhaps indirectly, it also celebrated the disciplines that fostered those
values. The natural sciences were represented by physics, chemistry and medicine – all worthy

fields that through practical applications at that time had led to immense improvements of people's well-being. Humanities were represented through literature, acknowledging the power of words to uplift and inspire. Finally, the social sciences were included for their potential to move the world in the direction of peace, offering healing in the aftermath of several deadly wars. Thus, the Nobel Prize awards were based on these values and their related disciplines, without change, for most of the 1900s. In 1969, however, a newcomer joined the field: economics.

The inclusion of economics in this prestigious award reflected broader changes in society generally and, more particularly, in economic sciences and how it was perceived by the public.

Finance theorists had by this time gradually moved away from objective economics to subjective (or neoclassical) economics. That is, they had moved away from the presumption that value can be determined based on the cost incurred in its production (raw material, energy, labour, and so on) to one where value is "the regard to what it is held to deserve" (Carney, 2020). In other words, the theorists transitioned to a so-called equilibrium value, where value not only reflects an average of supply and demand of something of utility, but also reflects what people generally think something is worth. Thus, value takes on a subjective element – a concept some readers might have experienced first-hand during the toilet paper shortage at the start of COVID-19. Suddenly toilet paper disappeared from shops, and people started hoarding and selling toilet paper for exorbitant prices. The ensuing frenzy was owing to (incorrect) assumptions related to the production of personal protective gear that was in short supply after the declaration of the COVID-19 pandemic.

In a society where the population lives according to subjective economics, anything and everything becomes negotiable, as the only thing that matters is how much somebody else is ready to pay for something they want. In earlier times trade unions and regulators could peg prices for services and products at certain levels, but with free-trade agreements across borders and consumers accustomed to price subjectivity this is no longer possible.

The inclusion of economics in the Nobel Prize awards has another significance. Seen from an axiological hierarchy perspective, four of the five original prizes commemorate achievements related to either intrinsic or extrinsic values. This sixth prize in economics joins the literature awards in celebrating systemic values. The laureates of medicine or peace, for example, have in many cases achieved breakthroughs that have directly saved people's lives (intrinsic values). Many of the discoveries are also directly enhancing and creating ways, such as tools and actions (extrinsic values), by which intrinsic values are improved. Economics, with its assumptions of a predictable future and faith in ideas about actions and timelines that can enhance people's lives, represents systemic values. The correlation with literature awards highlights the challenge; modern society sees itself as "economically rational" but puts too much trust in ideas that are not that different from outright fiction.

CONVERSATION STARTER

Nick Naumov asks students in his two teaching cases on Tourism and World Heritage Sites to think about how economic values in the world affect locations and sites that are supposed to represent specific cultural heritages. In the first one, a conversation starter, he asks students to think of social or cultural values they hold dear and discuss how willing they would be to see these intangible elements turned into world heritage, which in many cases means that they will be commercially exploited (see Activity 25).

ACTIVITY

In Nick Naumov's second teaching case, which is an activity, the emphasis is more directly aimed at the so-called economic benefits of world heritage tourism. The case and the assessment outline how economic values influence, change and even transform the sites (see Activity 26).

STORIES, TRUST, FAITH AND MONEY

As discussed in Chapter 5, our societies are made up of social realities that we both accept and create, shaping through our actions how they appear to others (Lawson, 2019). It works like a dress code in different social contexts. We see how others dress, and adapt accordingly, whereby we create an example for others. This circularity of cause and effect is invisible to the naked eye because it is part of our lived values, of the way we make sense of our lives and our roles in society. One factor that makes societies possible in the first place and that accounts for human coexistence as a powerful force on earth is trust: the trust we place in one another and the trust we place in the stories we tell ourselves and one another about reality (Harari, 2014). Trust is essential for cooperation. Without it, we cannot function in society. With it, we can accomplish incredible feats. The prosperity, well-being and developed state of our societies would not be possible without the trust we place in our fellow humans. This trust takes different forms, but it is typically the reason for our decision to believe what another person says, based on their experience or simply on their word: "Don't touch a hot stove", "This bridge can hold a maximum weight of five tons" and "I will repay my debt to you" are some examples.

In order to make human cooperation more efficient, for millennia we have placed our trust in something called money, a convenient shorthand for an entity that represents some kind of value. Historically this value correlated with some physical entity that had actual value to human sustenance, such as grains of cereal, but over time the correlation has become ever more abstract, something we will return to later in this chapter. Part of the trust we place in money comes from certain properties connected to it, such as the design and look of physical pieces of money that selected authorities are assigned to issue. That a piece of paper, with different colours and signs printed on it, magnet-strips inside it, holograms, watermarks and miniscule filigree printing would be more valuable than any other piece of paper is purely a result of trust, stories we believe in and rituals we follow. Monetary value and, by extension, economic value are therefore essentially not that different from any other faith that we might have. It is the surrender of rational thought that allows us to trust blindly and happily in whatever faith brings us contentment and conviction of our actions in life – but only if our faith stays strong. In this sense, economic value – the value that dominates thinking and action in modern societies – is an abstraction.

None of this is new for critical economists, who have long pointed out that the "emperor's new clothes" do not exist. Nonetheless, economic value remains a commonly accepted reality (Lawson, 2019). Carney (2020) points out that economists are suffering from physics envy:

they long for the certainty and determined outcomes that the mathematical formulas in physics provide. But these outcomes will always be elusive because economics is inherently tied to two factors that work against them: human behaviour and the "three lies of economics". The latter are (i) the complacency that comes with the assumption that "this time is different"; (ii) the distortion of markets, which goes against the presumption that "the market is always right"; and (iii) the presumption that "markets are moral" or, at least, their values are neutral and objective.

CONVERSATION STARTER

 Seek out some pictures from a natural disaster where homes have been destroyed by the impact of water, wind or fire, and explain to your students that people might find money that they had at home has been damaged or (almost) destroyed. Let the students discuss if the exchange value of that money is lost forever, or if people can regain it somehow. Let them investigate how this is handled by central banks in your region.

TAX, DEBT AND EMPLOYMENT: STRONG ECONOMIC VALUES

Modern societies depend on taxes to function – at least they did in the past, when societies still operated according to objective values, and each entity of value abstraction, such as money or shares in a company, was directly connected to something in the physical world. Nations still keep accounts and proclaim how a lion's share of the public services and investments that are needed, and expected, come from direct and indirect taxes. Politicians highlight how it is a nation's right to determine what taxes need to be paid and on whom they should be levied. The latter group, who inhabit that nation (either physically or virtually), are then obliged to pay their taxes. Tax is thus seen as a process of exchanging entities of value, where all services and infrastructure expected in the society are provided in exchange for shares of the money that people and organisations hold. This process follows the ideas of Hobbes, Locke and Rousseau expressed in "the social contract". At the same time, globalisation is radically changing how taxation works, enabling, for example, multinational companies to avoid paying any taxes whatsoever through clever, but unethical, tactics.

An argument that diverges from the traditional model of productive workers who receive salaries and pay taxes to fund social expenses is Universal Basic Income (UBI) (Kerstenetzky and Punzo, 2008). UBI takes into account the different expenses and services that nations provide to their citizens and highlights how the system of maintaining these welfare states is built on outdated assumptions. For example, people do not restrict themselves solely to salaried work in our societies. They might also perform a range of voluntary, creative and social roles that are necessary for thriving communities, or they might be engaged in lifelong learning activities outside formal educational institutions, which also indirectly contribute to the health of their communities. Old-fashioned economic models do not incorporate these activities. UBI would also be positive for ecological reasons. With people no longer being pressured to engage in salaried work, there would be no reason for states to commit to full employment and thus no need for an eternal growth cycle – the pursuit of which continues to cause grave damage to our natural environment (Andersson, 2009). In poorer countries, UBI could facilitate more equitable living conditions. Here, tourism is a suitable sector of the economy where wealth redistribution could take place (Kerstenetzky & Punzo, 2008). In short, this model could lead to new ways of imagining societies. These new ways, though, face a formidable barrier: deeply held economic and social values based on assumptions that no longer hold true but still hold sway.

Politicians favour comparing national accounts and debt with households. Debt is issued by governments as bonds sold to private or institutional investors. However, the comparison to households is faulty on several levels. Households cannot issue more money in the same way that states with their independent currencies can, as evident during economic downturns when central banks' "stimulus packages" essentially mean that money has been added to a ledger without any physical equivalent appearing to counterbalance it. Neither can households raise taxes, change laws or introduce any other measures that are at the disposal of independent nations. However, maintaining the concepts of taxes, debt and trade balances with other nations creates stability through reinforcing common beliefs in the system. These common beliefs are especially important regarding employment as an institution of social stability.

Employment is the final feature that is taken as a constituent part of society, and it is therefore given much value in people's minds. "Employment" and "work" are almost synonymous, referring to the actions people take to earn entities of value (often money, but not always) that they can exchange for other goods and services they need. To be employed and to earn one's living is therefore presented as something valuable, and as evidence of being a well-adjusted member of the society one belongs to. People are born, are schooled, they work and receive thereafter a pension. However, employment and productive activities in society are not always the same. Voluntary work and household work are not "productive" in a financial definition, but they are productive for maintaining quality of living. All these everyday concepts are so self-evident to us as educators that we hardly ever think about them. Our work, to prepare students for a future where they become productive (and hopefully critical and engaged) members of our societies, stems from a belief that work, employment and productivity are what reality must be like. This resembles the thoughts of Fisher (2009) in his classic work *Capitalist Realism: Is There No Alternative?* He explains that concerned and intelligent people accept capitalism and neo-liberalism not because they endorse these systems but because they can see no possible alternatives. He relates this to our field of leisure and tourism:

> The power of capitalist realism derives in part from the way that capitalism subsumes and consumes all of previous history: one effect of its 'system of equivalence' which can assign all cultural objects, whether they are religious iconography, pornography, or *Das Kapital*, a monetary value. Walk around the British Museum, where you can see objects torn from their lifeworlds and assembled as if on the deck of some Predator spacecraft, and you have a powerful image of this process at work. In the conversion of practices and rituals into merely aesthetic objects, the beliefs of previous cultures are objectively ironized, transformed into *artefacts*. Capital realism is therefore not a particular type of realism; it is more like realism in itself. (p. 4; emphasis added)

CONVERSATION STARTER

Let your students imagine what a society would look like that had no capacity to collect taxes from the people and organisations inhabiting it. Imagine further that there would be no employment in that society. What kind of society do they imagine? Is it a utopian or a dystopian society? Why?

Looking at the past decades with their large market failures, economic crises and public money bailouts of companies believed to be "too large to fail", one would imagine that things would be done differently afterwards. Just imagine the Boeing 737 MAX produced with a distinct fault that made it crash, or a pilot who has repeatedly been in accidents or near-accidents. The authorities around the world would forbid that plane from flying and that pilot from having a licence. All systems would be recalculated and any training programme of such negligent pilots would be redone, until it was certain that the same faults would not happen again. And still, the trust in people's minds of that plane type or of that pilot might never be fully restored. However, after a financial crash, business schools continue teaching the same material as before, bankers and financiers continue making similar decisions and we continue having more economic crashes.

According to Carney (2020), this blind adherence to a system that does not work stems from the economic values that are held in such high regard in society:

1. The idea that "markets are complete". Thus, in a state of perfect competition, rational financiers will finance that which will have a sufficient demand, and rational consumers will make the right choices. Consequently, all markets will "clear"; that is, everything that is offered for sale will be sold at a price that the markets consider to be right, regardless of what that entity cost to produce. The countless enterprises that have closed their doors for good when no tourists did visit, despite feasibility studies suggesting that they would, stand as examples of this folly in practice.

2. Humans are rational beings. Indeed, we even call ourselves "wise" (*Homo sapiens*), despite all the evidence to the contrary. One of the most striking pieces of evidence occurred when people rushed to stock up on toilet paper in spring 2020, as a response to COVID-19, even after being assured that sufficient supply existed. We tend to rationalise our behaviour and support past decisions as being right, even when shown evidence to the contrary. We think that singular examples can be generalised, and we are irrationally impatient.

3. Markets are moral, which is to indicate that all values have been "flattened", and all is neutral and of equal value (Carney, 2020). However, the evidence shows over and over that markets' morality has diverged far from human morality. Shareholder value is emphasised above and beyond values and disvalues (that is, negative values in an axiological sense) to employees, local communities and living environments. Societies have steadily abandoned any structural recognition of the human values that make life worth living, including those networks of community connections and respect which allow people to judge and esteem themselves by measures other than financial ones, in the pursuit of market freedoms. Many companies are no longer part of financing social goods and services, but are rather competing directly with public services, or even suing public sectors for "distorting markets" through measures put in place to care for the weakest in society (McMurtry, 2013).

INVESTMENT AND GROWTH

Investment is an interesting and very peculiar feature of societies. The idea of investing is often connected to finance, but viewed from a wider perspective it can be related to most things that humans, and even animals, do on earth. We all invest time, effort and care in events that we participate in – such as the intangible investment you are making right now by reading this book. To invest, therefore, is to take something of value and engage it in an action that has the capacity to create even more value – to make the valuable entity grow.

  However, investment always carries an element of risk, too. The money, time, effort, feelings or whatever we have invested might be wasted if the outcome of our investment is less than what we had intended. We might plant a seed in the ground, thereby investing in the future with the expectation that the seed will germinate, grow and produce a harvest that is more valuable than the original seed. But, at the same time, we know that a flood might wash away the seed, a storm might destroy the plant before we harvest it or somebody else might take the harvest. And in all those cases we are left empty-handed. We would have been better off consuming the seed ourselves in the first place, rather than investing it for the future.

  The ultimate reason for any investment is growth, and this is one of the economic values that our societies hinge on the very most. Growth is an incredibly powerful value because of all the benefits it can bring but, at the same time, growth for the sake of growth threatens to destroy everything that comes in its path. Uncurbed growth as an economic value is unfortunately ingrained in society. Governments set policies with growth as the central goal, and they win or lose elections based on the public's perception of how successfully they have achieved that goal.

  As evidence of how deeply embedded these values are, we can look at the rationale of the Sveriges Riksbank Prize committee in awarding the "Economic Sciences in Memory of Alfred Nobel" 2020 prize to the laureates who had "improved auction theory and invented new auction formats, benefitting sellers, buyers and taxpayers around the world" (Andersson et al., 2020). In other words, the theory that "won" this coveted award relates strictly to monetary utility value, benefitting societies where everything has a subjective value. Objective value – in terms of what it *actually* costs an employee in long workdays, sweat and minimum pay – is not accounted for and not compensated for. Yes, the lowest bid in these auctions might save a municipality upfront costs for some service, but it might simultaneously lead to an erosion of workers' rights, profits shifted to tax paradises and care of humans quantified, so that any additional needs can be billed for separately.

  In examining the application of these ideas, one can see that markets are by no means moral, because they do not exist on their own. Humans do, and humans behave as expected of them by the values in society. If the dominant values were care and stewardship for other living beings, then all would be fine. But when stock prices and share trader wealth as indicators of value are confused with values, then greed and egotism naturally follow.

What changed our communal values so radically in the late 1960s and early 1970s, away from the values of betterment of humankind to a single-minded focus on monetary value? Well, many things. It was the time of the Cold War, where two dominant ideologies were competing for global supremacy through different proxy wars. The space race was raging as an effect of the former, and the first human landed on the moon (Raworth, 2018). Large steps towards more equality were taken globally, and many former colonies gained their independence but then fell under the dominance of new powers. The world had its first oil crisis, and the United States went to war in Vietnam, the cost of which led to the scrapping of the "gold standard" of the dollar (McMurtry, 2013). GDP calculations, as a measurement of growth and well-being, started to include transactions in the "FIRE" (Finance, Insurance and Real Estate) sector as it outperformed the rest of the economy (Mazzucato, 2019). None of these factors was big enough on its own, but combined with the economic globalisation and deregulation that have dominated the last 40 years, they all coincided to reshape the ways in which the media and decision makers interpreted reality, creating the new era we now inhabit. The result has been a transformation of the state from a provider of public welfare to a promoter of markets and competition.

On the whole, society's faith in the economy as a factor leading to well-being brings along a need to shape how it is all measured, enhanced and rationalised. Deterministic economic models are created based on past experience, growth is taken as a measurement of improved standards, and excess is seen as an expression of success rather than waste. But growth models were created in the past century, when there were several billion fewer people on earth, when many companies were still committed to their social contract and when mass consumption was a goal, not a reality. So why should we continue to follow theories and assumptions created in a vastly different world to the one we inhabit today?

During the time of COVID-19, health officials pleaded with leaders of nations around the world to heed their call and close down activities in societies, but they were largely overshadowed by economic advisers claiming that the losses in lifestyle would be more severe than risks to lives. Contracting GDP figures, less direct employment and reduced tax-paying capacity all highlighted the cracks in our shared faith in the economic system. However, in response to financial losses for closed borders and businesses, governments the world over printed new money like never before. Or, more accurately, nothing was printed, only zeros added to balance sheets on central bank computers. Economists produced new estimates of when growth would start again, returning us to earlier levels of prosperity, but these estimates were based on assumptions, made in a time that had no precedent. That the emperor had no clothes was plain to see. Yet we refused to accept the sight, preferring instead to imagine lavish new clothes that promised more good times to come for us all.

Teaching Tourism asks us to accept a clear-sighted investment in our common future and in the well-being of all who inhabit this earth. All investments should be made based on the intrinsic values of each living being that is affected. The result will be less monetary wealth but much more value for all involved. It is time to reconnect our value creation with our human values.

ACTIVITY

Joanne Paulette Gellatly presents two assessments, one for individual students and the other for groups, both linked to the "Unfolding of
SARS-CoV-2" and aimed at rethinking tourism from a crisis management
perspective. Consequently, the lessons learned from the pandemic could be
used to rebuild tourism in a more ethical fashion. Joanne takes a humanistic approach as she
shows how students need to understand both economics and management in order to create
a better future in "Tourism resiliency post COVID-19" (see Activities 22 and 23).

ROLEPLAYING GAME

The first half round of "The Tourism Game" was played in Chapter 5 on
social values from the perspectives of social reality and class and inequality.
Here is the opportunity to play the second half round by asking students
once again to assume the roles of various participants in the debate. Their
job is to assess the costs and benefits of the development from the point of
view of their role and decide whether the project should proceed. The set-up is by Johan
Edelheim and the game itself is described by Stephen Fairbrass (see Activities 12 and 53).

8. Ethics

Marion Joppe; **Johan Edelheim**; **Joan Flaherty**; Xavier Michel; Kathleen Rodenburg

OBJECTIVES

This chapter provides readers with insights and engagement activities to help students:

1. Appreciate that the principles and fundamental convictions underlying morality are both universal and culturally relative
2. Identify the professions that are perceived as most trustworthy; and consider whether they agree, based on their own experience
3. Appraise how close to their authentic self they are, and how to get even closer
4. Explain why there is a need to think about justice when deciding where to go on holiday
5. Gain a basic understanding of different ethical traditions and principles

INTRODUCTION

Simply put, ethics is the principle of "good", and therefore it underpins all other values because the principle of "good" is the first principle of axiology (Edwards, 2010). More specifically, ethics concerns itself with what is morally right or wrong. It refers to the specific principles and values that guide our interactions in societies and shape our judgements about whether people's behaviour reflects these principles and values.

Ethical behaviour derives from specific value systems, meaning that different cultures, religions and societies have different conceptions of what it entails (Mihalič et al., 2015). In fact, our ethical positions can become so ingrained that they become almost immutable, even if we leave the familial, cultural or social environment that shaped them in the first place. Therefore, teaching ethics can be highly controversial and challenging, especially when we are confronted with ethical dilemmas where both positions are easily defended. Such dilemmas are particularly pronounced in tourism, due to social norm differences that arise from culture, religion, and so on. They can also be pronounced in classrooms that bring together students from diverse – internationally or otherwise – backgrounds. Therefore, our students need, for their personal and professional growth, to learn how to address these issues.

An additional teaching challenge is that discussions about ethics can engender cynicism. We live in a world that seems to be increasingly controlled by political and business interests that wield their power through financial and military means as well as corruption, essentially acting as if this power exempts them from abiding by the same "rules" as the majority. The pandemic, for example, highlighted many of these behaviours, with preferential treatment for those who were well connected or had the means to bribe their way to vaccination ahead of priority groups.

"Morality" refers to the norms and rules governing human behaviour in a given society. Edwards (2010) distinguishes between systemic, extrinsic and intrinsic dimensions of morality. At the systemic level are laws, policies and moral rules that are the foundation of each individual society. These are fundamental in any course, from human resource management to organisational behaviour to environmental studies. Adherence to these dictates is extrinsic morality, and there is an expectation that law-abiding citizens will respect, if not defend, them. Intrinsic morality defines an individual as an ethical person, and it is at this level that education can run into conflicting values, especially when dealing with a very diverse student body. To be an authentic self requires that the individual knows themselves. As instructors we can encourage the reflexivity and decolonisation of the self required to help our students live up to their self-ideals and self-expectations.

Relatively little research has been done to evaluate values-based education and learning as it relates to tourism, but the results of one study are particularly enlightening. Tourism students at an elite, three-country master's programme in Europe were asked about their perception of the presence of values in higher education and the importance of values in their industry. Their responses point to the need for improvement in how the topic is taught (Liburd et al., 2018). According to these students, the authentic self is one of the least important aspects of all values and their components in higher education. Furthermore, these researchers found that more European Union (EU) students think that the tourism industry is unethical than non-EU students (Mihalič et al., 2015), which could be the result of different cultural interpretations of what is "ethical". Yet Barber (2011), citing Sheldon et al. (2011), states that we need to recognise that good actions do not occur in a vacuum but are derived from specific value systems that further require understanding and respect for actions based on authenticity and authentic self.

In a tripartite study, Padurean and Maggi (2011) examined the mission statements of 84 graduate programmes in tourism around the world and 156 posts in international job search engines advertising for positions in tourism-related industries, and surveyed students in tourism and tourism-related programmes around the world. They reached the conclusion that, of the ethics sub-dimensions *honesty*, *transparency*, *authenticity* and *authentic self*, universities do not value *transparency* and the *authentic self*, but they do value *honesty*, while the industry is more interested in *transparency* and *honesty*. The students valued more the *authenticity* and the *authentic self*, both highest ranked overall.

One topic among several not captured by the Tourism Education Futures Initiative (TEFI) concept of ethics is justice, which is increasingly recognised as crucial in the context of tourism. There is greater awareness that the rights of local residents and industry workers are being short-changed by the private and public sectors' ever-increasing demands for more financial and economic returns on tourism investment. This is why the study of tourism development must be guided by principles of justice, responsibility and sustainability and an ethic of care (Jamal, 2019). For Fennell (2018), ethic of care seeks a balance between humans and their sociocultural environment. For Jamal et al. (2013), ethic of care denotes respecting and supporting "social differentiation and diversity, sympathy, mercy, forgiveness, tolerance, and inclusiveness" (p. 4606). These topics are further addressed in Chapter 6 on culture and Chapter 10 on mutuality.

If we are serious about the concept of sustainable tourism and its regenerative power, then it is crucial that the underlying ethical perspective be fully appreciated by students. This perspective, which will lead to more responsible tourism, requires ranking community benefits above individual benefits; decolonising our processes and governance; and placing community and environmental health at the centre of decisions. Only then can tourism hope to contribute significantly to achieving the United Nations Sustainable Development Goals. In a world dominated by corporatist economic interests that prioritise efficiency, growth and profit, the task before us is not an easy one. And the first step begins in the classroom: regardless of the specific subject matter, our courses must reflect, implicitly or explicitly, a worldview that values biocentricism and community well-being above individualism.

The exercises and activities in this chapter all focus on the intrinsic dimension of morality and offer different techniques to encourage students to reflect on and identify their own values and to assess the extent to which these values shape their decisions (Halstead and Taylor, 2000).

CONVERSATION STARTER

 In "The power of values to effect positive change 1", Joan Flaherty presents a foundational exercise aimed at fostering student awareness of their values (see Activity 28).

HONESTY AND TRANSPARENCY

Every child is taught about honesty at an early age, and yet when it comes to academic integrity we note stark cultural differences in how this concept is understood. Being honest also comes with consequences – again a lesson learned at an early age. We encourage team learning in many of our courses yet expect students to submit distinctly different individual assignments. Therefore, the whole concept of honesty is fraught with contradiction from a very early age.

Honesty and openness in a business and governance context can lead to trust in institutions and their leadership from the many roles we take on as economic actors (employees, investors, taxpayers, and so on). Transparency is necessary to allow us to determine whether the decision-making process is informed and equitable, and whether past injustices or cultural differences have been taken into account. With a clear understanding of the process, expectations can be managed, but leaders can also be held accountable for their decisions, the process itself, information shared or withheld, and any conflicts of interest that may arise.

Too much transparency, however, can have negative impacts. It can put businesses at a competitive disadvantage, unfairly target leaders in business and governance for criticism, create biased negative perceptions and lead to a loss of trust. Technology has provided much greater access to information but has also given rise to an unprecedented amount of misinformation, if not downright falsehoods. Examples of this arose throughout the COVID-19 pandemic, which has also been referred to as an "infodemic" or a "(mis)infodemic" due to the emerging nature of all knowledge connected to the pandemic and all the conflicting evidence, guesses and attempts at gaining political advantages from the situation (Williams et al., 2020). In short, discerning what is real and what is fake has become a significant challenge in our "post-truth" world. Helping students navigate this complex and challenging information environment is a task every instructor has to address, regardless of subject matter being taught, as disordered information has entered every realm from business to marketing to environmental studies.

CONVERSATION STARTER

For over 35 years Ipsos MORI's Veracity Index has been asking the public which professions they think are most likely to tell the truth. On its website under "Global trust in professions: Who do global citizens trust?"[1] is a table that shows some stark differences in our trust level of different professions, and how perceptions vary between countries. Almost without exception, politicians are among the least trusted people in the world, while scientists, doctors and teachers tend to be trusted by a majority, though certainly not all!

ACTIVITY

Joan Flaherty asks students to write an academic essay on an industry issue with ethical implications in "Industry ethics" (see Activity 29). Specific topics would depend on the course, but they could be narrowed down from broad issues such as impacts of tourism, industry hiring practices, tourism social entrepreneurship initiatives, resource conflicts, and so on.

AUTHENTICITY AND AUTHENTIC SELF

In a world where the majority of people have become disconnected from their roots in space and time, the search for authenticity has become a major driver in tourism's exponential growth. Every dip in demand – whether due to financial crises, terror acts or disasters – is followed by double-digit growth as pent-up demand is released. Trends such as a desire for local products, greater attention being paid to *terroir* – that is, how a particular region's climate, soils and aspect (terrain) affect the taste of its products – and an interest in experiencing traditions and cultural expressions different from our own are closely associated with this quest for the authentic. Yet we need to appreciate that what is considered authentic in different cultures and subcultures is very much determined by values held in those communities.

The authentic self is a logical continuation of the other subheadings we have dealt with in this topic: honesty and transparency. Being authentic means being honest with oneself about how one acts and what one claims to value. Large discrepancies between the two suggest that a person is not being authentic to themselves. Depending on the situation and the person, the result might be guilt, indifference or denial. For example, we are all aware that flying deepens our carbon footprint, contributing to climate change – an outcome that we are probably vehemently opposed to (Topham, 2019). As tourism educators, and as readers of this particular book, it is highly likely that we embrace environmental values. However, those values are directly contravened every time we get on a plane. That small, nagging feeling of discontent

– or guilt – we may feel as we book the ticket and board the plane is the authentic self, reminding us of its existence. Alternatively, we may feel no discontent, and instead indifference or perhaps even denial, as we tell ourselves that the actions of one person have negligible impact on climate change and are therefore meaningless. Humans are truly masters at rationalising cognitive dissonance when our wants collide with our values.

CONVERSATION STARTER

 Ask students if they believe they can have different authentic selves at different times of their life. Ask them to explain why they answered as they did and why the opposite cannot be true.

ACTIVITY

 Having students remember and relate their tourist experiences in phenomenological and humanistic approaches reveals their ways of being-in-the-world and thus their authenticity. Having students think about one or several personal tourist experience(s) encourages them to analyse how they engage with different milieux, how they approach otherness and their relationship with the environment. This is what Xavier Michel set out to achieve in "Mobilising learners' tourist memories towards a deeper, more authentic understanding and practice of tourism" (see Activity 7).

JUSTICE

Although we often equate justice with "what is fair", the approaches taken and variants on the theme make this another complex concept. "What is fair" has been debated by numerous philosophers: Aristotle's virtue ethics, Marx's distributive justice, Bentham's utilitarianism, Rawls' concept of justice as fairness and Sen's capability approach. There are many sub-themes within social justice, all attempting to promote equality or redistribute power and status between groups based on gender, race, age, religion, ability, ethnicity, and so on. These topics are also addressed in Chapter 10 on mutuality values, as diversity, inclusion and equity are closely linked to justice.

Two other dimensions of justice that are gaining attention are environmental justice and ecological justice. Environmental justice sees the economy as a subsystem within society and the wider natural world. It addresses inequities in the access and use of natural resources as well as the "fair" distribution of environmental benefits and burdens. Nonetheless, environmental justice remains very anthropocentric. Ecological justice affirms the sacredness of Mother Earth and addresses the justice between humans and the natural world. This focus reflects back to Chapter 2's introduction of "life-value" as the core intrinsic value (McMurtry, 2013). Another dimension of this discussion is found in Chapter 4 on ecological values, where nature is seen from four different perspectives, one of which defines nature as a person in its own right.

Justice-related topics often revolve around one theme: a redistribution of, or granting of access to, resources. Consequently, there are always "winners" and "losers" – a fact which leads to debates around privilege and "haves" versus "have nots". It also leads to discussions of power and how those who have it will try to influence decisions in their favour. In tourism development, operations and marketing, these justice issues are played out on an almost daily basis around the world. Many newspaper stories can be brought to class to initiate discussions. The conversation starter below serves as one example.

CONVERSATION STARTER

Having students examine the clash among the rights of traditional owners, colonists and tourists allows for a spirited debate that allows instructors to focus on many ethical concerns as well as justice, decolonisation and politics.

Uluru (or Ayers Rock as it was known previously) vies with Sydney Opera House as the most famous symbol of Australia. Yet to the original inhabitants of the surrounding area it is not just beautiful, but also sacred, the scene of holy rituals. Signs erected by the Anangu people at the base of Uluru declare, "Under our traditional law, climbing is not permitted." Yet climbing it has long been a favoured pastime of tourists. Some litter, defecate or strip while they scramble up. Thirty-seven people have died trying to reach the summit in sweltering heat. The Anangu have had enough: they own the site and since October 26, 2019 have banned visitors from ascending. It is "not a theme park like Disneyland", reasoned Sammy Wilson, one of its traditional owners, when the change was announced.[2] Some Australians complain they are being robbed of a birthright. The polarity of opinions was highlighted in the months leading up to the closure as thousands of visitors converged on one of Australia's most famous landmarks to make a final trek to the top, and often camped illegally on roadsides for kilometres because the local camping ground and accommodation were booked.

ROLEPLAYING GAME

Unions have accomplished much over the past century to improve remuneration, health and safety, working conditions and other benefits for the working and middle classes. In many companies and professions, joining a union may not be optional. However, the union's often rigid control over employee duties, work hours and other conditions of employment may hinder a workplace from adjusting to the fast-evolving realities of many businesses today. Johan Edelheim introduces "The dilemma of protecting workers in the face of entrepreneurship" through the case of the Finnish Hotel and Restaurant Workers' Union, and the challenges faced by micro businesses in Lapland trying to work within union rules provide an example of this dilemma (see Activity 27). In this exercise, students assume different workplace roles and attempt to reach a consensus that provides the necessary flexibility for these entrepreneurs to thrive without compromising the gains made by workers in larger establishments.

TEAM ACTIVITY

 Working in teams and through Kathleen Rodenburg's multistep project "Solving ethical dilemmas in the tourism industry", students are led to determine key ethical issues of the "right versus right" kind (for example, "truth versus loyalty", "justice versus mercy", "short-term versus long-term" and "individual versus community") faced by a destination community (see Activity 30). The ethical dilemmas are written up individually, ensuring different ethical lenses applied to similar contexts. Resolution is determined by teams working through a decision process for resolving ethical dilemmas. The exercise culminates in student presentations to a live panel that includes stakeholders from the communities where the dilemmas are present.

NOTES

1. www.ipsos.com/sites/default/files/ct/news/documents/2019-09/global-trust-in-professions-ipsos-trustworthiness-index.pdf.
2. www.economist.com/asia/2019/10/24/australians-resent-a-ban-on-climbing-their-countrys-most-famous-rock.

9. Stewardship

Marion Joppe; Johan Edelheim; Joan Flaherty; Karla A. Boluk; Alexandra Coghlan; Brynhild Granås; Tazim Jamal; Gunnar Thór Jóhannesson; Miranda Peterson; Outi Rantala; Bradley Rink; Sarah Ripper; Kaarina Tervo-Kankare

OBJECTIVES

This chapter provides readers with insights and engagement activities to help students:

1. Contrast the concept of sustainability with how it is used in a capitalist system of growth
2. Understand that all stakeholders of tourism have stewardship responsibilities
3. Describe what self-reliance is on both a personal and a communal level
4. Examine what it means to have the "right to be human" when talking about human rights
5. Judge how service to others could uncover a purpose for how to act as a steward

INTRODUCTION

The careful and responsible management of something or someone that has been entrusted to us is referred to as "stewardship". This concept also implies that we are accountable for how we manage what has been entrusted. Stewardship usually refers to the responsible use and protection of the environment through managing, recycling, conserving, regenerating, restoring and taking responsibility for choices made, including our own. Worrell and Appleby (2000) defined stewardship rather comprehensively as "the responsible use (including conservation) of natural resources in a way that takes full and balanced account of the interests of society, future generations, and other species, as well as of private needs, and accepts significant answerability to society" (p. 263). This biocentric view, which extends inherent value to all living things, human and nonhuman alike, is reflected in many cultural traditions and religions worldwide. It contrasts sharply with the much narrower anthropocentric position whereby environmental well-being is a priority only insofar as it serves the well-being of humans. According to this view, environmental preservation is a means to an end (that is, preserving the welfare of humans) rather than an end in itself.

Stewardship's connotations of an intimate connection with nature are often associated with Indigenous people. Indeed, all aspects of stewardship are intrinsic values of Indigenous worldviews and their belief that people, objects and the environment are all connected. This appreciation and understanding of humanity as part of a much greater whole distinguish the Indigenous from many groups of settlers from other regions. An important element of

Indigenous worldviews is reflected in the acute awareness that this earth we are living on, and the natural environment we are living within, are lent to us from future generations. What we do today should never diminish what we leave to those coming after us. This theme is further developed in Chapter 6 on cultural values, under the subheadings of *Sustainability* and *Responsibility* below, and in Chapter 10 on mutuality values.

One cultural "attraction" for people living in modern urban communities is to experience Indigenous people and their traditions. This experience, however, may be distorted by the fact that Indigenous people are often seen in a simplistic manner, their way of being and doing viewed as an earlier link in the evolutionary chain which different cultures have already gone through. This distorted view and its consequences are examined below under the subheadings *Self-reliance* and *Human rights*. If all stakeholders are to take responsibility for stewardship, then we must ensure that all are actually empowered to do so. Inclusivity and power sharing are necessary prerequisites if we are to reconcile the conflicting environmental, social and economic tenets that currently drive and divide our discourses about nature. Stewardship that engages everyone requires that we draw on shared values and beliefs about nature and legitimise knowledge based on an understanding of the planetary boundaries.

The great number and diversity of stakeholders involved mean that the above goals are challenging and long-term. Communities are rarely homogenous in their prioritisation. However, one core dimension of stewardship likely to be accepted by different stakeholders as their responsibility is service to others (Sheldon et al., 2011).

CONVERSATION STARTER

 Ask students to come up with an example of stewardship practised in their home community, either as a way of life or as an activity that people do voluntarily.

SUSTAINABILITY

Today, most students have been given at least a rudimentary introduction to sustainability, usually including the Brundtland Commission definition: "development that meets the needs of the present without compromising the ability of future generations to meet their own needs" (WCED, 1987). However, this definition often leads to a very flawed appreciation of the concept, starting with the belief that sustainability is achievable. In fact, accepting that sustainability can never be achieved may be an important step in understanding the complexity of our stewardship responsibilities:

> The very idea of striking a balance in which the environment, economy and social and cultural elements are in equilibrium can be seen as an oxymoron. Appreciating the complexities of socio-cultural values, quality of life aspirations, and the biophysical and economic systems in which tourism takes place over time, an integrated approach to stewardship is of importance. Consequently, also discarding the notion of sustainable development as a goal that can be achieved, a processual and holistic understanding is called for. (Sheldon, et al., 2011, p. 13)

Yet we will never be able to take this step toward a more comprehensive, impactful steward-ship role if neo-liberalism and consumerism continue to encourage unsustainable lifestyles and an "extract, make, discard" mentality that run counter to the very principles of stewardship.

The World Conservation Strategy (International Union for Conservation of Nature and Natural Resources, 1980) defined development as "the modification of the biosphere and the application of human, financial, living and non-living resources to satisfy human needs and improve the quality of human life" (p. 18). This notion of "quality of human life" does not imply growth in quantitative terms, but rather the qualitative improvement of potentialities. Unfortunately, when "development" is attached to "sustainable", it all too often implies growth as measured in economic terms (gross domestic product, employment, tax revenues, and so on). Therefore, when this concept is extended to "tourism sustainable development", it is often positioned as sustainable when the very essence of tourism – that it takes place elsewhere – means it will negatively impact the environment, if only through the carbon emissions of travel to the destination, and cause changes in the sociocultural life of the resident population.

The complexity of addressing sustainability is made apparent by the 17 United Nations Sustainable Development Goals (SDGs) with their myriad of objectives.

Although tourism is specifically mentioned in only three goals (Goals 8, 12 and 14 on inclusive and sustainable economic growth, sustainable consumption and production, and the sustainable use of oceans and marine resources, respectively), it has the potential to con-tribute to all 17 if properly planned and executed. This planning and execution, however, can be a daunting task – one that requires reaching consensus among a broad political, economic, technological and social spectrum of stakeholders. One way to introduce stu-dents to this challenge and its possibilities is to engage them in Climate Action Simulation (www.climateinteractive.org/tools/climate-action-simulation/), a highly interactive, online roleplaying game. Here, they can explore key technology and policy solutions addressing global warming. The game is conducted as a simulated emergency climate summit organ-ised by the United Nations that convenes global stakeholders to establish a concrete plan that limits warming to Paris Agreement goals.

In any case, the SDGs' approach – one that neatly confines tourism's role to its three boxes – is typical of a scientific approach that studies each "dot" within each goal to a great depth with measurable indicators. This approach is akin to scrutinising an object under a microscope. The results yield much information about that one particular object but are disconnected from all else. The results, in other words, are incomplete. In contrast, Indigenous knowledge has been gained over millennia by observing the interrelationships among the "dots" to develop a picture of the whole. That is, Indigenous knowledge enables us to see the entire "forest", while conventional scientists are all too often still stuck studying the individual "trees".

An additional challenge with the work done by the various United Nations commissions, whether leading to the World Conservation Strategy or the SDGs, is their anthropocentrism: it is essentially about human needs and human life. Even the need to protect our planetary ecosystems is seen exclusively from the perspective of protecting the future of human life and well-being. This positioning does not as yet take full advantage of the wisdom gained by Indigenous populations who view the human–nature relationship in kincentric terms; that is, both they and nature are part of an extended ecological family that shares ancestry and origins (Salmón, 2000).

ACTIVITIES

In her contribution "Using systems thinking and the UN's SDG framework as an opportunity for fostering critical dialogue", Karla A. Boluk has designed an activity using the principles of design thinking that challenges students to think more deeply about each of the SDGs, their relationship with tourism and potential responses (see Activity 32).

Alexandra Coghlan and Sarah Ripper have defined sustainability for the purpose of their exercises in "Reflecting on sustainable behaviour" as "a set of relationships – with our natural environment, with the resources we depend on, with our employees, our investors, our families, our community, and the governance structures that support our societies – and ourselves" (see Activity 5). To this end, they have devised a series of exercises that enable students to not only see multiple perspectives to interpret what is driving sustainable or unsustainable behaviours, but also assess their own behaviour in this regard.

RESPONSIBILITY

As noted above, stewardship also implies taking responsibility for our actions on an individual as well as collective level. Indeed, responsibility is central to Goal 12 of the SDGs. All stakeholders must acknowledge their responsibility for the environment and society, and then act accordingly. Tourism stakeholders include destination governments, generating country governments, tourism industry firms and organisations, employees, tourists, host communities, media and investors (Sheldon, et al., 2011). To this effect, the General Assembly of the World Tourism Organization adopted the Global Code of Ethics for Tourism in 1999 to guide the actions of the different stakeholders. It exhorts visitors to assume the following responsibilities: acquaint themselves, even before their departure, with the characteristics of the countries they are preparing to visit and be aware of and minimise any health and security risks. Obviously, they should not engage in criminal activity or what might be deemed so by the laws of the country visited, and should abstain from any conduct that could offend the local populations or damage the local environment. The public authorities are seen as responsible for providing protection for tourists and putting in place measures to ensure their safety. But host communities and local professionals are also called upon to get to know and respect those who visit them to ensure a hospitable welcome. Tourist destinations are expected to promote their offerings in a responsible way on behalf of all internal stakeholders. One of their tasks is to create a destination where tourists can make environmentally sound choices – such as using public transport. Finally, everybody engaged in tourism industries is responsible for ensuring that the services and products they provide are ethically produced and consumed.

CONVERSATION STARTER

A good way to get students to start thinking about their own responsibility with regard to stewardship is to have them calculate their carbon footprint using the website www.carbonfootprint.com and discuss the main contributors to its elevated level. Travel and meat consumption are often primary sources and can lead to animated discussions about different lifestyles and what individuals can do to lower their own carbon footprint. Marion Joppe outlines this in "Calculating a carbon footprint" (see Activity 33).

ACTIVITIES

A more complex individual assignment can be found under *Point 1: Carbon footprint and offsetting* in Tazim Jamal and Miranda Peterson's contribution, "Climate action for a climate-friendly educational destination", in- volving various websites and calculators to consider air travel and carbon offsetting, personal transport and its everyday impacts, as well as a closer look at energy and waste (see Activity 6).

Since humans dominate the earth's biosphere and we are running up against the limits of our planet's regeneration, it is important for students to understand nature's regeneration ability and how collectively we have overused the earth's natural capital. By analysing the ecological resource use and resource capacity of nations over time, and comparing countries graphically, students can quickly understand which countries have a biocapacity deficit or surplus, and which have the largest footprint, based on population. This is the topic of Marion Joppe's "The limits to biocapacity" (see Activity 34).

SELF-RELIANCE

Self-reliance might be associated with egoism and individualism, and these can indeed be dimensions of self-reliance. However, in the context of stewardship, the values of interest are those that allow us to create good in society. A self-reliant person might be forced to trust mostly in themselves and to act in ways that do not require a supporting network of others. But it is not necessarily out of egoism that a person is self-reliant; rather, they may find themselves in a situation where the only way forward is of their own making. When thinking of self-reliance in the context of stewardship, one might also think of how humans can live in harmony with nature by understanding what nature can give and what does not have to be sourced from elsewhere.

Self-reliance can also be seen in a broader scale where whole families, communities, societies or even nations are self-reliant, and not dependent on an outside source to survive. Indeed, for hundreds of thousands of years, humans have lived in small, intimate and self-reliant communities to survive; in the last few millennia, *Homo sapiens* – the only surviving human species – have formed ever larger collectives, largely through aggression and bloodshed. With the threat of nuclear war after World War II, efforts to establish a global order have also resulted in economic globalisation, creating complex interconnected networks that allow companies to produce, handle and distribute worldwide various goods and services to the public by taking advantage of cheaper costs of production, often at significant costs to human and environmental rights. However, the COVID-19 pandemic taught the world about the dangers of globalisation and outsourcing since it made countries increasingly dependent on others and therefore ever more vulnerable to disruptions in the supply chain. A disruption, for example, in the supply of personal protective equipment or vaccines during a pandemic could have disastrous consequences for the country dependent on those supplies. The awareness of these consequences has amplified calls for greater self-reliance and support for local manufacturers, businesses and farmers. As long as these local producers can maintain their output, local populations become more self-reliant, reducing the risks of a break in the supply chain. In terms of tourism, locavorism – the belief that local food is fresher and more flavourful – for instance, has been a growing trend as people are looking for greater connection with the hosts at their destination.

Whether for an individual or for a nation, self-reliance has significant implications for resilience and coping with severe challenges and disasters. It is what has allowed Indigenous peoples to survive for tens of thousands of years, even in the face of brutal colonisation. Here, too, the pandemic highlighted who is committed to cohesive communities and social accountability, the foundations of social self-reliance, as exemplified by the decisions about whether and how to protect the most vulnerable and who received access to the vaccines when they first became available. The downside of greater self-reliance is greater selfishness: wealthy countries monopolising vaccines and countries that were producing the vaccines in many instances blocking exports to other nations until their own populations were immunised.

CONVERSATION STARTER

Self-reliance implies self-knowledge as well as self-acceptance and the ability to think and act independently. These concepts can be explored with students by having them think about situations where they have been self-reliant, how they developed this and whether it was a conscious choice at the time. Through this discussion, students can then be led to think more broadly about their community, and how their own self-confidence can contribute to helping the particular community become more self-reliant. This conversation starter ties logically in with roleplaying games, such as "The Tourism Game", as it enhances participants' awareness of personal choices, interconnections and self-reliance.

HUMAN RIGHTS

The universal value of human rights is also addressed in Chapter 3 on political values. From the perspective of stewardship, human lives are quite limited. The earth has been around for approximately four and a half billion years, but the first human ancestors did not appear until five to seven million years ago. Humans, or *Homo sapiens*, are the only survivors among *Hominina*, but have been on earth for less than 200,000 years, a mere second in terms of a 12-hour clock. Aboriginal Australians have the oldest continuous culture on the planet at an estimated 75,000 years (Rasmussen et al., 2011).

An average human life expectancy is currently around 79 years globally, with quite large differences among countries. In just about every country, however, women tend to live longer (see Figure 9.1). Many factors account for these different life expectancies.

If we recognise human rights as stipulated by the Universal Declaration, then we must also support the notion that they are to be enjoyed by all people, regardless of who they are

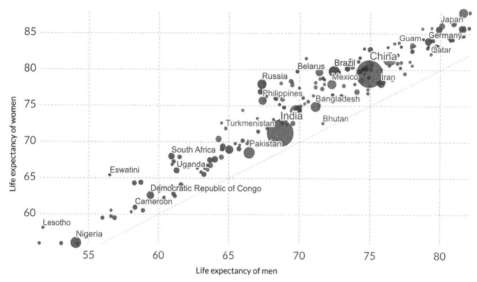

Note: Shown is the period life expectancy at birth measured in years
Source: UN Population Division (2019 Revision)

Figure 9.1   Global comparison of life expectancies by gender

or where they live. While this may sound self-evident in theory, when confronted with hard choices we often revert back to a hierarchy, with our family, community and nation coming first. This ranking is a natural tendency and the result of millions of years of evolution when we relied on small groups for survival. But in our global, interconnected world, that is a bias we must consciously work to overcome. The survival of humanity now depends on global efforts to address existential threats like nuclear war, the destabilisation of the global biosphere and, as witnessed with COVID-19, pandemics.

ACTIVITY

The roll-out of the first vaccines against the SARS-CoV-2 virus gave people hope that the pandemic would be controlled and that life would return to "normal" within months. But it also pitched wealthy countries against poorer ones in acquiring – and affording – vaccines as well as groups within countries as to which ones should be prioritised. In small groups, have students draw up a plan for the roll-out. Since mobility is a large contributor to viral transmission, should travel be a consideration? What are the implications of your answer for tourism from the perspective of both origin and receiving countries?

SERVICE TO OTHERS

The value of service to others might seem similar to other values we examine, like mutuality or ethics, but the core of service to others can be found in its creation of a ripple effect. Thus, when we receive a service from somebody, we can then pass it on to others, and they in their turn, over and over again. This ripple effect has become famously known in popular culture as "pay it forward". That is, rather than paying back a debt to somebody who already has enough, or who no longer can enjoy the debt settlement, we can pay it forward to someone who needs it. This concept has an ancient and deep meaning insofar as whatever we experience today is the result of actions (or inactions) of generations before us; similarly, our actions (or inactions) will have consequences for many generations to come. The Haudenosaunee (Iroquois) capture this value in their Seventh Generation Principle: every decision should result in sustainable relationships seven generations in the future (Clarkson et al., 1992).

Closely associated with service to others are the concepts of "servant heart" and "servant leadership". Having a servant heart means putting the needs of others ahead of your own, and is a virtue associated with spirituality. Similarly, a servant leader puts the needs of their employees first and shares power with them, thereby inverting the traditional view of leadership. The term "servant leadership" was first coined by Greenleaf in 1970 (Greenleaf, 1977). The concept has gained considerable traction in management studies since then.

As social animals, we rely on communities for our well-being, such as our family, our place of worship or associations of relatively like-minded people. The sense of belonging we derive from our communities allows us to cope better with stress and challenges, making us more resilient. But we must also reciprocate that feeling to others in our communities. Service to others is thus integrally linked to "care", which is such a strong word because it sums up our humanity like nothing else. As a service to others in the frame of stewardship, care is an act that needs to be made freely, in the spirit of giving, not because one has been forced to do it. Again, it is about understanding one's role as a steward of a greater good, even if that great good does not arise until long after one is gone. In these ways, the act of serving others gives us something that each of us needs: a purpose. This concept of an ethic of care is also discussed in Chapter 8 on ethics values.

People with a strong self-transcendent value orientation are highly motivated to engage in prosocial behaviours, such as caring for others' welfare, and they are also more concerned about environmental issues, and more willing to take responsibility and to behave in environmentally friendly ways (Liobikienė and Juknys, 2016). Unfortunately, these human traits are often undermined by our business world, which is built on the foundation of capitalism and has created a culture that values extrinsic rewards and self-serving behaviours (Coyle et al., 2016).

ACTIVITY

 The service sector, and particularly businesses in the hospitality and tourism industry, has raised service to others in the form of exceptional customer service to great heights. Stories abound about how service providers will try to exceed guest expectations. Ask students to search out these stories and share them with the class. They could even vote for the one they find most compelling.

SCAFFOLDED PHOTOGRAPHIC ESSAY

Not all students have experienced tourism themselves, but through capturing photographs of what might seem otherwise as familiar and banal
landscapes, students can learn to "see" tourism in the everyday, while also
critically reflecting on tourism's positive and negative impacts. In Bradley
Rink's "Seeing tourism landscapes: teaching tourism at the confluence of
theory and practice", tourism is approached in evaluative, analytical and interpretative
ways. Students become ethically, environmentally and socially aware and active, and become visually and textually more literate (see Activity 45).

FIELD COURSE

Outi Rantala, Brynhild Granås, Gunnar Thór Jóhannesson and Kaarina
Tervo-Kankare have developed an in-field dialogue model for learning
about northern tourism entitled "Stewardship: an in-field dialogue model".
The model is based on an idea of knowing-with, which is about being sensitive to different forms of knowledge, materially and in embodied ways.
By creating mutual trust and helping to develop a sense of belonging, students learn how
stewardship can emerge in relations with diverse actors, including more-than-human parties (see Activity 35).

10. Mutuality

Marion Joppe; **Johan Edelheim**; **Joan Flaherty**; Mette
Simonsen Abildgaard; Stefanie Benjamin; Blanca A.
Camargo; Sisko Häikiö; Emily Höckert; Outi Kugapi; Tanja
Lešnik Štuhec; Monika Lüthje; Carina Ren; Maja Turnšek;
Minna Väyrynen

OBJECTIVES

This chapter provides readers with insights and engagement activities to help students:

1. Understand how diversity is a building block of all humanity and how information technology might be undermining it
2. Contrast inclusion with exclusion, and consider the impacts of both in organisations
3. Illustrate why equity is preferable to equality
4. Determine how humility is expressed, and what inner strengths it suggests
5. Summarise the main features of collaboration

INTRODUCTION

Mutuality or mutual respect is a value grounded in our relationships, both human and non-human. It involves acceptance, self-awareness of structural inequalities, open-mindedness, empowerment and the ability to revisit one's cultural understanding of the world. These attributes require us to be in a dynamic, evolving state of attitudinal development, which is, needless to say, a long-term learning process. Mutuality can be developed at the individual level all the way to the societal and global levels. Its inclusion of human–animal relationships, particularly in the context of how animals are used in tourism, helps shift the dominant anthropocentric view to a more biocentric one that values stewardship of our ecosystems.

Mutuality, therefore, starts with self-awareness and understanding of one's values, cultural drivers and behavioural patterns. To help students gain this understanding, teachers must first recognise, question and revisit their own values. Indeed, instructors should understand that their role as positive change agents does not preclude them from being learners themselves, engaged with their students in continuous training to understand diverse cultural backgrounds and value systems (Boluk and Carnicelli, 2019). This understanding opens the door to an acknowledgement that structural inequalities involving race, sex, gender, religion, and so on, exist. Only then can there be a discussion of how to eliminate the bias and stereotypes that accompany these inequalities.

Mutual respect is about behaviours and attitudes, which involves recognising and acknowledging other people's views. It involves open discussions and appreciation of diverse opinions. It is critical, therefore, that the learning environment is inclusive, safe and dynamic, so that students are not afraid to open up about their values and biases. Classes with international students offer a great opportunity for this kind of exchange and learning – again, not just for the students, but for the instructor as well. However, it must also be realised that tolerance is not a natural trait; indeed, *Homo sapiens* have survived over the millennia because of *in*tolerance towards others – both human and non-human (Harari, 2014). Therefore, conscious thought is required to overcome what might be considered a natural instinct.

Since mutuality is a process of self-development unique for every individual, it cannot be taught, but only facilitated through self-awareness and conflict-resolution exercises and modules that emphasise diverse social and cultural values and behaviours and that encourage a positive attitude towards diversity. Tourism as a subject is an obvious study area to address these issues. For example, tourism courses that embed an appreciation of traditional knowledge and processes, inclusive of Indigenous content and references, can teach how to avoid the homogenisation and standardisation of culture that is too often the outcome of tourism merchandising. This commoditisation becomes particularly problematic when the Indigenous culture has very different worldviews, traditions and understandings from those of the dominant, largely industrialised market targeted by the promotional efforts. For instance, Indigenous people see nonfatal ways of resolving human–grizzly bear interactions, whereas conservation officers will not hesitate to kill the bear (Holiday, 2020). This may be equally true for ethnic communities who tend to inhabit an area they have migrated to (for example, in settler countries) as opposed to Indigenous people who are native to a destination region and are "pre-existing peoples". Developing respectful relationships through sharing and understanding values and attitudes is foundational to ensuring greater cultural competence in all graduates.

Mutuality celebrates diversity in society, which means working for inclusion of people of different kinds and abilities to do whatever it is they want to do in their lives. Mutuality is also connected to equity, which, as later explained, should not be confused with equality. O'Boyle (2020) clearly outlines how all these attributes enrich our lives and societies, and the questions we should keep in mind to ensure inclusivity in our daily reality. Mutuality also emphasises the need for collaborative actions to reach goals; and for the humility to realise that honouring our own strengths should never come at the cost of dismissing or ignoring someone else's. Consequently, mutuality sometimes requires a willingness to "unlearn" what we thought to be true; to challenge the "white gaze" that permeates our education, societies and value systems; to deeply listen to the viewpoints of others; and to understand that labelling people diminishes both them and us.

DIVERSITY

When considering the value of diversity, we can easily think back to Chapter 2 on axiology, where we examined intrinsic and extrinsic values, as the two are connected. It is only by knowing ourselves, by realising what values we have, and what biases we live with, that we can start to empathically see through the eyes of others. Differences appear in so many forms. We think differently because of our age, education, sex, gender, class, body shape, employment, ethnicity, nationality, and so on. It is easy to list all the demographic differences, but many of these differences are so subtle that we do not acknowledge them until we ask ourselves why we reach different conclusions than others on the same topic.

It is important, then, that we become aware of, and honour, this richness in ourselves and in others. However, artificial intelligence (AI), social media, cookies in websites and search algorithms from our web browsing thwart this effort. They make us less aware of the rich diversity existing within and around us by bombarding us with information that concurs with our established opinions and behaviours. Modern technology is designed to be "user friendly" by smoothly adapting itself to the needs and patterns of the user. What this means simultaneously is that we are steered away from things we do not habitually search, browse or "like", and steered towards things that reinforce what we have already searched, browsed and labelled as "like".

The result is less input that challenges our worldview, which means we are less familiar and less comfortable – and more likely to get annoyed – with input that does challenge our worldview, such as someone expressing an opinion completely different from ours. Thus, the reality we all build for our virtual selves is so fundamentally blinkered that we never see realities from other perspectives. When somebody else reaches a different conclusion, then it is simply the logical conclusion based on the reality they inhabit, just as our conclusion comes from our reality. The same premise applies to our "non-virtual" lives: at university, at work and during leisure time, we tend to congregate with people who are similar to us, not different from us.

Mutuality depends on us acknowledging and embracing real diversity. This is why it is so important to discuss things in person with others. Face to face, we are offered more than just the words being said. We can also discern the subtle reactions and interpret more closely the nuances of body language – possibilities not easily offered by the synchronous online environment. Finally, diversity should not be confused with multiculturalism, which simply recognises the various cultures that make up humanity, since in every culture we will find divergent viewpoints and people who challenge the status quo. True diversity aims to give voice to these viewpoints, not just the dominant view of the culture.

CONVERSATION STARTER

 Many people are unwilling to acknowledge, or completely unaware of, their biases and stereotypes. The Implicit Association Test (Project Implicit., n.d.) allows students to discover their implicit associations about race, gender, sexual orientation and other topics. Depending on the topic under discussion, ask students to find the test online and complete one or more of its sections. The ensuing discussion can focus on what aspects of their background led to the result received and whether their conscious self reflects the same results.

ACTIVITY

Present students with a number of negative stereotypes of younger generations commonly found in popular culture and media. Contrast these stereotypes with examples from popular culture and media that question the
older generation's willingness to listen to their younger counterparts. Help
students find scientifically valid proof for contrasting such generational blame. The aim of
Maja Turnšek's "Combating negative prejudice against young people" is twofold: to help
students start the process of writing an essay in which they respond to the generational
stereotyping with scientifically valid evidence; and to help students understand that to be
heard, one must first be willing to listen (see Activity 39).

INCLUSION

"Inclusion" refers to the characteristics and processes that increase participation, but one way
of understanding it is by looking at its opposite – exclusion. Exclusion is rather straightforward: somebody is excluded from a community. It happens for all sorts of reasons, but at its
core are two themes discussed earlier: diversity and our desire to socialise with those similar
to us, not different. This can also be called "tribalism", and it is deeply rooted in our minds.
Humans love to feel a sense of belonging to something larger than themselves. They join
associations. They are fans of sports teams. They cheer for their nation in large tournaments,
happily dressing in costumes indicating their group. Being part of a group might make us feel
"at home", providing a feeling of safety and support because we share a common sense of
purpose with our group members. In this particular moment, we are all there, in the group,
for the same reason. But exclusion and tribalism have hidden aspects, too. They prompt us to
make decisions we imagine are unbiased and free of value, when in reality those decisions are
biased and value-laden, excluding some people from environments we can control.

A common example comes from hiring practices in companies. When an organisation
needs a new member to fill a vacant role, it puts together an advertisement where the features
of the role are described, the corporate values of the organisation are set out, and the new
staff member's preferred qualities are listed. Applicants then apply for the position. Now, if
several applicants meet the criteria, perform equally well during the interview, and provide
comparable references, how will the company decide whom to hire? Research has shown that
hiring *always* privileges those who are similar to the ones doing the hiring. This result holds
true across a range of variables: gender (Koch et al., 2015), ethnicity (Ziegert and Hanges,
2005), age (Finkelstein and Farrell, 2007), education (Chua and Mazmanian, 2020), and so on.
Organisations are therefore self-replicating, and exclusion becomes a norm, even if it is unconscious. A way of changing this is by allowing for portals that create CVs without names, ages
or pictures. This measure forces those who are shortlisting candidates to focus on features they
can compare and that they have listed in their criteria. This leads us into the topic of equity.

CONVERSATION STARTER

In Chapter 8 on ethics, students wrote an academic essay on an issue with ethical implications (for example, impacts of tourism, industry hiring practices, social entrepreneurship) as part of Joan Flaherty's "Industry ethics" (see Activity 29). Ask them to reflect on why that issue matters to them – or to any industry professional – both personally and professionally.

ACTIVITY

Imagine that you are on the board of a university association. You have advertised the association and urged new students to join it. Now your task is to select those who will be part of the association because you received more applications than spaces available. How can you ensure that you act in an inclusive manner when choosing who will be allowed to join your association?

EQUITY

Students may easily understand the concept of treating people equally as the term can be found in numerous laws, regulations and policies. It even appears in the famous French slogan "liberty, equality, fraternity!" The concept of equity is much thornier and will likely lead to intense debate as not everybody agrees that groups who have been long disadvantaged might need targeted preferential treatment. This is the opportunity to delve deeply into topics of privilege ("male", "white", and so on). Discussion is likely to become quite heated. Figure 10.1 illustrates what is meant by equity and equality and may lead to a fruitful debate about policies that have contributed to inequities and policies that attempt to rectify them. "Attempt" is the key word here. We know that equity intentions do not always translate into measures that lead to culturally sustainable, equitable impacts.

The risk, of course, with Figure 10.1 lies in the interpretation. Looking at the cartoon, some people might imagine that the "reality" has been predetermined and attempts to reach equity are therefore futile. Introducing the topic of affirmative action is particularly appropriate at this point. Good-faith efforts to include particular groups, based on their gender, race, creed or nationality, in areas where they have been excluded such as education and employment, are still hotly disputed. The famous Harvard Admissions case provides an excellent context for a discussion about equity (see the conversation starter below).

CONVERSATION STARTER

Students for Fair Admissions (SFFA) accused Harvard of discrimination by putting a cap on the number of Asian Americans admitted to the university, making it harder for Asian applicants to get in, even though they comprise almost 23 per cent of Harvard's freshman class but are only 5 per cent of public high school students.[1] Have students do an online search for some of the arguments brought forth by both sides and why the lawsuit was ultimately dismissed. Ask students

Figure 10.1   An illustration of equality vs equity vs reality

how they feel about Harvard's approach. Do they think admissions should be based on grades alone? Is there a better way to ensure diversity of the student body? Could more be done to help underrepresented groups?

ONLINE COURSE

Ongoing changes in the Arctic require us to rethink the way Indigenous and other local cultures are represented, marketed and visited. A self-study course has been produced by ARCTISEN (Culturally sensitive tourism in the Arctic) and its collaborators Mette Simonsen Abildgaard, Emily Höckert, Outi Kugapi, Monika Lüthje and Carina Ren. "Enhancing culturally sensitive tourism in an online learning environment" underlines the role of recognition, respect and reciprocity in responsible tourism encounters (see Activity 17). In addition to reports and ethical guidelines, testimonies and advice from small tourism entrepreneurs are particularly insightful for the appreciation of mutuality.

HONESTY-HUMILITY

The basic trait of honesty-humility in the HEXACO[2] Model of Personality reflects "the tendency to be fair and genuine in dealing with others, in the sense of cooperation with others even when one might exploit others without suffering retaliation" (Ashton and Lee, 2007, p. 156). To be a good leader requires humility. Ironically, choosing to be vulnerable and unconcerned with how others perceive you makes it easier to show courage and take risks. Humility is not a weakness. It means being less aggressive, less manipulative and, importantly, being honest. Humble people are mindful of themselves and of being humane to others. They often have a high sense of self-worth, with a clear idea of their strengths. But they are equally clear-sighted about their limitations. That is one reason servant leaders, as discussed in Chapter 9, ensure that their employees develop to their fullest. Servant leaders recognise the wisdom of sharing power. They recognise that their employees may have greater knowledge and capability in some areas than they themselves do. Therefore, they will defer to those employees. This type of leadership requires a fair amount of humility.

Humility is often a difficult concept to convey to students, depending on their cultural background and upbringing. But humility and courage are particularly important when it comes to data creation and management, information management, and knowledge creation and management. Opening your mind to other viewpoints encourages you to delve deeper into the data, information and knowledge you encounter. It encourages you to explore new intellectual territory and to be brave enough to consider its value – even when it appears antithetical to what you have been taught. For example, ancient cultures developed worldviews over millennia largely driven by observations of their surroundings. Until relatively recently, the Western world generally ignored, and even belittled, these ancient ways of learning and knowing in favour of a scientific approach. But with humility comes wisdom: the Western world, while it still has a way to go, is beginning to take a less judgemental attitude towards the ancient ways. And our intellectual, physical and spiritual lives are thus enriched through the knowledge gained from studying complementary ways of learning and knowing the world.

CONVERSATION STARTER

Think of a person other than a family member who is important to you. Now imagine what your life would be like if you had never met this person. What qualities are you grateful for having as a result of knowing this person?

ACTIVITY

Incorporating improvisational theatre games into our teaching can help students learn how to be transparent and honest around mistakes which helps to normalise and humanise failures. Embracing this culture of failure allows for more "realness" within conversations – and groundwork to let go of "always being right". This is described by Stefanie Benjamin in "Yes-and: how to create a brave space by incorporating improvisational theatre games" (see Activity 2).

COLLABORATION

Collaboration is naturally related to how we work with others. We use the term "naturally" here because there is something intrinsic that propels us to reach results by building alliances. One of the most important elements of true collaborations is trust, and trust is earned through reciprocity. For a collaboration to work, each party (whether an individual, an organisation or a country) must feel the arrangement is mutually beneficial, with each bringing their own strengths to the table. If these conditions are not met, the two parties might still work together, perhaps for reasons of expedience or pressure, but theirs would not be a true collaboration and would likely yield lesser outcomes than those of a collaborative effort. Collaboration is built on trust, and both parties are better off for working together. What happens in collaboration is described as synergy, which can be defined as 1+1=3. That is, both parties contribute something of their own and the complementarity of their contributions makes something greater than the sum of the two. Lawson (2019) refers to this outcome as "emergence": the coming together of different entities forms new entities with different attributes to the original constituent parts. In other words, something new and better is generated through true collaboration. Thus, both parties always win, both parties are always better off, for having collaborated.

ACTIVITY

Service-learning projects can help instil citizenship, humility, collaboration, inclusion and responsibility when involving students in addressing the real needs of a community. Blanca A. Camargo's case study "Promoting mutuality through service-learning: La Santa Catarina restaurant" outlines the activities, challenges, opportunities and transformations resulting from the collaboration between students and local entrepreneurs, potential clients and suppliers, and community partners (see Activity 36). La Santa Catarina is a restaurant concept for a group of low-income women from a community adjacent to a private university in Monterrey, Mexico. Originally designed to raise students' awareness of the food entrepreneurial needs of a low-income group and develop their abilities to work with, and for, people from a different socio-economic background, the case serves as inspiration for adaptation to other locales and community needs.

COMPLEX ACTIVITIES

ROLEPLAYING GAMES

Time to play the third and final round of "The Tourist Game"! This is the opportunity for students to reflect on how and why their initial impression of their chosen values might have changed when playing the game, and whether this will also change the way they view that value in society (see Activity 12).

Students usually do not have experience with the real business world, but it is imperative that they learn to think openly and holistically and to communicate their ideas as part of a project team, whether as a leader or collaborator. By solving concrete projects with mentorship from destination representatives, students gain insight into stakeholder collaboration and relationships (tacit knowledge). They also gain the motivation to work in a specific workplace and build competencies related to values-based learning experiences – social intelligence, political, economic, social and ecological values of strategic and critical thinking as well as knowledge, complexity, professionalism and management skills. Tanja Lešnik Štuhec provides this opportunity in "Cooperation between students and the tourism industry to solve project challenges in sustainable rural destinations" (see Activity 38).

NOTES

1. www.vox.com/2018/10/18/17984108/harvard-asian-americans-affirmative-action-racial-discrimination.
2. Honesty-Humility (H), Emotionality (E), Extraversion (X), Agreeableness (A), Conscientiousness (C) and Openness to Experience (O).

11. Knowledge

Marion Joppe; **Johan Edelheim**; **Joan Flaherty**;
Barkathunnisha Abu Bakar; **Karla A. Boluk**; Elin
Bommenel; Helene Balslev Clausen; Richard Ek; Brynhild
Granås; Maria Huhmarniemi; Gunnar Thór Jóhannesson;
Outi Kugapi; Maggie C. Miller; Giang Phi; Outi Rantala;
Stuart Reid; Bradley Rink; Kaarina Tervo-Kankare

OBJECTIVES

This chapter provides readers with insights and engagement activities to help students:

1. Understand the value and power of knowledge as opposed to data or information
2. Challenge what is taken for granted, and differentiate between critical thinking and critique
3. Explain why an improvement cannot be counted as an innovation
4. Illustrate how creativity is intimately connected to life and leads to new ways of thinking and collaborating
5. Critically examine who is part of their various networks

INTRODUCTION

How do we know what we know? And how sure are we that what we know is true? Students rarely pause to think about these critical questions unless they are asked at the graduate level to reflect on their epistemological positioning about how they gained their knowledge and beliefs about reality. The English word "knowledge" combines concepts that are expressed with greater nuance in other languages: for instance, in French "to know" is either "*connaître*" (in the sense of being acquainted with) or "*savoir*" (in the sense of being able to do something as a result of practice, skills or experience). The process by which we arrive at knowledge is also multifaceted: "Knowledge is created through processes of selecting, connecting and reflecting. Knowledge is always already predicated by existing knowledge, which means that knowledge involves interpretation and contextualisation and existing knowledge should be challenged" (Sheldon et al., 2011, p. 10). There is also debate between the social and natural sciences. Philosophers like Kant and Weber first challenged the natural science way of knowing, which is focused on *erklären* (explaining); in contrast, social science, with its focus on knowing and explaining human behaviour, relies on *verstehen* (understanding) (Apel, 1982).

Facts are not knowledge. At best, they are data. At worst, they are values that someone, for some reason, wants you to believe in. We are living through a period where "alternative facts" are being used to explain events that most people would call "untruths", yet if enough people repeat these "alternative facts" enough times, sooner or later a surprising number of people will come to believe and even fervently defend them. After all, humans are the only animals that tell stories to make sense of their lives, and which stories we believe in depends on where and when we were born and which communities we belong to (political, religious, and so on).

The field of tourism studies is no different. Our scientific community has also its set "truths" and "facts" that all of us build our lectures and research upon, that we refer back to, and that we shape our perceptions of reality through (Belhassen and Caton, 2009). One comprehensive model describing how tourism knowledge is created is by John Tribe and Janne Liburd (2016). Their model shows how tourism knowledge comes from the disciplines that study and research the topic, as per Belhassen and Caton's argument (2009), but also from extra-disciplinary sources (see Figure 11.1).

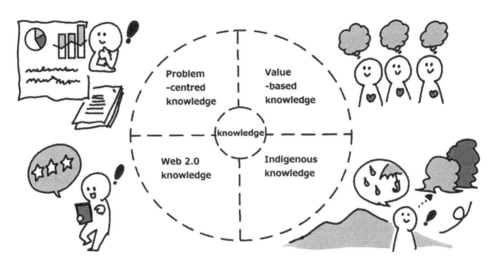

Source: Adapted from Tribe and Liburd (2016, p. 47)

Figure 11.1   Excerpt from "The Tourism Knowledge System"

These extra-disciplinary sources contain *Problem-centred knowledge*, which refers to reports and research conducted for a specific purpose, often commissioned by authorities or other tourism stakeholders; *Web 2.0 knowledge*, which refers to all the user- and owner-generated comments on social media platforms and review sites; *Indigenous knowledge*, which emphasises the holistic knowledge accumulated over generations of embodied connections with land

and environments; and, finally, *Value-based knowledge*, which has close links to the axiological framework we create in *Teaching Tourism*:

> Value-based knowledge harnesses the importance of values and meaningful interpretation. It engages human qualities and dispositions, authentic presence and meaningful participation in the context of world-making. Hard disciplinary knowledge has objectivity and value neutrality at its core, but value-based knowledge puts values at the heart of the project. (Tribe and Liburd, 2016, p. 50)

Although we always use interpretations of the past to explain the present, to truly understand the value and power of knowledge we must also be open to new knowledge, to different ways of perceiving knowledge and to communicating across community boundaries and disciplines. We also need a bit of humility as we often know a lot less than we think we do. After all, new discoveries are frequently changing what we thought we knew, such as the discovery of *Homo luzonensis* on Flores Island who disappeared, like all our human-like kin, fairly soon after we – *Homo sapiens* – showed up (Détroit et al., 2019). Long dismissed by scientists, some of the songlines of Aboriginal Australians dating back tens of thousands of years have recently been corroborated (Nunn, 2018), giving credence to their way of knowing.

Tourism scholars have problematically signalled how tourism reproduces colonial ways of knowing (for example, Ateljevic et al., 2007; McGehee, 2012) and "not yet readily apparent […] is engagement with indigenous and local peoples and epistemologies in the co-creation of tourism knowledge" (Chambers and Buzinde, 2015, p. 2). Chambers and Buzinde importantly draw attention to how host communities are treated as *objects* of research rather than *producers* of tourism knowledge, supporting what Spivak (1988) refers to as "epistemic violence" (p. 280). As such, epistemological decolonisation is required to pursue other ways of thinking, being and knowing about tourism (Chambers and Buzinde, 2015).

Building on the work above, Boluk et al. (2019b) offer a six-theme conceptual framework from their reflections on both reformist and radical pathways to sustainable transitions in tourism. Specifically, the authors propose the following core themes: critical tourism scholarship, gender in the sustainable development agenda, engaging with Indigenous perspectives and other paradigms, degrowth and the circular economy, governance and planning, and ethical consumption. Imperative to engaging with Indigenous perspectives is an open-mindedness stemming from an interest in engaging with diverse views and voices, with a commitment to understanding different ways of being, knowing and doing tourism (Boluk et al., 2019b, p. 849). Importantly, tourism scholars have recognised that diversity is imperative for sustainable futures.

Questioning the "colonial legacies reproduced in the governance, design, delivery and assessment of the curriculum" (Hall and Smyth, 2016, p. 18) is one way for us to engage in emancipatory approaches. Freire's (1970) work recognising humans as beings of praxis in their pursuit of activities, based on action and reflection oriented to achieving radical transformations in the world, is important here. Emancipatory praxis, stemming from action and reflection in the tourism curriculum, is vital. Boluk and Carnicelli's (2019) model for an emancipatory approach for tourism curriculum drawing on Freire's work engages three pillars which they argue should be "embedded within, and guide, the emancipatory approaches of tourism curriculum: Collaboration and Shared-Power; Experiential Praxis for Freedom; and Socio-Political Critical Reflectivity" (p. 173).

Real knowledge comes from critical thinking, innovation and creativity. These concepts involve the capacity to learn about different matters, evaluate those matters rationally, query why and how somebody has come to these conclusions and, finally, synthesise new ideas based on old knowledge and thus expand the thinking of those coming after you. Social networks can create knowledge or assist in refining the use of existing knowledge. And in our connected world it is ever more critical that these networks be open and accessible because problem-identification and problem-solving increasingly take place through sharing and cooperation (networking). Knowledge is also about creating new ideas that transform the way we imagine reality to be. This is something we will call "worldmaking".

CRITICAL THINKING

Critical thinking is a reflective and analytical process that involves recognising the assumptions underlying one's beliefs and behaviour, identifying alternative theories and imagining creative solutions (Fisher, 2017). It is a "purposeful, reasoned and goal directed" (Halpern, 2014, p. 4) inward process that shapes information into knowledge and then examines that knowledge in light of personal and communal experience in a search for wisdom. Critical thinking embodies three components: identifying and challenging assumptions, being aware of how context influences thoughts and actions, and developing and exploring alternatives to existing ways of thinking and living (Broomfield, 1997). Critical thinking encourages students to engage with multiple realities, deliberate their own dominant assumptions through various sources of knowing and explore multiple perspectives.

Paul and Elder (2008) define critical thinking as "self-directed, self-disciplined, self-monitored, and self-corrective thinking. It presupposes assent to rigorous standards of excellence and mindful command of their use. It entails effective communication and problem-solving abilities, as well as a commitment to overcome our native egocentrism and sociocentrism." Critical thinking takes practice to become a systematic habit that accounts for ethnocentric bias and prejudice.

Three types of foundational philosophies underpin critical thinking. The most common is epistemology, the philosophy of knowledge. Epistemology relates to truth claims (Steup and Ram, 2020). Science, education and, well, almost anything in society are based on the idea that some things are true and others are false. We learn about "truth" when we are growing up. We learn about it in school. And we learn about it from the media. However, we should never forget that much of what we consider to be true is actually just stories we have collectively chosen to believe in order to live in very complex societies.

We value epistemology, therefore, very highly as it is aimed at uncovering truth for us. In our post-truth era, however, propaganda and disinformation can have greater appeal than factual information for some people because the propaganda and disinformation confirm their personal beliefs.

The second foundational philosophy is ontology. It relates to meaning and being and investigates how our thoughts shape our reality. When we examined social reality in Chapter 5, it related to ontology.

The third foundational philosophy is axiology, the topic of Chapter 2. Axiology relates to values, and the idea that our actions are determined by our values (Edelheim, 2020).

One approach to fostering critical thinking in the classroom is through using humanities sources and spiritual responsive pedagogy. Here, students practise critical reflection and reflexivity to overcome habitual patterns of the mind, transcend towards openness and engage in meaning-making of the world (Caton, 2014).

Elin Bommenel et al. provide guidance on how to conduct an introductory week of meta-pedagogical thinking on teaching and learning regimes, drawing from experiences with a class of international students participating in a new university programme (see Activities 1, 10 and 42). The aim is to foster student awareness of the learning approach that has characterised their personal and academic life so far, and to consider whether their current university programme takes a different approach. Their contribution is divided into six phases, two of which are in this chapter, with the four others divided between Chapter 1 on didactics and Chapter 5 on social values.

CONVERSATION STARTER

A teaching and learning regime that favours a surface approach to learning will tend to see students feeling confident when they are expected to receive and store knowledge, when there is a strong focus on facts or content, when the knowledge per se does not affect them personally and when the knowledge is disseminated by an authority who conveys "the truth". A deep approach to learning, on the other hand, will tend to make students feel secure even if the knowledge affects their worldview, when they are challenged on an intellectual level and when they are invited to express their understandings of, or reflections upon, the topic. The first step to help students transition from a surface to a deep approach is to clarify the distinction between the two approaches – thus, the following exercise. Have students discuss in smaller groups the type of learning they are accustomed to primarily, and ask them to reflect upon whether the two different approaches really rule out each other or if they can be seen as complementary. Is a surface approach perhaps a precondition for a deep approach? Have them also discuss in what way they regard themselves as individual learners detached or not from the knowledge offerings or truth claims they encounter. This discussion can be introduced or concluded with key insights from philosophy of science in both ontological and epistemological terms.

Helene Balslev Clausen and Maggie C. Miller describe two field trip scenarios to point out the value of having students confront the unintended, pivot quickly by employing their critical thinking skills and develop resilience through reflective practice (see Activities 11 and 46). The Nepal trip gives rise to a conversation starter and a reflection activity in Chapter 5 on social values, while the Mexico trip is captured below.

CONVERSATION STARTER

Integrate the unintended into deep learning experiences by facilitating spaces for dialogue, openness and reflection post-mishap. Starting points for this conversation might include such questions as:

- How did you experience and perceive the unintended scenario? Why do you think you experienced or perceived it in that way?
- What was uncertain about the trouble? Why was it different from what you might be used to?
- What did you learn from the scenario? How can you use these experiences and insights in your future?

ACTIVITY

 Throughout a field course, students should be encouraged to develop their own reflective practice around their personal development, the unexpected and unintended, and wider global issues. But even if the field trip scenarios are treated as case studies in a classroom setting, students could be asked to write journal entries as though they had gone through these experiences themselves. Journal entries should include analysis, not just a description of what has occurred. Encourage students to be honest and articulate gut feelings, emotional reactions and responses to encounters with the unintended/unexpected.

CRITICAL INCIDENT QUESTIONNAIRE

 In "Fostering critical thinking utilising Brookfield's Critical Incident Questionnaire", Karla A. Boluk demonstrates how this tool can be used throughout the duration of a course (see Activity 41). This presents an opportunity for students to practise and explore critical thinking *in situ*, as well as enhancing their critical reflection skills.

REFLECTIONS ON ROLEPLAYING GAMES

 Students will have played the role play "The Tourism Game" as described by Johan Edelheim through three rounds (Chapters 5, 7 and 10), which means that they have had to think of the case in three different ways (see Activity 12). Role plays are forcing us to live somebody's reality, and the only way this can be done is by critically thinking about how that reality is perceived from the inside. Ask students to think back to the game and contrast the ways they thought in their different roles. What changed?

INNOVATION

"Innovation" has come to refer to the introduction of any novel concept, whether new to customers, a sector or an organisation. However, the broadness of this definition means that the term is overused and therefore often misunderstood. While the definition of "innovation" depends on a respective discipline's dominant paradigm (Baregheh et al., 2009), it is usually presented as a binary: either incremental or radical, depending on whether it occurred within, or departed from, existing practices (Abernathy and Clark, 1985). From a tourism business perspective, innovation entails introducing novel concepts potentially valuable to both existing and new customers that provide differentiation for an organisation at three different levels: incremental, liminal and radical.

Tourism operators tend to be risk-averse, and therefore what they consider to be innovations are merely incremental improvements or adjustments to an existing situation designed to improve performance, increase efficiency and, where possible, boost short-term profits. At the other extreme, radical innovation introduces the "next new idea" that disrupts current conventions with unique value propositions. These innovators are usually outsiders to the sector (Brooker and Joppe, 2014), because conventional thinking is a limiting factor. Liminal innovation is situated between these two extremes and refers to taking existing ideas from other contexts, shifting and adapting them to fit local situations, and thereby introducing new concepts. Liminal innovators are thus early adopters of new ideas, as they envision their value in advance of the majority.

The Burns et al. (2015) model stresses the social embeddedness of innovative agents and entrepreneurs, either as individuals or groups. Taking advantage of their social roles and positions while at the same time responding either to incentives or seizing opportunities, they manipulate symbols, rules, technologies and materials that are socially derived and developed.

Einstein is claimed to have said, "We cannot solve problems by using the same kind of thinking we used when we created them." In other words, we need to rethink matters, not just from new perspectives, but totally anew. The COVID-19 pandemic presents an opportunity to do just that. Pre-pandemic, far too many destinations relied on an industrial model of mass tourism, largely fuelled by low-cost carriers and cheap vacation packages. Tourism stakeholders now need to think critically about these dominant tourism discourses and structures and recalibrate the role of tourism as a worldmaking transformative force (Sheldon, 2020). Innovation and creativity will be key in how these destinations rethink the type of tourism they offer, the number of tourists they attract and the strategies they develop to ensure a better quality of life for local residents. Higgins-Desbiolles et al. (2019) call for tourism to be "redefined and redesigned to acknowledge, prioritise, and place the rights of local communities above the rights of tourists for holidays and the rights of tourism corporates to make profits" (p. 1927). In this scenario, "tourism operators would be allowed access to the local community's assets only under their authorisation and stewardship" (p. 1937). This approach requires new business models and practices, and one of the fastest growing social movements in this regard has been social entrepreneurship (Sheldon and Daniele, 2017). These types of entrepreneurs have been shown to play a particularly vital role in the development of rural tourism destinations (Mottiar et al., 2018).

CONVERSATION STARTER

Ask students to identify some radical innovations (past and present) in the tourism sector. Who were the people behind these innovations? What made them so disruptive? What does their future look like, especially post-pandemic? Repeat with liminal innovations and compare with radical ones to identify key differences.

GROUP ACTIVITY

 In Maria Huhmarniemi and Outi Kugapi's "Co-designing creative tourism activities for preserving and promoting local cultural traditions", art and tourism entrepreneurs and students collaborate to co-design craft-based services (see Activity 20). Co-design of new services is innovative: new services transform traditions while they also keep them alive.

CREATIVITY

Creativity is closely associated with innovation in that it is the ability to develop and express ourselves, our ideas and how we experience life in new ways. Indeed, its definition is "the ability to transcend traditional ideas, rules, patterns, relationships, or the like, and to create meaningful new ideas, forms, methods, and interpretations" (Pherson and Pherson, 2020, p. 405). A common misconception suggests creativity occurs only in the arts, but according to Dietrich (2004):

> Advances in the field of cognitive neuroscience have identified distinct brain circuits that are involved in specific higher brain functions. To date, these findings have not been applied to research on creativity. It is proposed that there are four basic types of creative insights, each mediated by a distinctive neural circuit. (p. 1011)

The four types of creativity are as follows: deliberate and cognitive creativity, which requires a high degree of knowledge and lots of time; deliberate and emotional creativity, which requires quiet time; spontaneous and cognitive creativity, which requires stopping work on the problem and stepping away from it; and spontaneous and emotional creativity, which is essentially the artistic kind that first comes to mind for many of us when we hear the term "creativity". These four types can be pictured as a matrix with an example for each quadrant (Figure 11.2).

		Knowledge Domain	
		Emotional	Cognitive
	Deliberate	Edison	Personal "a-ha" moment
Processing Mode	Spontaneous	Newton	Artists

Source: Authors' design

Figure 11.2   Four types of creativity

Today the importance of the creative industries and their contribution to the creative economy and human well-being are well recognised, and tourism has associated itself closely with this evolution. Florida (2002) was one of the early pundits who suggested that creativity is an essential asset for contemporary cities, particularly if they want to attract the "creative class", which adds a much-prized bohemian flavour to cities. According to Richards (2012), such ideas are also permeating the field of tourism "not only because creativity has become an important element of tourism experiences in cities, but also because creativity is seen as one potential solution to problems of commodification and serial reproduction, both of which seem particularly prevalent in cities" (p. 2).

Expressing creativity presupposes a willingness to take risks, which in turn requires being prepared to fail. We often talk about celebrating failure as a way to encourage creativity. As Edison famously said, "I have not failed. I've just found 10,000 ways that won't work." But the reality is that, whether in educational or corporate settings, we mainly penalise people for not succeeding. While children are creative by nature, parents and society, in well-meaning but misplaced actions, often dampen or even kill much of that spirit by encouraging children to work towards predetermined solutions. Similarly, employers may say they want "out of the box" thinking, but all too often there are manuals and protocols that must be strictly observed and leave little room for proposing different solutions. This is where design thinking and design-based learning truly come into their own: "At the heart of design thinking is a humancentric, structured, collaborative problem-solving approach that produces innovative products, processes, or experience solutions to address wicked problems" (Jamal et al., 2021, p. 3). The educational approach that is grounded in these processes of inquiry and reasoning towards generating innovative solutions is called design-based learning and lends itself well to engaging students in solving real-life problems.

ACTIVITY

As Barkathunnisha Abu Bakar points out in "Tourism teaching and learning using spiritual pedagogy", creativity requires nurturing the reflective capacity for an inner consciousness and a deepened awareness of environmental and societal issues in tourism (see Activity 40). Here, the learner gains an expanded understanding of knowing, which leads to a deeper development of the cognitive, affective and spiritual domains that give tangible form to creative ideas.

PHOTOGRAPHIC ESSAY

A powerful pedagogical approach to engage students in responsible and reflexive tourism place-making as well as reflecting on the importance of values and beliefs that underpin both their own self and tourism is through the combination of photos and narrative. A form of visual storytelling, a photo essay can be thematic (that is, dealing with a specific subject) or narrative (that is, telling a specific story), but in both cases provides endless creative freedom. See Joan Flaherty's "Field trip findings presented through a photo essay" (see Activity 43).

Bradley Rink's scaffolded photographic essay "Seeing tourism landscapes: teaching tourism at the confluence of theory and practice" is another approach that encourages students to "see" tourism in the everyday, while also critically reflecting on tourism's positive and negative impacts (see Activity 45).

TEAM ACTIVITY

 Design thinking is used today across many disciplines as this human-centric, structured, collaborative problem-solving approach can result in innovative solutions, especially in relation to wicked problems. It helps in questioning not only the problem, but also the underlying assumptions and the implications of adopting various solutions. The COVID-19 pandemic brought to light many issues: how tourism has evolved over the decades, the urgent need to rethink the experiences offered to tourists, how to minimise tourism's negative consequences without undermining its economic contribution and how to accomplish all of this while keeping guests, employees and residents safe and secure. By applying designed-based learning to this context, students will come to understand the interrelatedness between creativity, critical thinking and networking in the innovation/knowledge-generation process. This is outlined in Giang Phi's "Design-based learning and design thinking for innovation education" (see Activity 44).

NETWORKING

The dissemination of knowledge take place in offline and, increasingly, online social environments. The skills required to do so successfully with different audiences and media are highly valued in both professional and personal spheres. Each type of organisation – public sector, academia, private corporation – has its own way of communicating knowledge, which may not necessarily be understood by "outsiders". Hence the need to "translate" knowledge in non-technical terms and deliberately and strategically transfer it to broader audiences. This need to communicate knowledge connects to the need for our teaching to take into account multi-modality, as discussed in Chapter 1 on didactics. It is no longer sufficient that students just read and write texts: they need to be multiliterate, across all five modes of semiotic systems – linguistic, visual, audio, gestural and spatial (Anstey and Bull, 2018).

The amount of data produced every day is beyond comprehension, but that does not mean much unless this basic and generally unfiltered information is put in context with other pieces of data. Only then can this flow of information become actionable and create knowledge as coloured by the values, beliefs and disciplinary lens of its holder. Therefore, we are busily connecting knowledge holders and repositories through networks of people, machines and media. In this ever more complex world, big data can help identify patterns of behaviour that would go unnoticed without the help of algorithms and networks. At the same time, humans still need to live in real communities for their mental well-being. As we learned through the pandemic, while we can cope with the virtual environment, most of us much prefer spending physical time with people we care about and collaborate with.

SCAFFOLDED ACTIVITIES

By working through a series of activities, students are able to bridge different disciplines, institutions, cultures and subjects. The activities help them
reflect on the links between theory and practice in their knowledge creation.
In sharing their experiences and values, students develop their sense of criticality and reflexive sense of identity. Working collaboratively across universities and diverse countries is extremely challenging as each will have its own teaching
and learning regime, as discussed by Elin Bommenel, Richard Ek and Stuart Reid. Hence,
the activities developed by the team of Arctic/Northern researchers Kaarina Tervo-Kankare,
Gunnar Thór Jóhannesson, Brynhild Granås and Outi Rantala in "Value-reflexive engagement and dialogue" work as tools for value-reflexive engagement and dialogue in an online
environment (see Activity 50).

COMPLEX ACTIVITIES

In six phases, Elin Bommenel, Richard Ek and Stuart Reid provide guidance on how to conduct an introductory week of meta-pedagogical thinking
on teaching and learning regimes, drawing from experiences with a class of
international students enrolled in a new university programme (see Activity
42). The aim is to make students not only aware of their personal background and the institutional learning context in which they have grown up, but also to help
them understand how the learning regime of their new university differs.

12. Professionalism

Marion Joppe; **Johan Edelheim**; **Joan Flaherty**; Elin Bommenel; Blanca A. Camargo; Helene Balslev Clausen; Émilie Crossley; Richard Ek; Outi Kugapi; Maggie C. Miller; Stuart Reid; Kathleen Rodenburg; Maja Turnšek

OBJECTIVES

This chapter provides readers with insights and engagement activities to help students:

1. Compare and contrast the skills linked to professionalism in the tourism and hospitality industry to those in management generally
2. Appreciate the importance of relevance, timeliness and reflexivity
3. Illustrate why it is important to seek to understand another party's relevance before any joint activities are undertaken
4. Summarise what can be gained through engaging in partnerships, networks and teamwork
5. Explain the major trends in self-learning and deep learning technologies and how they will affect our industry's future

INTRODUCTION

"Professionalism" is a broad term that includes the skills, competencies or standards associated with a given profession as well as the attitude and behaviour that reflect these. It refers to how someone conducts themselves at work and, increasingly, outside of work, as the boundaries between these two spheres become more and more blurred. Professionalism also extends to appearance. Many hospitality and tourism positions come with code-of-conduct manuals and dress codes, even if the latter can be quite casual in sunny destinations where Hawaiian shirts or Cuban *guayaberas* may be deemed appropriate. Nonetheless, the "aesthetic labour" required to present a professional service image can add an unfair burden on employees, particularly female frontline workers, because it often requires effort, time and financial investment during time off work (Tsaur and Tang, 2013).

A professional is expected to be confident, polite and well spoken at all times, calmly dealing with customers, suppliers or co-workers. Confidence comes from developing skills, knowledge and understanding based on different forms of learned behaviour, including learning from experience.

All these elements of professionalism are an expected part of service jobs generally. However, those in tourism-related jobs face the extra pressure of having to be cheerful at all times, since they are part of a "feel-good" industry where guests are transported in time and space from the stresses of their home environment. The emotional dissonance that can result from suppressing one's actual emotions in order to present only a positive disposition can make the emotional labour – and the management of emotions (Hochschild, 1979) – required of tourism workers particularly stressful. Therefore, students need to be taught how to prevent, identify and address this particular work-related stress should they or their co-workers fall victim to it. The inclusion of co-workers here is deliberate. In their professional lives, our students are likely to deal with not only customers but also co-workers from different ethnicities, cultures and socio-economic backgrounds, which makes empathy a key skill to be learned and improved (Schumann et al., 2014). While the topic is well studied from a managerial and organisational perspective, little has been done to date about potential interventions to help service employees engage in effective emotional labour strategies and deal with emotional exhaustion (Lee and Madera, 2019).

The importance of emotional intelligence (EQ) as a predictor of leadership potential has long been confirmed (Higgs and Aitken, 2003). Therefore, by incorporating EQ into our students' education, we can help prepare them "to function effectively in a global workplace with its complex informal networks, intercultural issues, team emphasis, and participatory leadership" (Sigmar et al., 2012, p. 301) and encourage higher levels of critical thinking and reflexivity.

Cheng and Wong (2015) identified eight elements of professionalism: passion, sensitivity and open-mindedness to new trends, team-oriented attitude, competence and skills, emotional self-control, professional ethics, leadership by example and perfectionism. While a number of these themes recur throughout the literature, Sheldon et al. (2011) cite two more elements: proactivity and leadership. In other words, every employee has the responsibility to take control over matters that are within their control. We do not have to be leaders in a formal sense to assume leadership. According to Bateman and Crant (1993), "[p]roactive people scan for opportunities, show initiative, take action, and persevere until they reach closure by bringing about change" (p. 105).

Other features connected to professionalism are relevance, timeliness and reflexivity. These words are close to the core of excellent behaviours in any area. Professionals assume accountability for their actions at all times, and are reliable. That is, they respond to people promptly and follow through on promises in a timely manner. This practice requires professionals to reflect regularly on their workplace performance, identifying and sharpening those skills and behaviours that lead to excellence.

Some final features of professionalism are partnerships, networks and teamwork. The collegiality of working together in a professional team that may draw on employees ranging from frontline to senior management and across functional responsibilities has become indispensable in effective workplaces to take full advantage of complementary skills and ideas. There is also an expectation that someone who is professional has the ability to pass on professional knowledge and skills to others. But tourism is unique in its requirement for partnerships and teamwork to stretch across what might be deemed competitive businesses in order to create a larger presence in the cluttered world of competing destinations.

CONVERSATION STARTERS

Using cards that identify future challenges to be resolved in the areas of health, technology, society, environment and the economy helps students think beyond job titles in looking at what professional skills are required to address these challenges. See Kathleen Rodenburg's exercise "Solving wicked world problems" (Activity 49).

Helene Balslev Clausen and Maggie C. Miller describe in their reading "The value of the unintended in tourism education: Mexican case" how students coped with an unexpected mishap during a field trip to Mexico (see Activity 46). The result was a learning opportunity that helped students appreciate what it means to maintain a professional demeanour, even when expectations based on Western norms are not met.

LEADERSHIP AND PROACTIVITY

Managers assume responsibility for working with others to achieve organisational goals, whereas leaders help to develop the goals in the first place. In other words, managers concern themselves with the administration of processes, systems and structures, while leaders focus on people and how to align them to achieve the vision. Further, "manager" is a title with a given set of responsibilities, whereas "leader" is about exercising influence and can be displayed by anyone within the organisation. According to Bennis (2009), leadership is always about character and authenticity, the kind of integrity that creates trust. Key to exhibiting leadership skills is being proactive rather than reactive, and being comfortable with ambiguity and uncertainty. Therefore, any employee who thinks critically about their work and, based on that analysis, takes initiative can be valued for their leadership – no matter what position they hold.

CONVERSATION STARTER

Ask students whether they think that people are born with a tendency to take leadership or if people learn to become leaders (that is, can everyone learn to become a leader?). Have students develop a list of skills and qualities they would expect a leader to exhibit. Discuss how students could develop these skills and qualities and what role good communication might play in enhancing their own leadership potential.

ACTIVITY

Emotional self-control, an important aspect of EQ, has been identified as one of the core elements of professionalism (Cheng and Wong, 2015; Lee and Ok, 2012). Controlling one's emotions has long been recognised within tourism and hospitality studies as the essential definitional element of what

Hochschild (1983/2003) referred to as the "commercialisation of human feeling". Thus, emotional labour is defined as the labour to enhance, fake or suppress emotions to comply with an organisation's rules prescribing the feelings and emotions displayed by an employee when providing service to customers (Grandey, 2000). Maja Turnšek proposes a number of exercises in "Emotional labour and the future of automation" to help students understand the concept and discuss it in light of increasing automation in service jobs (see Activity 51).

RELEVANCE, TIMELINESS AND REFLEXIVITY

Relevance is an important – and challenging – aspect of professionalism. It requires that students place themselves in the position of someone else, such as their customer, their co-worker or their supervisor, in order to understand the other person's goals and priorities and, based on that understanding, create a win–win situation. This ideal outcome is possible only if each party knows what the other party is aiming for and is willing to adjust their own expectations to highlight common goals. At this point, both parties are likely to achieve relevant results from the interaction. Note, however, that this scenario is not meant to encourage unthinking deference to someone else's point of view. Risk aversion and a desire for harmony or conformity, which can be very strong in some cultures, can lead to "group-think", whereby social and cultural values are not challenged, and the resultant information collected is biased against leading-edge or innovative approaches. There are numerous examples from the consumer electronics industries, for instance, where this has happened. Leading manufacturers of, for example, photographic equipment or music players have found their products irrelevant to the market they dominated after developments by others changed consumers' preferences. Some among these producers knew about the changes taking place, but rather than upsetting the harmony of the group by challenging ruling practices, kept the knowledge to themselves.

The demand and supply characteristics of tourism are fast-changing, largely because our technological and communication systems have been accelerated by the global pandemic, as innovative responses to disruptions tend to do. To keep up with this fast pace and the changes that accompany it, we need constant upgrading of knowledge, competencies and skills. With so much data available at a click, it is critical that students learn how to discern which information is relevant, and how to gather this relevant information in a timely manner for decision-making purposes. Technology has also reduced the time allotted for most tasks, forcing a choice between two approaches: gather as much information as possible to support decisions (that is, take longer to complete the task), or narrow the information search to only the most relevant data (that is, complete the task more quickly). Deciding which approach is most appropriate at any given time is a challenge that every industry professional faces and addresses regularly. A balanced approach is therefore needed so that the focus on "timeliness" does not compromise "relevance".

Facilitating learning so that it contributes to these aspects of professionalism, allowing students to activate their repertoire of relevant skills and knowledge, is always challenging. Figure 12.1 addresses this challenge by integrating two models, one relating to curriculum space (Dredge et al., 2012) and the other to a curriculum design teaching–research nexus (Healey, 2005). The model can be read from bottom-left towards top-right, indicating a gradual move from basics to practical wisdom, where students have learned to think on their feet, their actions shaped by reflection (top-left corner) and critical thinking (bottom-right corner). This integrated model highlights simultaneously how students need to be active participants in their learning, and how their own research should be an integral part of their inquiry-based learning.

Each quadrant also indicates effective means of incorporating research as an active part of all teaching. The model is thus an extension to the idea of teaching as transmission, transaction and transformation presented in Chapter 1 on didactics. Research-led teaching is often transmission of best practices and basic concepts. Research-tutored and research-oriented teaching builds on transactions between learners and instructors. Finally, research-based teaching is a transformative practice where students develop new understandings for themselves and their surroundings. Research should in this context not be understood simply as an academic practice but rather as an active search, evaluation and reflection on all issues of relevance to the individual. The model is thus an illustration of how well-planned curricula and teaching can facilitate research-based learning that leads to practical wisdom and professionalism.

CONVERSATION STARTER

 A service-learning project that requires students to develop a realistic project for a marginalised community brings to the forefront the many considerations and professional skills that students need to think about and develop. Blanca A. Camargo describes this in "Promoting mutuality through service-learning: La Santa Catarina restaurant" (see Activity 36).

While the value of reflection has long been acknowledged and is anchored in Kolb and Kolb's reflective model (2009), it is often ignored in today's time-poor environments. One way to introduce reflection into your life is to take stock of what you know or do not know. In this case, reflecting or taking stock is not just to think of *what* you know, but to ask yourself *how you came to know* what you know, and *why* you know what you know (Hinett, 2002). This process is inherent within humans, a natural reflex that helps us survive. In many cases, it takes place unconsciously: we experience something that has a good or bad outcome, and next time we are in a similar experience we tend to select a pattern of behaviour that should lead us to a good outcome.

Now, reflexivity is different. It is a conscious process, intended to help us learn from our experience about what we do, why and how we do it; challenge our assumptions, social and cultural biases; and find alternatives. Reflexivity is where proactive acts are born. Reflexivity is where we create relevance. Reflexivity is how we become professionals.

A certain amount of confidence in one's professionalism is required in order to determine which information is relevant, use that information to analyse and understand the situation, and then learn from the results. Reflexivity fosters this confidence and its beneficial outcomes. It does, however, require that we step beyond a culture of deference while, at the same time, assuming responsibility for our own actions and mistakes. In other words, reflexivity can challenge us, especially when the situation we face is uncomfortable or undesirable.

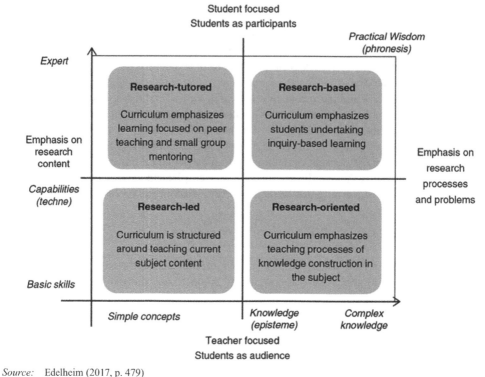

Source: Edelheim (2017, p. 479)

Figure 12.1   *The curriculum space and design teaching–research nexus (TRN) Model*

ACTIVITIES

The writing of a business proposal that reflects values that students have identified as important to them requires them to reflect on and articulate what they would do if they were a decision-maker. The proposal can be for any type of organisation students have worked at or volunteered for. This is the second part of Joan Flaherty's "The power of values to effect positive change 2" (see Activity 48).

Émilie Crossley provides a guided reflective assessment in "Professional practice review of learning" that is suitable for postgraduate learners and practitioners who wish to develop critical self-awareness as a foundation for enhancing their professional practice (see Activity 47).

PARTNERSHIPS, NETWORKS, TEAMWORK

Competition between business and destination is fierce in tourism, and becoming increasingly so as more and more actors enter the field. But since most tourism-related businesses fall into the micro-to-small enterprise categories, cooperation – especially in terms of marketing – is vital to compete effectively in a global marketplace. This need has given rise to "coopetition" or collaboration between business competitors, in the hope of mutually beneficial results. The marketing of destinations in particular requires coordination of efforts of a large number of stakeholders in the private, public and non-profit sectors, each with different individual goals. The aim is to increase performance of both stakeholders and destination, and thereby appropriate the value produced by the group (Chim-Miki and Batista-Canino, 2017). According to Chim-Miki and Batista-Canino (2017), "coopetition is a hybrid behaviour resulted from competitive cooperation that occurs between networks and organizations, or within organizations, including relations among competitors, suppliers, complementary businesses, government agencies, local people, and customers" (p. 384).

Since the actors in a tourism network are not just highly interdependent but also have competing individual goals, the decision to enter into coopetition requires a significant amount of trust among the partners that none will behave opportunistically and try to gain an unfairly large part of the benefits. Building trust among the various partners requires not just a cognitive component – that is, observing behaviour and being aware of reputation – but also an emotional component built through social and personal bonds between actors (Czernek and Czakon, 2016). Formal and informal networking is immensely useful in establishing the high level of trust required to work effectively as a team in an environment that relies heavily on cooperation.

Teamwork, as well, takes on an additional connotation in the tourism realm in the form of experiences that are co-created between tourism workers and customers. Here, a different kind of team approach is required, one that might be deemed performative work. The "experience economy" where "work is theatre and every business is a stage" – popularised by Pine and Gilmore (1999) – has led to an explosion of experiences being created that not only repackage the tourism products but also the service providers; thus, both consumers and producers might engage in performances. A destination's residents might also be co-opted, willingly or unknowingly, as actors in the dramaturgy of local life. For example, Old Order Mennonites (a religious sect active in North America) often practise a lifestyle without some elements of modern technology, dress plainly and retain horse-and-buggy transportation, making them an "attraction" to curious visitors intrigued by these communities. These performative encounters raise issues around authenticity, cultural representations and the essence of professionalism. They also point out the importance of positioning tourism so that it is relevant to the economic, political and social infrastructure of the host community, contributing to the destination's quality of life and its residents' well-being.

At the opposite end of the spectrum are managerial strategies that reduce or even eliminate interactions between tourism employees and customers – an unfortunate development that significantly accelerated during the pandemic. Thus, deskilling, routinisation, increased reliance on technology, robotics and artificial intelligence have all played a role in stripping tourism encounters of cultural meanings of concern, care and attention (Crang, 1997).

CONVERSATION STARTERS

Reflecting on the roleplaying game "The Tourism Game" played at various points throughout this book, ask students whether they felt uncomfortable at any point having to be in roles with others or having to negotiate with other groups. What contributed to this feeling and how did they overcome it? What strategies did they adopt and how would they approach similar situations in the future?

Phase four of the introductory week of meta-pedagogical thinking on teaching and learning regimes by Elin Bommenel, Richard Ek and Stuart Reid provides students with an opportunity to reflect on communities of practice, their motivations for joining them, their behaviour and actions as a member, and what they expected as outcomes (see Activity 1). This discussion can easily be stretched to identify communities within their chosen field of study and their approach to becoming a contributing member.

ACTIVITY

In small groups, have students research examples of how technology is changing various sectors both in front and in back of the house. Sharing these examples with the rest of the class, have students discuss how they feel about this evolution, the impact on the workforce, labour costs, health, safety and security. How do they personally feel about having robots as team members?

13. Activities

ACTIVITY 1: META-PEDAGOGICAL MELIORISM 1: DIDACTICS

Elin Bommenel, PhD,[1] Richard Ek, PhD[2] and Stuart Reid[3]

DESCRIPTION

The metaphysical concept of meliorism pivots on the idea that progress leads to improvement and that by partaking in processes, humans can improve themselves and, at the same time, improve the world they are embedded in. As a cornerstone concept in liberalism, meliorism is primarily associated with liberal political philosophy and philosophical pragmatism. In this contribution, as well as in Part 2 (Social values) and Part 3 (Knowledge), we transfer the spirit of the concept into the classroom.

USAGE SUGGESTIONS

The three contributions on meta-pedagogical meliorism all relate to an introductory week for a newly arrived class of international students with pedagogically heterogenous learning backgrounds. However, the concept of teaching and learning regimes is equally applicable to industry professionals and undergraduate and graduate classes, and also to more homogenous groups who are meeting for the first time. Learning is a personal journey, but teaching seldom makes meta-pedagogy overt. All activities involved with these contributions aim to highlight this fact.

LEARNING OBJECTIVES

By the end of this activity, participants should be able to:

1. Acknowledge that their personal background (nationality, ethnicity, age, gender) is an individual resource, but what matters most in a university learning context is the prior teaching and learning regime they have been a part of
2. Explain and make visible the teaching and learning regime at their home university for the benefit of an international group of co-learners with different learning experiences

THEORETICAL FOUNDATION

In our university's teaching and learning regime, dialogue is seen as critical for learning. It encourages the student to be active, which is central to pedagogics at Lund University (as in Northern Europe in general). This approach also reflects the Vygotsky-influenced belief that learning is a collective endeavour (Daniels, 2016). As learning is a social and active process, it tends to transform the learner, who is therefore not only a vessel to be filled with knowledge, but also a vessel whose form changes due to the gained knowledge. In post-structural terms (for instance, in Donna Haraway's work) we could see it as a change in subject position, a dialectics of de- and re-subjectification.

TIME PLAN

We have divided the introduction week into six phases with some online preparations. This contribution on didactics covers phases four, five and six. Phase one is covered in Chapter 5 on social values, and phases two and three in Chapter 11 on knowledge. In our case we dedicated one week to this process, but it is possible to tailor the time and resources dedicated to this programme task.

STEP-BY-STEP PLAN

Phase Four: Critical Dialogues (Student Subjectification)

Learning is personal and thus interactive. It is a social practice surrounded by a set of implicit and explicit rules – a spatio-temporal specific community of practice and habitus. This is perhaps most clearly showed in, but not limited to, classroom discussions.

The students need to be aware of this approach in order to be able to contribute constructively to classroom discussions, and to contribute to a community of practice where they can learn and be shaped together with their classmates. They need to ruminate somewhat on their motivations for entering the community of practice at hand (ego-oriented learning, task-oriented learning, extrinsic motivation or intrinsic motivation). That makes it possible for them to see the extent to which their motivation fits the current teaching and learning regime.

Extrinsic motivation invites a surface approach and one based on a fear of failure – qualities that do not align with a teaching and learning regime that stresses deep learning. (Deep learning practices aim to foster intrinsic motivations for learning. This requires feeling secure enough to be challenged by, and to challenge, knowledge claims encountered in learning processes).

Moving from an extrinsic motivation towards an intrinsic motivation carries within it a realisation of the learner's own agency in the learning process. Seeing a possible gap between extrinsic and intrinsic motivations makes it easier for the students to become empowered to act constructively. This relates to how a recognition of teaching and learning regimes can increase one's sense of comfort and personal security in a classroom or, indeed, in facilitating learning processes in general.

Phase Five: Seminar and Discussion Culture

A key skill for a student to possess in an academic community of practice is the learning-oriented interaction with other students, in group work, at seminars and in other collective tasks or work.

Arrange a seminar with the students; for instance, reading a master's thesis written by a student from the programme. Allot different roles within the seminar group: a chair, a subject secretary, a process secretary (who documents active listening, reading, how critical thinking was displayed and how group practice/dynamics evolved during the seminar), a manager who guides the group so that all tasks are covered within the allocated time, and active participants; that is, everyone else.

All roles are needed to empower students to contribute to the collective process by making at least two comments, listening in an active way and showing that they have read the assigned material and can discuss it critically.

Hand out a sheet of paper for each active participant so that they can make notes about their own participation in the discussion according to the following criteria:

- "I acknowledged and expanded upon an argument by a previous speaker"
- "I showed that I had read and grasped the material"
- "I contributed to a critical analysis by making a reflective comment, associated comment/ question or taking an idea further"

Plan the seminar so that not only is time devoted for discussing the reading material, but there is also time for the secretaries to share and discuss their notes with the class.

As the sociology of science research field, from Merton and Storer (1973) and beyond, informs us, the science community is just another social and cultural setting with spatio-temporal specifics when it comes to behaviour, understandings and performativities. It is important to make the students realise how a safe and inclusive learning environment is beneficial for all. It is also important to make the students aware that, as in all societal settings, power asymmetries and capital of different kinds are at play in the construction of power differentials: like "socio-capital-splaining" – a powerful metaphor made out of a pun upon the term "mansplaining". See, for example, Kubota (2020) on epistemological racism or Lange and Young (2019) on rebalancing feminine and masculine pedagogies.

Specific performativities beneficial for the situation need to be discussed, like active listening, inclusive techniques and the rotation of different functions among a group of discussants. Seminar culture is an elusive concept but has to be pinpointed down in order to address strengths and weaknesses in a group of learners.

At this stage it is also important to clarify that it is in the seminar moments in which the critical incidents so crucial for learning unfold. Incompatibilities between different teaching and learning regimes often remain latent and do not surface until critical incidents occur.

These critical incidents are not in themselves inherently unfortunate but need to be highlighted and addressed in a constructive and inclusive way in order to work as epistemological insights for the students.

Phase Six: Grading and Designing Exams

One appropriate way to get a grasp of a certain teaching and learning regime is to study the examination forms used, how they are designed and what they contain. The design of the exam will decide how the students study. A teacher who wants a deep and active approach to the material will make sure the exam encourages just that behaviour in the students' preparations.

TEACHING TIPS

Showing and discussing the different examining activities and how grading systems work in the programme, and looking at the different criteria for different degrees, is a way to reveal the epistemological contours of the teaching and learning regime at hand. It all comes down to, and relates to, the earlier phases in this introductory package, as the nature of the examination distils the characteristics of the teaching and learning regime at the current university.

ACTIVITY 2: YES-AND: HOW TO CREATE A BRAVE SPACE BY INCORPORATING IMPROVISATIONAL THEATRE GAMES

Stefanie Benjamin, PhD[4]

DESCRIPTION

Improvisation, or improv, along with other theatre techniques, is a communal art form that requires not only spontaneity but also sharing of offers and generous mutual support. It forces us to get out of our heads and access deeper parts of ourselves that help us manage change. Doing so, we learn how take the focus from ourselves and suspend personal judgement. Incorporating improvisational games into curriculum, workshops or training sessions can foster a "brave space" where people become more aware of their own speech, body and behaviours in order to observe, listen and respond to their environment (Benjamin and Kline, 2019). By doing so, we can learn how to lead and communicate in the moment – to keep the conversation, and the relationship, on a productive trajectory.

USAGE SUGGESTIONS

Improv theatre games can be used by any audience, including students (K–12; higher education) and industry/practitioners. For instance, improv can be interwoven within class discussions to break up the monotony of a passive lecture, at an industry workshop or as a way to diffuse difficult conversations/topics. The tools and experiences of improv theatre help with slowing down conversations to separate reactions from responses. Understanding how to respond to our own emotions – and recognising what triggers them – can help us become more empathetic and active listeners. The highest we can achieve from a difficult conversation is to understand the other person's point of view and remain respectful. Thus, improv can reinforce an open and curious mindset, which, in turn, helps foster critical and creative thinkers who work towards inclusive and diverse understandings.

Three major tenets of improv help unpack our emotions, open space for reflection and slow down conversations: (1) empathetic and active listening, (2) saying "Yes-and" and (3) embracing vulnerability.

Empathetic and active listening

- Most people are waiting for the other person to stop talking, so they can interject their opinion. However, with improvisational games focused on listening, participants learn how to listen to both verbal and non-verbal cues, which help with actively and empathetically listening to what their partner is saying. This amounts to having to listen to *understand* as opposed to just listening merely to *answer* or act in response – avoiding miscommunication and potentially leading to deeper discussions
- Encouraging listening around the non-verbal cues helps when there may be an emotional outburst triggered by a partner's comment or response. Instead of running away, learning how to identify those emotions, process them and discuss them empathetically helps to better understand a different point of view. Most importantly, staying present, maintaining eye contact and actively listening signal to the other person that they are heard, validated and seen

Saying "Yes-and!"

- Yes-and means not being afraid to contribute. It helps us to build upon people's ideas in a supportive way and to boost creativity and innovation. In a culture where the default answer is no, in order to avoid risk and possibility of failure, incorporating a yes-and mindset allows for a fast-paced, energetic, forward momentum
- This opens a space for opportunity, allows an idea to grow and, most importantly, forces us to let go of our ego! Respect what your partner has created and at least start from an open-minded place. Start with a yes and see where that takes you. Because if we do not say yes … then we are denying the scene
- Yes-and gives the people who practise it the "confidence that, come what may, in business or their personal lives, they can create something out of nothing and make something wonderful out of it" (Leonard and Yorton, 2015, p. 49)

Embracing vulnerability

- Improv teaches people to learn how to let go of self-judgement and become confident innovators. It also allows for risk-taking and failing
- Learning how to be transparent and honest around our mistakes helps to normalise and humanise our failures. Failure is not something to be feared; in fact it is something to embrace. Sometimes, you have to accumulate a series of failures in order to succeed. This does not mean you are a failure. Instead, you were brave enough to take risks – and willing to jump back in the saddle after epic failures. Ask yourself, what did I learn from this failure to lead me towards success?

LEARNING OBJECTIVES

Improvisation and, more importantly, the number-one rule of Yes-and as a relational tool are strategies to support the other person, even if we may disagree about a specific issue. By embracing a yes-and mentality, our students can achieve three major learning objectives:

- Participate in a dynamic alternative to traditional classroom discussion, capitalising on creative, nonlinear expression and idea exchange
- Learn how to make themselves fully present – stay in the moment to help improve their emotional intelligence and sustain focus
- Foster skills towards listening empathetically and actively that embrace a curious and open attitude

MATERIALS LIST

Depending on the game, paper and pen(cil)s may be needed. Physical space to move around and room for personal reflection are important.

PRE-WORK REQUIRED BY STUDENTS

No prior work is needed. Just an open mind and judgement-free attitude – which, of course, might be difficult to achieve. However, see my teaching tips for guidance.

THEORETICAL FOUNDATION

Self-efficacy theory is used to explore how improvisation workshops potentially help individuals feel confident about their work and improv(e) their collaborative learning environments. Within this theory, one's perceived ability to exert influence over one's own actions or over circumstances that affect one's life is a key determinant of the motivation, effort level and perseverance towards a goal (Scholz et al., 2002, p. 242).

TIME PLAN

Time frames can range from a 15-minute game to a four-hour workshop.

STEP-BY-STEP PLAN

Below are some examples of improvisational games appropriate for a class, workshop or training session:

1. One-word response (10–20 minutes)
   Have participants gather in one large circle (or multiple smaller circles, if there are more than 30 people). As the moderator, stand in the middle and ask for a one-word noun. Instruct the participants to answer only with a one-word response when they hear the prior response, and that they cannot duplicate a response. For example, we start with "school". As moderator, point to one person in the circle to give a one-word response based on their

interpretation when they hear the word "school". Let's say that they respond with "pencil". The person to the right of them in the circle will respond, using one word only, based on what comes to their mind when they hear the word "pencil". Let's say they respond with "eraser". Then the person to the right of them has to respond with what they think of when they hear the word "eraser". Do this at least twice around the circle, making sure that nobody repeats the same word

- The meaning behind this game is that everyone holds their own truths, and as such has their own interpretation and worldview. Thus, making sure that we truly listen to what a person is saying, and holding space for them to share their own feelings, helps us to suspend our own judgement, as we all come from different lived experiences

2. Saying "Yes-and"

In groups of two, identify who will be Partner A and who will be Partner B. Partner A starts the game off by planning a party or activity with Partner B. Everything Partner A suggests to Partner B, Partner B must agree and add to it. For instance, Partner A says, "I want to plan a party with a dinosaur theme." Partner B responds with "Yes, and we should provide dinosaur-themed hats!" After three to seven minutes, have the partners switch, where Partner B plans the party and Partner A agrees and adds. The next step is having Partner A plan a party or activity but Partner B says "No-but …" For instance, Partner A says she wants to plan a dinosaur-themed party. Partner B replies "No – since dinosaurs are super lame." Repeat this again with the roles reversed

- This game helps with letting go of control and caring less about our own egos. It helps to create a positive approach to disagreement or conflict. By agreeing and adding to an idea, we feel heard and seen. This helps us to feel good about ourselves, invested in the mission/vision and like we are contributing to the cause by adding our voice. Additionally, students feel different emotions with the yes-and the no-but response. Ask them: "How did it feel to be told 'no' compared to your partner agreeing with you? Was it more difficult to plan your party? What does this mean for collaborating with others?"

3. Having the last word

With this game, have Partner A state a sentence. Partner B must respond with the last word from that sentence. (This conversation does not need to make sense.) For example, Partner A says, "I love to go downtown for dinner." Partner B responds, "Dinner is something you eat at night." Partner A then responds with "'Night' is another word for evening." And so forth

- So many times, when we are in a discussion or argument, we tend not to truly listen to what is being said. We are so irate or so excited to respond, we do not actually listen to the person in front of us. Instead, we are in our own mind, thinking of a response or finding a way to prove that we are correct! Unpacking how to actively and empathetically listen to our partner is challenging. However, it forces us to sit in moments of discomfort, which, in turn, helps us to be open to critique and to challenge our own biases and perceptions

TEACHING TIPS

Facilitating improvisational games in the classroom can be daunting. As someone who has faced some pushback from students, I offer some tips to help ease folks into this process:

- Creating a community with your students is essential. Try to establish a classroom environment that is considered a "brave space" where we, as a class, can suspend judgement, act silly and foster a yes-and mindset where everyone's voice is heard and valued. This can mean creating a GroupMe (mobile messaging app) for your class and asking for silly photos of your pets or integrating ice-breakers/fun videos at the beginning of class
- Provide some reading material on improvisation or YouTube videos on why this form of engagement helps us become more creative, empathetic and flexible. Do this before you implement the games
- As an instructor, participate with your students – perform along with them in the games and exercises. Allow the students to experience your vulnerability and willingness to look silly
- After each game, explain the *why* behind each exercise. What would you like for the students to get out of that game? *Why* is this important within your field/discipline?
- Ask students to write a reflection, record a video or keep a blog/journal about how they are implementing what they learned during these games. Be clear that you do not want a summary, but instead an example of how they applied the skills learned in their everyday life

Using some key principles of improv, we as instructors can keep an open mind, suspend judgement and stay present. By doing so, we can promote an inclusive learning environment where our students feel brave enough to share their lived experiences without fear of attack. By helping our students become emphatic and critical thinkers, we can help diffuse some difficult conversations and promote social equity.

ACTIVITY 3: TOURISM TO PROMOTE POLITICAL RESPONSIBILITY

Jaume Guia, PhD[5]

DESCRIPTION

The aim of this assignment is to foster political awareness among students, prompting them to take action against structural injustices.

   This specific contribution describes a ten-day field trip to the Sahrawi Refugee Camps in Western Sahara. Travelling to places where human rights are clearly violated or some type of structural injustice, whether social or environmental, is rampant puts students in a paradoxical position. They become not just privileged tourists visiting a unique place, but also witnesses of structural injustice. Here, simply paying for tourism services does not seem to be right. The situation demands political responsibility, which by nature cannot be monetised – it must be acted upon. Students are thus expected to learn that structural injustices are everywhere and that when we travel we are often blind to them. Tourists mostly travel self-focused in search of a value-for-money service or in search of personal growth and transformational experiences. The consideration and care for the host communities is often romanticised or, at most, moralistic, but seldom political. Consequently, even with the best moral intentions, tourism loses its potential for curbing structural injustices. In fact, visitors may return home oblivious to the structural injustices of their destination, simply happy to have been on holiday. This outcome indirectly reinforces the neo-liberal system at the base of the structural injustices.

USAGE SUGGESTIONS

In our case we address this activity to master's-level students, but it could also be done with undergraduate students. Because it is a long activity, it should be positioned in the middle of the unit, where there is preparation before the trip and discussion and reflection upon return. This way, students engage in the activity aware of the conceptual tools around the ethics of travel, the commodification of travel, the depoliticisation of travel, and so on. In the case of a lockdown, the physical trip obviously cannot be done. However, the activity could still be carried out by means of "virtual travel". This option could also help solve the problem of students not being able to afford the field trip. A third option would be for someone from the community to visit the university instead, or a combination of both virtual travel and community visitor to the classroom.

As stated earlier, structural injustices are everywhere. Therefore, identifying a suitable destination for this field trip assignment is not likely to pose a problem.

LEARNING OBJECTIVES

- Become more aware of the destinations' structural injustices of all sorts, instead of focusing only on their attractions and romanticised views of their cultures and landscapes
- Be less self-focused and travel with openness to difference in search of genuine transformation
- Be committed to act with political responsibility, which means establishing a "political" relationship with the place and its people after the trip
- Identify what ethical approaches underlie different ways of visiting a destination, and to what extent their contribution is purely utilitarian, sociocultural responsible, humanitarian or political

MATERIALS LIST

All the characteristic arrangements of a multi-day (and likely international) field trip.

THEORETICAL FOUNDATION

The contribution builds on ethical theories in tourism, specifically within the context of justice and tourism. It highlights the essential role of posthumanism in shaping our political action as tourism students and scholars against structural injustice (Guia, 2021). In terms of pedagogical foundations, the contribution's reflective and applied nature borrows heavily from Experiential Learning Theory (for example, Kolb and Kolb, 2009).

TIME PLAN

International field trips are ten days long for a minimal significant immersion.

STEP-BY-STEP PLAN

- Conceptual background phase: it is essential that before the trip students are acquainted with concepts like commodification, depoliticisation, neo-liberal capitalism, utilitarianism, moralism, ethics of care and posthumanism
- Preparation phase: getting acquainted with the place through materials, meetings with activists, teamwork, and so on. Also, discussions about what the trip should include and should not, and so on
- The trip: implementation of the prefigured set of activities
- Post-trip: reflection and discussion about the main concepts of the course, how the experience may affect the way one will travel and whether students will keep related to the place and to the structural injustice; for example, by engaging in activism for the communities and their types of injustice

TEACHING TIPS

The field trip requires plenty of preparation. It also requires plenty of follow-up. A key learning objective is that the participants keep involved in different ways after the course, maintaining their commitment to address structural injustice. As instructors, we are obligated to work alongside our students in this effort, contributing with our own political activism.

ACTIVITY 4: UNINTENDED CONSEQUENCES OF POLICY IMPLEMENTATION

Marion Joppe, PhD[6]

DESCRIPTION

In democratic societies, government policy is usually the result of a deliberate process that includes consultations with stakeholders that might be affected or have an interest in the issue. Often, the result is a compromise that allows the political party in power to advance its agenda while toning down the most objectionable aspects of the policy proposal. However, there are times when that party is caught off guard by an event and, in an effort to quickly cover its negligence, will rush into implementing a policy without first receiving sufficient input. The result can have quite devastating consequences that were not intended but are not rectified.

That was the case of Canada's worst-ever outbreak of E. coli contamination, in the small rural town of Walkerton, Ontario. Almost half its population fell ill, and seven people died after a preventable breakdown in the local water system. As part of its deficit-reduction agenda, the Conservative government had been severely cutting the Environment Ministry's budget, and regular oversight of water-quality testing at the local level was one of the victims of these cuts. To restore the public's faith in the quality of the province's drinking water, the government imposed a multi-pronged approach that included forcing any business that makes drinking water available to the public and does not get it from a municipal drinking water system to invest in a small system of its own at a minimum cost of $50,000 plus training and certification of the operator. This policy forced many businesses that were supplementing their income through tourism-related activities, such as farm stores, bed and breakfasts, small RV parks and campgrounds, and so on, to close as the investment far exceeded the income, even on a multi-year basis.

USAGE SUGGESTIONS

The audience can be undergraduates, graduate students or practitioners since the aim is to make the audience aware of how an event apparently unrelated to their own business can have impacts well beyond those apparent at first glance. This conversation starter should lead to discussions about the challenge for operators to stay abreast of policy developments and pending legislation. This leads to probing the need for operators to belong to advocacy associations that have strong relations with elected officials and civil servants to get advance notice of regulatory developments as well as reasons for collaborating with other sector associations and power relationships. Inviting a government relations representative from one of the leading industry associations to speak about these challenges and strategies can lead to much greater understanding of the political systems and a willingness to become more engaged with them.

LEARNING OBJECTIVES

- Understand the process of how policy is developed and laws are made
- Appreciate the role of government relations and advocacy organisations
- Analyse political platforms from the perspective of tourism operators and society at large

PRE-WORK REQUIRED BY STUDENTS

Aside from reading up on the Walkerton case by following its timeline (for example, www .cbc.ca/news/canada/inside-walkerton-canada-s-worst-ever-e-coli-contamination-1.887200), it would be a good idea to have students research the long list of government initiatives that an industry association has to follow.

THEORETICAL FOUNDATION

Any discussion of the policy process needs to be grounded in an understanding of the nature of power and power relations (Hill and Varone, 2014). Power is rarely evenly spread, even in democracies, and, depending on the political system, may not even be openly contested. There are also great variances in the scope for public participation. Thus, the policy process is firmly grounded in the values held by the party in power, which may well conflict with those of other actors concerned with the process. Dredge (2018) probes tourism network research to gain a better understanding of "what [is] really going on in tourism policymaking" (p. 2) and criticises much of the existing research for its lack of theoretical discussions of concepts such as power, influence and knowledge. But she also admits that policy is "messy, dynamic, non-scalar and [a] value-laden set of relations, issues, agendas and actions in which actors engage, directly and indirectly" (p. 6).

TIME PLAN

Conceived as a conversation starter, this contribution can easily be built into a fairly major component of a course by expanding on underlying themes such as power, power relations, political ideologies and platforms, networks, and so on.

STEP-BY-STEP PLAN

1. Assign pre-readings: ask students to familiarise themselves with the Walkerton case
2. Open class discussion with a brief summary of the case highlights
3. Pose questions of the class as to whether they believe the government's response was warranted, at what point businesses in rural areas should have become alert to the potential impact of new legislation, steps businesses could have taken to make their concerns known and who they might have aligned themselves with to exert more influence on the final decisions

ACTIVITY 5: REFLECTING ON SUSTAINABLE BEHAVIOUR

Alexandra Coghlan, PhD[7] and Sarah Ripper[8]

DESCRIPTION

The activities set out in this section are designed to enable students to bring their authentic selves to a course on sustainability in tourism. In teaching the course, we have defined sustainability as a set of relationships – with our natural environment, with the resources we depend on, with our employees, our investors, our families, our community and the governance structures that support our societies. And ourselves. To understand if what we are doing enhances or harms our relationships is to understand whether what we are doing is sustainable or not. Each of the activities here is designed to be an easy and safe way to understand other perspectives, our diverse ways of seeing and understanding the world, and the various needs that we are looking to fulfil through the decisions that we take.

USAGE SUGGESTIONS

The activities described here were undertaken during an undergraduate field studies course. Some have also been used in three-hour workshops that required creative work by students to solve problems in their campus community and seek feedback from their peers. The activities can be used in a range of contexts with students at either undergraduate or graduate level.

All the activities are designed to be undertaken in small groups or pairs, and most involve some reflective activities.

LEARNING OBJECTIVES

- To see multiple perspectives to interpret what is driving sustainable or unsustainable behaviours
- To appraise one's own response to sustainable and unsustainable behaviours
- To voice one's views in a way that facilitates ongoing discussions of sustainability

MATERIALS LIST

- Reading on Appreciative Inquiry (AI), with some sample questions (for example, "An overview of AI" from www.imaginechicago.org/appreciative-inquiry-resources)
- AI workshop cards: www.michellemcquaid.com/product/appreciative-inquiry-cards/
- Pen and paper
- A bespoke travel journal
- Smart device for vlogging
- A whiteboard
- The signature strengths quiz: www.viacharacter.org/survey/account/register

PRE-WORK REQUIRED BY STUDENTS

Students should complete the signature strengths quiz available at www.viacharacter.org/survey/account/register.

THEORETICAL FOUNDATION

The foundation is Kolb's experiential learning cycle, with the various activities targeting different stages of the cycle. It also uses an AI approach (www.imaginechicago.org/appreciative-inquiry-resources) and takes elements from Positive Psychology around character strengths (Niemiec, 2017). Mary Gentile's (2010) *Giving Voice to Values* book is also a useful resource.

TIME PLAN AND STEP-BY-STEP PLAN

The approach is scaffolded through a multitude of smaller activities:

Activity	How to do it	Time and location
The initial ice-breaker	After brief introductions, ask students to anonymously write five things they would want someone to know about them. Shuffle the notes, hand back one to each student, and ask them to guess who is who. Move to the person whose name has just been correctly guessed. And include yourself	10–15 minutes for a group of 10, in class, face to face
Signature strengths test	Ask students to complete the strength quiz and reflecting on how they plan to bring their strengths to the course. Discuss in class to get a feel for the diversity in the room	1 hour, at home

Activity	How to do it	Time and location
Bring a gift	List all the people who will contribute to the field studies course and ask the students to each pick a host to bring a gift for. Help them consider the culture and context of the gift receiver, so that they have to really think about who they are meeting, and so on	20 minutes to list and pick, multiple discussions via email to discuss appropriate gifts
The 6 Rs of service-learning	Using the activity above, segue into the concepts of reciprocity, reflection, research, respect, recognition and reflection	45 minutes of discussion in class
The code of conduct	Ask the students to brainstorm their own code of conduct, collate the ideas and collectively agree on a code	45 minutes in class
GLADs	This is a daily reflective piece on what am I Grateful for, what did I Learn and Accomplish, and what Delighted me	Students can use their diary (with a daily GLAD prompt) to make notes either prior to or after having shared it with the group, usually at the end of the day A group of 10 students will usually take 10–15 minutes
AI-based vlog	The main assignment is a vlog, which is creative and narrated (thus personal expression) based on observation and interactions (including with other students). The vlogs are shared with other students at the end of the course	Explain what AI is and use the Imagine Chicago worksheet and cards to practise an AI approach to discussions and listening Role play what this would look like with hosts The vlog itself is 5–7 minutes long, and students are instructed to capture at least 5 concepts from the taught course material. The filming of the vlog is limited to one community-based ecotourism host site (where the hosts are briefed on the assessment beforehand), but we have a practice run at another site prior to the main assessment, with teacher and peer feedback
Post-trip debrief	Hold a trip debrief workshop to reflect on what they learned and how has it impacted them	2-hour guided session reflecting on what they have learned personally and professionally

TEACHING TIPS

- As part of using relationships as a way to operationalise sustainability, the entire trip was organised by the primary convener (no agent) with the help of in-country friends and colleagues. The intent was to emphasise that the trip is not just a commercial transaction, but based on relationships. The outcome was that students did start to see destination communities as consisting of people in their own right, who *host* us rather than providing a paid-for service
- As an introvert, I found the activities were sometimes intimidating but always worthwhile. Even the other introverts in the group said that this approach helped them integrate their experiences, reflections, learning and emotions during the trip, and build the 6 Rs (reciprocity, reflection, research, respect, recognition and reflection). It is important to start

early (hence the ice-breaker activity) and be consistent with this approach, never missing an opportunity to recast an interaction through the Rs. Daily GLADs were never missed, no matter how busy the day, but their timing was flexible – over breakfast or dinner, waiting for the bus, waiting in line

- The course content was strongly integrated into the assessment – the vlogs brought together theory/concepts, with individual interests, reflection and creativity. I believe that the structure (focus on four concepts that you see in action, capture them in video, try to triangulate across various sources, narrate your observations and have a take-home message) was important, and also looped back to the 6 Rs. Practise, practise, practise with the AI approach. It can be uncomfortable to use AI for people used to a deficit approach (what is the problem and how do we fix it?), and practising it as a group with teacher feedback before applying it is incredibly important
- Set aside plenty of time for the post-trip debrief – ask them to review their vlogs, journals, social media posts, and so on, to remind them of what they saw, learned, felt. If possible, have them write their daily GLADs down so that they can review them in the debrief. Allow plenty of time for open discussion, but also have a structured exercise to focus their attention. I have a facilitator assist me on this, so that the students are telling the (outside) facilitator about their experience, so that he or she can probe for information. We use desirable graduate attributes and the STAR (situation, task, action, result) interview technique to get students to articulate how they have changed and grown from the experience
- One other trick that I have used in the past, but not on this course, is to get them to write themselves a postcard on the last day about what they want to take home from the experience, which I collect and mail back to them just prior to the debrief

ACTIVITY 6: CLIMATE ACTION FOR A CLIMATE-FRIENDLY EDUCATIONAL DESTINATION

Tazim Jamal, PhD[9] and Miranda Peterson[10]

DESCRIPTION

This assignment illustrates the importance of solution-based learning on climate change, enabling not just climate literacy but also constructive climate action by college students. The assignment is set up to be carried out individually and shared widely using online tools. However, doing this collaboratively in small groups is highly recommended. Facilitating student engagement and informing the student population are critical if Intergovernmental Panel on Climate Change (IPCC) 2030 and 2050 goals are to be met.

USAGE SUGGESTIONS

This action-oriented assignment is targeted at undergraduate students interested in making their college or university a climate-friendly and carbon neutral educational destination. It encourages them to be action-oriented and engaged in constructive praxis (critical action for constructive change) on climate change.

LEARNING OBJECTIVES

- Understand one's own contribution to climate change as well as the contribution of air travel in relation to tourism
- Apply learning from simulation and carbon footprint exercises plus other online searches to a real-life situation (for example, identify strategies to make a college/university a carbon neutral or carbon zero educational "destination" by 2030 or 2050)
- Analyse and evaluate various strategies to identify some key strategic priorities
- Create a final report that compiles learning and discusses (argues) the merit of key strategies recommended to enable the climate-friendly educational destination

MATERIALS LIST

- Chapters 4 and 5 plus cases 6.1 and 7.1 from *Justice and Ethics in Tourism* (Jamal, 2019)
- The En-ROADS website at www.climateinteractive.org/tools/en-roads/
- A workshop on the En-ROADS simulation exercise could be helpful to the students and the instructor. Details can be found on its website

TIME PLAN

The following task is highly flexible and can be tailored to class needs. It can be an individual or group assignment or term project. Separate forums can be set up for Points 1, 2 and 3 if it is a term project over the course of the semester.

STEP-BY-STEP PLAN

1. Students undertake three tasks (Points 1–3) individually and share them in a discussion forum with peers, focusing on Point 3 and drawing on Points 1 and 2 as needed
2. They develop an individual report based on Points 1–3 below
3. The final report should be between 1,200 and 1,300 words, excluding references and the appendix
4. A summary report compiling results from Point 3 could be made and distributed to administrators too

POINT 1: CARBON FOOTPRINT AND OFFSETTING (30 MARKS)

This exercise helps to familiarise students with some of the websites and programmes available for calculating and offsetting greenhouse gas (GHG) emissions of air travel and everyday living.

(a)   Air Travel and Carbon Offsetting

Calculate the global-warming-related impact of a future air travel activity using the calculator available at www.carbonfootprint.com/. Go to the "Calculate" tab, select "Individual" and use the Flight tab to calculate your carbon footprint for one international destination you would like to visit in the future (use round-trip, economy class). For example, you might wish to visit an ecolodge in the Canadian Rockies to do some backcountry hikes. Or you might wish to engage in volunteer tourism to help with community-based projects for clean water and women's empowerment in a less developed country.

Make notes of all relevant information, including trip origin/destination, distance flown and pounds of total warming impact of your trip. How much would it cost to offset your carbon emissions? (Write this down too.)

What does all this mean? Visit the "Offsetting" tab on the above site and read about carbon offsets. Browse the various projects where you can offset your air and car travel impact by purchasing carbon offsets on different projects.

(b)   Personal Transport (No Air Travel) and Everyday Impacts

On the same website (www.carbonfootprint.com) calculate only your personal transport impacts (car, motorbike, any public transit) over the course of one year (estimate for the past 12 months). Then look at the carbon offset options offered, which let you offset the carbon emissions from your transport activities. How many dollars would it cost to offset your personal transport impacts over the course of a year? What offset programme looked interesting?

(c)   Energy, Waste and Another Look at Transport

The US Environmental Protection Agency site has a carbon footprint calculator that allows you to calculate emissions from waste generated: www3.epa.gov/carbon-footprint-calculator/. Calculate your current emissions from waste as well as home energy and transport. Make a note of your calculations.

(d)   Report and Discuss Your Findings

- Discuss your findings from 1(a), (b) and (c) above (one–two paragraphs). Comment on your resource use and activities based on the results obtained. Where does the majority of your carbon footprint come from? What carbon offset programme would you select? Why?
- Include in your reflection any climate-friendly actions you might decide to take after undertaking the climate footprint exercise. Make this week "My Climate Action Week" and reduce your carbon footprint. For instance, walk or ride your bike, take public transit instead of driving, take your own shopping bags to the store rather than bringing plastic shopping bags home, and buy local produce and products made close to home. Support your local businesses as well as reducing carbon miles
- Report all your calculations in an appendix in your paper

TEACHING TIPS

The En-ROADS simulation exercise is a great "visioning" and literacy exercise. A trained En-ROADS facilitator could do a workshop exercise. (I have had one do a 60-minute face-to-face workshop as well as a 30-minute online workshop.) However, the En-ROADS exercise above can be done without the facilitator. It is a short, self-administered task.

POINT 2: POLICY ACTIONS FOR GLOBAL TO LOCAL SUSTAINABILITY (20 MARKS)

Climate change is affecting many destinations, ranging from low-lying coastal places to ski resorts and ecosystems worldwide. Review cases 5.1, 5.2, 6.1 and 7.1 in *Justice and Ethics in Tourism* (Jamal, 2019). Also read about the United Nations Development Programme's Sustainable Development Goal 13, which can be found on the undp.org website. Recall, too, the example of the Great Barrier Reef (GBR) provided in Chapter 4 of Jamal (2019). Check out some facts and video on the GBR, tourism and climate change impacts at www.gbrmpa .gov.au/the-reef/reef-facts.

Following the GBR example in *Justice and Ethics in Tourism* (Jamal, 2019), it can be argued that the Australian government, reef tour operators, local businesses and visitors, too, bear varying degrees of responsibility to manage climate change and conserve the reef. But what policy actions (implemented globally and domestically) are most effective to help towards destination sustainability? Do the En-ROADS simulation to gather some ideas and insights.

En-ROADS Interactive Tool (Policy Level)

En-ROADS is a transparent, freely available policy simulation model. Go to the website to find the En-ROADS simulator tool. Notice in the graph to the right that the black line represents business-as-usual policies. The blue line represents the policy scenario you will produce by adjusting the sliders below. The dotted grey lines indicate climate goals of limiting warming to +1.5°C and +2°C. Your goal in this assignment is to get the current scenario (blue line) to fall below or at the climate goals (dotted grey lines). Once you have achieved this goal, respond to the following questions:

(a)   Under the Energy Supply section, what did you decide to tax and/or subsidise?
(b)   Under the Land and Industry Emissions section, what do they mean by "Methane and Other"? (Hint: you can see an explanation by clicking on the three dots to the right)
(c)   Under the Energy Supply section, what do they mean by "Carbon Price"? (Hint: you can see an explanation by clicking on the three dots to the right)
(d)   In the Transport and Buildings and Industry sections, how important was "Energy Efficiency" and "Electrification" in your policy scenario?
(e)   Drawing on your insights from the En-ROADS simulation exercise above, list and briefly discuss three action areas (or policies) that need to be implemented to address climate change for a sustainable future. In other words, what three policy actions could be highly effective to reduce carbon dioxide (GHGs) overall and atmospheric temperature, thereby helping to reduce adverse impacts on vulnerable populations and at-risk destinations like low-lying small island nations? See case 5.1 and Chapter 4 in Jamal (2019)

POINT 3: A CLIMATE-FRIENDLY EDUCATIONAL DESTINATION (50 MARKS)

This is a continuation of the same Teaching Case assessment as in Points 1 and 2 above.

(a)   What has your college/university done in terms of environmental sustainability and reducing GHGs? List three actions that you feel are the most important to follow up on. Discuss your choices, drawing up various information sources, as well as the En-ROADS exercise and carbon footprint exercise above

(b)   Do a search online and see what other universities in the United States are doing. Provide and discuss three examples of actions other universities are taking that you feel would be good to implement at your college/university. Cite and reference the sources you use

(c)   List and discuss three other actions that your college/university can implement to become an environmentally sustainable destination. It is a "destination", hosting educational visitors (students), as well as parents and other visitors for social, cultural and educational events. Think also of connectivity of your college/university to airports, cities, and so on; and the carbon footprint of students, staff and visitors, and so on

(d)   Consider the IPCC recommendations on carbon reduction in the 21st century. Should your college/university aim to become a carbon neutral or carbon zero destination by 2030 or 2050? Discuss your response. Helpful sources are:
  •   Tollefson (2018): "IPCC says limiting global warming to 1.5C will require drastic action"
  •   IPCC Special Report on Global Warming of 1.5°C (just for your information – peruse the headline statements below): www.ipcc.ch/sr15/
  •   www.ipcc.ch/site/assets/uploads/sites/2/2019/06/SR15_Headline-statements.pdf

ACTIVITY 7: MOBILISING LEARNERS' TOURIST MEMORIES TOWARDS A DEEPER, MORE AUTHENTIC UNDERSTANDING AND PRACTICE OF TOURISM

Xavier Michel, PhD[11]

DESCRIPTION

Analysing the tourist experiences allows us to be aware of what tourism is in terms of being and dwelling (Palmer, 2018; Pernecky, 2010) in another place for discovery and leisure purposes. However, when we teach tourism, we often confine ourselves to classroom lectures, implementing a top-down, sometimes dryly academic, approach that does not always engage students in their own learning. In order to foster our students' deeper and more authentic understanding of tourism as a human phenomenon, we suggest involving them in the learning process by starting with their own tourist experiences. This approach leads us to consider the role of teacher as one who actively integrates the learners' personal lives and backgrounds into the learning experience. The approach is, thus, phenomenological and leans heavily on students' accounts of their tourist experiences, which are then related to different theories and conceptualisations in the field. The final learning objective moves beyond an academic understanding of these theories and concepts as students are asked to consider their own responsibility in fostering sustainable, ethical forms of tourism.

USAGE SUGGESTIONS

Any teaching/learning approach that leans heavily on student engagement requires a certain level of commitment and maturity of its participants. For that reason, this approach may be more suitable for graduate students or practitioners. However, depending on the nature of the students and the particular course, this approach may also work with undergraduates.

This workshop dedicated to the mobilisation of learners' accounts of experience is included within a learning unit dealing with humanities in tourism. In a whole degree plan, it is connected to other training unit(s) of travel projects. The mobilisation of these accounts has to be organised during several sessions: at least two or three two-hour sessions is a good option, to enable learners to get used to the initiative. Without having the opportunity to do a residential or itinerary trip, the sessions have preferably to be in different settings close to the learning institution. The implementation is better in pleasant surroundings to help prompt personal memories and good interactions among participants. We suggest an outdoor environment if weather conditions allow it. Depending on opportunities, one can use the outdoor area of the school/the higher education institution, and/or a particular place (in a residential centre, a museum) and/or public open place(s). Thanks to the sky and other natural and built components in a landscape, learners are often more willing to open their imagination and share their memories. Being located outdoors, the group of learners is in more of a position to develop connections in their minds between this lived learning place and their personally lived tourist places. In case of a lockdown, the workshop could be conducted online; online and outdoor, weather permitting; or using a hybrid approach, partly online and partly outdoor, again weather permitting.

LEARNING OBJECTIVES

The objectives aim to help future tourism professionals design and develop tours that will provide a meaningful, authentic experience to the participants, in no small part because they are based on ethical, sustainable principles. More precisely, these objectives aim to help students:

- Realise that every participant has different experiences, preferences and abilities in terms of tourist mobility and perception of the environment
- Know how to recognise personal authenticity in tourist experiences, even towards landscapes apparently commodified
- Identify participants who create and promote authenticity during tourist experiences, and others who have to be encouraged to perceive and experience authenticity in tourism. Both have implications in terms of conceiving, promoting and guiding tours
- Develop tours that honour the different perceptions, preferences and expectations of each participant, while adhering to the principles of ethical, sustainable tourism

PRE-WORK REQUIRED BY STUDENTS

Students should have completed one or several course(s) in human or social sciences (anthropology, human geography, philosophy, sociology) in order to thoughtfully complete the exercise. This/these course(s) can be specific to tourism studies or not.

THEORETICAL FOUNDATION

We are all connected, not just to each other but also to the places we inhabit and visit. This connection helps shape our identity. Augustin Berque (2010) writes about the human condition in connection with a milieu, arguing that we are made up partly by our own body and mind, partly by our surrounding milieu. Thus, we would not exist without this milieu, which has major implications in terms of authenticity. Authenticity is referred to as the ability to engage with every milieu, and to be open to things without imposed categories (Bonnett and Cuypers, 2003). In a learning process, "authenticity" refers to the relationship between instructors and learners, and to an engagement with the object of study (Humberstone and Stan, 2012), hence the importance of relying on outdoors to raise perceptions and memories. Tourist experiences raise global consciousness (Lew, 2018) which, in turn, can be (re-)mobilised during the learning steps. To deal with environmental ethics during the workshop, the framework of non-anthropocentric or anthropocentric ethics (Gardiner and Thompson, 2017) serves to help us think about our mode(s) of relations to the environment. The aim is not to judge every personal behaviour, but rather to think about the ways by which learners engage with the environment, given that authentic relations can be found in different environmental ethics. These ethics are connected to the tourists' authenticity in the sense that they reveal their ways of thinking, feeling and acting towards the natural and even social environment.

TIME PLAN

The exact time plan depends on the number of learners (for example, for a group of 20 learners the exercise would consist of two or three sessions of two hours' duration each).

STEP-BY-STEP PLAN

- Ask learners to think about one or several previous tourist experience(s), in order to lead to a discussion on how they lived these experiences in terms of mobility and engagement with the natural and social environments
- Organise an individual reflection time in an appropriate place (see *Usage suggestions*) to enable each learner to remember and think about their experience(s) in its dimension of being-in-the-world elsewhere and paying attention to the environment in this context
- Carry out a group discussion: each learner is asked to share their memories, and what those memories mean. Interact with the learner to facilitate their expression and to provide insights regarding personal authenticity. Here, the instructor has to draw on theories in tourism and mobility to highlight the theoretical scope revealed from these memories
- At the same time or later, compare the differences between the individual accounts, highlighting what authenticity is for each individual, and taking into account the similarities among them
- With the entire class, apply these personal accounts and meanings to the professional skills (see *Learning objectives*) needed by tour operators: their accounts and the meanings derived from them can be applied to organising tours, welcoming tourists and in some cases supporting them in their mobility trajectories (for instance, in social tourism)

TEACHING TIPS

This workshop leads learners to remember experiences, think about themselves and interact with others. You may have to know the learners' personalities to anticipate different levels of engagement with the exercise: some of them can be less able to remember, imagine, think, analyse and share what they have in mind. Conversely, others can be very talkative, the trainer having to moderate them to allow everyone to participate.

ACTIVITY 8: EXPERIENTIAL LEARNING IN NATURE-BASED RECREATIONAL SETTINGS

Sudipta Kiran Sarkar, PhD[12]

DESCRIPTION

This experiential learning activity focuses on a day field trip to a nature-based site. The objective of the trip was to engage in a nature-based activity, so that students obtain real-world knowledge (and skills) relevant to their future careers as leisure service professionals. Further, this immersive activity helps students understand and analyse the ecological and social surroundings. In the end, the main learning expectation was for the students to develop an understanding of the importance of environmental advocacy and stewardship as embedded elements of their professional field.

USAGE SUGGESTIONS

This activity is appropriate for a wide audience of tourism students (both undergraduates and graduates) and industry practitioners.

LEARNING OBJECTIVES

The objectives can be modified, according to the nature of the course, the participants and the site visited. Essentially, however, the assignment aims to help students:

- Understand the ecological and social impacts of an ostensibly benign tourism activity, such as hiking
- Acknowledge their own responsibility both as tourists and as (future) industry professionals for mitigating any negative ecological or social impacts
- Develop concrete strategies to minimise or eliminate the negative impacts and to capitalise on the positive impacts
- Foster a deeper sense of, and appreciation for, the importance of working as a team and honouring one's own and others' leadership attributes

MATERIALS LIST

Participants need appropriate clothing and footwear for a field trip to a nature site. A camera and video-recorder (for example, a cellphone) for each participant is recommended.

THEORETICAL FOUNDATION

The assignment is based on Kolb's experiential learning model (Kolb and Kolb, 2009). An important part of Kolb's model involves the student being exposed to new experiences – which may contain an element of risk insofar as the learner is required to venture outside their comfort zone. Leaving behind the urban classroom in order to hike for the better part of a day through forests, boardwalked marshes and pebbled lake shores satisfies those learning requirements for most of our city students. The group discussion afterwards on what the hike has taught us about tourism's impact and the extent to which each of us contributes to that impact satisfies the reflective and conceptualisation stages of the model. Lastly, Kolb's active experimentation stage is addressed by having students develop strategies to apply what they have learned.

TIME PLAN

The assignment is a field trip; therefore, depending on the site destination, it may require a half to full day.

STEP-BY-STEP PLAN

1. Students are introduced to the ecological and social impacts of tourism through classroom activities. The depth of, and amount of time devoted to, this introduction will vary, based on the nature of the course and the students
2. Students participate in the field trip
3. Guided by the learning outcomes listed above (and any others that individual instructors have added to suit the particular nature of their course), the instructor leads the students in a debrief of their experiences. (See *Teaching tips* for further information)

TEACHING TIPS

One of the striking observations made in my class's field trip was that the conditions provided by the natural settings led to enhanced student participation and social engagement. The challenging conditions of the terrain (that is, the hiking trail and the stream crossings) led to a range of learning opportunities for the students. Firstly, they displayed qualities of cooperation and kinship in the form of helping each other in forming human chains to make the difficult river crossings easier. Secondly, the process of engaging with the difficult terrain enabled them to have a deeper understanding of the heuristic and epistemic aspects of nature-based recreation. Another significant observation made was the display of leadership skills by some students who had prior expertise of negotiating with difficult conditions in similar natural settings.

The field trip activity also involved a post-trip reflection of the students' experiences. They were made to observe their activities by referring to photos and short videos taken by them and the instructors during the trip for observational purposes. Based on the reflections, they were required to engage in further understanding, analysing and synthesising of the key functional and critical aspects of nature-based tours and ways to engage with the ecological elements of such tours. This activity involves both lived values (social and ecological) and aspirational values of stewardship, knowledge and professionalism.

ACTIVITY 9: IOMANTE RITUALS: ECOLOGICAL AND ECONOMIC VALUES MEET CULTURAL VALUES

Chiaki Shimoyasuba, PhD[13]

DESCRIPTION

This is a conversation starter that illustrates competing ecological values between non-human animals, modernity and Indigenous traditions and beliefs.

Wildlife is an interesting and valuable tourist resource. However, conflicts between wild animals and human life, particularly in ecotourism contexts such as natural parks and agricultural, forestry and fishing areas, frequently occur. This contribution is based on the author's experience in Hokkaido, Japan, where in recent years this conflict has escalated because of maintenance of the road network and the invasion of human activities into the wilderness areas of Hokkaido. For example, brown bears have come down from the mountains in search of food and attacked humans who have entered their living space. Deer and seals who have similarly encountered – and caused damage to – humans, crops and fishing resources are being eradicated by hunters.

On the other hand, the Indigenous Ainu, who live mainly in Hokkaido, have worshipped the brown bear for generations as a god who brings food and fur to humans. They had a sacred ritual called Iomante where they killed a bear cub and sent its soul back to the world of god to thank him. This ritual was temporarily banned due to animal welfare concerns, but it is now allowed as part of Ainu folk culture. In the past, brown bears were a valuable food source for the Ainu people, and it was important to recognise the value they brought and at the same time understand the balance needed to live in harmony with wildlife in their habitat.

What lessons can be learned from Indigenous views of nature and what measures are needed for wildlife and humans to coexist in leisure and tourism settings, considering the current wildlife problem?

USAGE SUGGESTIONS

This conversation starter is suitable for both undergraduate and graduate students in tourism, biology and cultural studies programmes. It can also be used in community workshops where the aim is to highlight how different values can lead to disagreements between separate stakeholders.

LEARNING OBJECTIVES

By the end of the conversation starter, participants should be able to:

- Evaluate how wild animals and humans could and should coexist in communities and in tourism settings
- Explain the meanings that Indigenous peoples associate with nature, which are being lost in modern society
- Apply their knowledge on how wild animals should be protected and appropriately included in ecotourism

MATERIALS LIST

- Library and Internet access for information searches
- If necessary, present photos and videos of cases where the relationship between wildlife and human life is at stake

THEORETICAL FOUNDATION

This conversation starter, insofar as it presents a modern challenge related to ecological, economic and cultural values, functions as a case study of a real-life situation. Shoyama and Yamagata's work (2016) describing a regional community's residents' perceptions of competing values can be used to frame this discussion. For insight into eco literacy and postcolonial ecocriticism related to the Ainu people, see Sung and Sakoi (2017). The texts by Bricker et al. (2013) and Honey (2008) contextualise this discussion in the fields of ecotourism and sustainable tourism debates.

STEP-BY-STEP PLAN

- Ask your students to collect information on the Internet regarding the conflict between wild animals and human life
- Based on the information obtained from them, hold a group discussion as part of a workshop and discuss what kind of problems (where, when and why) are occurring
- If possible, conduct a field survey of the area where the problem is occurring, and an interview survey with stakeholders

ACTIVITY 10: META-PEDAGOGICAL MELIORISM 2: SOCIAL VALUES

Elin Bommenel, PhD,[14] **Richard Ek, PhD**[15] **and Stuart Reid**[16]

DESCRIPTION

The metaphysical concept of meliorism pivots on the idea that progress leads to improvement and that by partaking in processes, humans can improve themselves and, in the process, improve the world they are embedded in. As a cornerstone concept in liberalism, the concept is primarily associated with liberal political philosophy and philosophical pragmatism. In this contribution we transfer the spirit of the concept into the classroom. Our foundational idea is that students can improve themselves (and indirectly the world) by being aware of all that they have learned.

USAGE SUGGESTIONS

The three contributions on meta-pedagogical meliorism all relate to an introductory week for a newly arrived class of international students with pedagogically heterogenous learning backgrounds. However, the concept of teaching and learning regimes is equally applicable to industry professionals and undergraduate and graduate classes, and also for more homogenous groups who are meeting for the first time. Learning is a personal journey, but teaching seldom makes meta-pedagogy overt. All the activities involved with these contributions are aimed at highlighting this fact.

LEARNING OBJECTIVE

By the end of this activity participants should be able to:

*   Acknowledge their own individual "baggage" when it comes to knowledge, and the institutional learning context they have been inculcated into during earlier university studies

THEORETICAL FOUNDATION

This contribution is based on insights from the research on teaching and learning regimes, as proposed by Trowler and Cooper (2002). The teaching and learning regimes originally were a way of explaining why university teachers experienced problems when moving between the learning environment of an educational development programme and the teaching environment of their home department. The crash of different value systems and of hardened practices caused confusion, anger and resistance towards new ways. The experiences of the students, journeying from one learning environment to a new one, may be understood and facilitated using Trowler and Cooper's tools. Knowledge that is usually created and elaborated upon backstage (among university teachers and in courses for university faculty) is, in our meta-pedagogical meliorism, brought frontstage among the students, as we share with them our views on learning and the production of knowledge.

TIME PLAN

We have chosen to divide the introduction week into six phases with some online preparations. This contribution on social values covers phase one. Phases two and three are covered in Chapter 11 on knowledge, and phases four to six are covered in Chapter 1 on didactics. In our case we dedicated one week to this process, but it is possible to tailor the time and resources dedicated to this programme task. It is, however, our experience that the students need a full week to allow time for contemplation, reflection and engagement in different learning tasks. This is particularly the case if the student cohort comes from all parts of the world (as in our case), bringing all sorts of teaching and learning regimes with them.

STEP-BY-STEP PLAN

Phase One: When Did You Learn Something?

The first step is to introduce the notion that "learning" is a verb, something all humans actively engage in. Furthermore, learning is also a social activity, involving both formal and informal interactions with people and resources. Learning can be a collective effort, as in class. Learning can also take place seemingly in isolation, as an individual process, but it nevertheless relies on resources that are produced with a purpose. A concrete learning experience is individual in the sense that an individual conceptualises and admits that it is a learning experience. Consequently, the learning experience is a social construct, whatever its form or content: understanding a specific concept, realising a cause and effect, gaining a new corporal skill, finding out that a certain procedure does not work, and so on. These are all fundamentally social processes.

The introduction week is mostly seminar based but complemented with online films on generic concepts, online reflections with peer review, lectures, and individual and group-based assignments.

To have a common language on Day One, students have watched short films where we define concepts like learning, knowledge, teaching and learning regime, conceptual change, the deep approach and surface approach to learning, communities of practice and motivation. They have reflected on the content and commented on the reflections of other students.

On Day One they thus have a basic but shared vocabulary about learning – the vocabulary of their teachers.

A morning session on Day One offers an opportunity for the students to reflect over their own vocabulary and their experiences, when we encourage them to speak up and mull over when in life they learned something:

- What did you learn?
- How did it happen?
- Who was important to the learning?

TEACHING TIPS

The seminar can be organised differently depending on the number of students, the localities, and so on, and may also be done as a discussion in pairs on the web, should restrictions make face-to-face meeting impossible. The key here is to communicate the importance of dialogue in these settings, to show how talking, listening and learning are intertwined. It is an opportunity for the students to "take place" orally; that is, to consciously create their own persona in relation and response to others, and experience that they are in a social setting of people with diverse understandings and experiences.

The pedagogical insight the student should take away is that learning is, besides a collective endeavour, something that each decides on their own; that is, socially constructed. This should create an awareness that learning is an enterprise, or an active undertaking, something that they have to work with in an active way. Traditional lectures are a possibility, but perhaps not what works best in this context.

Different categories of knowledge and other insights from the field of epistemology can instead be revealed in the dialogue of the seminar/webinar, unfolded in responses to the students' recapitulations of different learning occasions.

ACTIVITY 11: THE VALUE OF THE UNINTENDED IN TOURISM EDUCATION: NEPAL

Helene Balslev Clausen, PhD[17] and Maggie C. Miller, PhD[18]

DESCRIPTION

Before departure, we as field course educators seek to plan, control and organise a comprehensive and intentional travel and education itinerary. We identify the predictable as well as acknowledge potential situations and events that might undermine or enhance learning experiences for our students. Yet even in overly intended, well-planned educational contexts, there is always a chance for the unintended to occur. That said, our purpose here is to resist the temptation to oversimplify the unintended, and instead draw attention to its inherent pedagogical value. Thus, we use this contribution to explore "trouble" – the "unintended" and "unexpected" – in experience-based and field course learning scenarios.

USAGE SUGGESTIONS

This activity would be relevant for a wide range of learners: both undergraduate and graduate students in various programmes, as well as practitioners.

LEARNING OBJECTIVES

- Appreciate how unintended situations in field courses can become deep learning experiences
- Reflect upon the learning opportunities presented by "trouble" in the field
- Identify the personal values that help foster the above two learning objectives

THEORETICAL FOUNDATION

It is critical for tourism education to emphasise the importance of contextual learning, such as field-based activities, whereby teaching and learning become embodied, emplaced, sensorial and empathetic (Clausen and Andersson, 2018; Pink, 2015): a notion understood by Wenger (1998) as "knowing in practice" (p. 141). Rather than simply facilitating opportunities and providing tools to engage and critically analyse from a distance (that is, within the walls of a university), we suggest that field courses, and more specifically "unintended" encounters that emerge in these contexts, are pivotal for students' intellectual and critical development. Indeed, knowing in practice affords opportunities for students to unpack their privileges and reflect on their roles as future tourism practitioners and, more broadly, as responsible citizens of the world.

FIELD SCENARIO: AN ENCOUNTER WITH INFRASTRUCTURE AND ACCESS CHALLENGES IN DHORPATAN, NEPAL

In the spring of 2019, 15 undergraduate management students took part in a two-week field-based course to Nepal as part of a "Tourism in Practice" module. Working closely with a variety of community-based tourism initiatives, as well as local teaching and learning partners (for example, Tribhuvan University, Outdoor Adventure Centre) throughout Nepal, students were exposed to the potential impacts and challenges of tourism development in a less developed region. A major component of the field course involved comparing and analysing two regions of Nepal as sites for adventure tourism development and management (trekking, mountain biking, and so on). The Annapurna Conservation Area Project (ACAP), the first conservation and protected area in Nepal, was designated as the first region students would appraise; ACAP had already been recognised for its careful management, sustainable development and positive contributions to local communities. On the other hand, the second region students visited to appraise was the Dhorpatan Valley, which is still in its infancy with tourism development.

The trip was to conclude with a multi-stakeholder consultation forum with various community and government representatives in Burtibang, a regional town within the Dhorpatan region. Here, based upon their research and findings, students were to present proposals for future tourism development opportunities for the Dhorpatan community. Hours before this stakeholder forum, however, the expected direction of the field course took an unintended turn. En route to the forum, the wheel on the students' bus came off, unexpectedly stranding the entire group in the middle of the remote mountains of Dhopatan. As the situation unfolded, they were not only growing anxious about their previously arranged multi-stakeholder presentations (which were also to be graded), but the gravity of the situation that could have been also began to sink in ... luckily for all, the unintended wheel mishap did not occur on a cliff's edge!

TEACHING TIPS

After safely returning from the "unintended" bus incident, the course leaders hosted a briefing for students to discuss and reflect upon their experiences and feelings. Though reflective briefings were hosted most days, this one felt particularly eye-opening: students spoke of increased feelings of fear and anxiety, but also of a heightened awareness of the infrastructure challenges throughout Nepal.

As a pedagogical practice, dialogue and discussions encourage students to draw connections between academic content, their own lives and society more broadly (Peterson, 2009). Additionally, exploring one's feelings is an integral aspect in reflection (cf. Gibbs, 1988; Jasper, 2013), yet apprehending and then articulating such sentiments can sometimes feel difficult and perhaps make the speaker feel vulnerable (cf. Johnson, 2009). Thus, it is important for leaders to cultivate a safe space for students to explore and identify "what happened", their feelings and thoughts about these experiences as well as any key learnings that can be carried forward.

Finally, field courses and contextual learning provide learning enhancement outcomes for the students including increased student satisfaction, greater "classroom" participation and engagement, as well as opportunities to create an international learning community. For instance, this field-based trip afforded students opportunities to directly interact with local stakeholders from university, community, practitioner and various NGO groups, which facilitated cooperative and integrative teaching and learning.

ACTIVITY 12: THE TOURISM GAME 1

Johan Edelheim, PhD[19]

DESCRIPTION

The activity involves a roleplaying game, "The Tourism Game", adapted from Stephen Fairbrass' (n.d.) original concept. It takes place in a hypothetical country called Latasica and brings together a number of different issues connected with tourism and values. The activity aims to show the good that tourism can bring to communities, but it simultaneously emphasises the need for a holistic perspective that is grounded in a range of lived and aspirational values, rather than being built on one exclusive (that is, economic) set of values.

USAGE SUGGESTIONS

The game has 12 roles (see Fairbrass), and in order to have a multitude of opinions one should try to use as many of them as possible. In cases where the class is bigger, students can be divided into pairs, or groups of up to five members, each group given one role to play. Playing in small groups adds a level of reality, as groups of people inherently will have a range of different interpretations of their reality, even when being placed in the same situation.

The point of the game is to imagine the realities lived in a developing country where a new (mass) tourism development is proposed, and to negotiate between the groups on what is an acceptable way to proceed as a society. The roleplay basis is simple. It is designed for high school students, but has been played by both undergraduate and graduate students. The role play can be played once, if there is a workshop that needs a half-day programme, or it can be played as a recurring activity in a 15-week course, as was the case when I used it.

LEARNING OBJECTIVES

By the end of the exercise, students will have acquired:

* A deeper understanding of social roles and inequities that shape individual decision-making
* An appreciation of tourism as a phenomenon that signifies modern society

MATERIALS LIST

For a full set of "The Tourism Game" with an outline of the case, the roles and how to moderate it, see Activity 53.

Ahead of class, print out the different roles and give each group the one-sheet explanation of that role's priorities and interests. If possible, let the participants choose their role in advance, and send them the sheet by email ahead of class. In cases where the roles are given in class, let the participants read through their role for 10–20 minutes, take notes and discuss within the group what that role might think of the tourism development that is proposed.

PRE-WORK REQUIRED BY STUDENTS

If your students are not tourism majors, an introduction into academic tourism studies can be given through a lecture explaining the Whole Tourism System (WTS) theory (Leiper, 2004). It is common among non-tourism students to imagine that "everyone knows tourism", since most people in developed nations have at some point of their lives been a tourist – this theory gives an insight into why that perception might not be true.

THEORETICAL FOUNDATION

Holistic education is linked to philosophies that emphasise the interconnection between people and their contexts, freedom of thought and the inherent good that each person can strive for (Miller, 2019). A majority of holistic education practitioners work in the field of primary education, and even preschool pedagogy, but there are also examples in secondary and tertiary education (Palmer et al., 2010). There are so far very few published accounts of holistic education in tourism higher education (Inui et al., 2006), and even fewer set in a virtual context.

The role play was not assessed on its own, as the intention with having the game in the course was to allow all students to assume the mindset of different kinds of value positions that diverse groups in society hold, live by and draw on to shape their actions. The assessable item was based on the students' reflection on the game, and if, or how, the game changed their views of tourism and values that shape tourism around the world. Reflexivity and reflections are integral components of holistic learning (Alvesson and Sköldberg, 2009). By taking stock of our assumptions and attitudes, we come to understand better the values that shape our actions – and those of others.

TIME PLAN

The roleplay case and functions are explained in the first joint session. All participants get a printout of the case, so that they can familiarise themselves with the premises of the situation.

The first round of the game is often where participants need most support to get going. It is useful to ask all roles in advance for a list of three other roles that they would like to negotiate with ahead of the next round. This speeds up the allocation of negotiating parties and makes the process of switching negotiation partners more fluent.

Allow for each meeting between two roles to take approximately ten minutes (it generally takes a shorter time with fewer participants in each role), and signal to the whole class when it is time to change over to the next negotiation. Let two, or a maximum of three, negotiations take place per session; this keeps all participants alert.

At the end of the second session where a round is played, call the whole class together and determine if the planned development should be allowed or not. This determination can be done in many ways, and each has its own strong points. One way is to have a vote between all roles and let the highest number rule. For this option it is necessary to decide if the "international" roles have a say in the country's internal affairs, or if it is only the "domestic" roles that get to vote. Another option is for the "government" role to implement a decision based on evidence (and lobbying) that they have received.

Allow for 20–30 minutes to debrief after the decision is made so that different roles can explain how satisfied or dissatisfied they are, as well as why they feel that way.

New roles can be chosen for new rounds whereby the same role play is played out. Even though the roleplay case and the roles are simple, this role exchange still gives the participants plenty of opportunities to "live" and think of the world from different perspectives.

Based on my experience, the COVID-19 pandemic in 2020 gave the role play a totally new dimension, as the students could follow first-hand what happened to communities dependent on tourism at a time when no tourism took place.

STEP-BY-STEP PLAN

The evaluation component of the game requires each student group to write a reflective report that shows how their perception of two given values changed during the course of the game, if they changed. The group report requires students to negotiate internally what to reflect on. The unit where the game was implemented was at the first-year level, and the reflective report was therefore stipulated to be less than 1,000 words. The grade breakdown was as follows:

- Structure and format (10 per cent)
- Description of the group and how they played together (brief overview of group and how different group members contributed; explain also how the group made decisions and decided on what other groups you needed to negotiate with) (20 per cent)
- Presentation of two chosen values (give a short explanation of any two values that were discussed in the unit; use own definitions, explanations and comments to peers as a basis) (30 per cent)
- Reflection of what has changed during the course of the game (explain how and why your initial impression of your chosen values changed or did not change when playing the game; reflect on whether this influences the way that value is viewed in society, too) (40 per cent)

TEACHING TIPS

It is important to highlight at the start that simulations and role plays are always abstractions of reality and, therefore, never perfect illustrations of real life. The point is not for the role play to illustrate exactly a situation in one place, but rather to act as a metaphor for how something works in many places.

It is important for the teacher to be familiar with the case, to plan role interactions in advance, and to pick up on clues from discussions between roles that might need to be debriefed after the game has been brought to a conclusion, such as power relations between international and domestic actors.

ACTIVITY 13: FILM AND TOURISM: CONSTRUCTING SOCIAL REALITIES

Johan Edelheim, PhD[20]

DESCRIPTION

"Film and Tourism" is an elective master's-level course offered university-wide, thus attracting students from various disciplines. The course is not related to film/media-induced tourism, but rather the other way around. Media-induced tourism focuses on how tourist destinations and attractions are construed and promoted through different media portrayals. This course investigates instead how tourism as the central phenomenon is portrayed and understood in films. What tourism does, is and has as its purpose is by no means self-evident. The core of the course circles around social constructionism and foundational philosophies. Students are given readings relating to paradigms, epistemology, ontology, axiology, constructionism and visual methods. These readings are coupled with the viewing of different films (both fiction and documentaries). The ongoing assignment that students have is to write reflective pieces on the films that are viewed together in class, using the theories presented in their readings as their basis. The final assignment is for all students to create their own mini film in which they investigate a tourism-related matter from the perspective of one of the theories discussed in class.

USAGE SUGGESTIONS

This contribution is suited for graduate students or final-year undergraduates, as it links research methods and investigations of knowledge creation to a deeper understanding of how tourism is understood in society. The teaching is based on a flipped-classroom methodology where students prepare for class by summarising given readings and then alternately lead the class discussion about the methodological or philosophical implications the readings have on social constructs and realities.

LEARNING OBJECTIVES

Students should be able to:

- Explain the research paradigm they feel comfortable in, and evaluate why they value that paradigm
- Differentiate between textual, intertextual and discursive elements of films viewed, to pinpoint how understandings of tourism are created
- Create a mini film that uses a foundational philosophy to reflect on how some aspect of tourism is valued in society

MATERIALS LIST

- A book of readings with selected articles and book chapters aimed at highlighting and questioning different theoretical concepts as a basis for film reflections
- A list of suitable films and documentaries that are to be viewed in class. This course uses *The Art of Travel* (2004), a filmatisation of Alain de Botton's philosophical thoughts about tourism; *Only Yesterday* (1991), an animated fiction film directed by Isao Takahata; *My Long Neck* (2013), a documentary about ethnic tourism and identity by Shalom Almond; *The Beach* (2000), a fiction film about backpacking by Danny Boyle; and *Total Recall* (1990), a science-fiction film by Paul Verhoeven. *Bye, Bye Barcelona* (2014) by Eduardo Chibás Fernández was used at an earlier stage but was later replaced
- Audio-visual equipment in a classroom, or a streaming device for virtual classrooms
- Students will need smartphones or digital cameras to film with – smartphones have been found to be quite sufficient for most tasks
- Film editing software such as iMovie or Adobe's Premiere Pro. If the university has computer labs with software installed, it might be offered to students who have not got access to free software on their own computers
- Classroom version: preferably a room that can be made totally dark, and moveable tables/chairs, so that the initial part of the class can be conducted in seminar settings with discussion across the room easily facilitated. The latter (major) part of all film viewing classes should allow for a full immersion in the film
- Online version: a learning platform (or platforms) where readings and recordings are provided, as well as a live streaming system to discuss theories and watch films together. (Note: there are limitations to streaming copyrighted films on many teaching platforms, so some inventiveness is needed to facilitate this)

PRE-WORK REQUIRED BY STUDENTS

Understanding how paradigms and the foundational philosophies (ontology, epistemology and axiology) form each researcher's own research projects would be beneficial.

THEORETICAL FOUNDATION

This course combines readings from social constructivism, philosophy, research methodologies and visual methodologies. For relevant sources, see Hillman and Radel (2018) as well as Rakic and Chambers (2012).

TIME PLAN

The course has been offered both as a two-week intensive course, and also spread over a full semester (15 weeks). Both versions function, though the intensive course was challenging for all involved, and alterations of assessments might be necessary. Note, the films are between 49 and 119 minutes long, so you need double classes, or classes scheduled at the end of a day (and flexible students), in order to run both the discussion before the film and the full film in one go. The step-by-step plan below is based on the full-semester alternative.

STEP-BY-STEP PLAN

1. Make a list of your own each time you come across films, documentaries, TV series or games that construe tourism based on different societal values
2. Review your list, re-watch the film and determine if it can be screened in a classroom setting. Have warnings ahead of screening films that contain violence, sex, nudity, alcohol or drug use. Your students will giggle at the warnings, but it might save you a lot of trouble down the line
3. Match films with good readings that allow students to apply the theories presented in their reflections
4. Lay out the classes with five films interspersed fortnightly from the second session onwards
5. Use the alternate weeks to discuss the students' reflections in class. This is crucial for students to reach beyond the textual to intertextual and discursive levels of the films
6. Schedule two or three workshops without theory content where students are to present their (a) film idea, (b) film script and (c) pre- and post-production preparations
7. Have a final session where the students' own films are screened. Hand out an evaluation sheet where students are asked to evaluate their peers' films based on their ability to clarify a foundational philosophy and to deconstruct a tourism-related issue in society. You can even make it a "cinema event" where other students and colleagues are invited too

TEACHING TIPS

Some students will initially struggle to go beyond the textual level (the storyline of the film). Ask them to think of the film as a metaphor: it is not its direct representation that is of interest. Instead, what is under examination is the shadow it reflects of the society it is created in. Ask students to think of what, how and why tourism is construed as it is.

Tom Barrance's excellent website Learn about Film can be used as a reference. The media package for sale on the site might be purchased for educational settings for students to learn film making step-by-step: www.learnaboutfilm.com/making-a-film/organising-filmmaking-process/.

ACTIVITY 14: VALUES-BASED LEARNING AND STORYTELLING

Brendan Paddison, PhD[21]

DESCRIPTION

This activity seeks to illustrate how values-based learning can be achieved through storytelling. The latter is a pedagogical approach to help students develop criticality, empathy and reflectivity. As part of this activity, students collect and interpret stories of past encounters in tourism. These stories are then used as a resource for understanding of, and reflecting upon, experiences of travel within the context of authentic learning. This activity provides opportunities for remembering, conversation and reflection, enabling positive social change by facilitating cultural awareness among learners. The intention is for a community of practice to emerge, which is concerned with the collaborative engagement of stakeholders (for example, students, academics and community members) through shared knowledge and understanding.

USAGE SUGGESTIONS

This activity would be relevant for undergraduate and graduate students in tourism or tourism-related programmes. The activity is ideally positioned within a seminar/workshop and would be facilitated over a number of weeks, involving a combination of field work and in-class activities. The activity can easily be adapted for online delivery, with both the field work and class-based activities delivered online. The narratives and stories collected could be based on any type of holiday or travel experience and do not necessarily need to focus on overseas travel.

LEARNING OBJECTIVES

On completion of this activity, learners will have:

- Evaluated the historical development of tourism through self-reflection and knowledge co-creation
- Developed an understanding of, and applied key skills in, data collection, analysis and the presentation of findings
- Demonstrated their comprehension of capturing, developing and understanding storytelling
- Synthesised conversations, stories and reflections to develop cultural awareness of the evolution of travel through an audio presentation

MATERIALS LIST

- Audio recorder
- Sticky notes
- Pens

PRE-WORK REQUIRED BY STUDENTS

In advance of this activity, students may wish to explore the following:

- The historical development of tourism: with a specific focus on the period after World War II, which experienced a significant expansion in domestic and overseas leisure travel and the development of mass tourism. The beginning of this period in modern tourism was characterised by new destinations, infrastructures and travel by air, leading to new experiences for both travellers and host communities
- Storytelling: tools, techniques and approaches to storytelling

THEORETICAL FOUNDATION

Storytelling informs nearly every aspect of social and cultural life, allowing for the sharing of customs, values, perceptions, memories and knowledge. Stories are reconstructions of experiences, remembered and told from a particular perspective (Coulter et al., 2007). They do not present "life as lived". Instead, they are representations of those lives. Storytelling has the ability to educate, inform, motivate and provoke a response, whether emotional or action-oriented. Stories and storytelling can associate understanding, organise information and interpret past events. It enables those engaged to begin to understand the world around them and the values and experiences that guide those interpretations (Deniston-Trochta, 2003). Consequently, complex patterns, identity construction and reconstruction, and evidence of social discourses that impact a person's knowledge creation from specific cultural standpoints, may emerge. Stories can be therapeutic and catalysts for change (Koch, 1998).

As a pedagogical strategy, storytelling is not a new phenomenon. Yet, as an approach to teaching and learning, the potential of storytelling in education has been underestimated (Landrum et al., 2019). As an educational tool, storytelling allows for a wider appreciation of the external influences that shape our understanding, facilitating transformative pedagogy and developing critical and multicultural understandings. Storytelling can contribute to the dialogical educational development of students and facilitate the processes of self-reflection and knowledge co-creation. Storytelling is a powerful means of communication (Koch, 1998) and is not necessarily limited to the written word. Performance, narratives and imagery are also methods of capturing stories (Christensen, 2012).

TIME PLAN

This contribution could be completed over four weeks or could be shortened, depending on access to data.

STEP-BY-STEP PLAN

1.   Field Work (1–2 Weeks)

Students should collect primary data on travel and holiday experiences, ideally between 1950 and 1975. Conversational interviews should be conducted which draw on the thoughts, memories and stories of people's holiday experiences as a topic designed to capture memories of travel as a tool for reminiscence. Respondents could include parents, grandparents, family members and friends. It is recommended that these interviews be audio-recorded.

Respondents should be encouraged to "tell their stories" and to reflect upon their first experience of travel either at home or abroad. The focus here is on finding out how it felt to be in a different place – that is, a town, region or country – for the first time and the instances that people remembered most about their experience of travel and of being in a new environment. Topics of conversation could include the journey, the food, the weather, the people, the language, funny incidents, the hotel, how it felt then and how they feel now.

2.   Looking for Themes (2-Hour Workshop)

Using the data collected from the conversational interviews, working in small groups listen to the audio and identify key themes emerging from the data. These themes could focus on the following: the journey, the food, the weather, the people, the language, funny incidents, the lodging, how it felt then and how they feel now.

Use these themes to create an audio summary of each interview. For example, students should take sound bites from each interview which help to tell the story for each respondent of their first holiday experience.

3.   Students' Stories (Depending on Size of Group, up to 2 Hours' Workshop Activity)

Set-up
Divide the class into small groups of 4–6 people. Each group is to have sticky notes and pens. The goal of this activity is to connect stories in an interesting way. Students are to tell their own story of their first experience of a holiday. These stories should be shared with the group in a round-table-style activity and discussion.

Activity
The first student begins by sharing an interesting memory or experience that they have of travel or a holiday. Members of the group are to write a few memorable words or phrases on a sticky note about each story.

Once each member of the group has shared their stories, the group should connect together the memorable words or phrases to create one story linking all experiences shared.

You may ask the group to share the entire story with the whole class.

4.   Comparing Stories (Depending on Size of Group, up to 2 Hours' Workshop Activity)

In small groups, students are to compare their stories with the stories collected as part of the field work.

Topics for discussion may include:

- How do the stories of those who travelled from the 1950s onward compare to your own travel experiences?
- Are there any examples which stand out as being very different?

- Can you identify any similarities?
- How has travel evolved since the 1950s onward?
- What might the future of travel and tourism look like?

TEACHING TIPS

Students should feel comfortable sharing their travel experiences with their peers. Some form of ice-breaker activity may be needed to create a sense of community and a safe space to share stories.

ACTIVITY 15: EXPERIENTIAL LEARNING IN GASTRONOMY TOURISM

Sudipta Kiran Sarkar, PhD[22]

DESCRIPTION

This assignment helps students identify values that enrich and sustain a community's culinary-based culture. Working in small groups, students visit and experience first-hand popular street food "trails" (including farmers' markets) in order to assess the extent to which the street food operations preserve the community's culinary cultural heritage and contribute to its overall well-being. The groups then identify the social, economic and environmental values associated with positive outcomes – as well as any infrastructure, logistical or marketing issues that may influence the values.

USAGE SUGGESTIONS

This assignment primarily targets undergraduates in a food- or culinary-based programme. The assignment's activities and learning outcomes, however, would also be appropriate for a range of related courses and programmes (for example, in social sciences or business).

LEARNING OBJECTIVES

The assignment aims to help students:

- Identify qualities (or "wow" factors) of food vendor operations that reflect the community's culinary tradition and heritage
- Determine what social, economic and environmental values are reflected in those qualities (or "wow" factors)
- Identify the infrastructural, logistical and marketing issues within which food entrepreneurs operate – and their impact on the operation's values
- Develop strategies to foster strong social, economic and environmental values within street food operations

MATERIALS LIST

Visiting the street food sites means eating at the street food sites. The costs are relatively inexpensive; nonetheless, students should be prepared for this expense. If the sites are local, transportation costs will be minimal. Out-of-town sites will require that each student group arranges (and pays for) its own transportation. A camera (for example, a cellphone) per group is recommended.

THEORETICAL FOUNDATION

The assignment is based on Kolb's experiential learning model (Kolb and Kolb, 2009). An important part of Kolb's model involves the student being exposed to new experiences – which may contain an element of risk insofar as the learner is required to venture outside their comfort zone. Leaving behind the classroom in order to visit and assess various street food operations, either local or out-of-town, satisfies those learning requirements for most of our students (that is, they are being asked to "see" the street food vendor from a different perspective – less the perspective of consumer and more that of detached scholar). The discussion afterwards on what has been learned about gastronomy tourism's impact on a community's culinary cultural heritage and the extent to which that impact revolves around values satisfies the reflective and conceptualisation stages of the model. Lastly, Kolb's active experimentation stage is addressed by having students develop strategies to apply what they have learned.

TIME PLAN

The visit to the street food sites takes place out of class (that is, each student group arranges to visit the sites on its own time; depending on site proximity, the groups can expect to spend anywhere from several hours to one full day for their visit). The amount of time spent in class (see *Step-by-step plan*) will vary, depending on the nature of the course and the class size. It is, however, a major assignment; therefore, an appropriate amount of time should be spent on the pre-visit material re food entrepreneurship, culinary heritage and values.

STEP-BY-STEP PLAN

1. Students are introduced to food entrepreneurship and its relationship to a community's culinary cultural heritage
2. Students are introduced to values, the different ways values are reflected in gastronomy tourism and the impact of values on the well-being of the business and its community
3. In preparation for the food vendor visits, students select their groups and the sites they will visit:
   • For my particular course, the sites were selected primarily based on class discussions and informed by recommendations laid down in the online platforms – websites and blogs – of city-based and national tourism promotion agencies
   • The number of groups created was proportionate to the number of sites to be visited, and the sites were allotted to the groups based on the principle of a "pick the chit" game; that is, each site is written on a piece of paper, which is then folded, and each group gets to work on the site identified in the paper chit it picks up

4. After the site visits, at least one session (preferably more) should be devoted to organising and writing a 1,500-word reflective report, and at least one session to presenting the report findings

TEACHING TIPS

In case of a lockdown, the learning objectives could be achieved through virtual tours of the sites, online meetings with entrepreneurs and local communities involved in food heritage of the sites, as well as analysis of websites and social media content – vlogs, Facebook and Instagram content.

A combination of these elements will ensure an engagement process for the students that aligns with the assignment's theoretical foundations.

ACTIVITY 16: ACCESS RIGHTS TO THE COMMONS

Chiaki Shimoyasuba, PhD[23]

DESCRIPTION

This conversation starter is a case study that exposes students to the importance of building consensus among stakeholders on the ecological and social values of local resources. This local consensus is essential for the conservation and utilisation of a community's natural and cultural heritage.

In recent years, rural areas of Japan, including Hokkaido, have been experiencing serious regional problems stemming from aging landowners and a declining population that has led to an increase in abandoned cultivated land, absentee landowners, vacant houses, a decline in economic activity and the disappearance of villages. These challenges are jointly leading to a loss of the region's social customs.

In order to address these problems, we need input and consensus from various stakeholders on how to conserve and utilise the local natural and cultural heritage; and also, an agreement on whether promoting these regions as tourist destinations would address the problems mentioned above. However, ownership of land and buildings is strongly embedded in the Japanese culture, which creates a challenge in terms of conserving and utilising tourism resources since these resources include a large amount of private property. One way to deal with this challenge is by creating an access to common resources by evoking a concept prevalent in the UK: the Commons; that is, resources held in common by a community (Berkes et al., 1989). This solution entails regulating private property of resources to some extent.

Regarding the social value of local resources, another important issue is how to coordinate with landholders and other stakeholders to promote ecotourism and green tourism that ensures sustainable development of local resources.

USAGE SUGGESTIONS

This assignment targets both undergraduate and graduate students in tourism, policy and area planning programmes.

LEARNING OBJECTIVES

*   Define and distinguish among basic concepts of "the common lands" of Japan, "the Commons" in UK and "Nordic access rights" (Ostrom, 1990)
*   Elucidate the causes of conflicts between landowners and stakeholders (for example, tourists who hike on footpaths and trails)
*   Consider measures to reach consensus on the social value of ecological resources

THEORETICAL FOUNDATION

This assignment, insofar as it presents a modern challenge related to social and cultural values, functions as a case study of a real-life situation (McHarg, 1992). The teaching/learning approach follows the Saitou pedagogy (Miyazaki, 2011) by creating a joint, equitable dialogue among all participants, where no one voice is given prominence over another. The combined outcome is therefore polyphonic.

TIME PLAN

The assignment can be spread out over three separate lectures: the first one introducing the concept and setting the research task for students, the second where the actual dialogue happens in class and a third where the polyphonic voice is revisited and reflected upon.

STEP-BY-STEP PLAN

Ask your students to collect information from academic literature, newspaper articles and the Internet. This case is based on the Japanese example, but similar set-ups would be appropriate for other locations, too.

*   Gather information on Japanese common lands, UK Commons and footpaths, and Scandinavian access rights from academic and popular literature and the Internet
*   Gather case study information about walking tourism, such as footpaths, long trails and pilgrimages to sacred sites

Set the following task for students to consider: to what extent can land and building owners' rights be restricted according to the same logic as British footpaths and the Commons for the sustainable development of local resources? Ask the participants to consider concrete examples.

TEACHING TIPS

It is noticeable that Saitou pedagogy allows for disagreement and contradictions in its process, but that it aims for a harmony to be restored. Miyazaki comments (2011) that there are four contradictions in play in Saitou pedagogy classrooms: (1) among students, (2) between students and material in use, (3) between students and the teacher and (4) between the teacher and the material. Finding a true polyphonic voice is therefore a skill honed with practice.

ACTIVITY 17: ENHANCING CULTURALLY SENSITIVE TOURISM IN AN ONLINE LEARNING ENVIRONMENT

Mette Simonsen Abildgaard, PhD,[24] **Emily Höckert, PhD,**[25] **Outi Kugapi, MSocSci,**[26] **Monika Lüthje, PhD**[27] **and Carina Ren, PhD**[28]

DESCRIPTION

As global interests increase in the Arctic, there is a pressing need to rethink the ways Indigenous and other local cultures are presented and visited in the region (Olsen et al., 2019). Through an online learning environment, we wish to foster knowledge and reflection about culturally sensitive tourism encounters among different kinds of tourism actors. Cultural sensitivity is understood here as a framework for developing tourism products and services, and for approaching tourism encounters in general, in ways that enhance recognition, respect and reciprocity towards otherness (Viken et al., 2021).

The content of the online learning platform is produced within the ARCTISEN – Culturally Sensitive Tourism in the Arctic project through extensive desk studies and stakeholder interviews across Arctic Norway, Finland, Sweden and Greenland, and desk studies in Arctic Canada (Olsen et al., 2019). The course draws focus to harmful legacies of stereotyping, assimilation and appropriation in Arctic tourism, and sensitises the students to recognise cultural values and diversity and possibilities of intercultural collaboration. Hence, our aim is to enable the course participants to work in culturally sensitive ways with local cultures in order to make tourism more culturally sustainable. The open-access online platform contains versatile materials in a modular course format that are easy to approach by both practitioners and students regardless of their physical location. The online platform is accessible at www .learn-cultural-tourism.com.

The core component of the course environment is eight videos addressing cultural sensitivity in tourism under different themes. During the videos, the stakeholders share their views, challenges and solutions for culturally sensitive tourism. The platform also contains Prezis (visual presentations) about challenges and opportunities of culturally sensitive tourism, a map of ethical guidelines for tourism in the Arctic area, tests, blog posts and other materials offering versatile learning possibilities for different students with different learning styles. Self-reflective writing assignments form a central component of the course, as several studies on intercultural sensitivity emphasise reflection (see Bennett, 1986; Hurst et al., 2020; Saari et al., 2020, pp. 103–104). Exchange of ideas is enabled by Padlets (online notice boards) where students can share their reflections anonymously and learn from others' thoughts.

USAGE SUGGESTIONS

Our online learning environment welcomes anyone interested in learning about cultural sensitivity in tourism. The participant must, however, be able to study in English. The learning environment is developed for people working in the tourism business, planning and development as well as tourism students from vocational school to university undergraduate level. The online course consists of modules that can be studied for free at any time. All who pass the course receive a certificate to acknowledge their skills.

The online course is structured around five practice-oriented modules and one module with more academic content for university students. Tourism companies can integrate any number of the modules in the training of their staff, as can educational institutions in their curricula.

LEARNING OBJECTIVES

After the course, the participant will be able to:

- Identify the meanings of cultural sensitivity in tourism and develop skills related to them
- Recognise, describe and reflect upon challenges related to cultural sensitivity in tourism and particularly in their own tourism-related work
- Create and apply culturally sensitive approaches in their tourism-related work by using practical tools given during the course

MATERIALS LIST

To study in the online learning environment, the student needs an open mind and a computer with Internet access. Moreover, we recommend pen and paper for self-reflection and taking notes.

PRE-WORK REQUIRED BY STUDENTS

Since the online course is meant for participants with varied backgrounds, no pre-work is required. Nevertheless, the participants are expected to join with some background knowledge about tourism practices.

THEORETICAL FOUNDATION

Theoretically, our learning environment draws inspiration from Milton J. Bennett's (1986) model on developing intercultural sensitivity. Bennett's writings clarify why and how we experience cultural differences and attach meanings to them. Drawing on Bennett's theory (1986, p. 180), we define cultural sensitivity as an orientation that we can develop and strengthen by enhancing both cultural self-awareness and other-culture awareness. This means that cultural sensitivity simultaneously shapes, and is shaped by, different kinds of intercultural tourism encounters (Viken et al., 2021). More on Bennett's model, and intercultural development research, can be found through this site: www.idrinstitute.org/dmis/.

TIME PLAN

The course is divided into six modules. The scope of the course is 1 ECTS[29] for practitioners, translating into 27 hours of studying, and 2 ECTS – or 54 hours – for university students.

STEP-BY-STEP PLAN

The six modules are divided in the following way:

1. Module 1: a video featuring a word of welcome to the online course; here the content of the course and its learning outcomes are explained
2. Module 2: introduction to cultural sensitivity
3. Module 3: cultural sensitivity in the Arctic
4. Module 4: business innovations and cultural sensitivity in tourism companies
5. Module 5: digitalisation, responsible marketing and cultural sensitivity in tourism companies
6. Module 6: academic discussion

TEACHING TIPS

Teachers are encouraged to take advantage of the flexibility of the online course format to expand or condense the modules as needed and adjust the course individually to match differing needs of students. Teachers are also encouraged to complement the online course with group discussions with the students to increase peer learning or with learning-diary-type assignments to add more self-reflective learning.

COPYRIGHTED MATERIAL

All course materials are produced by the ARCTISEN project team and its collaborators.

ACTIVITY 18: DEEP CULTURAL INTERPRETATION MODEL: A TOOL TO UNDERSTAND THE TOURISTS' CULTURE

Linda Armano, PhD[30]

DESCRIPTION

The Deep Cultural Interpretation Model (DCIM) (Armano, 2018) systematises, in a language understandable to management and marketing, cultural values and worldviews collected through ethnographic research. It codifies culturally modelled knowledge that a human group has of the reality in which they live. It is effective for comparing different worldviews of different social groups. By photographing and codifying the cultural vision of different groups it is possible to focus attention not only on the contents of the DCIM categories, but also on the relationship between different worldviews in order to highlight any value-related gaps and possibilities.

USAGE SUGGESTIONS

The DCIM is aimed at university students. It can be suitable for students of various levels of preparation. It is recommended, however, that undergraduate students should already have some exposure to the underlying theory and methodology of qualitative research. Nonetheless, the DCIM is especially suitable for graduate and senior students, who, having acquired more skills in qualitative research, are able to use the data they have collected to elaborate concrete projects in the field of tourism to present to professionals in the tourism business. The DCIM may involve either a long or short journey, and it may be carried out both in distant sociocultural environments different from the student's original cultural context or in the student's own community, because cultural values can be investigated in any human context. In addition, in case of lockdown, the use of DCIM can also be adapted to online survey, without the need to move to other locations.

The DCIM can be either an individual or group assignment.

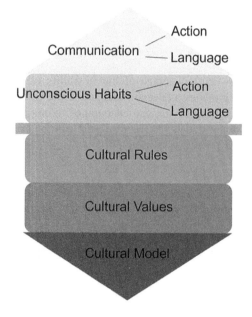

Source: Armano (2018)

Figure 13.1   Deep Cultural Interpretation Model

The DCIM is made up of Cultural Models that could be explained through the concept of "world vision", which guides people to classify the world they live in on the basis of specific defining traits (such as cultural values and norms). Cultural Values are ideals towards which people in a particular culture tend, and which influence behaviour. Cultural Rules are norms, such as procedures that explain what is right or wrong to do or not to do in order not to violate the cultural values. Unconscious Habits are the implicit behaviours (understood as *habitus*) that group members regularly express without necessarily being able to articulate why. Finally, Communication refers to the explicit behaviours that manifest, with words or deeds, people's thoughts and feelings.

Notably, these two latter categories differentiate information emerging from actions and spoken language to achieve a deeper understanding of the complexities that appear through personal stories.

The traits that fill the DCIM categories can correspond to a keyword or to a phrase present in an interview, which refers to certain sociocultural meanings discussed by interviewees. This aspect encapsulates the assumption that the discourses developed in the interview are always imbued with value aspects. Consequently, a word or phrase extrapolated from interviews has the power to represent both an experience that the interviewee knows, has seen or experienced directly, and a series of social attitudes shaped by particular cultural values.

LEARNING OBJECTIVES

By the end of this activity, the student will be able to:

- Understand how an individual or group's worldview conditions their choices and actions
- Create empathy with interlocutors with whom the student can co-construct a deep understanding of the context of analysis
- Analyse in detail the cultural values embedded in social behaviours
- Analyse, thanks to the comparison of information collected and systematised in two or more DCIMs, the cultural gaps between different worldviews typical of different social groups
- Concretise proposals capable of creating an encounter between the mission of a tourist stakeholder and the cultural values of the local inhabitants in order to respond to the needs of both

MATERIALS LIST

- A computer and Internet access
- A camera, a video camera or a smartphone
- Notebook

PRE-WORK REQUIRED BY STUDENTS

The following pre-work is essential:

- Students are expected to have acquired at least the essential qualitative methods useful in collecting data to proceed with the development of ethnographic research. In particular, students will be expected to know what a semi-structured interview is, and possibly conduct one; and to understand when it is appropriate to use the method of observation (silent and participant)

THEORETICAL FOUNDATION

The DCIM is a tool based on the "Cultural Iceberg" Marie Skłodowska-Curie project (Armano, 2018). The "Cultural Iceberg" allows systematising, in a language understandable to marketing, interpretative categories of anthropology. The method brings depth to the marketing comprehension of the cultural, social and situational determinants of cultural behaviours by employing an anthropological lens on how individuals' identities are forged and co-evolve with the cultural context. Thus, different business contexts can acquire a new key to the interpretation of the target and the co-construction of the possibility of an encounter between consumers and the company. Increasing the "Cultural Iceberg", the DCIM also analyses actions (such as corporal attitudes) from information that emerges from spoken language. The result is a deeper understanding of the complexity arising from comparing different cultural contexts.

TIME PLAN

The exercise can be carried out either in a classroom or in a workshop divided into ten sessions – approximately 20 hours of face-to-face instruction.

STEP-BY-STEP PLAN

- First session: students will be invited to understand how cultural values shape not only their behaviour, but also their thoughts, judgements, choices and priorities. Examples of cultural values are taken from ethnographic studies (Ren and Qiu, 2019; Wikan, 1992)
- Second session: the biggest differences between Western ways of thinking and other ways of thinking are explained, and the principle of non-contradiction, according to which it is not possible for something to be itself and its opposite at the same time. To better understand this particular cultural way of structuring knowledge of reality, other examples are introduced for students to use a comparative method of analysis. It is crucial to introduce different assumptions than Western ones
- Students can consider the specificities of all the cases compared in order to avoid producing erroneous conclusions which, if wrongly assessed, impact both the cultural vision of the local inhabitants and that of particular groups of tourists. Provide a handout with case studies explaining how cultural values that take shape are in reality manifested not only through conscious attitudes explicitly referable by the people, but also in the incorporated and unconscious habitus (Sapiro, 2015)
- Third session: the DCIM and the ethnographic case to be developed are introduced and, if the contribution implies the consideration of a real case study, provide the contact details of the informants who will be involved in the interviews. In this phase of the exercise, the students should formulate some questions to structure interviews
- Fourth session: students will be invited to connect online with the chosen stakeholder and proceed with the interview. Each interview will last about 60 minutes
- Fifth session: students will conduct two online interviews with two locals, and two interviews with two tourists
- Sixth session: students will analyse and systematise the data collected from the interviews within the categories of three DCIMs. If the exercise is aimed at several students, the cul-

tural gaps between the different worldviews as they emerge from the data systematised in the three DCIMs will be analysed in depth
• Seventh session: students will analyse the cultural gaps and the possibilities of meeting the different points of view systematised within the DCIM categories
• Eighth to tenth sessions: students will analyse how the stakeholders interviewed can approach the point of view of local inhabitants and tourists, and will draw up a business plan with a tourist offer, filling cultural gaps that emerged in the analysis of data

ACTIVITY 19: CULTURAL AWARENESS

Jonathon Day, PhD[31]

DESCRIPTION

This is a two-part exercise to increase cultural awareness and build a shared understanding of the meaning of the term "respect". The activity can be done in pairs or in small groups in a classroom setting.

In the first stage of the exercise, have participants work with a partner or a small group whom they do not know. Ask them to spend five to ten minutes talking about respect. Pose questions that elicit reflection on the importance of respect in their lives. For instance, "What does it mean to show respect? How do you show respect? What does it mean to you to be respected?" Afterwards, bring everyone together to discuss the topic.

The second stage of the exercise is designed to raise awareness of the learner's cultural self. Versions of this activity were originally developed by Berardo (2012) and Vande-Berg (2014) and can be easily modified for specific circumstances. Begin the exercise with a discussion of possible cultural groups in which participants may belong. Let the participants know that a wide range of possible answers are expected here. Groups may include gender and sexuality, family or social roles, profession, race, ethnicity and religion, to name a few. Then ask learners to write their name, a quote that is meaningful to them or in some way defines them, and a cultural group they identify with. Have the students share their responses. Following this discussion, ask them to add two or three additional cultural roles with which they most identify. Once again, have them share their responses and add probing questions that encourage reflection on the influence of cultural groups on our lives: "How easy was it to answer the culture question? How have these roles impacted your core values (or vice versa)? What behaviour is rewarded in each group? What is challenged or discouraged? Are you the same person when you are in each of these groups? How do you manage any contrasting behaviours or priorities in your cultural groups?"

Understanding ourselves and our roles is an important step towards cultural awareness. Often, we are oblivious to the cultural influences of our own unique heritage and how it impacts our perspective. This activity helps learners to be conscious of a range of cultural contexts in which they find themselves, and raises an understanding of the unique experiences of their peers and colleagues.

USAGE SUGGESTIONS

This exercise is appropriate for a wide variety of learners: undergraduate and graduate students, and practitioners. It can be useful with groups that have established a degree of trust and a respectful dialogue. These activities can also be good ice-breakers and build mutual understanding in small groups and classes. Respect is the foundation on which future discussions about racism and sexism can be approached. Similarly, understanding our own cultural context provides a strong foundation for discussions on recognising, understanding and appreciating cultural differences.

Of course, each part of this programme can be done as a stand-alone exercise, but I like the balance of the two exercises. Together they can be conducted within a 40- to 45-minute group session or class.

LEARNING OBJECTIVES

These activities have a number of useful learning outcomes. They are useful ice-breakers and provide a foundation for future activities. Specifically, they are designed to help the participants:

- Build mutual understanding and empathy as they gain insights about their team members and practise interacting in personal ways about cultural differences
- Increase their awareness of cultural identities
- Explore ways in which values and behaviours can change in different cultural contexts and introduce ways participants cross cultures

THEORETICAL FOUNDATION

These exercises introduce learners to cultural self-awareness, an important type of knowledge for effective intercultural competence. They can be the first step towards intercultural knowledge and competence, defined as " a set of cognitive, affective, and behavioural skills and characteristics that support effective and appropriate interaction in a variety of cultural contexts" (Bennett, 2008, p. 97). In addition to cultural self-awareness, the Association of American Colleges and Universities has identified knowledge of cultural worldview frameworks, together with the skills of empathy and communication, and the attitudes of curiosity and openness, as key to developing intercultural knowledge and competence (Rhodes, 2010).

ACTIVITY 20: CO-DESIGNING CREATIVE TOURISM ACTIVITIES FOR PRESERVING AND PROMOTING LOCAL CULTURAL TRADITIONS

Maria Huhmarniemi, PhD[32] and Outi Kugapi, MSocSci[33]

DESCRIPTION

Creative tourism includes arts- and craft-based activities that have, at their best, the potential to enhance cultural revitalisation and act as mediators of traditions, cultural values and discussions. These activities, often carried out as crafting workshops, increase the appreciation of local traditions and crafts as well as Indigenous and similarly situated knowledge. They also transfer heritage and cultural capital in general in a way that respects cultural continuity and cultural identities and promotes social inclusion. It can be said that creative tourism breathes new life into cultural traditions and fosters appreciation for handicraft skills and designs.

In this group activity, art and tourism entrepreneurs and students collaborate to co-design craft-based services with an aim to preserve and promote local, place-based business practices. Co-design of new services is innovative: new services transform traditions while they also keep them alive.

USAGE SUGGESTIONS

This contribution is targeted for practitioners and/or students in the fields of arts, design and tourism. This could be also carried out as interdisciplinary joint studies in arts and tourism fields.

LEARNING OBJECTIVES

This contribution aims to help the students/tourism practitioners:

- Understand more deeply the value of local cultural heritage
- Examine how tourism can support cultural continuation, cultural pride and regional vitality
- Collaborate with local crafters/artists/art entrepreneurs to evaluate and design new ways of making arts and crafts for culturally and socially sustainable tourism

MATERIALS LIST

- Sticky notes, pens, paper
- Crafting materials chosen by the collaborators

PRE-WORK REQUIRED BY STUDENTS

- Basic knowledge of tourism and how to create tourism activities
- Identification of artists and/or entrepreneurs as potential collaboration partners

THEORETICAL FOUNDATION

Dialogue, knowledge exchange and creativity in tourism can be achieved in several ways (see for example, Duxbury and Richards, 2019; Kugapi et al., 2020; Richards and Wilson, 2006). Creativity and co-designing new services with local artists also set an excellent foundation for developing services that are based on local culture. In creative tourism, arts- and crafts-based activities offer "presumption", meaning "production by consumers". Thus, creative tourism can shift the focus from artefacts to the production process of arts and crafts.

Creative tourism also has the potential to impact sustainability on many levels: economic, social and cultural. Here, cultural sustainability can be understood as the respect for heritage and continuation of traditions and local authorships. Culture acts as an enabler and a driver of the economic, social and environmental dimensions of sustainable development. Therefore, cultural sustainability can be seen as an important fourth pillar or even interwoven into all other aspects of sustainability.

Revitalisation is an intentional effort to renew and remake cultural traditions. It is often understood as creation of cultural continuation from one generation to a new one, reconstruction of forgotten skills and/or a boost to cultural identities rooted to villages, towns and wider regions. This can give traditional elements, such as crafts, new meanings. Therefore, it can be said that creative tourism services can be a way to keep traditions alive and transform them for new societal and economical contexts. Creative tourism, that involves designer-makers, does not only generate deeply relevant experiences for tourists but also sustainable livelihoods for local designer-makers (Sarantou et al., 2021).

Co-designing creative tourism services follows an approach of project-based learning aiming to step away from teacher-led learning situations and enhance the learners' individual agencies and collaborative skills, and creates possibilities for prosumption. In project learning, students respond to a challenge and gain experience of interdisciplinary activity. The pedagogical approach is also motivated by theories of transformative education for achieving sustainability.

TIME PLAN

This could be done in a day or a couple of days.

STEP-BY-STEP PLAN

1. "Pre-work" task: identify possible artists with whom to collaborate
2. Tourism students and/or entrepreneurs are invited to the workshop together with the local artists/art entrepreneurs; the main aim of the workshop is to co-design craft-based services to tourism purposes that will preserve and promote local crafting traditions and cultural values
3. General introduction to creative tourism and the main aim of the workshop
4. Get to know each other (warm-up exercise)
5. Brainstorming session
6. First wrap-up, conclusions of the first brainstorm
7. Break
8. Second round of brainstorming session, starting from the best idea from the first round

9. Co-developing a creative tourism service in collaboration, following the steps on how to produce a tourist service
10. Discussion on how to collaborate in the future, what to do next, how to test the product with customers, ask for customer feedback

TEACHING TIPS

- Warming up and introducing the main aim to the audience is important
- Trust and empathy among the participants support successful co-design. This can be enhanced with a clear aim of the workshop, supported by knowledge of the participants and their backgrounds and a warm atmosphere during the workshop
- Make sure that the activities are done in real collaboration and crafters/artists are consulted carefully so that the outcomes will be culturally sustainable

ACTIVITY 21: TOURISM AND INTANGIBLE HERITAGE

Nick Naumov, PhD[34]

DESCRIPTION

This is a conversation starter that seeks to illustrate how tourism can be a powerful force that brings a number of cultural changes to society. The context of intangible heritage is ideally suited to stimulate a critical and engaging discussion on the extent to which tourism has the potential to revitalise cultural values and tradition while, at the same time, contributing to their exploitation for commercial purposes.

1. Preliminary task: students explore the definition and characteristics of intangible heritage assets and identify ones that have a particular importance to them (for example, customs, language, religion)
2. Discussion point: working on a selection of intangible heritage practices, students discuss the interrelationship between intangible heritage and tourism and analyse tourism's positive and negative influences on society; and, most importantly, discuss how the perceived benefits of tourism development influence the sociocultural values

The development of tourist resources often challenges the conservation of heritage assets. This is even more complex for intangible heritage practices as they are often commercialised for economic purposes. The main purpose of this contribution is to critically examine the balance between commercialisation and preservation of local culture. The goal is for the students to (1) critique how tourism changes the understanding of local culture from a holistic perspective and (2) identify both positive and negative impacts of tourism development over intangible heritage practices.

USAGE SUGGESTIONS

This conversation starter is suitable for undergraduate and graduate students, particularly those studying tourism, cultural studies, anthropology and cultural geography. Ideally, the activity should be placed at the beginning of a teaching session/seminar, but it can also be used as a part of a larger discussion or individual/group activity. In case of a future lockdown, the tutor can select a number of intangible practices, locate videos online and ask the students to use virtual whiteboards to present their comments.

LEARNING OBJECTIVES

*   Develop an understanding of the power of tourism to bring sociocultural change
*   Critique how tourism can be a driver for positive/negative sociocultural changes to society
*   Identify challenges of intangible heritage revitalisation and preservation and be able to discuss heritage commercialisation in the context of tourism development

PRE-WORK REQUIRED BY STUDENTS

It is expected that students have gone through the pages of UNESCO Intangible Heritage domains and in particular the Convention for the Safeguarding of the Intangible Cultural Heritage (2003).

THEORETICAL FOUNDATION

The task promotes interdisciplinary and thought-provoking debates around authenticity, commercialisation, cultural change and acculturation. Students can find relevant articles in many academic journals, particularly the *International Journal of Heritage Studies*, *Journal of Heritage Tourism* and *International Journal of Intangible Heritage*. A highly recommended edited collection on intangible heritage is Smith and Asagawa's *Intangible Heritage* (2009).

TIME PLAN

The conversation starter should take around 15–25 minutes depending on the size of the class.

STEP-BY-STEP PLAN

*   The tutor to select a set of intangible heritage practices and present them to the rest of the class
*   Students to discuss positive and negative impacts of tourism development
*   Critical discussion in which students present their standpoints/arguments
*   Critical tutor-led summary

TEACHING TIPS

Expect students to need some guidance and a contextual introduction to intangible heritage in general and the Convention for the Safeguarding of the Intangible Cultural Heritage (2003) in particular. Depending on the course objectives, class time could also be spent asking students to identify an intangible heritage practice that belongs to their country/place of origin and/or is related to their local culture.

ACTIVITY 22: THE UNFOLDING OF SARS-COV-2

Joanne Paulette Gellatly, DBA, CTC, TIA[35]

DESCRIPTION

This assignment asks students to investigate the impact of COVID-19 on the tourism industry worldwide by analysing and interpreting real-world data. Requiring largely online research, this activity can be carried out asynchronously but lends itself to a debriefing and discussion session as a group.

The unprecedented crisis of the pandemic had a devastating impact on people's lives, especially the travel and tourism sector, globally. The early months of the crisis pinpointed the vulnerabilities of the various industries within the tourism sectors. The World Travel & Tourism Council (WTTC, 2021) put the loss of tourism-related jobs between 100 million and 200 million worldwide in 2020, with an estimated decline of 1 billion international travellers and a global loss of 1.3 trillion USD. However, measures to address the pandemic taught nations how to coexist in collaborative safekeeping activities, which created new alliances. The communication strategies adopted by the international community to combat the health and economic impacts were complex.

USAGE SUGGESTIONS

This assignment sets the scene for the more complex strategic management assignment ("Tourism Resiliency Post COVID-19"; see Activity 23) and would be particularly useful to undergraduate students who may not have followed the pandemic's evolution and impacts closely. It can be done wholly online and out of class, while the assignment debrief and discussion could be an in-class, an online or a hybrid session.

LEARNING OBJECTIVES

- Demonstrate your ability to identify and synthesise relevant information
- Create a timeline that clearly communicates key events
- Discuss the unfolding of events and demonstrate comprehension of the impacts on the travel and tourism sector
- Analyse the global economic and social impacts due to the unprecedented loss of tourism and travel activities (option: focus on one country or one region within a country)

MATERIALS LIST

• Online access

Table 13.1   *World tourism statistics*

Year	Travelers in millions	Increase in millions	% increase
1950	25.200		
1960	69.700	44.500	176.6%
1965	113.120	43.420	62.3%
1970	166.180	53.060	46.9%
1975	222.410	56.230	33.8%
1980	286.105	63.695	28.6%
1985	327.118	41.013	14.3%
1990	435.262	108.144	33.1%
1995	528.403	93.141	21.4%
2000	675.475	147.072	27.8%
2005	798.679	123.204	18.2%
2010	940.919	142.240	17.8%
2015	1,184.000	243,081	25.8%
2020F*	1,400.000F	216.000F	18.2%
2030F*	1,800.000F	400.000F	28.6%

Notes: Adapted from the World Tourism Organization (UNWTO, 2020) and Gellatly (2016). According to the UNWTO, there were 1.4 billion arrivals worldwide in 2018. Growth was originally forecasted to be between 3 and 5 per cent per annum, reaching 1.8 billion international arrivals by 2030.* However, COVID-19 in 2020 shut down international tourism due to the World Health Organization's (WHO's) declaration of a worldwide health crisis, which led to a drop of 1 billion arrivals worldwide in 2020. Recovery was anticipated to be slow with a resilient global tourism industry not expected before 2024.

PRE-WORK REQUIRED BY STUDENTS

Students should have a general understanding of the impact of COVID-19 on jobs within the various sectors of the industry, particularly the travel sector, which could be facilitated through an online search of popular media/news sites. For example:

• https://globalnews.ca/video/6673064/coronavirus-outbreak-officials-say-up-to-50-million -jobs-at-risk-in-international-travel-tourism-industry
• https://globalnews.ca/news/6939140/travel-will-never-be-the-same-thanks-to-covid-19/
• UNWTO Barometer (2021, March 7). Impact of COVID-19 on global tourism made clear as UNWTO (World Tourism Organization) counts the cost of standstill. Retrieved from www.unwto.org/taxonomy/term/347

THEORETICAL FOUNDATION

According to self-determination theory (Reeve, 2012), students' engagement with their learning increases with real-world impact work. This assignment encourages that engagement by exposing students to real-world data sourced from the UNWTO and various countries/regions. Thus, students are provided with real-world meaning and context and given an opportunity to learn the relevance of data interpretation. This, in turn, enhances their motivation to learn about the related impacts of risk management and contingency measurements to gain an understanding of how the tourism economy may or may not contribute to the creation of tourism-related jobs and foreign exchange earnings.

TIME PLAN

Depending on how detailed the tracking of the spread and evolution of COVID-19 is expected to be, the exercise will likely require one to two weeks to complete individually. At least one to two hours should be allotted for the class debrief in a group discussion or online discussion board.

STEP-BY-STEP PLAN

1. Ask students to review postings by WHO (World Health Organization), UNWTO, WTTC, International Air Transport Association (IATA), Cruise Lines International Association (CLIA) and any other official resources to establish a timeline of the spread and impact of COVID-19
2. Major events and milestones should be captured by reviewing the communications of these organisations
3. Describe the evolution of timelines and communication strategies led by UNWTO that aligned in historical collaboration with WHO, ensuring the safety and essential protection of people while combating a community-spread pandemic that affected almost 200 countries
4. The impact on the travel and tourism sector in terms of job and revenue losses by sector should be highlighted, as well as the timelines of progressive recovery
5. Findings are presented to the class through a discussion of the impacts and future prospects for this sector

ACTIVITY 23: TOURISM RESILIENCY POST COVID-19

Joanne Paulette Gellatly, DBA, CTC, TIA[36]

DESCRIPTION

This assignment asks students to develop appropriate recommended courses of action to work towards resiliency of the tourism industry, and to forecast the positive impacts of an integrated tourism system based on collaboration and reciprocity.

It is becoming increasingly clear that the SARS-CoV-2 virus will not disappear but rather continue to spread for years to come, albeit with less deadly effects due to the number of vaccines that have been developed. However, this means that resiliency of the travel and tourism industry will become a primary concern over the next quarter century. In providing a longer-term vision of a 2050 integrated system, lessons learned from the unprecedented COVID-19 crisis that devastated the industry can serve as a basis for collaborative activities that will keep both those employed in the industry and its guests safe. Reciprocity is a part of humanity, and soul servitude is part of our core system: human connectedness will be ever more important as the industry rebounds and restructures. The vibrancy of destinations depends on human interaction among guests, residents and employees. The desire to explore and find the uniqueness in every existence is part of why people want to travel, and this desire will ensure the rebound of tourism demand.

USAGE SUGGESTIONS

This assignment builds on the data interpretation assignment "The unfolding of SARS-CoV-2" (see Activity 22); however, it is aimed at a more senior level that has some knowledge of strategy development. This online assignment task can be conducted in class or in a hybrid format to address how a tourism region may potentially rebuild by creating reciprocal and ethical constructs for the evolution of a renewed tourism system.

LEARNING OBJECTIVES

* Understand how integrating people and processes into a proactive workforce that encompasses values-based alignment to service delivery can re-imagine tourism at the destination level in a more regenerative form
* Apply analytical research and critical thinking as a team
* Demonstrate an understanding of ethical constructs and inclusive reciprocal business philosophies in the rebuilding of tourism resiliency
* Describe policies that pertain to tourism customers, employees, services and enterprise assets
* Analyse how markets are affected by various tourism services
* Explain how global tourism can be rebuilt through a management plan for a specific tourism region to regain consumer confidence in travel activities

GROUP TOPIC APPROACHES: GROUPS (4/5) FOR TEAM ANALYSIS AND KEY SOLUTIONS-RECOMMENDATIONS

1. Identify local challenges and find solutions for designated destination tourism branding
2. Define the unique positioning of a local cultural tourism destination within a global marketplace
3. Attract human resources and create a Retain Talent Plan for sector service delivery models
4. Competitive strategies for target marketing for leisure markets and business meetings
5. Global expansion strategies for multinational and collaborative tourism development products
6. Trends in international hotel industry sustainability and its marketing

7. Create a tourism cycle timeline for a renewal strategy for destination market positioning

PRE-WORK REQUIRED BY STUDENTS

Some suggested reading for students to review:

- Hall, C. M., Timothy, J., and Duval, D. T. (2012). *Safety and Security in Tourism: Relationships, Management, and Marketing*, Routledge
- Harvard Business Essentials (2009). *Crisis Management: Master the Skills to Prevent Disasters*, Harvard Business School Press
- Mitroff, I. (2009). *Why Some Companies Emerge Stronger and Better from a Crisis*, American Management Association
- United Nations World Tourism Organization, retrieved from www.unwto.org/taxonomy/term/347
- World Travel & Tourism Council, retrieved from https://wttc.org/Research/Recovery-Dashboard

Suggested videos:

- https://globalnews.ca/video/6673064/coronavirus-outbreak-officials-say-up-to-50-million-jobs-at-risk-in-international-travel-tourism-industry
- https://globalnews.ca/news/6939140/travel-will-never-be-the-same-thanks-to-covid-19/
- https://globalnews.ca/world/

THEORETICAL FOUNDATION

In keeping with self-determination theory (Reeve, 2012), students' engagement with their learning increases with real-world impact work. By working with real-world data that provide real-world meaning and context, students learn the relevance of data interpretation. This, in turn, enhances their motivation to learn why tourism can cultivate global exchanges for both job creation and influential economic activities. The opportunity to develop the tourism system as a united whole provides students with an opportunity to conceptually plan for emergent processes, linking the various sectors of tourism to determine an evolved structure for a global exchange with linked policies and market reciprocity.

TIME PLAN

Depending on how detailed the tracking of the spread and evolution of COVID-19 is expected to be, the exercise will likely require up to a month to complete in teams. At least two to three hours should be allotted for the class debrief and group discussion of each tourism region.

STEP-BY-STEP PLAN

1. Teams will be working in small class groups (a minimum of three or four to a maximum of five per group)
2. Class groups will be acting as a strategic management committee charged with developing an overall strategy for one of the contemporary global tourism topics as listed above

3. Encourage students to review postings by the World Health Organization (WHO), the World Tourism Organization (UNWTO), the World Travel & Tourism Council (WTTC), the International Air Transport Association (IATA), the Cruise Lines International Association (CLIA) and any other official resources to establish as a team a timeline of the spread and impact of COVID-19
4. Ask students to document the major events and milestones through the communications by these organisations
5. Discuss how futurity planning of industry policy may be developed for better systems
6. Student teams discuss the evolution of timelines and communication strategies led by the UNWTO that aligned in historical collaboration with the WHO, ensuring the safety and essential protection of people while combating a community-spread pandemic that supervened almost 200 countries, globally. To achieve better strategic approaches to integrating people and industry structure, plan how to bring united regions and a global system into collaborative and resource-based aligned systems
7. Trace the impact on the travel and tourism sector and create timelines for futurity planning towards an integrated system vision for 2050
8. Student teams present their findings to the class through an instructor-led discussion of the impacts and future prospects for this sector as a connected global supply system that is integrated and aligned for a united purpose
9. Teams submit a written report of their recommended tourism policy (see the project outline below) and present their tourism team design policy through a six-slide summary PowerPoint online. Suggest teams also provide a one-page topic summary of a problem area overview and recommendations script

PROJECT OUTLINE: GLOBAL TOURISM

Working in teams, students are asked to create their own approaches to resilience planning for rebuilding the hospitality and tourism sector. The final submission should contain:

- A definition of the crisis' spheres of activities within the chosen topic area. Who are the stakeholders? Who should be overseeing the tourism committee? What qualifications are needed? What should local certification strategies be?
- A review of the potential risk factors, including the likely behaviours of consumers and habitual patterns of industry attitudes
- A description of the source of risk areas and the potential crises design plan that includes a review of the early warning signals and situational crisis management structures in relation to lessons learned from COVID-19
- An incident/accident reporting plan that details different risks, how these are captured and processes for corrective action
- A description of the purpose for risk-crisis management analysis and safety system design that covers responsibilities of various stakeholders/the chain of command and recommended risk instruments, the information or procedures relating to potential emergency response processes and/or safety equipment (communication strategies, sample press releases, waivers, agreements to participate, and so on), and different levels of crises (search and rescue or evacuation plans, and so on)

- An outline of the Policies and Procedures Manual with discussion of who is responsible for its review as well as when, where and how this occurs, and considerations for adaptation for a particular tourism region

TEACHING TIPS

Describing tourism as a global system has its challenges since tourism and related industry sectors seemingly operate in a decentralised manner. Determining just how regionalised elements of the tourism industry may be brought into a network that is aligned at all levels is the main objective of this particular assignment. Discussion on developing interpersonal skills with an emphasis on customer service culture may cultivate better understanding of the global origins of complexity that are part of a connected system of the tourism community. The ability of the industry as a whole to deliver responsible and authentic products and services that ensure the safekeeping of operations and guests is paramount. Thereby, the integration of people and processes is part of the collective system which can be envisioned through an evolved system and lessons learned from the pandemic.

ACTIVITY 24: AUTHENTIC ASSESSMENT: ACTIVATING PURPOSEFUL LEARNING FOR A DIVERSE STUDENT COHORT

Ece Kaya, PhD[37] **and Deborah Edwards, PhD**[38]

DESCRIPTION

Villarroel et al. (2018, p. 850) advocate that authentic assessment requires components of "realism, cognitive challenge and evaluative judgement". In this particular contribution, aimed at master's students, the assessment includes a reflective journal, a presentation and an industry research report. All assessments are individual, and students are supported by a team-based teaching approach. Game and Metcalfe (2009, p. 46) argue that team teaching can radically transform the learning environment, where "there are no longer individual sources of energy and knowledge, the dialogue involves everyone as learner and everyone as teacher".

The major assessment is an industry research report, worth 50 per cent of the students' final grade, that addresses an issue impacting the industry sector in which they will be working post their degree. The issue can involve any or all of social, cultural, political, economic, ecological and technological considerations for the firms and the communities in which they operate. Students are required to consider their own values as well as the values of the stakeholders affected by the issue. Students are encouraged to work on issues that are considered wicked, and to reflect on a human story that gets to the centre of the industry issue. Their research is to be based on secondary data; the final report must include about 40 academic and industry references.

The presentation and reflective journal are designed to set the ground for the final report. They enable students to develop their arguments with active feedback and individual discussion, leading them to the completion of a substantial report. Identifying and exploring their industry issue and generating impactful recommendations to respond to organisational and professional needs prepare students to apply theory to practice. The assessment is cognitively challenging as students become aware of the real challenges happening in their industries.

The authentic assessment enables students to synthesise their learning in the context of their chosen issue, and teaches them the processes of making a practical contribution to their field.

USAGE SUGGESTIONS

Students are required to independently identify a contemporary issue impacting their industry, synthesise salient information, articulate original ideas and provide a valid set of recommendations to address the industry issue.

The assessment is positioned as a final piece for master's students in management discipline programmes such as event, sports, human resources, strategic supply chain management and management to complete before they graduate. It encourages a high level of independent work. The subject is best delivered in workshop mode. Scaffolding of the assessment is provided via group and independent activities. Although the subject is best facilitated face to face, it was easily adapted for online delivery during the COVID-19 isolation period.

LEARNING OBJECTIVES

Once final-year graduate students complete the authentic assessment, they will be able to:

1. Critically analyse complex theoretical business concepts in a global context and apply them in a local context to discuss and solve a complex industry issue
2. Use relevant information and data from academic and professional sources as well as the skills gained in previous subjects to critically analyse complex issues in business and engage with a variety of concepts and theories
3. Apply strategic and critical thinking, influence, creative and problem-solving skills effectively within management practice
4. Incorporate examples, evidence and personal interpretations for and against a particular position, and articulate and pursue well-reasoned, strong, valid and logical arguments
5. Provide a valid set of recommendations to address an industry issue, and create a professionally presented industry research report

MATERIALS LIST

While there is no specific text required for this subject, the materials below are to provide guidance on how to develop a business research report:

- Bell, E., Bryman, A., and Harley, B. (2018). *Business Research Methods* (5th edition), Oxford University Press
- Maurer, T. J., and London, M. (2018). From individual contributor to leader: A role identity shift framework for leader development within innovative organizations. *Journal of Management*, *44*(4), 1426–1452
- Quintanilla, K., and Wahl, S. (2020). *Business and Professional Communication: Keys for Workplace Excellence* (4th edition), SAGE

Students are required to draw on their knowledge of relevant industries and sectors and to apply their understanding of professional business report writing.

They are directed to university library resources specifically available for the study of business management, human resources management, sports management, events management and other managerial subfields. Students also have access to other library resources, such as a list of key databases for company, industry and country information.

PRE-WORK REQUIRED BY STUDENTS

Students are required to work on individual activity sheets that are designed to narrow their topic, to understand the audience of their report, to work on a systematic literature review and to have a clear grasp of their understanding about knowledge construction. The activities involve mind mapping, empathy mapping, cataloguing knowledge and skills, and a literature spreadsheet.

THEORETICAL FOUNDATION

Gulikers et al. (2004) define authentic assessment as "an assessment requiring students to use the same competencies, or combinations of knowledge, skills, and attitudes that they need to apply in the criterion situation in professional life" (p. 69). In authentic assessments, students engage with real-life tasks and apply the knowledge and skill sets that they developed in those real-life tasks (Khaira and Yambo, 2005).

The core element that supports students in developing authentic assessments is team teaching. Team teaching accords students "the opportunity to hear multiple perspectives on the same topic and to learn from experts" (Minett-Smith and Davis, 2020, p. 582). This has several benefits for the students. It enables the teaching team to work collaboratively to facilitate creative and effective learning experiences for the students. The team can draw on their individual and collective knowledge and strengths. It opens the way for supportive relationships to develop between teachers and students, and between the students themselves.

TIME PLAN

The 12-week plan includes nine hours of weekly workshops as a combination of face-to-face sessions and individual working time.

STEP-BY-STEP PLAN

Identifying an industry issue and refining it to a research question is a demanding intellectual exercise that takes students out of their comfort zones. We developed resources and curricula to support this journey, including: "clearness committees", where students support each other to interrogate their research topics; human stories to identify tensions and crystallise issues; empathy mapping to dive deeper and harness multiple perspectives; steps for crafting the research question; concept mapping to generate ideas; and literature reviews. Through individual dialogue with teaching staff and student colleagues (McArthur and Huxham, 2013;

Metcalfe and Game, 2006) students discuss their ideas and make their own decisions about their industry research report; that is, the issue, approach and content.

The first week introduces the subject, explains the assignment details and explores students' industry interests. In clearness committees, students work to observe and describe industry issues from multiple perspectives – global, historical, personal, cultural, financial, societal – and present these ideas to the class. A clearness committee supports authentic enquiry and is based on the relationship between meaningful reflection, action, context and relationships. Ideas are shared in a supportive non-judgemental environment. The purpose is not to give advice or "fix" people from the outside in, but rather to help people remove the interference so that they can discover their own wisdom from the inside out. In a clearness committee each person (through question prompting) will reflect on these three areas:

- A contemporary, complex industry issue, even if it is not clear – this process works equally well with murky or clear issues
- A recounting of relevant background factors that may bear on the issue
- An exploration of any hunches the focus person may have about what is on the horizon regarding the issue

The clearness committees are a supportive way in which students can share their ideas and uncover their inner resources to address a complex issue.

Starting from Week 2, students engage with their peers, working in group activities. They also receive individual feedback from the teaching team. They pick news/media articles, read and think about the industry issue(s) and use them to identify two or three issues related to their industry that are considered to be wicked problems. Students are encouraged to think about their own industry-related experiences and human stories that get to the heart of the industry issue and find a topic about which they are passionate.

Students create mind maps for the industry issues they have identified. This activity is to assist them in translating their ideas into possible research questions. Applying problem-analysis tools, they identify relevant evidence to justify their industry issue. Students read different sections of a business research report and complete quizzes. This activity helps them understand how to structure their assignment. Students also work on how to deliver a structured presentation.

TEACHING TIPS

The subject involves a team-teaching approach in the design, delivery and evaluation. "Super tute" has been developed to support the approach and students in preparation of their authentic assessment. The super tute generates a new dynamic in the classroom, which fosters collaboration between students: to share ideas, research and findings, and to generate discussion, ideas and meaningful feedback for each other.

Following Game and Metcalfe (2009), the class is best broken into structured components, which include activities, discussions and one-to-one assistance. Designing in time for individual attention is a significant component. Students should be able to approach any or all of the team to discuss their industry issue. A team member may bring in or refer a student to another team member depending on the expertise required. This has several benefits for the students. Students feel more at ease when they have the freedom to approach the team member with whom they feel most comfortable. The approach enables the teaching team to work collaboratively to facilitate creative and effective learning experiences for the students. We can draw on the individual and collective knowledge and strengths of the team. It opens the way for supportive relationships to develop between teachers and students, and between the students themselves.

ACTIVITY 25: TOURISM AND WORLD HERITAGE SITES 1

Nick Naumov, PhD[39]

DESCRIPTION

This is a conversation starter that seeks to illustrate how economic values bring sociocultural changes to the society. The discussion around world heritage and tourism is a particularly good fit as it stimulates a thought-provoking discussion on how economic interests often challenge social and cultural values.

1. Preliminary task: students identify sociocultural values that particularly influence their own lives, based on their own culture, heritage, ethnicity, and so on
2. Discussion point: working on a selected example of a World Heritage Site, students discuss how economic development in general, and tourism development in particular, bring positive and negative impacts to the society and most importantly, how economic benefits influence and even change sociocultural values

As we know, every society has a set of values, beliefs and traditions, collectively known as sociocultural values. This contribution illustrates how these values often change as a result of economic development and economic interests. The context of world heritage and tourism is a good arena for thought-provoking discussions as it enables students to think more critically about their own values and the influences that shape them. The problematic nature of heritage conservation allows the students to critique how tourism often changes the sociocultural values at a given destination and identify some concerns in the context of heritage preservation and development. In addition, the contribution is designed to provide a discussion platform that students use to recognise the economic significance of heritage for the local stakeholders and identify some of the main challenges to manage World Heritage Sites in the era of mass tourism and over-tourism.

USAGE SUGGESTIONS

This conversation starter is suitable for undergraduate and graduate students, particularly those studying modules/units as part of multidisciplinary programmes (for example, tourism, anthropology, cultural geography).

Ideally, the activity should be placed at the beginning of a teaching session, workshop or seminar as a "setting the scene" activity, but can also be used as a part of a larger research individual/group activity. In case of a future lockdown, the tutor can prepare a "mini case study" with the most essential site information, or locate a video online and ask the students to use virtual whiteboards to record their comments.

Expect students to need some guidance and a contextual introduction to World Heritage Sites and what "outstanding universal values" they represent. Depending on the course objectives, class time could be spent to provide an example of a World Heritage Site that has gone through a radical transformation as a result of mass tourism development (for example, Venice, the Old Town of Dubrovnik).

LEARNING OBJECTIVES

- Develop an understanding of the power of economic values to alter and even change sociocultural values
- Critique the conceptual nature of World Heritage designation and be able to understand the controversial impacts on the local society
- Identify challenges of managing tourism at World Heritage Sites

PRE-WORK REQUIRED BY STUDENTS

It is expected that students have gone through the pages of the UNESCO World Heritage Centre and in particular the World Heritage List (https://whc.unesco.org/en/list/).

THEORETICAL FOUNDATION

Students can find relevant articles in many academic journals; in particular, the *International Journal of Heritage Studies*, *Journal of Heritage Tourism* and *Journal of Cultural Heritage*. A highly recommended review of world heritage and tourism is Takamitsu Jimura's (2019) *World Heritage Sites*.

TIME PLAN

The conversation starter should take around 15–25 minutes depending on the size of the class.

STEP-BY-STEP PLAN

- The tutor to select a World Heritage Site and present it to the rest of the class
- Students to discuss positive and negative impacts of tourism development
- Critical discussion in which students present their standpoints/arguments
- Critical tutor-led summary

ACTIVITY 26: TOURISM AND WORLD HERITAGE SITES 2

Nick Naumov, PhD[40]

DESCRIPTION

This is an in-class individual/group activity that seeks to demonstrate how economic values create forces of change in society in the context of tourism development at World Heritage Sites. The contribution is aimed at stimulating a critical and constructive discussion about how economic benefits influence the meanings and values attached to material representations of our past and, most specifically, World Heritage Sites.

1. Preliminary task: students examine how tourism development brings economic benefits to heritage sites and prepare a list of those benefits based on their research
2. Main activity: working individually/in small groups, students identify two World Heritage Sites (ideally one from a developing country and one from a developed country) and compare/contrast positive and negative impacts of tourism development at World Heritage Sites

This contribution enables students to understand how economic values play a crucial role in the context of heritage management and development. Students shall recognise the financial pressures put on the conservation of heritage sites and also examine how tourism contributes to those challenges. The activity is a good opportunity for the students to enrich their knowledge about World Heritage Site management and practise their critical analysis, reflecting on how economic values influence, change and even transform world heritage, and also understand more about how tourism contributes to the changing values and meanings attached to our past. In addition, the activity also allows students to demonstrate their critical thinking by proposing solutions to address the negative impacts.

USAGE SUGGESTIONS

This individual/group activity is suitable for undergraduate and graduate students, particularly those interested in heritage studies, heritage tourism and urban geography. The activity may be used separately but also form the basis of a larger research individual/group activity. In case of a future lockdown, the students can still complete this activity though tutor-led online discussion using online tools for video communication such as Zoom or Microsoft Teams.

LEARNING OBJECTIVES

- Foster understanding of how economic values create forces of change in society in the context of tourism development at World Heritage Sites
- Explore how economic values contribute to the changing discourse of (world) heritage management and development
- Recognise the conservation challenges and financial pressures of World Heritage Sites and explore solutions to addressing these challenges

MATERIALS LIST

Students should bring their own device (for example, laptop, tablet) for the research part of the activity.

Some suggested readings are:

- Hampton, M. (2005). Heritage, local communities and economic development. *Annals of Tourism Research*, *32*(3), 735–759
- Van Blarcom, B., and Kayahan, C. (2011). Assessing the economic impact of a UNESCO World Heritage designation. *Journal of Heritage Tourism*, *6*(2), 143–164

PRE-WORK REQUIRED BY STUDENTS

It is expected that students have gone through the pages of UNESCO World Heritage Centre and in particular the World Heritage List (https://whc.unesco.org/en/list/).

THEORETICAL FOUNDATION

Students should read the journal articles under *Materials list* as an introduction to economic impacts and World Heritage Sites.

TIME PLAN

The activity shall include preparation time (research), in-class oral/virtual presentations and sufficient time for critical discussion depending on the size of the class.

STEP-BY-STEP PLAN

- The tutor to explain the task and provide instructions
- Students to conduct desk research
- Critical discussion in which students present their case studies and analyse the positive and negative impacts of tourism development
- Comparative analysis and group discussion
- Critical tutor-led summary

ACTIVITY 27: THE DILEMMA OF PROTECTING WORKERS IN THE FACE OF ENTREPRENEURSHIP

Johan Edelheim, PhD[41]

DESCRIPTION

This case provides the opportunity to learn more about the labour movements in various countries; understand the contributions they have made, which are all too often taken for granted in more industrialised countries but are still battles to be fought in poorer or emerging economies; and appreciate the limitations they represent when the rules are applied to all workers in a sector, regardless of the operating realities. By taking on the different roles (union representative, large employer, entrepreneur, government, and so on) and having to develop as well as defend a position, students gain great insight into the constraints faced by each stakeholder and the difficulty of achieving compromise solutions.

Unions have, since the Industrial Revolution, developed into formidable forces in many nations, jointly putting pressure on other stakeholders to further the rights of their members. Employees in many Western countries can thank trade unions for rights and privileges that nowadays many take for granted, such as standardised work hours, holiday entitlements and occupational health and safety regulations. However, to remain relevant, unions need to collect a substantial number of the available workforce as their members, and they need to deliver perceived benefits to them. Almost 75 per cent of Finns, for example, are members of a trade union, a high percentage by international standards. The International Labour Organization (ILO) has ranked Finnish unions as among the most effective in the world (Allt, 2020).

USAGE SUGGESTIONS

The audience could be undergraduates, graduate students or practitioners, as negotiations are a critical component of any managerial position.

The case itself can be implemented either in class or through virtual classrooms.

LEARNING OBJECTIVES

* Gain an understanding of labour movements and the role played by labour unions in establishing decent work and working conditions
* Appreciate the policy implications of protecting workers versus protecting jobs
* Enhance negotiation skills

MATERIALS LIST

It would be helpful to provide students with background material and/or a lecture for a better understanding of the objectives pursued by each stakeholder and how these impact unionism. This is also the opportunity to bring in guest speakers from a union representing hospitality workers as well as an association representing hospitality and tourism businesses and/or a representative of the Ministry of Labour.

PRE-WORK REQUIRED BY STUDENTS

Students should familiarise themselves with some of the historic background of the labour movement in Finland, the tourism offerings in Lapland and current labour legislation.

Finland has traditionally had a strong workers' movement and unionisation of workplaces. The first unions were established in the 1860s, and the initial central union organisation in the early years of the 20th century. The Hotel and Restaurant Workers' Union was founded in November 1933 (Pohls, 2016). The provision of hospitality services and the monopolised sale of alcohol, both instilled after the abolition of prohibition rules in 1933, led to strict rules about services available, with only international-standard – in many cases state-owned – hotels being given the right to serve stronger alcohol in their restaurants, with wine- or beer-serving privileges strictly controlled and enforced. Employees in the industries were unionised to a high degree, and unions dictated the rules regarding compensations for working odd hours, and required social areas for staff, such as cafeterias and changing rooms.

National minimum salaries, social benefits and other work agreements, as well as tax details, have been negotiated in "three-party negotiations" (with representatives from workers' unions, employer organisations and the ruling government) since 1940. These negotiations still act today as reoccurring agreements where the three parties agree on salary raises or caps for the following two to three years, although these are now negotiated by each profession.

The changes that have occurred in the Finnish hospitality and tourism industries since the 1980s are forcing this industry to evolve, and at the same time have created large challenges for trade unions to stay relevant. Deregulation of air traffic, a successful branding of Finnish Lapland as the official home of Santa Claus, good snow conditions and a growing interest in aurora borealis (the Northern Lights) viewing have all led to an unprecedented growth of tourism demand and supply. Lapland makes up a third of Finland's landmass, but is home to just 3.7 per cent (approximately 200,000 people) of the country's total population.

There are over 900 hospitality and tourism businesses registered in the region – but these companies' average size is only 1.4 employees on a full-time equivalent (FTE). While there are some larger ones, which employ the bulk of employees, most are very small, with an average of only 0.7 FTE (Regional Council of Lapland, 2017). These micro businesses operate season-ally, drawing on family or hired rush-helpers only during peak demand, from mid-November until Easter. Although there is a desire to address seasonality so that a larger workforce can be employed on an ongoing basis, union rules for employment make this extremely difficult. The unions' expectations of employers to hire full-time year-round employees do not make sense, nor do their strictly enforced work hours during peak demand. One compromise has been reached: workers in some destinations are now allowed to work more hours than the average 112.5 hours per three weeks, which is the rule elsewhere. This means that employees can work even double shifts when needed and are paid for the extra hours after the season is over. Employers do not incur overtime payments for this arrangement, and therefore do not have to employ two people to do the job during peak seasons, which, while desirable, is difficult to do because of the small population in the region.

Other union demands are not as flexible – such as assigned social areas for employees. Dressing rooms, lunch-break areas and toilets make perfect sense in a city hotel, but not for a family-owned safari company wanting to hire out a husky dog-sled guide for aurora borealis tours in the non-light-polluted wilderness. Also, new fledgling companies avoid employing staff due to having to pay social benefits connected to full-time employment. It is in such examples that originally just and ethical rules create challenges for local entrepreneurship.

Mobilities, open borders and globalisation have also increased the challenge for unions to protect workers. For example, an entrepreneur can buy services from a company in Latvia, which is allowed inside the European Union. The Latvian company, following Latvian rules, pays travel and salaries, which are just a quarter of Finnish salaries (Simoska, 2017). The entrepreneur avoids hiring Finnish-born staff, and ensures no unionisation takes place at the resort, by actively hiring first-generation immigrants or by buying outsourced services.

This case illustrates both the importance and challenges created by union rules aimed at protecting employees from unjust employment practices. The rapidly changing landscape for hospitality and tourism businesses requires compromises between protection and entrepreneurship, while being mindful of the fierce competition within the industry as well as among destinations.

THEORETICAL FOUNDATIONS

According to Reigeluth and Keller (2009, p. 37), role play is an instructional method "in which key ideas and skills are illustrated or practiced by learners assuming roles and contexts in which the ideas and skills would typically be applied" and is based on Experiential Learning Theory. Applying such a problem-centred method of instruction is particularly suited to adult learners (Cranton, 2000) and situations where practising required skills directly in the field is not practical, such as this setting of labour negotiations.

TIME PLAN

It would be ideal to allow students to gain an appreciation of the labour issues, legislation, conditions and entrepreneurial challenges over a two- to three-week period, approximately six hours in total. A negotiation session would be the culmination of the roleplaying game.

STEP-BY-STEP PLAN

- This assignment forms one component of a course on tourism policies. The marking of the assignment is based on students' ability to argue for their assigned viewpoint, based on research conducted
- Provide students with background on labour legislation pertaining to hospitality and tourism, labour movements and unionism, international industrial relations systems and transnational bargaining-coordination policies from the perspectives of government, employers and labour unions
- If possible, bring in guest speakers to address these various perspectives either in person or virtually
- Choose one issue, preferably identified by guest speakers, that requires solving. Ideally, students would discuss various issues that were highlighted and collectively reach agreement on which one will be the object of the roleplaying game
- Set up students in groups of three to five and assign the role to be assumed by lottery. Depending on class size, more than three stakeholder groups can be identified (for instance, large year-round employers versus small seasonal ones, or by adding a government representative from economic development/tourism)
- Allow students time away from class to develop their negotiation strategy, determining their base position as well as which aspects they are to compromise on
- During the actual negotiation, allow each group to present its position (wish list) and then open up discussions moderated by the instructor as arbitrator
- Help students reflect on their experience developing their position and strategy and the negotiation itself

TEACHING TIPS

Although this case lays out the situation in Finland, labour regulations tend to be thorny issues globally for hospitality and tourism businesses because of the irregular working conditions, staffing flexibility needs, high labour costs and low profit margins. It can therefore easily be adapted to any country, providing students with more concrete knowledge of the issues that prepare them for workplace settings. The background can be further expanded to include international industrial relations systems, transnational bargaining-coordination policies and the challenges that they represents. An example would be the eurozone (cf. Glassner and Pochet, 2011).

ACTIVITY 28: THE POWER OF VALUES TO EFFECT POSITIVE CHANGE 1

Joan Flaherty, MA, MSc[42]

DESCRIPTION

A foundational exercise aimed at fostering student awareness of their values and the power of those values to effect positive change (see *Theoretical foundation* below).

1. Students are asked to participate in a visualisation exercise: "Imagine yourself ten years from now walking into a large room, filled with people who are important to you (relatives, friends, co-workers, and so on). As you walk into the room, you become aware that each person is there to honour you. Now, take two minutes to write an answer to this question: 'What impact do you want to have had on their lives?'" Note: they will not be asked to share what they have written
2. Instructor debrief: "What you have written is important – so important that it merits revisiting – because it reflects your good values. Consider how to make every communication effort – written or spoken – reflect those good values that you just wrote about. Doing that consistently ensures that your actions are likely to have positive outcomes for both you and the people you are dealing with, both personally and professionally."

USAGE SUGGESTIONS

The exercise is best suited for a mature audience (for example, graduate students or practitioners). Age and experience make it easier to explore the notion that one can have a meaningful, long lasting impact on others. (And two minutes of uninterrupted writing can also seem unreasonably long for a younger group of learners.) I have, however, also used it with undergraduates. It can be well received with this group if a classroom culture of engagement and active learning has already been established.

  As described here, it is intended as a preliminary exercise, setting the stage for any written or oral presentation assignment that requires awareness of one's values.

See Flaherty's "The power of values to effect positive change 2" under the Professionalism contributions (Activity 48) for an example of how this foundational exercise can then be applied to a written assignment.

LEARNING OBJECTIVES

- Identify significant values and beliefs that shape how you see yourself and how you see others
- Consider the power of those values to effect positive change

MATERIALS LIST

Each participant requires writing materials (laptop, tablet or paper and pen or pencil).

THEORETICAL FOUNDATION

This is a modification of an activity from Covey's *The Seven Habits of Highly Effective People* (1989). In terms of pedagogical theory, the assignment aligns with the increasing emphasis on the need for our students to understand and articulate their values as preparation for their professional lives – a theme which likely resonates with you in light of the text you are reading right now and which recurs throughout Palmer's work (2007).

TIME PLAN

The exercise takes 15–20 minutes.

ACTIVITY 29: INDUSTRY ETHICS

Joan Flaherty, MA, MSc[43]

DESCRIPTION

A two-part writing assignment: a research essay on a topic re industry ethics, and a reflective piece on the topic's professional/personal relevance to the student's life.

1. Students write an academic essay on an industry issue with ethical implications. Specific topics would depend on the course, but they could be narrowed down from broad issues such as impacts of tourism, industry hiring practices, tourism social entrepreneurship initiatives, resource conflicts, and so on
2. Students write a shorter, corresponding reflective piece on why that issue matters to them – or to any industry professional – both personally and professionally

If you are reading this book, you care about this challenge: how to convince students that the material matters. This two-part assignment, which I first encountered through reading one of Parker Palmer's blogs, addresses that challenge. It asks students what they think about the material based on the facts, figures and conclusions they have uncovered. In doing so, it stays within the realm of conventional learning outcomes. However, it then ventures outside that realm by giving students permission to write about their personal feelings re the material. It asks them, in other words, to link the cognitive with the affective – a synthesis exercise that helps foster their engagement with the material by exploring the intersection between it and what Palmer calls the "inner landscape" of their lives.

USAGE SUGGESTIONS

The two-part writing assignment is suitable for a wide range of learners (undergraduate, graduate and practitioner). Depending on the course and context, instruction may be required on how to write a research essay. It will probably be required on how to write the shorter, reflective piece. In terms of structure, my own expectations for this piece are not sharply delineated. As long as their reflection is thoughtful and coherent, I like to give students freedom to explore their feelings about the topic without being constrained by structural requirements. (I think that ground is covered in the essay assignment.)

LEARNING OBJECTIVES

* Demonstrate your ability to engage in academic research through identifying and accessing relevant information on your essay topic
* Synthesise key themes from your secondary source research with your own reflections
* Develop and present your material thoughtfully and coherently in an appropriate written form

THEORETICAL FOUNDATION

Pairing a conventional academic essay with a reflection on the essay topic's personal relevance draws on a fundamental principle of modern education: student engagement is more meaningful, and learning more profound, when the material is relevant to the student's life. Of course, as instructors we explain to students all the time why the material is relevant, but self-determination theory (as well as common sense) tells us that this lesson is more effective when they figure it out for themselves (Palmer, 2007).

TIME PLAN

Both assignments are intended to be completed out of class, based on guidance provided during class time. That class-time guidance could take the shape of mini lectures, workshops and/or hands-on exercises re how to narrow the essay topic, research secondary source material, outline the essay and write the essay. The amount of time spent on these activities will depend on the context of your course. (That is, more time class time will be spent if these activities are reflected in your course's learning outcomes, less time if they are not.)

STEP-BY-STEP PLAN

The sequence for teaching how to write an essay is provided in the time plan. For courses where writing instruction does not figure prominently, a guest speaker from your institution's writing support services could be invited to provide the necessary details.

TEACHING TIPS

Do not assume that your students will know how to write an essay. In particular, they will likely need help narrowing down the topic. (In my experience, students often gravitate towards broad, all-encompassing topics.) And they will probably need reassurance about the unstructured nature of the reflection piece. A grading rubric detailing your expectations would be particularly helpful here.

ACTIVITY 30: SOLVING ETHICAL DILEMMAS IN THE TOURISM INDUSTRY

Kathleen Rodenburg, PhD[44]

DESCRIPTION

The need for sustainable business practices within the industry requires teaching and learning to extend beyond basic skills (Stoner and Milner, 2008) and include the development of ethical decision-making and values-driven leadership (Gentile, 2013, 2017). This is not an easy task as most students arrive on campus with pre-established value systems (for example, ethnic origins, family values, cultural and religious affiliations) that influence the lens through which they view ethical dilemmas. The proposed project applies Experimental Learning Theory (ELT) to ethics education. Research has shown that applying ELT to ethics education has resulted "in increased empathy, better understanding of how decisions trigger consequences, better understanding of power relationships and their possible abuses, increased ability to defend one's views in a group, and increased alignment of personal and work value systems" (Balotsky and Steingard, 2006; Rodenburg, 2020; Trevino and Brown, 2004; Weaver and Agle, 2002). The culminating task at the end of this activity requires a public demonstration of competence which provides an additional catalyst for transformational learning (CTE, 2015).

USAGE SUGGESTIONS

Tourism industry practitioners face ethical challenges daily. As such, this teaching practice has a broad application within any tourism curriculum. The activity can be completed by an individual student or by a team of students and can be facilitated in a face-to-face classroom, field study programme or virtually. Although initially developed for undergraduate students, it has a broad application and relevance for graduate-level courses and industry practitioners.

LEARNING OBJECTIVES

* Acquire the skills and knowledge to conduct a situational analysis using secondary- and primary-source research
* Recognise what constitutes an ethical dilemma
* Research and identify ethical dilemmas that occur in the tourism space
* Identify the steps to resolve ethical dilemmas
* Identify and evaluate one's own value systems and recognise the consequences of using one's own ethical lens when making ethical decisions
* Analyse consequences of using the ethical lens employed by others
* Accurately voice one's values (Gentile, 2013) through a public presentation

MATERIALS LIST

1. Ethics literacy; that is, definitions of ethics, business ethics and ethical dilemmas; various ethical/philosophical orientations found in literature; and the difference in orientations among cultures, demographics and individuals
2. Tools and tips for conducting secondary-source research to complete a situational analysis of an industry, region and/or place
3. Tools and tips for conducting primary-source research to identify ethical dilemmas faced by key stakeholders within the region and/or place of study
4. Decision-making tools, checkpoints and criteria to assist with ethical dilemma resolution

PRE-WORK REQUIRED BY STUDENTS

1. Conduct secondary-source research to complete a situational analysis of a pre-assigned region
2. Conduct primary research to uncover an ethical dilemma faced by this same region that needs resolution

THEORETICAL FOUNDATION

1. Four phases of the Experiential Learning Theory process (Kolb and Kolb, 2009): students are provided with a concrete experience and must apply theories and concepts taught through the curriculum, are required to reflect on and identify ethical dilemmas in the context of the experience, are required to conceptualise how they would approach solving the dilemma, and engage in active experimentation when they present their resolution for implementation to industry practitioners and faculty
2. Constructivist Theory: student-directed project-based learning, deep-dive exploration of ethical dilemmas in context
3. 4E Cognition Theory: context-based learning activity beyond the classroom
4. Transformational Learning Theory: complex systems thinking and public demonstration of competence provide a catalyst for transformational learning

TIME PLAN

One semester project that can be condensed and modified for an in-field study.

Activity	Week	Hours
Project overview and introduction	1	1
Mini-lesson: secondary source research methodologies	2	1
PESTEL submission*	4	20
Mini-lesson: ethics, ethical dilemmas and primary-source research methodologies	5	3
Complete primary-source research	8	20
Submit written ethical dilemma	10	20
Ethical dilemma resolution event	12	30

Note: * A PESTEL analysis is an acronym for a tool used to identify the macro (external) forces facing an organisation. The letters stand for *Political, Economic, Social, Technological, Environmental* and *Legal.*

STEP-BY-STEP PLAN

Project Overview

Students are integrated into a community as an industry consultant (role play) and collect necessary information to write their own case study (case method) describing the environment and the ethical dilemma pertaining to the tourism industry. Once the context is established, students exchange their identified ethical dilemma with another student or team to resolve.

Specifically, students are required in teams or individually to conduct secondary and primary research to complete a situational analysis and to identify an ethical dilemma facing the tourist industry in a specific region that needs resolution. Using their completed situational analysis as context, and tools and checkpoints for ethical decision-making taught in class, these same students must also resolve an ethical dilemma written by another student team. Teams present their recommendations and compete for best-in-class status in front of a live panel consisting of industry stakeholders and faculty.

1. Pre-select one region for the entire class to study. The region selected should be heavily dependent on, or impacted by, the tourist industry
2. Provide students with skill sets/tools to conduct secondary research to complete a situational analysis. Specifically, provide tools that will assist students in broadening their understanding of the political, economic, sociocultural (ideologies), technical, environmental and legal constructs binding the chosen region. This step provides the students with the context necessary when writing and resolving ethical dilemmas
3. A mini-lesson and readings to define ethics, business ethics, ethical dilemmas and the various ethical orientations that lead to different decisions made in the ethical dilemma space. Ensure that students understand that the dilemma they identify must contain a right-versus-right paradigm; that is, an issue that requires a choice between "truth versus loyalty", "individual versus community", "short-term versus long-term" and "justice versus mercy", making the resolution both challenging and context-dependent

4. To narrow their focus, ask students to identify a specific destination/attraction from the region to study. (This should be different for each team/student)
5. A mini-lesson and readings pertaining to primary-source research methods to assist them with ethical dilemma identification
6. Ask students to identify and interview key stakeholders from the community to determine key ethical issues faced by the chosen destination
7. Provide a template (one to two pages) with examples of written ethical dilemmas for students to write their own dilemma pertaining to their selected destination/attraction
8. A mini-lesson and readings to provide tools, checkpoints and key criteria for resolving ethical dilemmas. See *How Good People Make Tough Choices: Resolving the Dilemmas of Ethical Living* (Kidder, 2009). You are providing students with a process to enable them to make better thoughtful decisions, and not providing them with the "right" decision
9. Distribute the completed ethical dilemma from one student (team) to another student (team) for resolution. Resolutions must be made in the context of the local community, as ethical responses will vary depending on this situational context
10. Invite industry-relevant individuals to adjudicate the student (team) resolution presentations. This is where students practise and learn to effectively "voice their values" (Gentile, 2013)

TEACHING TIPS

1. The situational analysis can be completed as one class project with each team contributing to the final product. This will allow open dialogue in a flipped-classroom setting with an overall objective for all students to get immersed within the community. The ethical dilemmas identified and the recommendations for resolution will be enhanced by ensuring all students have detailed and relevant context
2. Industry practitioner inclusion in the discovery steps and on a panel elevate student performance as they are solving real ethical challenges
3. Select the region, conduct the situational analysis and even have students select the destination within the region before contacting industry representation (alleviating the project's dependency and success on industry participation). Past experience with this exercise reveals that practitioners will participate after their destination has been chosen as they are eager to see how students view their operation through available information

ACTIVITY 31: INTRODUCING CRITICAL TOPICS TO TRANSFORM OUR PRACTICE

Karla A. Boluk, PhD[45]

DESCRIPTION

Addressing sustainability in the tourism industry places an important responsibility on graduates. Students should not merely be aware of contemporary tourism issues, but also view these issues with a critical lens, equipped with the skills to anticipate problems that may arise (for example, contributors to climate crisis and potential responses, and the industry's role in helping rebuild economies following economic downturns, specifically post COVID-19). Furthermore, students must consider their own accountability in responding to sustainability and well-being challenges. Exposing students to an array of critical sustainable tourism topics may provide insight into the various impacts of the tourism industry and further expose opportunities for students to formulate ideas and practise their responses to pressing global challenges. Introducing an array of critical topics may encourage thought around opportunities for the tourism industry to be a conduit for equity, justice, agency and sustainability. Such topics draw awareness to more complex problems that require broader systems thinking and action from various stakeholders.

USAGE SUGGESTIONS

The audience for this conversation starter is undergraduate students. Careful consideration is required by the instructor to integrate topics of critical importance to the understanding of sustainability in the syllabus. Specifically, the instructor may provide opportunities for students to explore how the industry intersects with socio-ecological systems and opportunities to analyse positive and negative impacts, comprehending reality versus market messages, and the quality of life for local destination stakeholders monopolised by corporations. The instructor's task is to create a learning climate where students are willing to consider their own accountability and engage in thought-provoking topics that challenge their assumptions. The instructor must be flexible, integrating important topics into the course that arise throughout the term. The instructor must also be mindful of topics of interest to students. To empower students to engage with critical topics, instructors should encourage them to raise such topics in class and then be willing to devote class time to discuss these topics.

LEARNING OBJECTIVES

- To identify and critically reflect on contemporary topics that have a positive and/or negative impact on tourism
- To critically reflect on tourism's role in shaping quality of life, community and nature
- To realise one's agency within the contemporary topics discussed and consideration of critical responses

MATERIALS LIST

Students should follow the news online, on TV, in print or via applications. For example, students could use a news app such as Flipboard and share and/or refer to articles pertinent to tourism with their peers and instructors.

PRE-WORK REQUIRED BY STUDENTS

Keeping abreast of the news and engaging in course content through class discussions will help students in identifying contemporary issues, appreciating their relevance to tourism and recognising their own capacity to respond to such concerns.

THEORETICAL FOUNDATION

Exposing students to an array of critical sustainable tourism topics may provide insight into tourism impacts, affording opportunities to mutually formulate ideas and responses to pressing global problems. This approach may also prompt students to consider their own personal agency. The introduction of critical topics requires a responsibility from both educators and students. Educators bear a responsibility to bring forth challenging topics which may present opportunities for challenging the positive status quo images of tourism. Creating spaces for such topics may create mutual discomfort, yet, at the same time, it may encourage students' engagement with their own critical ideas (and those of their peers, educators, scholars, the media), providing opportunities to consider viewpoints that run counter to the conventional image of tourism (Boluk, Cavaliere and Duffy, 2019). Novice learners are responsible for identifying essential contemporary topics to master (Young and Olutoye, 2015) and engaging in dialogue about these topics. Introducing an array of critical topics may encourage thought around opportunities for the tourism industry to be a conduit for equity, justice, agency and sustainability. Such topics may draw awareness to complex problems requiring systems thinking.

TIME PLAN

Identifying critical topics will take some planning when designing the course syllabus before the course is offered, and throughout the course in response to new contemporary issues that may be integrated as examples.

ACTIVITY 32: USING SYSTEMS THINKING AND THE UN'S SDG FRAMEWORK AS AN OPPORTUNITY FOR FOSTERING CRITICAL DIALOGUE

Karla A. Boluk, PhD[46]

DESCRIPTION

Sustainable development has been used as a popular conceptual framework in tourism, yet tourism interests are recognised as an omission in the 1987 publication of *Our Common Future* (WCED, 1987). Similarly, the tourism industry is mostly absent from the United Nations' (UN's) Sustainable Development Goals (SDGs) (albeit 8, 12, 14) (Boluk, Cavaliere and Duffy, 2019; Boluk, Cavaliere, and Higgins-Desbiolles, 2019). While the broadly written approach may lend to open interpretation across fields, the size and impact of the tourism industry highlights the importance of sustainability considerations. Broadly acknowledging the nuances of the SDGs such as well-being and considering different perspectives are essential to challenge the status quo and actively progress sustainability. Many scholars have noted the difficulty in teaching interdisciplinary topics – such as sustainability – calling for critical thinking and systems thinking to effectively address the complexities (Capra, 1996; Coops et al., 2015). That is, "the more we study the major problems of our time, the more we come to realise that they cannot be understood in isolation. They are systematic problems and are interconnected and interdependent" (Capra, 1996, p. 4). The activity introduced here requires a systems-thinking approach in order to engage students in critical dialogue.

USAGE SUGGESTIONS

This activity may be best facilitated following a few foundational lectures, mainly on critical thinking and critical dialogue, systems thinking and design, and a discussion on the UN's SDGs, emphasising the targets in the three goals directly signalling action on behalf of the tourism industry (8, 12, 14). Following a discussion on the SDGs, students would then assemble in small groups (of three or four) and self-assign themselves to an SDG. Using the principles of design thinking, students would be responsible for identifying the concerns/contributors of tourism to the problem and potential responses. For example, SDG 4 is Quality Education. Currently the field or subject of tourism does not exist in primary or secondary curriculum. While the scholarly literature emphasises the various impacts of tourism (on host communities, peoples, environments and economies) there is no translation of this to future travellers and citizens. As such, students may develop a curriculum intervention envisioning quality/responsible/sustainable tourism.

LEARNING OBJECTIVES

- To critically reflect on course literature and peers' contributions, and formulate critical arguments and contribute to dialogue
- To understand the attitudes of others and assess divergent viewpoints regarding critical tourism topics to develop an informed perspective
- To learn the skills required to iteratively and critically engage with the literature, peers, instructor and potential stakeholders
- To appreciate the time required to contribute to critical dialogue and its relevance to progressing sustainability
- To appreciate the opportunities of adopting a systems-based approach to understanding sustainability

MATERIALS LIST

- Lectures on engaging in critical thinking/dialogue, systems thinking and the UN's SDGs

PRE-WORK REQUIRED BY STUDENTS

Students will need to understand the basics of critical thinking/dialogue, systems thinking and the UN's SDGs. The foundations would be ideally presented in a couple of lectures at the outset of the semester. Students would be required to familiarise themselves with the SDGs prior to self-assigning a specific one to research.

THEORETICAL FOUNDATION

Systems thinking has the potential to facilitate students' ability to embrace and understand the complex and intra-dependent issues surrounding sustainability that ultimately depends on complex solutions through engagement with other perspectives and disciplines. The incorporation of critical topics (for example, on climate change, refugee crises, environmental and social justice issues and the impacts on tourism) provides a platform to imagine potential creative solutions to address contemporary challenges facing the tourism industry. Crossley (2017) contends that critical content should be "accompanied by an equally important creative and dialogical pedagogical context" to which learners can be nurtured (p. 429; also see Schwarzin, 2013). Boluk, Cavaliere and Duffy's (2019) empirical research proposed that facilitating student group interaction and engaging in critical dialogue were pivotal in fostering "Critical Tourism Citizens". Encouraging critical dialogue provides space to practise and engage in oral articulation of opinions and to contemplate one's thinking (Paul and Binker, 1990), but also to learn the language of the tourism profession. The practice of critical dialogue requires a skill set including curiosity and inquiry, quietude and active listening, suspending assumptions, expressing one's viewpoint and reflection.

TIME PLAN

An initial lecture on critical thinking and critical dialogue, systems thinking and the SDGs is required at the outset of the semester. To promote critical reflection/thinking it would be ideal if this activity took place over a few weeks to allow students to adequately study the SDG selected, discuss intervention with peers and prepare for an in-class critical dialogue.

STEP-BY-STEP PLAN

Initially a lecture on critical thinking, critical dialogue and systems thinking may be useful in order to help students understand the complex and intra-dependent issues surrounding sustainability. Secondly, an introduction to the SDGs is needed, recognising the targets that are explicitly related to the SDGs (in SDGs 8, 12 and 14). Next, students should self-assign themselves to an SDG (aside from 8, 12 and 14), research it and discuss its dependence across sectors and industries. They should critically reflect on the applicability of the specific goal to the tourism industry and consider ways in which the tourism industry may be a conduit for progressing the specific SDG. Students should prepare a specific intervention and present their findings to their peers and engage in a critical dialogue.

TEACHING TIPS

Students must reflect on the process of unpacking their thinking, and this may be facilitated via a Socratic approach whereby educators provide questions, not answers, and thus model inquiry and facilitate critical thinking. Modelling questions categorised as procedural (those with a right or wrong answer), preference (those with no correct answer) and judgement (questions requiring critical reflection to obtain the best answer; Paul and Elder, 2006, p. 1) are important in facilitating critical thinking. A Socratic paradigm aids in the analysis of information "requiring clarity, logical consistency, and self-regulation" (Oyler and Romanelli, 2014). Socratic tactics may be challenging from the educator's perspective so as to not impede the direction of the discussion, and from the student's perspective to avoid groupthink. A Socratic approach may facilitate self-generated knowledge and an ability to regulate thinking, which may aid in recognising one's role in responding to sustainability challenges. Although critical dialogue could generate uncomfortable feelings, such practice will foster critical engagement.

ACTIVITY 33: CALCULATING A CARBON FOOTPRINT

Marion Joppe, PhD[47]

DESCRIPTION

The purpose of calculating a carbon footprint is to have a consistent measure of the total output of greenhouse gas emissions for an individual, organisation, event, product, city or country. This measure provides a better understanding of which practices contribute the most to these emissions, which then allows initial steps to be taken to reduce these emissions. "Carbon" is used as shorthand for all greenhouse gases because it is the most dominant of them.

USAGE SUGGESTIONS

This is an excellent conversation starter at all levels of teaching, from undergraduate to graduate and professional, as it should generate divergent results in terms of emissions due to lifestyles.

LEARNING OBJECTIVES

- Understand the two scopes for considering and measuring carbon emissions, namely emissions that are created (for example, by using a car, air travel, commuting, waste) and emissions that are consumed (for example, electricity usage, natural resources, food)
- Determine where the biggest impacts are (for example, transport and meat consumption) and set an annual reduction target
- Assume personal responsibility to effect change

MATERIALS LIST

Many different types of carbon footprint calculators are available online, depending on the level of sophistication required for the exercise. Most are free, and many, like www.carbonfootprint. com/calculator.aspx, provide a lot of additional information on topics such as climate change, carbon offsetting, deforestation and the United Nations Sustainable Development Goals.

THEORETICAL FOUNDATION

Originating from the concept of the ecological footprint (that is, the measure of human demand on the Earth's ecosystems), the carbon footprint and assessment standard is one of the most basic and crucial areas of focus in low-carbon research. Wiedmann and Minx (2008) defined it as "a measure of the exclusive total amount of carbon dioxide emissions that is directly and indirectly caused by an activity or is accumulated over the life stages of a product" (p. 4). Although the term itself has become widely established, there is still much controversy on precisely how the carbon footprint should be measured, what is to be included and which methodology is most appropriate for its calculation.

TIME PLAN

If a fairly simple footprint calculator is used, students will require no more than 15–30 minutes to come up with their results. This exercise could be done prior to class, with class time dedicated to discussion. The discussion itself can take between 30 and 60 minutes, depending on class size and the number of questions students are asked to explore.

STEP-BY-STEP PLAN

- Ask students to look up the average global carbon footprint calculated in tons or in "number of Earths"
- Ask students to look up different countries and compare their footprint to the global average. What is the students' idea of fairness? How do they justify their understanding?
- Have students calculate their own carbon footprint and compare it to both their country and the global average. How do they compare?
- Have students reflect on what contributes to their carbon footprint and consider steps they are prepared to take in order to reduce it
- What if governments mandated certain actions, like not allowing the use of private vehicles on certain days, discouraging short-haul air travel, perhaps even limiting the amount of meat a household could purchase?

ACTIVITY 34: THE LIMITS TO BIOCAPACITY

Marion Joppe, PhD[48]

DESCRIPTION

The purpose of this activity is to help students understand nature's regeneration ability and how collectively we have overused the Earth's natural capital. By analysing the ecological resource use and resource capacity of nations over time, and comparing countries graphically, students can quickly understand which countries have a biocapacity deficit or surplus, and which have the largest footprint, based on population.

USAGE SUGGESTIONS

This activity lends itself to all levels of teaching, from undergraduate to graduate and professional, as its complexity can be tailored to the audience by focusing on one or more countries, and total versus per person results, and delving into current management practices that account for the divergent positioning of countries.

LEARNING OBJECTIVES

- Understand the concepts of ecological deficit and ecological reserve
- Compare and contrast countries based on their footprint and biocapacity at the national and per person levels
- Explain the geopolitical realities and management practices implemented that lead to country differences

MATERIALS LIST

The Global Footprint Network has developed an interactive website that tracks a number of indicators and allows for the calculation of a diverse range of analyses at different levels of sophistication (https://data.footprintnetwork.org/#/).

THEORETICAL FOUNDATION

Building on the early work of Mathis Wackernagel and Bert Beyers on ecological footprint accounting, the concept of a biocapacity budget, one that compares overall human demand on nature with what our planet can renew, is translated into one number: how many Earths we use.

Biocapacity and its management increasingly determine humanity's future in the face of climate change and resource constraints. Wackernagel and Beyers (2019) posit that humanity's only option when faced with these challenges is to run our economies on nature's regeneration, not on natural capital liquidation.

TIME PLAN

The Global Footprint Network open data platform provides rich opportunities to explore time-series at a global, national and regional level since 1961. It tracks overall demand on nature and biological capacity, but also footprints by land type, the ecological wealth of nations and sustainable development as measured by combining the ecological footprint with the United Nations Human Development Index (HDI). Students should be given sufficient time to explore the platform, although the amount required depends on the sophistication of the activity and analysis students will be asked to undertake.

STEP-BY-STEP PLAN

- Ask students to look up the open data platform on the Global Footprint Network website and familiarise themselves with the various tabs under "Explore Data"
- Be sure to have students check the terms, record types and common questions under the "About the Data" tab to fully understand what data they are working with
- Help students understand the HDI, which measures how well a country's citizens live by tracking the country's achievements in longevity, access to education and income. Details

for each country can be found under the United Nations Development Programme's Human Development Reports at http://hdr.undp.org/en/countries
- Students should be familiar with the concept of the ecological footprint and can now review in greater detail what contributes or detracts sustainable development over time and in various countries. This can be undertaken in small groups or individually
- The depth of the analysis, the number of countries to be compared and contrasted and relationships with other variables such as population or gross domestic product/capita can be adjusted based on course objectives

ACTIVITY 35: STEWARDSHIP: AN IN-FIELD DIALOGUE MODEL

Outi Rantala, PhD,[49] **Brynhild Granås, PhD,**[50] **Gunnar Thór Jóhannesson, PhD**[51] **and Kaarina Tervo-Kankare, PhD**[52]

DESCRIPTION

Over the years, seven core universities of the University of the Arctic's thematic network on northern tourism have developed an in-field dialogue model for learning. The model is an outcome of our annual field course, taking place in different Arctic destinations and run in cooperation with local actors (for example, Mäkinen et al., 2018). Our ambition to provide for learning through participation is pursued through varied activities, taking place in different safe and supportive environments that serve for multiple and overlapping dialogues where students, researcher-teachers, local actors and more-than-human parties[53] are involved. The value-reflexive emphasis of these dialogues has enabled broad and active engagement in promotions of meaningful tourism futures. The in-field dialogue model of learning has emerged and found its (preliminary) shape within a network of trust – in a process marked by competent improvisation and discovery, while being founded theoretically on ideas about becoming- and knowing-with (Haraway, 2008; Jóhannesson, 2019).

USAGE SUGGESTIONS

The dialogue model is targeted for graduate-level teaching, taking place in a field setting. It can accommodate 15–35 students, depending on the number of teachers/facilitators (two to five teachers are required). Different mobility funding (such as Nordplus Higher Education), research project funding or support from local stakeholders can be used to cover the expenses. The model paves way for subsequent courses that might take place online, since it creates mutual trust and helps to develop a sense of belonging and group spirit among both students and teachers. These emotional bonds decrease the need for social get-to-know activities during the online courses.

Possible further lockdowns due to pandemics provide obvious limitations for the in-field model. Indeed, during the spring 2020 we applied the model by performing parallel, internationally co-organised field work sessions within each country, accompanied with online workshops before, during and after the empirical sessions – including online webinars with local stakeholders from each country.

LEARNING OBJECTIVES

Upon completion of the field course the students should be able to:

- Identify stakeholders and networks engaged in tourism development in the field course setting
- Identify research themes relevant to the field course setting
- Design and conduct a small-scale tourism development research project
- Create new knowledge by engaging in a dialogical discourse
- Understand how stewardship can emerge in relations with diverse actors, including more-than-human parties
- Critically reflect on research ethics

THEORETICAL FOUNDATION

The model is based on an idea of knowing-with, which is about being sensitive to different forms of knowledge, materially and in embodied ways (Ulmer, 2017). Pedagogical theories and historical discussions about the value foundation of university education relate to such (feminist) philosophical articulations. Altogether, the research-based education that the field course relies on pursues fewer instrumental and more educational and dialogical-oriented ideas about university education, as promoted by the Humboldt tradition (see, for example, Strømsø, 2016, p. 41). Among the attitudes we aim at fostering is one connected to the encompassing "participation metaphor" in educational research that values "knowing" before "knowledge" and acknowledges the learner "as a person interested in participation in certain kinds of activities rather than in accumulating private possessions" (Sfard, 1998, p. 6). Furthermore, learning and knowledge creation require dialogue and interaction where more-than-humans take part and where partial knowledge can become completing.

TIME PLAN

The model has been constructed in a context of a five-day international field course, during which the time plan is approximately the following: Sunday – arrival; Monday – course introduction and familiarising with the field; Tuesday – field work and mentoring/lectures/facilitation; Wednesday – field work and preparing for the workshop with stakeholders; Thursday – whole-day workshop and dinner with stakeholders; Friday – summing up and departure.

STEP-BY-STEP PLAN

Pre-Work

Careful preparations are needed to facilitate the learning as participation-process, and the becoming-with-many. A flexible time plan is crucial to allow for dialogues and participation, as are carefully designed activities that prepare for communication between multiple groups of participants, in environments that also allow for engagements with more-than-human parties. In most cases, the preparations start – often a year before the actual course – with sketching an idea related to a development or research task in a specific setting, including sketching the possibilities of either applying for funding or planning how to connect the field course with existing funding (see, for example, the prefaces in Müller et al., 2020, and Rantala et al., 2019 for a more detailed description of the possibilities). This is followed by contacting relevant tourism actors and stakeholders in the chosen setting and involving research partners in the sketching of the content and outline. Once the content and idea are figured out – as well as the core stakeholders and participants – the outline of the course can be planned in more detail. This is followed by preparation of the instructions and prework-materials for the students and preparation of the instructions for the final assignment of the course/any assignments related to the course. Preparations also include many practicalities, such as booking facilities, accommodations, meals, activities, and so on.

During the Field Course

The activities during the field course include facilitating and mentoring the multiple dialogues where students, researcher-teachers, local stakeholders and more-than-human parties are involved – and coordinating all the practicalities.

After the Field Course

Stewardship, taking responsibility and caring for the more-than-human parties, local stakeholders and students continue to develop after the in-field experience. Therefore, it is important to make sure that the dialogue continues when supervising the individual work of the students and evaluating their assignments, and also when writing research reports and/or disseminating the outcomes.

TEACHING TIPS

The in-field-dialogue requires time and engagement from all the participants, and a high degree of trust between the collaborating universities and flexibility for bypassing some of the bureaucratic barriers that our systems seem to create.

ACTIVITY 36: PROMOTING MUTUALITY THROUGH SERVICE-LEARNING: LA SANTA CATARINA RESTAURANT

Blanca A. Camargo, PhD[54]

DESCRIPTION

This award-winning service-learning project implemented in the Restaurant Design and Management class of the International Tourism Program was designed to raise students' awareness of the food entrepreneurial needs of a low-income group and develop their abilities to work with and for people from a different socio-economic background. It details all the steps that were taken to design "La Santa Catarina", a restaurant concept for a group of low-income women from a community adjacent to a private university in Monterrey, Mexico.

Collaborating with local entrepreneurs, potential clients and suppliers, and community partners allowed students to gain real-life experience while creating economic opportunities and psychological empowerment for vulnerable women, thus contributing to social change.

USAGE SUGGESTIONS

This project is suitable for undergraduate tourism, hotel and/or restaurant management students taking a restaurant design and/or management class, but it can be adapted to other courses that require developing a business plan.

LEARNING OBJECTIVES

*   Develop an understanding of community (food and nutrition, entrepreneurial, tourism) needs
*   Propose a research design to examine the culinary habits of a low-income market segment
*   Apply different data collection methods to obtain primary and secondary market data
*   Design healthy menus for low-income customers
*   Apply restaurant design and management concepts for a real-life restaurant
*   Forecast financial performance of a (restaurant) business
*   Communicate respectfully with community stakeholders
*   Analyse primary and secondary data from a market study to propose avenues for the economic and psychological empowerment of vulnerable women

MATERIALS LIST

*   Restaurant and design management textbook (or the book that applies to the course you are teaching)
*   Kitchen and/or restaurant facilities (at school or community kitchens)
*   SPSS Statistics software to analyse surveys
*   Local restaurant industry statistics

PRE-WORK REQUIRED BY STUDENTS

It is expected that students participating in this project have taken introductory management classes and been introduced to the foundations of the restaurant industry.

THEORETICAL FOUNDATION

This project is grounded on service-learning, an experiential pedagogical approach that integrates service into a course, balancing learning goals and services outcomes (Sigmon, 1994). Applying theoretical concepts to real-life situations and being exposed to real experiences in non-academic settings help foster students' critical thinking and positive values (for example, active citizenship, respect, responsibility). Community members also benefit by obtaining knowledge, expertise, resources, capacity-building and networking to address their challenges and improve their quality of life. Service-learning has been applied in tourism (Jamal et al.,

2011; Longart et al., 2017; Mak et al., 2017) and hospitality (Lin et al., 2017) courses but has found little room in restaurant courses.

TIME PLAN

It is suggested that the project be implemented throughout the whole semester as all theoretical aspects of the course are put into practice for the opening of the restaurant (in our case, "La Santa Catarina") and several visits to the community are needed to obtain primary data to inform different aspects of the restaurant business plan. However, the instructor and students can also undertake individual phases of the project, as needed by the beneficiaries of the project.

STEP-BY-STEP PLAN

Topic	Service-learning component
History of restaurants	N/A (Instructor lecture)
Foundation of the restaurant industry	N/A (Instructor lecture, students' presentation)
Franchises	N/A (Instructor lecture, guest speaker)
Market study	Based on government data and field research, analyse the characteristics of the existing restaurants in the community Conduct a survey to explore potential customers' food habits and restaurant preferences
Legal aspects of opening a restaurant	Research the permits, licences and regulations required for opening a restaurant in the community; gather documentation and fill out relevant forms
Restaurant concept	In consultation with the female entrepreneurs and based on the market study, develop the restaurant concept (name, location, logo, degree of service)
Menu design	With the support of nutrition experts, design a healthy menu for a low-income community that incorporates the food preferences and purchase power of the target market Facilitate cooking workshops for the female entrepreneurs Organise a menu-sampling event and obtain feedback from potential customers
Kitchen planning and equipping	Design the kitchen layout, select the equipment and determine initial investment in kitchen equipment
Kitchen operations	Develop product specifications and quality standards for all food items in the menu Design a product purchasing, receiving and storing system Prepare food sanitation, cleaning standards and safety manuals for the restaurant

Topic	Service-learning component
Human resources	Create job descriptions and tasks for the restaurant
	Interview the female entrepreneurs to assess their experience, interests and skills; match them to restaurant positions
	Identify training needs
Financial aspects	Determine initial investments
	Forecast restaurant sales and expenses
	Prepare an income statement for the first year of the restaurant
	Research small business seed capital grant and loan options

In subsequent semesters students can create sales and marketing strategies for the restaurant, service quality training for the staff and/or organisational development programmes.

TEACHING TIPS

A service-learning project takes time and preparation to implement. Several challenges will also be encountered in the implementation, ranging from students' apathy, unwillingness to visit the community and conflict with classmates to difficulties in communicating with community members. Below are some tips that can help overcome such challenges:

- Inform them of the pedagogical approach and course expectations from the beginning of the course. Emphasise the importance and benefits of service-learning for the students and the community, so they are motivated and willing to work with others
- Create groups and assign well-defined, meaningful tasks for each one of them. Hold groups accountable for their performance and progress towards the class goals. Promote communication if conflict arises
- Closely monitor students' interaction with community members, in particular if students are from a better-off socio-economic background, as they may assume low-income people have the same needs and preferences. Foster equitable interactions. Coach students as needed
- Involve the community as much as possible in the project decision-making. They should not be passive recipients of information
- Invite other professors to participate in the project. They can provide additional knowledge and expertise to enhance the learning outcomes and community impacts
- If necessary, create partnerships with local organisations. We worked with a group that empowers women to help us approach community members, facilitate meetings, mediate any conflict among participating women and deliver the results
- Do not promise quick results; and follow up on commitments made with members of the community. If possible, give continuity to the project

ACTIVITY 37: VIDEO PROJECT "ENJOY LAPLAND SAFELY"

Sisko Häikiö, MA[55] and Minna Väyrynen, MA[56]

DESCRIPTION

This learning activity develops students' cultural awareness and mutual understanding and respect. The activity was to create a safety video for a certain cultural target group of tourists coming to Lapland. The project, carried out in multicultural teams, develops awareness of one's own culture, the cultures of the other team members, the tourism target cultures and the local culture of the operating environment. Through being exposed to cultural diversity in this way, students gain an understanding of how cultural values affect one's behaviour and attitudes.

USAGE SUGGESTIONS

This activity is appropriate for first-year undergraduate students. Our activity was carried out with Finnish and international first-year tourism majors as part of their larger study unit. It was worth 30 hours of student work. English was used as the common language. In making the video, students were encouraged to choose and arrange the filming locations themselves.

If there are no international groups available at your university, classes from international partner universities could be combined to participate in the exercise through online meeting platforms. (That is, the activity, from the start to finish, can be conducted virtually; the outcome (video) can be distributed virtually.) In that case, note different time zones and possible administrative tasks involved.

LEARNING OBJECTIVES

- To recognise cultural values that affect one's behaviour, attitudes and communication style in multicultural teamwork
- To work respectfully and productively with others towards achieving a common outcome
- To select and use relevant cultural information for the target culture in order to cater to different cultures in the tourism field

MATERIALS LIST

- A common forum for drafts and coaching, where the teams and instructors can share and comment on the drafts; this can be on a Learning Management System or on a social media or project management platform preferred by the students
- Material for the brainstorming workshop (sticky notes, markers or an online environment)
- At least one camera (smartphone) per team, and an editing tool/app (free and downloadable)
- A distribution channel for sharing the final videos (organised by the instructor)
- A form for voting for the best video (online or printed)

PRE-WORK REQUIRED BY STUDENTS

The following pre-work is useful:

- A brief introduction to the concept of culture, cultural values and intercultural communication, which could be offered as a lecture or video or an article
- Assessing one's own cultural preferences through different dimensions (an online form with feedback; for example, Meyer's (2014) "What's your cultural profile?")
- Assessing one's skills and expectations for multicultural teamwork based on the cultural profile (form)
- For achieving the learning outcomes, managing basic, freely available filming and editing tools will suffice
- Previous media studies or technical support during the project are recommended, but not necessary

THEORETICAL FOUNDATION

This quotation summarises our idea of facilitating cultural awareness:

> Tourism education is a medium through which mutual respect can be promoted. However, we believe that mutuality is a process that starts from self and therefore cannot be taught directly as a subject but rather facilitated through the whole variety of general self-awareness and conflict resolution courses […]. Another way of incorporating mutual respect in tourism curricula is to ensure that students are exposed to diverse social and cultural values and behaviours, and to encourage positive attitude towards diversity. (TEFI, 2010, pp. 20–21)

Our contribution builds on the concepts of intercultural competence and cultural values. According to Arasaratnam (2016, p. 6), an "interculturally competent person […] is mindful, empathetic, motivated to interact with people of other cultures, open to new schemata, adaptable, flexible, able to cope with complexity and ambiguity. […] Further, she or he is neither ethnocentric nor defined by cultural prejudices."

Cultural values influence how we interact, communicate, plan and execute tasks. By understanding and reflecting on our own preferences, and by comparing them to the preferences of those with whom we interact, we will develop mutual understanding and enhance our interaction.

Our pedagogical approach is based on transformative learning (O'Sullivan et al., 2002).

TIME PLAN

After being introduced to the project, students spend approximately 30 hours working in their teams during a period of three to six weeks. This includes independent work in the teams and coaching meetings with the instructors. The project ends with students presenting their videos, followed by reflection and discussion.

STEP-BY-STEP PLAN

1. Plan a timetable (recommended duration three to six weeks) that includes student project meetings and coaching sessions
2. Inform the students about the start of the project. Assign pre-work:
   * Assessing one's own cultural profile (online form with feedback)
   * Based on the cultural profile, assessing one's skills and expectations for multicultural teamwork (form)
3. Organise a project kick-off:
   * Instructors: project goals and general timetable with deadlines, divide the teams as multiculturally as possible
   * Instructors: show some examples of videos:
      * *E Komo Mai, Enjoy Hawai'i Safely!* – www.youtube.com/watch?v=tvYpI4ozzsI
      * *Pack Warm Stay Happy | Iceland Academy* – www.youtube.com/watch?v=ano1nvxGADc
   * Students: choose a target culture for the team, get to know each other by sharing information about one's cultural profile and expectations for the teamwork
   * Students: agree on team rules and time management, brainstorm ideas for the content of the video
4. Hold project meetings and coaching sessions according to the general and teams' own timetables throughout the project
5. Teams return the first draft: a script with text and some illustrations on a storyboard
   * Feedback is given by the coaches, reminding students about user rights for audio-visual material from sources
6. Teams return the final script for the video; coaches provide feedback and permission to start the filming
7. Teams film and edit their videos independently according to their plans and scripts
8. Teams return the final videos
9. Assess the videos. Give students a possibility to modify them if necessary (user rights, appropriate content, data-protection regulations)
10. Showtime! Teams present their videos and tell others about their process of working together to produce the video
    * Students vote for the best video
11. Reflection
    * Use discussion methods encouraging students' active and open discussion on the learning process
    * Students reflect on the emotional and other experiences of working in the multicultural team. Assist discussion with a set of questions (slide show, form or other)
    * Students compare experiences between the teams
    * Collect feedback individually (form)
    * If needed: a concluding discussion led by the coaches

TEACHING TIPS

Most likely there will be communication or commitment problems in the teams. Try to support and facilitate teamwork throughout the process, but let the students find the solutions themselves. Keep in mind that transformative learning involves both rewarding and frustrating experiences, and the process is typically more valuable than the mere outcome (video).

The students will likely need consistent reminders to stay focused on their goal: to produce a culturally targeted video. (The novelty of producing a video may tempt some of them to deviate from that goal, pursuing their own artistic visions.)

Finally, when it comes to the various technical tools and applications needed, do not worry! We have noticed that the students are ahead of us in using videos as an everyday means of communication. They will find the latest apps from the vast selection offered; for example, free apps such as Filmora and Vimeo.

ACTIVITY 38: COOPERATION BETWEEN STUDENTS AND THE TOURISM INDUSTRY TO SOLVE PROJECT CHALLENGES IN SUSTAINABLE RURAL DESTINATIONS

Tanja Lešnik Štuhec, PhD[57]

DESCRIPTION

After reviewing the theoretical background on sustainable rural destinations, students are confronted with a real-world example from the tourism industry. Based on previous experience and interests, students apply to take part in a working group that tackles specific challenges in the respective destination in cooperation with its stakeholders. In this way, they gain direct insight into the behavioural patterns of the working group members, who are tasked with solving a specific case, common in the profession; they test it out, or play a role in the working group. Students work with the destination stakeholders and present the results of their work at the end of the assignment, with the objective of growing mutually and exchanging views.

1. Preliminary task: students explore the destination, and gain knowledge of the project content and the activities that the working group members are engaged in. Thus, they are involved in the process, directly recognising the expected behavioural patterns of individual working group members (leader, coordinator, and so on), as well as the roles of individual members in addressing the issue. Assignment: as a group, and in cooperation with the destination stakeholders, students create a "project study". Each student plays a different role, and this is how they get to explore each project working group member's behavioural patterns. In the project development phase, results are presented to the stakeholders and discussed with them in a workshop, as well as later, at the presentation of final results
2. Learning outcomes: students are put to the test through role play in the field. By observing behavioural patterns, they familiarise themselves with requirements for a potential job in a project working group

It is uncommon for students to have extensive experience in real-world business before they get a job. For this reason, it is vital for students to start learning the communication methods in the world of business and behavioural patterns in project working groups during their studies. It is essential for them to be able to think openly and holistically, and have the opportunity to carry out different roles within a project team, ranging from collaborator to leader. They need to learn how to present their standpoint to fellow students and to destination stakeholders who have been entrusted with solving a challenge (for example, design green tourism products for identified target groups in the selected destination, together with stakeholders who represent the value chain of a guided experience) and who have given their valuable time.

USAGE SUGGESTIONS

The assignment is suitable for all levels: undergraduate, graduate and part-time students, under the condition that the students have reviewed study material and got to know the chosen destination and the project challenge in the field. Examples are mentioned above.

The preliminary task is carried out in the lecture hall, where students are visited by representatives who describe the destination and the challenge in the field. Once students have learned about the destination and the content related to the project challenge, the second phase is carried out. It takes place at the destination, in form of a workshop with stakeholders. The cost of sightseeing and accommodation are covered by the destination. The destination, in turn, receives proposals for implementation of relevant project studies. During COVID-19, the task was carried out remotely, using an online classroom, and the results were very satisfactory.

The lecturer prepares a template that the students use as a basis for creating a snapshot of the current state of the destination, as well as for solving the project challenge. The first day in the field is dedicated to presenting the destination and the project challenge. In the evening and during the second day, students work on the project idea together with the stakeholders. At the end of the visit, the first results are presented to the stakeholders. After one week, the final task is presented to the representatives of the destination at the faculty headquarters. The last coordination is carried out, and then the final project study is shared with the destination.

A lecturer and an assistant tutor guide the students and are available for them throughout the whole process. A contact person is also appointed at the destination to resolve any potential queries. Students learn how destinations operate and get to know the companies and organisations involved in the projects.

Through participation, students get acquainted with the representatives of the destination, which presents them with an opportunity to arrange for student or volunteer work.

LEARNING OBJECTIVES

- Working in a team and solving concrete examples from practice gives students an insight into stakeholder collaboration and relationships; that is, tacit knowledge
- Gain motivation to work in a specific workplace
- Build competencies related to values-based learning experiences, such as social intelligence, political, economic, social and ecological values of strategic and critical thinking, as well as knowledge, complexity, professionalism and management skills

MATERIALS LIST

Introduction to theoretical starting points, project idea, template for writing a project study (guidelines for creating a destination snapshot and solving a specific project challenge).

PRE-WORK REQUIRED BY STUDENTS

Specific prior knowledge is not required. Experience has shown that students take on the group leader role confidently and boldly and are able to communicate openly with stakeholders and teammates.

THEORETICAL FOUNDATION

This assignment relates to Kolb's Experiential Learning Theory (Kolb and Kolb, 2009).

TIME PLAN

The task is worked on for a minimum of eight weeks. In the lectures, theoretical starting points of destination management are given, and the destination and the project idea are presented (five weeks). Tutorials cover the creation of a destination snapshot and project challenges, based on a prepared proposal (three weeks). These activities last for a total of six weeks, since lectures and tutorials overlap in time. In addition, two days are spent in the field.

STEP-BY-STEP PLAN

1. Tutors work with destination representatives to create a student work plan and an itinerary for the first day of the visit to the destination. They also establish the workshop methodology with stakeholders. This is followed by a presentation of the template for the destination snapshot and solving the project challenge
2. Classroom lectures allow students to learn the theoretical foundations of rural green destination management, and about the ways of connecting and participating with stakeholders in the destination, and various stakeholder roles
3. The destination representative presents the destination and the project idea after the students have had a chance to review several examples of successful destination businesses in the lectures
4. Tutors divide the students into groups and assign different roles to them. In the tutorials, the groups then work on a snapshot of the destination's current state and the project challenge. (A template for the snapshot and the final results are prepared in advance and the process is guided by tutors.)
5. Visit to the destination. On the first day, the guide presents the destination and the stakeholders concerned with the project challenge. During the same day, students continue to work in groups and look for solutions to the project challenge. They are also allowed time to discuss solutions on the second day, until the beginning of the workshop with stakeholders. This is where they present their solutions and work on tailoring them to the destination stakeholders' opinions

6. With feedback from the workshop, students further develop their solutions to the project challenge. After one week at the faculty, they present them again to the destination representatives, with whom they then finalise the solutions

7. After an additional week, the final project studies are presented to the tutors, who send them to the destination

TEACHING TIPS

It is important for the teachers/tutors to be very familiar with the destination and the project challenge.

ACTIVITY 39: COMBATING NEGATIVE PREJUDICE AGAINST YOUNG PEOPLE

Maja Turnšek, PhD[58]

DESCRIPTION

Young people have in the past often been perceived in two opposing dichotomies. On the one hand, they have been hailed as the bearers of some of the most important progressive movements. On the other hand, the public discourse has long debated political apathy of young people. As we have pointed out elsewhere (Brlek Slaček and Turnšek, 2010), even in the 1950s scholars were concerned with the apparent apathy of young people and their apparent difficulty in deciding upon worthy causes to address.

It seems, however, that the young people of today have very much consensual views on what issues are to be addressed. Bowels and Carlin (2020) and Bowels and Cohen (2019) argue for a profound change in the way economics is taught around the world. Between 2016 and 2018, they asked 4,442 students from 25 universities in 12 countries what questions economists should be addressing today. Recurring themes were inequality, climate change, instability and robots. What our students thus need from us is not to help them find a cause, but to help them build internal efficacy in advocating for tourism as a strong social force in our post-COVID, politically and economically unequal, climate-change-eroded world.

In other words, we need to help them dispel the negative labels (for example, "snowflake generation") that hinder their political expression. The exercises presented here aim at building the students' capacity in finding their political voice via discussing the historical and sociological roots of blaming the young. We present the students with some common negative judgements of the younger generation as reflected in current and historical media and popular culture (for example, Ruggeri, 2017). Such current negative judgements are then contrasted with the historical line of such critiques and video examples (see, for example, Evans, 2017). Students are asked to find scientifically valid proof for such generational blame via analysing the so-called Flynn effect and its relation to the future of the tourism and hospitality professions.

USAGE SUGGESTIONS

The proposed exercises are primarily suited for participants at the undergraduate level, assuming they belong to the younger generations. However, if the groups are of mixed ages, the discussions will be enriched since participants from various generations can share how they themselves were subject to negative labels in their youth.

LEARNING OBJECTIVES

- Help the students understand generational blame as a form of power struggle between younger and older generations
- Provide insights into how generational blame is a form of judgemental, critical communication that hinders open communication
- Aid the students in thinking about the differences every new generation faces within its work processes and what these different trends might mean for the future of their profession

MATERIALS LIST

The exercises assume that students have Internet access during the workshop in order for them to be able to look for examples. Additionally, YouTube access is required in order to show the students the TEDx videos used as prompts for discussions.

THEORETICAL FOUNDATION

The theoretical underpinning of the presented exercises is based on the classical knowledge that one of the most important preconditions of political action is one's internal political efficacy: personal beliefs regarding the ability to achieve desired results in the political domain through personal engagement and an efficient use of one's own capacities and resources. Internal efficacy mostly concerns the degree of influence that people perceive to be able to exert due to their own capacities. External efficacy, on the other hand, concerns the degree of influence people perceive to be able to exert due to the actual functioning of the political system (Caprara et al., 2009). The proposed exercises are designed in a way to help students build their own internal efficacy while at the same time realising how these negative labels are part of the power struggle – thus a reflection of the functioning of the political system (external efficacy). Labels such as "snowflake generation" are methods used by those in power to decrease the internal efficacy of young people and keep them out of political discussion – thus denying them a voice in the future of tourism as a social force.

TIME PLAN

The exercises have been set up to be composed of 45- to 90-minute workshops with a relatively small group of participants (10–15 people). However, if the group is larger it is advisable to extend the time frame so that everyone has a chance to express themselves and the discussion is appropriately in-depth.

STEP-BY STEP PLAN

Below are some examples of exercises that you can include in your class, workshop or training sessions:

1.   Current versus Old Generational Blame (90 Minutes)

- Have participants use their Internet access (for example, via their phones or laptops in the classroom) to search for a number of current generational blame examples in the popular media; for instance, the "snowflake" generation, "avocado toast stereotype", "generation me". Discuss what they found and how they understand it. Put special emphasis on listening to their feelings about these negative labels. Discuss their own experiences with being the victims of such prejudice in their everyday life: at home, in the pedagogical process
- Next, have participants use their Internet access to search for historical generational blame examples and quotes from famous figures in history. (For a list, see, for example, Ruggeri, 2017.) Discuss what they found and how it compares to the current versions of the stereotypes of young people. Discuss the role of authority and power struggles reflected in these quotes. What difference in values can we see from these historical examples? What could the fears of the authorities hidden in these negative labels be? What needs are these authorities expressing? Should young people give in to these needs at the time?
- Discuss what they know and think about Greta Thunberg. Have participants look for examples of negative media and political backlash towards Greta Thunberg – what examples of generational blame can they find in these examples? Are there any other young political activists today that your students admire – why? What are the stances of these heroes on travel and tourism?

The meaning behind this exercise is to help students perceive the relative "historical universality" of negative labelling of young people and to reflect on the fact that rather than saying much about the young people as objects of these stereotypes, such labels say more about the people who express them.

2.   What Are They Really Saying When They Are Blaming? (45 Minutes)

- Show participants the TEDx Genova talk by Louise Evans (2017) about her own experience when visiting a jazz concert with a young friend. She noticed the friend scrolling on her phone instead of watching the concert. One of her possible reactions could be: "What is wrong with this generation?! I mean, they have the attention span of a fruit fly!" But would she be wrong if she reacted in that way? Watch the full video to see the full range of possible reactions she could have had
- Ask the students to identify the needs that Louise Evans had and the potentially hurtful ways she could have reacted. Discuss with participants the generational blame in some of the presented possible reactions. Discuss which of the reactions they themselves would have if they were in the same position
- Discuss with participants their perception of generational differences in media consumption. Can they reflect on the various examples where other generations do not seem to understand how exactly their use of media is beneficial rather than negative?

The meaning behind this exercise is again to help students reflect on the fact that rather than saying much about the young people as objects of these stereotypes, such labels say more about the people who express them. Additionally, the aim here is to discuss the media consumption as one of the most common generational differences between the younger and older generations.

3. **Every New Generation: Having to Work More in the Cognitive Domains (45 Minutes)**

• Show participants graphs as examples of the Flynn effect (an example of a graph is in Pietschnig and Voracek, 2015, p. 285). The Flynn effect refers to population intelligence increasing throughout the 20th century, although recent years have seen a slowdown or reversal of this trend in several countries (Bratsberg and Rogeberg, 2018; Trahan et al., 2014). In other words, younger generations have actually consistently showed higher IQs than generations before them. As Pietschnig and Voracek (2015) argue, this is mainly due to factors associated with life history speed, favourable social multiplier effects and effects related to economic prosperity

• Ask students to write down their first tentative answer to this question: "Why are our IQ levels are generally higher than our grandparents?" Then show participants the TEDx talk of the original author of the Flynn effect: James R. Flynn (2013), with a similar title

• Discuss with students the cognitive domains of work in travel and hospitality. How are the changes identified by Flynn reflected in the current travel and hospitality workforce? What changes do students expect in the future?

The meaning behind this exercise is to help students understand the historical changes in the IQ domains and how they relate to changes in expected workforce skills and the future of professions in tourism and hospitality.

TEACHING TIPS

Throughout the exercises, do not forget to share your own experiences and do not be afraid to show your own vulnerability regarding the topics addressed. When leading the discussions, be especially mindful of three values that facilitate personal growth according to humanistic psychology (Rogers, 1961/2016): (a) congruence: be what you are, without a front or a façade when discussing with your students; (b) unconditional positive regard: do not simply accept the students when behaving or arguing a certain way, but show outgoing positive feelings towards them without reservations and without evaluations; (c) show empathic understanding: try to sense your students' feelings and personal meaning when discussing their thoughts and feelings, and try as much as possible to communicate this understanding to your students.

ACTIVITY 40: TOURISM TEACHING AND LEARNING USING SPIRITUAL PEDAGOGY

Barkathunnisha Abu Bakar, PhD[59]

DESCRIPTION

While the cognitive capacities of learners are enhanced through readings, lectures and discussion of ideas, the use of innovative approaches such as drawing, poetry, drama, silent reflection and rituals helps to develop the spiritual, imaginative and symbolic dimensions in learners. With a spiritually oriented approach, the attention is not on the knowledge alone, but also on the knower and the process of knowing (Hart, 2014) to gain meaningful interpretation of the tourism phenomenon. The premise is that the knower cannot be separated from the known, and there is a mutually influential relationship between the two. The knower is able to influence the knowing process and thus the knowledge. The knowledge-production process of a spiritually oriented approach is grounded on perspectives of "subjectification and intimacy" rather than "objectification and distancing" (Palmer et al., 2010, p. 94). For example, the use of a community service programme in tourism aimed at improving the quality of lives of an Indigenous community can encourage learners to reflect on themselves and the world around them, promoting participative and empathetic ways of knowing. The understanding is that objectification and disconnection of learners from knowledge results in a disconnect from the consequences of one's actions and personal responsibility, resulting in global problems. For instance, when students undergo a lecture on the impacts of unethical tourism on the lives of the long-necked Kayan community in Thailand, the context and content may not be "experienced", and a deep understanding of the plight of the women may not be gained to facilitate self-reflexivity and personal responsibility in our students.

One of the pedagogical tools used in a spiritually oriented educational experience is critical thinking. To promote critical thinking, students need to develop a sense of focus and a deeper consciousness of themselves. The focus is on nurturing the reflective capacity for an inner consciousness and a deepened awareness of environmental and societal issues in tourism.

A spiritual pedagogy also employs engaged teaching that is inspired by experiences from a variety of sources – from what we feel, read, sense, observe, create, believe, intuit and test.

USAGE SUGGESTIONS

The target audience is undergraduates of tourism higher education. These activities can be conducted online if physical presence in the classroom is not possible.

LEARNING OBJECTIVES

These exercises are intended to help the student:

- Harvest from new knowledge intermediaries
- Question and challenge what is taken for granted
- Risk the adventure of creative journeys, using creativity tools and new ways of collaboration

- Strengthen critical thinking skills through interactive teaching processes

MATERIALS LIST

- Colour markers
- Flip charts

THEORETICAL FOUNDATION

The integration of spirituality in tourism education is proposed to direct students towards their inner selves, enable them to expand their consciousness and to see their lives as part of the universal human experience (Barkathunnisha et al., 2018). An educational approach that integrates spirituality aims to develop students' sense of interdependency and interrelationships with all aspects of life and centres on nurturing a deep sense of compassion and unity. The educational experience is focused on a movement towards a *metanoia*, a holistic intellectual, affective and spiritual shift from alienation into a deeper awareness of one's meaning and purpose (Vella, 2000).

TIME PLAN

- Activity 1: Breathing exercise: 5 minutes
- Discussion/journaling: 10 minutes
- Activity 2: Drawing activity: 15 minutes
- Discussion: 15 minutes

ACTIVITY 1

This activity could be used at the beginning of a class to develop students' presence of mind, to encourage them to focus and to be mindful of their thoughts. It is a useful way to help students transition from their busy day, disengage from the media that they are hooked on and introduce quiet and internal focus. It prepares students to be aware of visual sensory input and inner stillness and be observant to thoughts and movements. It is also a powerful exercise to enable students to acknowledge others' presence and experience their interconnectedness.

Step-by-Step Plan

- Ask students to sit in a "pedagogical circle" so that everyone can face each other. This seating arrangement lends to a sense of closeness and a non-hierarchical mode of transmission of knowledge where the educator is also a member of the learning experience
- Students are requested to close their eyes and breathe for about five minutes
- Ask students to observe their breathing and their thought processes during the few minutes
- Next, ask them to open their eyes and observe those sitting next to them and around the class. What were their observations, assumptions, feelings? Did they notice something that they could not have if not for the exercise? What domains (intellectual, affective, spiritual)

did they use in the process? You may want to facilitate a sharing session or request students to journal their thoughts and encourage reflexivity

ACTIVITY 2

Visual art (drawing and colouring) can be a very valuable pedagogical tool to facilitate the exploration of ideas, stimulate creativity and enable reflections and sharing in a non-intimidating environment. Students also learn to acknowledge and appreciate other perspectives without demonstrating judgements.

Step-by-Step Plan

- Distribute colour markers and flip charts to students. Alternatively, in an interactive classroom (with interactive whiteboards and whiteboard-finished tables) students can be encouraged to draw anywhere that they are comfortable. This activity can be used when the class topic centres on controversial issues in tourism (for example, wildlife tourism) or abstract and challenging concepts (for example, who is a "good" tourist?), or when facilitating creative strategies and ideas in tourism
- Provide 15 minutes for this activity and ask students to creatively draw their thoughts and perspectives. Play background music to facilitate the process. Students' ideas and thoughts can be encouraged to flow as there is no right or wrong in drawing and there are no judgements of anyone's perspectives. This activity can also encourage contemplation, which is an alternative way of being conscious in the world, to take a distant view from an issue and deliberate
- At the end of 15 minutes, break students into small pedagogical circles, and facilitate their sharing

TEACHING TIPS

If the educator is familiar with mandala art, this could also be used. Mandala art is a powerful tool to promote creativity, self-expression, concentration and deep connection within oneself.

ACTIVITY 41: FOSTERING CRITICAL THINKING UTILISING BROOKFIELD'S CRITICAL INCIDENT QUESTIONNAIRE

Karla A. Boluk, PhD[60]

DESCRIPTION

Steven Brookfield's (1987, 2012) Critical Incident Questionnaire (CIQ) is a five-item evaluation tool prompting students to reflect on their learning experiences, when they felt most engaged and distanced from the course, actions that were affirming or helpful in their learning, moments during the class when they felt puzzled or confused, and times when they felt surprised by something they learned or experienced. Boluk et. al (2019) included a sixth question, requiring personal reflection on actions taken by students to improve their learning in their courses. Utilising the CIQ as a tool throughout a course presents an opportunity for students to practise and explore critical thinking *in situ*, as well as enhancing their critical reflection skills.

USAGE SUGGESTIONS

The audience for this contribution is undergraduate students. It is important to introduce critical thinking, reading and writing at the beginning of the course. Following this introduction, the CIQ can be administered weekly or biweekly following specific discussions or exercises assigned to students. The CIQ may be administered in class or on virtual learning platforms. The time required for the surveys may range between ten and 20 minutes. The instructor should review the CIQs once submitted and present a synopsis of the reflections back to students, signalling evidence of critical thinking within the responses. Students could also review and reflect on their own critical reflection trajectories towards the end of the semester noting their critical progress. Specifically, students could reflect on what may have helped them throughout the semester (or more broadly throughout their degree to date) to enhance their ability to critically engage (specific formal class discussions, informal conversations, exercises, lectures, readings, visual materials, and so on).

LEARNING OBJECTIVES

1. To understand the meaning of critical thinking and critical reflection
2. To appreciate the time required to consciously, thoughtfully and critically reflect on information received, literature reviewed, experiences and processes
3. To reflect on and assess one's own critical thinking progress
4. To apply critical thinking and critical reflection capabilities in order to evaluate information consumed

MATERIALS LIST

Prior to administering the CIQ, a lecture on critical thinking and critical reflection is required. Next, the CIQ is a series of six questions that may be administered in a face-to-face setting or virtually (see questions below).

PRE-WORK REQUIRED BY STUDENTS

Students should have listened to the lecture/overview on critical thinking and critical reflection, and fulfilled the assigned course expectations – for example, course readings, assignments, participating in class discussions.

THEORETICAL FOUNDATION

Brookfield's (1987) CIQ is a five-question evaluation tool encouraging student reflection on learning experiences through probing questions about moments students felt most engaged, distanced, affirmed, confused and surprised. Boluk, Cavaliere and Duffy (2019) developed a sixth question, requiring reflection on actions students may take to improve their learning.

Limited scholarship has examined the CIQ to explore critical thinking and/or enhance critical reflection, aside from Gilstrap and Dupree (2008), who identified the CIQ as an effective tool to "assess student critical thinking" *in situ*, and as a formative assessment for educators highlighting opportunities to enhance teaching methods (p. 410; also see Glowacki-Dudka and Barnett, 2007). Another example analysed the CIQ after four years of organisational and academic use and notes the CIQ "should be adaptable based on learner and instructor needs" (Keefer, 2009, p. 181). The CIQ may also serve as a useful method of data collection to study effective teaching methods and a strategy for bringing criticality to the classroom through critical reflection.

TIME PLAN

The CIQ should be administered at the end of a class and/or virtual learning participation. Brookfield recommends its use weekly in a 12-week course. Boluk, Cavaliere and Duffy (2019) used it effectively biweekly (six times in a 12-week course). They (2019) noted that it is important to build in sufficient time for administering the survey when course-planning. Between ten and 20 minutes should be expected to complete the questions:

1. At what moment in class this week were you most engaged as a learner?
2. At what moment in class this week were you most distanced as a learner?
3. What action that anyone in the room took this week did you find the most affirming or helpful?
4. What action that anyone in the room took this week did you find most puzzling or confusing?
5. What surprised you most about class this week? (Brookfield, 1987; 2012)
6. What specific actions have you taken to improve the quality of learning in this class (either to improve your own learning, or to help others learn)? (Boluk, Cavaliere and Duffy, 2019)

TEACHING TIPS

As explained above, it is imperative that students understand the techniques for enhancing critical thinking and critical reflection. Therefore, the critical thinking/reflection lecture at the outset of the course is necessary. Furthermore, synthesising and presenting examples of critical thinking/reflection throughout the course is useful for students.

ACTIVITY 42: META-PEDAGOGICAL MELIORISM 3: KNOWLEDGE

Elin Bommenel, PhD,[61] **Richard Ek, PhD**[62] **and Stuart Reid**[63]

DESCRIPTION

Our foundational idea is that students can improve themselves (and, indirectly, the world) by being aware of all that they have learned, and by being aware that learning takes place in different ways. That awareness, in turn, produces different behaviour in learning situations within and outside the classroom. Consequently, a tolerance for, and understanding of, different learning techniques is established, which is a condition for a secure learning environment for all participants.

USAGE SUGGESTIONS

The three contributions on meta-pedagogical meliorism all relate to an introductory week for a newly arrived class of international students with pedagogically heterogenous learning backgrounds. However, the concept of teaching and learning regimes is equally applicable to industry professionals, undergraduate and graduate classes, and also to more homogenous groups who are meeting for the first time. Learning is a personal journey, but teaching seldom makes meta-pedagogy overt. All the activities involved with these contributions are aimed at highlighting this fact.

LEARNING OBJECTIVES

By the end of this activity participants should be able to:

• Acknowledge that the teaching and learning regime they will encounter at the current university is, to varying extents, different from what they have experienced, and that they need to understand and master the new teaching and learning regime in order to perform well in the new educational programme

THEORETICAL FOUNDATION

Teaching and learning regimes, a concept advanced by Trowler and Cooper (2002), imply a constellation of assumptions, rules, relationships and practices regarding higher education that shapes the performance of academic staff members in their profession. For Trowler and Cooper, teaching and learning regimes serve as a heuristic tool in a reflection process to help university staff become aware of their own situated knowledge. Thus, they are a tool for unpacking institutional and tacit, or more-or-less taken-for-granted, professional knowledge and for contemplating its implications for teaching. Depending on the teaching and learning regime that the individual teacher is socialised into, or even institutionalised in, they will have a certain teaching style, emphasising different approaches to knowledge and different ways to increase knowledge, that is acted out in the teaching situation, in the design of examining activities and in the grading. When the students understand this, they also realise that there exists a cipher to understanding an "incomprehensible" teacher – the teaching and learning regime the teacher departs from and the one they use in their practice. This is an empowering insight.

The divide between teacher and students is designed into the very organisation of higher education. But understanding the divide as a distinction between different learning regimes, rather than as, for instance, an asymmetric situation of intellectual or cultural capital, reduces the risk that the student finds the situation intimidating. This, in turn, reduces the risk that the student experiences the new learning situation as a threat to their identity, with anxiety and impeded learning following as a result.

Further to that, the students preferably realise that the experience of being a novice is partly a result of comparison. Some students are more familiar with the teaching and learning regime at hand than others. And it is just that, and not a differentiation based on other identity traits like social class and ethnicity, nor a reflection of individual learning capability. With this awareness in the class, an atmosphere of equality, solidarity and tolerance can be more easily realised. Understanding the cipher of the teaching and learning regime becomes a collective or social task, with great rewards regarding the possibility to learn.

TIME PLAN

We have divided the introduction week into six phases with some online preparations. This contribution on knowledge values covers phases two and three. Phase one is covered in Chapter 5 on social values, and phases four to six in Chapter 1 on didactics. In our case we dedicated one week to this process, but it is possible to tailor the time and resources dedicated to this programme task. It is, however, our experience that the students need a full week to allow time for contemplation, reflection and engagement in different learning tasks. This is particularly the case if the student cohort comes from all parts of the world (as in our case), bringing all sorts of teaching and learning regimes with them.

STEP-BY-STEP PLAN

Phase Two: Teaching and Learning Regimes and Learning Styles

In the second phase, following the first on learning, the teaching and learning regime as a concept is presented in depth and discussed. Some theoretical outline is necessary; thus, a lecture is needed, but one way to entangle different teaching and learning regimes is to include the lecture in a seminar where you ask the students what kind of teaching and learning they have encountered in previous studies at university. The lecture-seminar can be held via the Web if students can be asked to discuss in groups of three or four at times. A collective typology can then be developed, or some characteristic traits that the students can agree upon.

As the purpose of this second step is to invite and involve the students in reasoning from a pedagogical perspective, an interactive, dialogue-based lecture works better than an interactive and discussion-based seminar. The prime purpose of this second phase is not only to move the concept of teaching and learning regime from backstage to frontstage, but also to present the characteristics of the teaching and learning regime the students will encounter in the new programme.

In the teaching and learning regime at work at Lund University (as in Northern Europe in general) the core characteristics are active learning, self-motivation, focus on deep learning and critical thinking, and discussion. It may be important to share some content or at least vocabulary and models from the material in the university's teacher-training courses (in our case, for example, Ambrose et al., 2010; Biggs and Tang, 2011; McKeachie and Svinicki, 2013). In this literature, the theme for the next phases shines through and is thus introduced in its context: the distinction between surface and deep approach to learning, the importance of critique and the inherent change of subject position each student needs to make, to varying degrees depending on their familiarity with the present teaching and learning regime.

Phase Three: Surface and Deep Learning

Different teaching and learning regimes emphasise and facilitate one of the following: a surface approach to learning, a deep approach to learning or, more often than not, something in between the two. In each case, the learner is confronted with a challenge that creates cognitive or intellectual dissonance. Challenge and/or dissonance is necessary for development (if we listen to Piaget's cognitive approach). This is something the students need to be informed about, along with the fact that they, as sense-making beings, can reject or appropriate the challenge/dissonance. In other words, each student is empowered to determine for themselves when learning is taking place.

From a Heideggerian perspective we could say that the student's pre-understanding is challenged by exterior information, facts or viewpoints. Deep learning here fits better into this hermeneutic circle, as deep learning not only focuses upon the content but is also operationalised in questions like:

- What is the author's point with the text?
- In which spatio-temporal context is the text written?
- How does that relate to the meaning of the text as well as the "facts" presented in it?
- What kind of worldview is expressed in the text?

TEACHING TIPS

Students socialised into a teaching and learning regime that favours a surface approach to learning will tend to feel confident when they are expected to receive and store knowledge, when there is a strong focus on facts or contents, when the knowledge per se does not affect them personally and when the knowledge is disseminated by an authority who conveys "the truth".

Students socialised into a teaching and learning regime that favours a deep approach to learning will tend to feel secure even when the knowledge affects their worldview, they are challenged on an intellectual level and they are invited to express their understandings of, or reflections upon, the topic.

In our own pedagogical work, we have many students familiar with a teaching and learning regime that favours a surface approach who need to get acquainted with, and eventually master, engagement with a teaching and learning regime premised upon a deep approach to learning.

The first step of this transition is to make the distinction between a surface and a deep approach visible for all students. In sum, to take a meta-theoretical approach to learning, by learning how to learn, or how to learn in a different way than one is accustomed to.

ACTIVITY 43: FIELD TRIP FINDINGS PRESENTED THROUGH A PHOTO ESSAY

Joan Flaherty, MA, MSc[64]

DESCRIPTION

1. During the field trip: students are asked to take photos that reflect key lessons they are learning about the trip's tourism-related topic – or that simply grab their attention
2. After the field trip: students present their findings re the field trip in the form of a photo essay; for example, each key finding is accompanied by a photo(s). In addition, students deliver oral presentations, using the photos taken on the field trip

I used this exercise for a field course in Nepal and found that it led students to think about the topic – sustainable tourism – from both a macro and a micro perspective. (That is, while students took photos of iconic images, such as mountain peaks, temples, villagers in colourful dress, they also took photos of mundane, daily life experiences, such as a plastic water bottle discarded on the path or a donkey carrying an overloaded burden.) Integrating the two perspectives prompted them to make unexpected connections that suggested a more nuanced understanding of the topic than I had expected. Integrating photos with their own narrative on what they had learned also prompted the students' emotional engagement in the subject matter, laying the groundwork for them to reflect on the importance of values and beliefs – their own and those that underpin tourism.

USAGE SUGGESTIONS

This photo essay assignment is suitable for a wide range of learners (undergraduate, graduate, practitioners) and can be easily modified to address different tourism-related topics and contexts. Depending on the students' learning style, the teaching/learning approach can vary from self-directed to highly structured. Note, too, that a field trip assignment does not necessarily refer to a group field trip. The same learning outcomes could be addressed by having students visit a local site individually or a distant site virtually.

LEARNING OBJECTIVES

• Explore values and beliefs that shape your choice of photos and their accompanying text
• Identify and synthesise relevant key themes and information
• Develop and present material logically and coherently in appropriate written and visual and oral form

MATERIALS LIST

A camera is needed (for example, cellphone camera).

THEORETICAL FOUNDATION

The assignment is heavily influenced by Weimer's five characteristics of a learner-centred approach (2002): student engagement, explicit skill instruction, reflection, student control over the learning process and collaboration. Here, students are given the freedom to choose their own focus of attention, based on what they perceive as being important – a task (and a responsibility) that requires complete engagement and that gives them significant control over their learning process. "Significant" control, of course, does not mean complete control. Time is devoted to ensuring that each student understands the expectations and is guided towards successfully achieving them (see *Time plan*). The final oral presentation allows students a chance to share and debrief their experiences in a collaborative context.

The assignment also addresses the need for our students to be literate in a number of ways – in this particular case, in written, visual and spoken forms.

TIME PLAN

The assignment can be used in a wide variety of courses. Therefore, the time plan would be tailored to reflect the course's specific content. Generally speaking, though, the exercise would unfold in the following way:

- Before the field trip: establish a teaching/learning environment that reflects Weimer's five key characteristics of a learner-centred approach. A particular focus on "explicit skill instruction" might be in order – as a way of addressing any student preferences for a structured approach. For example, time should be spent discussing how to organise, write and present the photo essay
- During the field trip: the instructor acts as facilitator, encouraging student engagement and reflection while providing support and structure
- After the field trip: students deliver their oral presentations, with time for discussion and debriefing of the field trip and the key lessons learned

TEACHING TIPS

Despite the ubiquity of the term "learner-centred", it has been my experience that not every student is familiar or comfortable with the approach. Some students might be stressed by having to take responsibility for their own learning. That is why it is important to establish the approach before the field trip assignment and to pay particular attention to providing adequate structure.

ACTIVITY 44: DESIGN-BASED LEARNING AND DESIGN THINKING FOR INNOVATION EDUCATION

Giang T. Phi, PhD[65]

DESCRIPTION

Design-based learning and its hallmark, design thinking (DT), is one of the most popular pedagogies associated with innovation education. DT fosters deep empathy for the end-users by engaging them throughout the innovation process, a high level of creativity in the generation of ideas and solutions, and sound rationality in analysing the problem situation and evaluating its potential solutions. DT is thus often referred to as "outside the box" pedagogy that challenges the traditional divide between creative thinking and critical/rational thinking. DT is frequently carried out in the format of a sprint, ranging from two days to several months, and ends with a showcase event where new ideas/prototypes are presented to an audience. Through learning-by-doing via the participation in a DT sprint, learners acquire key innovation competencies such as creative problem-solving, system thinking and networking.

USAGE SUGGESTIONS

This contribution is suited for students at both undergraduate and graduate levels, as well as practitioners interested in using DT to innovate or generate user-centred solutions to existing problems.

DT sprint has been adopted both for physical and online learning environments, although most of the stages in the DT process take place outside the classroom. These stages can be through self-directed and facilitated group work, self-directed learning and self-directed in-person/online field work.

LEARNING OBJECTIVES

Students should be able to:

- Understand the interrelatedness between creativity, critical thinking and networking in the innovation/knowledge generation process
- Develop innovative solutions to existing problems utilising DT and a user-centred approach
- Evaluate the influences of self and universal values in innovations

MATERIALS LIST

- Classroom version: preferably moveable tables/chairs to quickly set up different formations and foster learners' creativity through removing rigid structures
- Online version: computer/Internet, a learning platform to host readings/videos/lectures and to communicate with learners; an online conference platform to host the virtual showcase event

- Optional: physical/virtual sticky notes to support brainstorming sessions; papers, tapes, pencils, strings or online drawing tools to create quick visualisations/prototypes

PRE-WORK REQUIRED BY STUDENTS

Students should have been exposed (in their previous studies or in the introduction unit of this course) to discussions on their own values and a diverse range of values embedded in the debates of sustainability, sustainable development and, when relevant, the United Nations' 17 Sustainable Development Goals.

THEORETICAL FOUNDATION

This contribution is based on design-based learning, a pedagogy which integrates DT and real-world challenges with the knowledge and skills of specific curricular subjects to foster learners' innovation competencies. Suggested sources include Raber (2015), Tschimmel (2012) and Brown (2009).

TIME PLAN

A DT sprint can be carried out via both:

- Short format as a training course or competition (for example, a two-day hackathon or four-day bootcamp)
- Long format of a teaching period in higher education (for example, a four-week intensive or normal 12-week semester)

STEP-BY-STEP PLAN

1. DT 101: introduce learners to DT principles, tools, key DT stages and key milestones for the DT sprint
2. Team formation: learners are asked to select their own team members (three to five per group) based on similar values and/or interests in particular issues they want to address during the DT sprint. This is guided by the pre-work section on values
3. Discover/empathy stage: in-person or online field work to generate insights on the problems by engaging with the groups directly affected. Learners can use diverse tools such as journey mapping, observation, interviews, surveys, and so on
4. Define/point-of-view stage: unique insights on the users' problems are generated based on the collected data
5. Develop stage: a wide range of ideas is generated through tools such as brainstorming/reviewing existing solutions, and so on, to solve the defined problems
6. Deliver/implementation stage: the team discusses and evaluates different options to choose ideas with the most potential to develop prototypes and test feasibility and usability
7. Showcase event: the sprint ends with a pitching/showcase competition where different teams pitch to both a panel of judges and the wider audience to receive more feedback
8. Report writing (optional for university students): students are asked to write a report on their DT sprint and reflect on DT, innovation and personal/professional development

These steps allow students to develop both divergent thinking (that is, via the Discover and Develop stages) and convergent thinking (that is, via the Define and Deliver stages), and better understand the interrelatedness between creative thinking, critical thinking and system thinking in innovations. By actively reaching out to relevant users in their networks and developing new networks throughout the sprint, students also develop important networking skills. These are further supported with the showcase event, which also serves as testing/validation for their innovations.

TEACHING TIPS

- As DT is very task-centred and focuses on learning-by-doing, teachers would have to adopt the coach or facilitator roles, instead of the traditional roles of a knowledge expert and controller
- Checkpoints (that is, consultation sessions, peer-to-peer feedback) should be established throughout different stages of the DT sprint, in order to provide tailored guidance that can improve learners' understanding and motivation. However, this will incur extra teaching hours outside the classroom that currently are not acknowledged by many higher education institutions
- While the DT sprint follows linear stages to support beginners' learning, it is important to emphasise to learners that the innovation process is rarely linear, and they can keep going back and forth or jump between any of the stages once they become more familiar with DT

ACTIVITY 45: SEEING TOURISM LANDSCAPES: TEACHING TOURISM AT THE CONFLUENCE OF THEORY AND PRACTICE

Bradley Rink, PhD[66]

DESCRIPTION

This contribution discusses a multilevel assessment task in an introductory tourism module that allows students to integrate theory into practice. The assignment that culminates the activity assesses students' skills in identifying and articulating sociocultural, environmental and economic impacts of tourism at various scales. Activities leading up to the assessed task provide an opportunity for students to engage geographical perspectives on tourism using the tourist landscape approach. Activities also challenge students to communicate visually and through texts. The assessment task takes a scaffolded approach facilitated by teaching and learning through tutorial or small-group interaction where students apply theory from the fields of geography and tourism into everyday "landscapes of tourism". Theory provides a means to unlock new ways of seeing otherwise familiar and banal landscapes. While the personal experience of tourism as a tourist is uncommon for the cohort of students at the author's institution, the semester-long, scaffolded assessment task allows students to "see" tourism in the everyday, while also critically reflecting on tourism's positive and negative impacts.

USAGE SUGGESTIONS

This activity is appropriate for undergraduate students within an introductory level of tourism and/or geography studies with a tourism focus. The activity was developed in the context of a semester-long introductory tourism module which students entered after one year of geography study. While the activity has been designed for use in face-to-face contact sessions, it can be adapted to an online or blended learning environment.

LEARNING OBJECTIVES

Upon completion of the activity, students should be able to:

- Describe the elements of touristic landscapes
- Apply geographical knowledge and theory to tourism studies
- Articulate the sociocultural, environmental and economic impacts of tourism at various scales

MATERIALS LIST

As noted below, students should have access to devices that allow capturing of photographic images (mobile phone, camera, tablet, and so on). For face-to-face activities using photographs, the facilitator should ideally have access to printing facilities where student-submitted images can be printed for discussion and peer review.

PRE-WORK REQUIRED BY STUDENTS

Given the context of tourism studies in this example, students are assumed to have some theoretical and conceptual knowledge related to geography, upon which tourism studies are introduced.

THEORETICAL FOUNDATION

This activity focuses on lived values that are part of the author's institutional graduate attributes, and illustrates concern for student learning needs that are inquiry-based, situated in spaces which enable creative and flexible teaching and learning facilitated through tutorial or small-group interaction. In the scaffolded approach of this activity, both the content and the assessment are built up through a range of learning activities through lectures and tutorials. This activity builds upon student-centred, constructivist and authentic learning pedagogies that emphasise "active and deep learning, increased responsibility and accountability on the part of the student, an increased sense of autonomy in the learner, an interdependence between teacher and learner" (Lea et al., 2003, p. 233). Herrington et al. (2010) offer an evaluation matrix for assessing authentic learning design, arguing that the ideal learning environment will:

1. Provide authentic contexts that reflect the way the knowledge will be used in real life
2. Provide authentic activities
3. Provide access to expert performances and the modelling of processes

4. Provide multiple roles and perspectives
5. Support collaborative construction of knowledge
6. Promote reflection to enable abstractions to be formed
7. Promote articulation to enable tacit knowledge to be made explicit
8. Provide coaching and scaffolding by the teacher at critical times
9. Provide for authentic assessment of learning within the tasks

Taken together, these benchmarks for situated learning environments help to ensure the delivery of authentic learning that is student-centred, applicable in real-world situations and socially embedded in practice.

TIME PLAN

This activity is designed for a semester-long undergraduate tourism module with one lecture contact hour per week, and one (hour-long) tutorial every second week. The activity is structured to take approximately six weeks (not including pre-survey) – from introduction of the assignment task to submission.

- Pre-survey: since the activity requires capturing and sharing of real-world examples of tourist landscapes in their surroundings, students are surveyed (using Google Forms or a similar platform) regarding their access to various technologies, equipment and connectivity; this survey is a critical initial step to ensure that all students have appropriate access and can engage in the activity as designed
- Tutorials: three tutorials over a period of six weeks
- Assignment: preliminary and final submission

STEP-BY-STEP PLAN

1.   Tutorial

The assignment is introduced to students during a tutorial session with the theme of "Introduction to Tourism Landscapes", along with theoretical concept of "tourism landscapes" as discussed by Zhang (2015).

2.   Tutorial

In the following tutorial session, "Photo Interpretation", students develop skills in describing, interpreting and explaining elements that articulate the sociocultural, environmental and economic impacts of tourism at various scales. The tutorial provides an opportunity to engage geographical perspectives on tourism using the tourist landscape approach while challenging students to communicate visually and through written texts.

Using photographs provided by the lecturer, students are asked to describe, interpret and explain (DIE) elements in the photograph related to tourist subjectivity, mobilities and destinations (amenities, attractions, access and ancillary services) – theoretical material that is delivered in an earlier series of lectures. The DIE approach can be broken down as follows:

- Describe: simply make a list of what you see, your sensory perceptions (I see "x", "y", "z")
- Interpret: decode and understand relationships between elements in the photograph
- Explain: assess and/or judge how the elements bring meaning, emotion, and so on

Students provide short descriptive sentences related to each element and their relationships, and are asked to describe the tourism landscape and its social, economic and environmental dimensions as explained by Zhang (2015, p. 119): "Landscapes can be attractions. Visually appealing settings, both natural and cultural, form the basis of tourism; soundscapes, smells-capes and therapeutic landscapes may relate to perceptual senses beyond vision, exuding additional appeal to attractions and destinations."
Students submit their responses as a group, with the names and student numbers of the group members present.

3.   Student Task

After completing an environmental scan of the area where they live or spend time, students source a photograph for use in the activity. The photograph is meant to illustrate a touristic landscape in any sense as described by Zhang (2015). The photograph may be sourced by cap-turing the photograph themselves (preferred), or by selecting a photograph from a secondary source that is properly cited and approved for re-use. The latter option is primarily for students who may not have access to a smartphone or camera. Students upload their photograph to a course portal for use in the tutorial activities.

4.   Tutorial

In the next tutorial, "Tourism Landscapes Peer Review", students are given opportunities to generate knowledge through group interaction and discussion. Learning activities allow students with different learning styles to gather and articulate knowledge in preparation for submission of the final assignment task. The tutorial requires students to take part in peer review of their class assignment photograph according to the following steps:

- One-by-one in their small groups, students share the photograph that will be used for the assignment. This may be done electronically, with all students accessing the uploaded photograph from Step 3 on their devices, and/or with printed versions of photographs provided by the lecturer
- Each group member takes turns to DIE elements in the photograph related to tourist sub-jectivity, mobilities and destinations (amenities, attractions, access and ancillary services). The DIE approach (as noted in Step 2 above) is used, and notations (electronically or using small sticky notes attached to photographs) capture student feedback
- Students are further prompted to consider:
  - What is visible and invisible in the photograph as it relates to tourism?
  - Tourism impacts that are visible/invisible

- The type of tourism landscape(s) that is/are shown in the photograph, aligned with Zhang's (2015) definition

5.   Preliminary Submission and Feedback

After rounds of peer review in tutorial setting, students submit a preliminary draft for which feedback is provided by the lecturer.

6.   Final Submission

Students consider feedback from peers and from the lecturer in crafting their final submission. This scaffolded approach enables the assessment task to produce formative outcomes. Students are provided with specific requirements and a marking rubric as below:

- Using your sourced photo, provide a written analysis of the photo. You may use the DIE approach as it relates to tourist subjectivity, mobilities and destinations (amenities, attractions, access and ancillary services). You should also discuss the environmental, economic and/or sociocultural impacts that are present in the image
- Your analysis of the touristic landscape might focus on the natural, heritage, manufactured or other dimensions of landscape, and should include a discussion of the elements that are present in the photograph that support your landscape analysis. Describe the tourism landscape and its social, economic and environmental dimensions as explained by Zhang (2015)
- The final submission of no more than 750 words of text and image should be uploaded using our Google Form. Criteria and mark allocation are as follows:

Criteria	Marks
Format, style and quality of photograph	20
Identification and analysis of photographic elements	40
Description of touristic landscape	40
Total	100

7.   Public Dissemination/Online Exhibit

The portfolio of evidence from the assignment is presented online using a project website found here: https://sites.google.com/myuwc.ac.za/tou223/home.

TEACHING TIPS

This activity is particularly suited for students who may not have experienced tourism themselves (as tourists), but who may live in a town/city/region where tourism is an important part of the economy. It is as much about bridging theory and practice as it is about opening students' eyes to the ways that tourism shapes landscapes.

ACTIVITY 46: THE VALUE OF THE UNINTENDED IN TOURISM EDUCATION: MEXICAN CASE

Helene Balslev Clausen, PhD[67] and Maggie C. Miller, PhD[68]

DESCRIPTION

Within this contribution we hope that educators learn to resist the temptation to avoid and/or oversimplify unexpected situations brought on by "trouble" in the field (that is, situations that, at first glance, seem dismaying). We argue that these instances can be learning opportunities that add value to higher education and can contribute to changes in students' attitudes and actions upon their return home.

Sustained by a shared vision for experiential education, this contribution explores the following questions:

- How can educators learn to use unintended mishaps and unexpected encounters as pedagogical tools?
- How can unintended situations in field courses support students' development as critical thinkers as well as actively engage them in societal challenges once back home?

USAGE SUGGESTIONS

This activity is relevant for a wide range of learners: both undergraduate and graduate students in various programmes, as well as practitioners.

LEARNING OBJECTIVES

- Appreciate how unintended situations in field courses can become deep learning experiences
- Reflect upon the learning opportunities presented by "trouble" in the field

THEORETICAL FOUNDATION

The unintended can be an opening, a space full of generative possibility. Therefore, we urge tourism educators to practise "staying with the trouble" (Haraway, 2016), using the unintended as deep learning experiences for their students and themselves.

Educators are typically not trained to stay with, or even sway towards, trouble, and thus are often unsure how to provide meaningful responses when anything unintended does occur. Further, unknown cultural contexts and behavioural interactions are important and should be reflected upon in relation to the decisions that are made and communicated while in the field.

FIELD SCENARIO: QUESTION POWER, PRIVILEGE AND WESTERN NORMS IN TULUM, MEXICO

In 2019, 18 masters' students went to Tulum, Mexico to conduct 12 days of field work. One of the primary objectives of this trip was to present proposals in collaboration with various stakeholders (including local authorities and non-governmental organisations) on solutions to minimise the growing mountains of plastic waste in the village due to increasing tourism and lack of adequate infrastructure.

After conducting field work (collecting material, analysing and writing a report), the students were to present their proposals to various stakeholders, including the regional tourism minister, who is managing a tourism budget of 70 million USD a year; the secretary of tourism in the region; the mayor; and the local tourism manager of Tulum.

The students spent hours preparing, rehearsing and discussing how to conduct their presentations, and were both very eager and nervous. In advance, they asked if they would have access to electronic media and PowerPoint, and the authorities answered: "Yes, of course."

Then, on the day for the presentation, the students were caught by surprise. They had to squeeze into a tiny room of approximately 10 square meters for their presentation, while also making space for the panel of four government representatives well dressed in suits, despite it being 35°C outside and the lack of air conditioning inside.

The students were shocked by the unfolding, unplanned situation: the limited capacity in the hot and tiny room, the missing (promised) PowerPoint projector, and the lack of tables and chairs for all left them panicked! They started to desperately reorganise, and decided that only four students should be in the room while presenting.

However, the governmental representatives insisted on everyone being present in the room, and the students once again had to reorganise before launching their final presentations.

TEACHING TIPS

"Staying with the trouble" entails resisting panic, recovering and learning, which all rest on both student and course leader resilience. To manage the presentation within the unintended contexts and circumstances, students cultivated responses that were empathetic and adaptive. This was expressed in course feedback after returning home:

> Being hands-on with the cases, how to approach the cases and adapt to the cases and the situated contexts. I think you may have a lot of ideas while you sit at your desk and do theoretical work but when you get into a context, you have to learn to adapt to it, how to handle it and take care of it. (Student L, March 2019)

> I also think our pre-understanding was rattled when we got into the context. We had some presumptions or pre-understandings about Mexico but when we got into the context we had to adapt it in a radical way. Not just small things but a whole new way of thinking which was good because it will shape our future understandings. (Student E, March 2019)

Reflection took place daily within creative workshops each afternoon. Here the course leaders (from Aalborg University and Colegio del Estado de Hidalgo) encouraged students to reflect on their experiences, both around the surprises and challenges encountered within their groups. Each workshop ended with open dialogue about the wider (sometimes uncontrollable) contexts, and why students perceived and experienced these as challenging, and, more importantly, how they might navigate such contexts.

This case study, along with its companion case study on our Nepal field trip, demonstrates ways in which the unintended – unexpected mishaps – can redirect our pedagogical attention to what and how students learn and can learn. These instances become part of transformative practices, affording opportunities to pause, reflect and rethink the ways in which we respond to differences and the evolving dynamics of the places we visit for education. The link between *what* and *how* we learn is pivotal in higher education, and mishaps within the field might be a way to strengthen this link, leading to deeper understandings of *why* this learning is necessary and valuable. Indeed, as educators open space to dwell in the unknown, they pave the way "for the continuous something coming together which is not rooted in fixed or pre-determined conditions but rather in the new lines or threads which are set in motion" (Tucker, 2018).

ACTIVITY 47: PROFESSIONAL PRACTICE REVIEW OF LEARNING

Émilie Crossley, PhD[69]

DESCRIPTION

The "Review of Learning" is a postgraduate professional practice assessment designed for experienced practitioners. The assessment can be applied to a tourism context as a vehicle for enhancing values-based leadership through critical reflection on work-based learning (WBL). Learners engage in autobiographical reflection, enabling them to (a) explain their career history and development of their professional identity, (b) critically reflect on their learning across educational/practice dimensions and (c) articulate their current/aspirational framework of professional practice. A 5,000-word written reflective commentary is produced with support from a learning facilitator that captures the Review of Learning. This exercise is potentially empowering for tourism practitioners, allowing them to validate learning gained in the workplace, strengthen professional identity, reflect on values guiding their practice and enhance leadership. This contribution is based on the Review of Learning used at Capable NZ, a leading provider of work-based and independent learning qualifications in Aotearoa/New Zealand (Ker, 2017).

USAGE SUGGESTIONS

The Review of Learning is a guided reflective assessment that can be facilitated at a distance. This assessment is suitable for postgraduate learners and practitioners who wish to develop critical self-awareness as a foundation for enhancing their professional practice. It is essential that learners engaging in this task have sufficient work experience in order to articulate their current framework of practice and reflect on WBL. Postgraduate learners at Capable NZ are expected to have a minimum of five years' professional practice experience, although it is conceivable that the Review of Learning could be completed by learners with tourism industry experience below this threshold (Capable NZ, 2020). It is anticipated that the assessment would generally not be suitable for undergraduates.

LEARNING OBJECTIVES

After completing the Review of Learning, learners are able to:

• Explain their career history and the development of their professional identity

- Critically reflect on their learning across educational and practice dimensions
- Articulate their current and aspirational framework of professional practice

THEORETICAL FOUNDATION

The assessment is underpinned by three theoretical foundations – lifelong learning, heutagogy and WBL:

- Lifelong learning: there is growing recognition that lifelong learning offers transformative potential to the tourism industry (Cuffy et al., 2018). However, tourism higher education still caters to a relatively small group of potential learners, with a predominant focus on undergraduate programmes for young adults. In contrast, this assessment, taken from a postgraduate professional practice programme, caters to experienced practitioners looking to develop or enhance values-based leadership
- Heutagogy: in professional practice, the learner, who is an experienced practitioner, is framed as the expert and determines to a large extent the learning that they wish to undertake. The Review of Learning assessment can thus be viewed as an example of heutagogy or "self-determined learning" (Hase and Kenyon, 2013). An extension of andragogy, or "adult learning", heutagogy is learner-centric and the approach fosters reflexivity regarding learning. In recognition of this level of self-determinacy, the Review of Learning embraces creative expression and diverse formats that allow the learner to best tell the story of their professional practice. The learner is supported by a "facilitator" rather than being taught by a "teacher"
- WBL: the Review of Learning assessment is conventionally undertaken by learners who are engaged in WBL, which denotes learning arising from activity within the workplace (Helyer, 2016). Professional practice learners typically study alongside full-time employment, which provides heightened relevance for their studies and opportunities to put new learning into immediate practice. Reflection is critical to WBL, and the assessment provides a chance for reflection on both past and contemporary learning that informs the practitioner's framework of practice

TIME PLAN

The time taken to complete this assessment will depend on the circumstances of the individual learner. Professional practice learners who are employed full-time are usually expected to complete the assessment within four months. Given that the Review of Learning is a deeply reflective and personal exercise, there is value in not rushing the learner.

STEP-BY-STEP PLAN

The Review of Learning commences with a meeting between the learner and their assigned facilitator, in which the assessment task is explained and resources on reflection are provided. The learner is then left to work independently, engaging in autobiographical and work-based reflection. A 5,000-word written reflective commentary is produced, with no set format in order to provide the learner with creative freedom to tell their story in a personally and culturally authentic way. The Review of Learning is expected to articulate the learner's

- Career history and development of their professional identity
- Existing professional knowledge, capabilities and competencies
- Learning across educational/practice dimensions, including key learning moments
- Development of professional values, ethics and philosophies
- Strategies for WBL and evaluating knowledge gained from practice
- Approaches for the application of theoretical knowledge to practice
- Reflexive understanding of how they learn and can manage their learning
- Current and aspirational framework of professional practice

This critically reflective exercise allows the practitioner to develop knowledge on their professional self and identity and to situate their current practice within the broader contexts of their profession and their own autobiography. What emerges from the Review of Learning is a framework of professional practice that begins to articulate how the practitioner operates within their professional setting and, crucially, *why* they operate in this way. Eschewing a narrow focus on professional skills and knowledge, learners are encouraged to delve deeper to uncover the values, ethics, philosophies and worldviews that underpin their practice. Having reflected on past and present practice, the learner then begins to formulate an *aspirational* framework of professional practice that expresses the growth and development of competencies that they hope to achieve throughout the remainder of the programme.

The Review of Learning is a pass/fail assessment that signals readiness to progress onto the next course of a postgraduate professional practice degree. It is assessed on the basis of how coherently, comprehensively and reflexively the candidate articulates the points listed above regarding their professional practice learning journey. Outside of the formal framework of professional practice, this assessment could usefully be integrated into tourism postgraduate programmes or adapted for practitioners not formally enrolled in higher education.

TEACHING TIPS

The purpose of the Review of Learning is to develop critical awareness of how the learner operates within their professional context and to review learning that has occurred within educational and work-based settings. However, facilitators should be aware that the autobiographical nature of this exercise may inadvertently trigger difficult memories for learners, including those of a more personal nature. The role of the facilitator at such moments is to determine the relevance of the memory for the task at hand by questioning whether learning, such as a renegotiation of professional values or identity, occurred as a result. If deemed relevant, the learner may choose to continue exploring the challenging episode as part of their reflection. It is important for facilitators to remind learners that they are not obligated to disclose details of their professional or personal lives if they feel uncomfortable doing so. Facilitators should be prepared to provide pastoral support to learners if required.

ACTIVITY 48: THE POWER OF VALUES TO EFFECT POSITIVE CHANGE 2

Joan Flaherty, MA, MSc[70]

DESCRIPTION

A writing assignment, grounded in a practical context, that illustrates the power of values to effect positive change.

1. Preliminary task: students identify values that are important to them, based on the visualisation exercise described in Flaherty's "The power of values to effect positive change 1" (see Activity 28)
2. Assignment: students write a business proposal: "a concrete, practical recommendation that, if implemented, could improve a business/organisation that you have either worked at or been a member of"
3. There is only one qualification: each student's proposal must implicitly reflect the value(s) they identified in the preliminary task (that is, the proposal must be based on good values)

In my experience, most students – most people, actually – are not philosophers. They prefer the concrete to the abstract, the clearly defined to the conceptual. Our task as educators, however, is to prompt our learners to venture outside the comfort zone of their preferences. Hence, this assignment. I use it to encourage my students to think about an abstract concept (the power of values) by embedding it within a concrete reality (a real-life operation or business). The goal, in other words, is not just to have students articulate what they would do if they were a decision-maker. For most of them, that is a straightforward task. The goal is to have them dig more deeply by identifying the values that are reflected in, and that shape, their decisions and the actions that follow those decisions.

USAGE SUGGESTIONS

The assignment is suitable for all levels (undergraduate, graduate and practitioner). As indicated in the description above, the visualisation exercise described in Flaherty's "The power of values to effect positive change 1" is used to introduce this writing assignment.

LEARNING OBJECTIVES

*   Develop an increased awareness of the power of values to effect positive change
*   Organise your thoughts in writing logically and coherently

PRE-WORK REQUIRED BY STUDENTS

Each student needs to have either worked at, or been a member of, a business or an organisation. A part-time job in a business (of any size or type) or extended involvement in an extra-curricular activity or volunteer organisation all qualify. The key is that the student must have some detailed knowledge of an operation or part of an operation.

THEORETICAL FOUNDATION

This assignment, insofar as it revolves around applying an abstract concept to a real-life situation, borrows from Experiential Learning Theory. For anyone not familiar with the theory, David A. Kolb's work is a good starting place (Kolb and Kolb, 2009).

TIME PLAN

The preliminary task takes up 15–20 minutes of class time. The proposal assignment is completed outside of class time, based on guidance provided during class. The amount and type of guidance provided during class will depend on the course's learning objectives. (That is, a course that emphasises the importance of writing skills will spend more time going over how to write a proposal than a course that focuses on other learning outcomes.)

STEP-BY-STEP PLAN

1. Students are led through the visualisation exercise
2. The instructor provides a mini lecture, explaining the relevance of the exercise, emphasising the role of values in shaping our decisions and actions both in our personal and professional lives
3. The instructor introduces the assignment and provides the appropriate level of guidance (see *Time plan* above)

TEACHING TIPS

Expect students to need guidance on how to write a proposal. Depending on the course objectives, class time could be spent going over how to do this, or students could simply be directed to a sample proposal, which acts as an example or template.

Expect, as well, some students to have difficulty identifying a business or organisation to write about. Those who have had no formal work experience may need to be prompted to realise that they can rely on knowledge gained from, for example, volunteering for a non-profit, participating in a leadership-in-training programme at a summer camp, or playing for an intramural sports team.

These types of experiences all provide insight into a specific business or organisation, which can be used to address the assignment.

What does not provide adequate insight, however, is experience as a customer. Patronising a particular coffee shop or clothing store does not give the student enough detailed information to write a business proposal for that operation. Check your students' topics right at the start to ensure they are based on in-depth knowledge from having worked at, or been a member of, the business or organisation.

ACTIVITY 49: SOLVING WICKED WORLD PROBLEMS

Kathleen Rodenburg, PhD[71]

DESCRIPTION

This exercise is designed to help students look beyond job titles when exploring potential future career options. The goal of this activity is to help them discover their passion in terms of solving a big world problem (broadening their career choice set) and help them recognise that the key goal of coming to university is to learn how to solve problems.

USAGE SUGGESTIONS

This is a great icebreaking exercise for first-year students. It encourages them to go beyond job title aspirations and focus on wicked world problems that they would like to help solve in their future careers.

LEARNING OBJECTIVES

- Look beyond job titles
- Help create a purposeful future
- Discover opportunities
- Showcase important challenges
- Flip the traditional career development model (www.sparkpath.com)
- Introduction to the 17 United Nations Sustainable Development Goals (SDGs)

MATERIALS LIST

The exercise utilises the challenge cards found at www.sparkpath.com. They include a deck of 30 cards. Each one identifies challenges in the future that need to be resolved in the areas of health, technology, society, environment and the economy. You can purchase decks of cards for the class or students can do the same exercise online.

PRE-WORK REQUIRED BY STUDENTS

Students could submit a half-page reflection on what wicked problem they hope to help solve in advance of their first seminar.

Students should familiarise themselves with the 17 SDGs set by the United Nations: https://sdgs.un.org/goals.

THEORETICAL FOUNDATION

1. Self-Determination Theory: learner-driven investigation, interest-based learning and a focus on real-world-impact work
2. Constructivist Theory: exploratory dialogues with classmates

3. Complex Thinking Theory: an additional design-thinking component can be added

TIME PLAN

A one-hour session or two one-hour in-class activities with the second centred on design thinking to assist with solving the previously identified wicked world problem within the context of the tourism industry.

STEP-BY-STEP PLAN

- Devise a process for each student to select one challenge card that they would like to work on in the future
- Think–pair–share
- Individually: "Why did I choose this card?"
- Find a partner with same challenge colour and discuss choice
- Share findings in groups of four or five with members who have chosen a similar challenge
- Ask students to reflect on what careers (not titles) would enable then to work on a solution to this challenge
- With what SDG(s) does this card best fit?
- Follow up with a design-thinking seminar that asks, "How might the tourism industry solve this wicked world problem?"

TEACHING TIPS

1. Pre-work for this session gives students more confidence in their card selections and when sharing with classmates and instructors for the first time
2. As an ice-breaker activity, it helps connect students with common interests at a deeper level

ACTIVITY 50: VALUE-REFLEXIVE ENGAGEMENT AND DIALOGUE

Kaarina Tervo-Kankare, PhD,[72] **Gunnar Thór Jóhannesson, PhD,**[73] **Brynhild Granås, PhD**[74] **and Outi Rantala, PhD**[75]

DESCRIPTION

Here, we describe three activities used in collaborative online courses of seven universities focusing on Arctic/northern tourism. The three activities – "My northern community", "Discussion statement" and "An opinion letter" – work as tools for value-reflexive engagement and dialogue in online courses. Their potential lies in enabling the students to relate their personal experiences, skills and expertise to the subject matters of the courses and thus reflect on the links between theory and practice in their knowledge creation. In addition, the three tools help us overcome several challenges related with the course composition and operation;

for example, the different time zones involved. They also aim in turning the diversity of the student material into an asset, as the students that enrol into our courses represent different universities, study fields (for example, tourism, geography, environment and resource management), nationalities and cultures.

USAGE SUGGESTIONS

The activities described here are designed to increase interaction in an online learning environment, but they can be used also in a normal face-to-face setting.

"My northern community" sets the scene and functions as an ice-breaker for the individual student to engage with an online learning environment and to initiate communication and dialogue between students located far apart.

The "discussion statement" used throughout the course is intended to underline the key elements in each of the course modules and to encourage the students to take the initiative on reflecting on discussed topics.

"An opinion letter" encourages the students to view tourism-development-related issues from another perspective, to create understanding of other stakeholders' points of view.

LEARNING OBJECTIVES

Upon completion of these activities the students should be able to:

- Contextualise tourism and its challenges relating to tourism development in diverse regions/contexts
- Explain where similarities and differences originate from
- Define solutions for overcoming challenges
- Develop a better understanding of the diverse stakeholders and their views on tourism-related issues
- Link conceptual discussion with their own experience and background knowledge
- Identify their own expertise and skills

THEORETICAL FOUNDATION

The three tools for reflexive engagement and dialogue support the metaphor of learning as participation and knowledge creation (Paavola et al., 2004) and put into practice the idea that knowledge creation is a social process. Hence, interaction is fundamental, and the participants' partial knowledge can combine to create something new. In the three activities, interaction among students is essential in creating understanding of the students' own skills and expertise, while teacher involvement mostly aims at supporting self-reflection and sense of achievement.

The students are encouraged to share their experiences and values, and to develop their sense of criticality and "a reflexive sense of identity that is both academic/conceptual and professional/applied" (Fullagar and Wilson, 2012, p. 3), in assignments that are not only based on "facts" and scientific knowledge. The facilitation of a comfortable and safe learning environment required for this sharing activity is another important factor, which is beyond this contribution but has been touched upon in our field course contribution "Stewardship: an in-field dialogue model" (see Activity 35).

TIME PLAN

The described activities can be time-consuming for the student.

To write and submit Activity 1 should in general not take much more than one hour of individual work, and one to three hours for the group work.

For Activity 2, the students can adapt the workload to their schedule, but, of course, those actively engaging in the assignment benefit the most from it. On average, the activity takes one to two hours per week.

For Activity 3, most time is spent on choosing the perspective from which to write the opinion letter. Still, the letter is kept rather short, so one to two hours should be enough. In the commenting phase, an additional 30 minutes to one hour is needed.

STEP-BY-STEP PLAN

"My northern community" includes the utilisation of a common platform (in this case, Padlet) to collect views, ideas and experiences concerning a northern destination/community familiar to each student. At the start, the students fill in information on the Padlet about this destination/community on the basis of their existing knowledge. They provide information about the name and location of the community; its resources, amenities, attractions and developments; its capacities; its stakeholders; and its vulnerabilities. This task is completed during one module. In the next module, the students go back to the Padlet, this time together with their discussion group. They go through the material to (1) reflect on the ways the concepts covered intersect and how they interface with other communities, and (2) search for commonalities and differences, and their origins. In addition, the group considers how the issues relate with what they have learned so far. The students then prepare a short presentation (for example, PowerPoint slides) that they share with the other discussion groups.

For the "discussion statement", the teacher of each module of the course posts a statement to the students at the beginning of the module. One example in relation to the topic of tourism governance in northern environments is: "What are the arguments for and against the active role of the state when it comes to tourism development and governance?" Students are organised into smaller subgroups. Each subgroup is to respond to the statement, reflect on it and engage in a written dialogue among the group members. The size of the subgroup is kept limited to encourage the active participation of all members. Each student is a member of only one group and the discussion is only visible for members of that same group. The teacher of each module also participates in the discussion.

"An opinion letter" aims to widen the students' perspectives and increase their understanding of diverse tourism stakeholders' standpoints and motives. The students first get a short (theoretical) introduction to the theme (here, reconciliation of livelihoods in a peripheral area, in this case nature-based tourism, mining and reindeer-herding). Then, on the basis of some additional context-related readings (for example, a development plan), they produce an opinion letter that is to be published in an imaginary newspaper. In the letter, the students provide a clear statement of who they represent and whether they support or oppose the development plan under study, and reason their positioning. The opinion letters are published in the course's discussion forum. During the next module, each student reads and comments on others' letters and tries to understand their viewpoints or give feedback about the reasoning, for example. This activity allows the students to show creativity and does not need to be too serious.

The students are encouraged to utilise the findings and ideas developed during all three activities in later assignments. Thus, they can "piggyback" the information and knowledge brought out by others as part of their knowledge creation.

TEACHING TIPS

The language in our courses is English, but the flexibility built into the online format, where discussion and commenting does not happen in real time, allows non-native English speakers to use time to check spelling and grammar and refine their arguments.

Test the platforms well beforehand.

If you have a possibility for in-person teaching as well, it is worthwhile having the "northern community" presentations in the form of live oral presentations (face to face here and/or via Zoom or similar platform), instead of only a written format. For the opinion letter, a real-life reflective group discussion would help the students get the full learning potential from the activity.

For the discussion statement, the active participation of teachers has a positive effect on student participation.

ACTIVITY 51: EMOTIONAL LABOUR AND THE FUTURE OF AUTOMATION

Maja Turnšek, PhD[76]

DESCRIPTION

Emotional labour takes a hard toll on tourism workers in the forms of exhaustion and burn-out (Lee and Ok, 2012). To address this problem, industry employees and their managers are advised to build their emotional and social intelligence, but few practical approaches on how exactly to do this are provided. Various reasons account for this gap, but it might be attributed to the fact that higher education's primary focus has been generally perceived as honing cognitive skills. Moreover, building one's emotional and social intelligence takes a lifetime of personal growth. It is therefore difficult to create a list of activities that could be used in the classroom. My primary "first step" advice is that, as teachers and mentors, we must first learn how to build our own emotional and social intelligence in our everyday work with students – work that also includes high levels of emotional labour (Constanti and Gibbs, 2004). I would advise learning via the set of directions that involve interactive workshop methods, including broader paradigms of humanist psychology, non-violent communication and active listening. The practical work of Rosenberg (2015) and Gordon (2001, 2010) is especially helpful, each having built long-standing professional training schools and philosophies.

Since such interactive emotional intelligence workshops and their paradigms are well beyond this contribution's scope, we limit ourselves here to a much easier task: providing examples of the set of directions that help students cognitively grasp the concept of emotional labour and critically discuss its role in their everyday work and the future of automation.

USAGE SUGGESTIONS

The exercises are suited for any level and any type of students.

LEARNING OBJECTIVES

- Understand the concept of emotional labour
- Critically discuss the role of emotional labour in the future of automation

THEORETICAL FOUNDATION

The activities presented here are intended to help students critically think about the concept of emotional labour and the historical critique of commercialisation of emotions, or "managed heart" as aptly described by Hochschild (1983/2003). Additionally, the future world of automation and artificial intelligence will still include work that we *want* humans (instead of machines) to perform due to our cultural expectations (Susskind, 2020). In tourism and hospitality, this does not mean the work that could easily be replaced by automation, for example, self-check-in options. Rather, the question of what type of work is specifically reserved for humans will be one of the main issues of the tourism futures. One such direction can already be seen with Airbnb Experiences – where emotional labour, described as experiences with human "connection", is the main value proposition of such products, interwoven with new types of human resource management: algorithmic management (Cheng and Foley, 2019).

TIME PLAN

The workshops here range from 45–90 minutes, with a relatively small group of participants (10–15 people). However, if the group is larger, the time frame should be extended, so that everyone has a chance to express themselves and the discussion is appropriately in-depth.

STEP-BY-STEP PLAN

Below are some examples of exercises that you can include in your class or workshop:

1. How does emotional labour feel? (30 to 90 minutes, depending on the size of the group)
   - Have participants discuss in small groups their own understanding of emotional labour, where in tourism and hospitality work you might witness it and whether they have had personal experience with it. Additionally, if the group is small enough and the students perceive it as a safe place of expression, ask them to share their own personal stories of situations where they felt they needed to control their feelings, how they managed and how they felt before, during and after
   This exercise help students express their emotions regarding situations that needed one's control of emotions, and to discuss the importance of emotion in everyday work
2. Is true kindness something you can buy? How about true hospitality?

- Discuss with students how they understand true kindness: "Is it something you can buy with money? How about true friendship? True love? True hospitality?" Continue to discuss with them the different meanings of the word "hospitality" in various cultures. This activity is especially suited if you have students from different cultural backgrounds – in that case, give special attention for each to be heard. For example, in Slovenian the word "hospitality" is translated as "*gostoljubje*", which literally means "loving your guest". The Slovenian language, however, has difficulties when it comes to translating "hospitality industry", since not only would it sound strange if translated literally as "the industry of loving your guest", but it would also sound like an oxymoron, since, just as true love, true hospitality is a value cherished beyond money exchange. In Slovenian we would therefore rather use the terms "hotel industry" or "catering industry" or just "tourism" to encompass all possible related activities (including "hospitality industry") when relating to the industry aspect. We reserve the word "*gostoljubje*" primarily as a professional and personal value

This exercise helps students think about hospitality both as an industry and as a value. Furthermore, it can introduce the commercialisation of emotional labour. Readings from Hochschild (1983/2003) and discussions on the concept of commercialisation are helpful here

3. What are the expectations that we need to live up to? The case of Airbnb
    - This exercise can be interconnected with students thinking about tourism's future, from the perspective of new types of human resource management within the platform economy: algorithmic management (Cheng and Foley, 2019). Present the examples below, and in small groups discuss Airbnb's "connection" quality standards: does Airbnb expect emotional labour from its hosts? How does the "connection" standard differ from professional standards of traditional hotels?

This exercise helps students understand that emotional labour is prescribed by organisational rules, either implicit or explicit. Class discussion might also focus on other examples of professional standards that either you or the students have found

Airbnb (2020) describes the quality standards for Airbnb Experiences with these words:

What are the quality standards for Airbnb Experiences?

Everyone who hosts an experience on Airbnb must demonstrate high levels of expertise and the ability to connect with guests. The experience itself must give guests insider access to places or things they could not find on their own

Every experience submitted to Airbnb is reviewed to make sure it meets these three quality standards: expertise, insider access, and connection. Once published, an experience must continue upholding these standards to ensure that it meets guests' expectations

- Expertise: Hosts are knowledgeable and deeply passionate about what they do. They go beyond the surface with personal stories and context that bring the experience to life.
- Insider access: Hosts unlock places or activities that the average traveller would not be likely to discover on their own. They invite guests to actively participate in the activity, community or culture.

- Connection: Hosts are dedicated to creating meaningful human connections. They go out of their way to make guests feel welcome and recognised. Guests come as strangers and leave as friends. Learn more about these quality standards in our blog post about the three pillars of a quality experience. Experiences that do not meet the above standards may be removed from Airbnb

In particular, the standard of "connection" relates to emotional labour. Find images on the Airbnb website that describe this standard in more depth. Have students analyse and discuss the visuals

Finally, it is important for students to understand that managerial standards relate to the ways the workers are evaluated both by the management and the guests. Many academic studies have undertaken surveys of former guests to determine their satisfaction with Airbnb. Ask students to analyse the criteria used to evaluate guest satisfaction with the standard of "connection". Discuss with students the impact of the survey findings on the experience providers.

4. What jobs of the future will be taken up by technology?
   - Provide students with a list of tourism jobs and ask them to do the following: identify those that include emotional labour; those that will likely be replaced by technology (self-service and automation, robots, artificial intelligence); and, finally, those jobs they themselves would be willing to pay an extra 30 per cent for if performed by a human instead of self-service. An extra 90 per cent?

This activity helps students think about the inherent value of human encounters in tourism and hospitality; and the future of emotional labour in the world of automation

TEACHING TIPS

These exercises address the cognitive aspects of emotional labour – understanding the concept and its contexts. A greater challenge is to teach the non-cognitive skills: the emotional elements of emotional intelligence. True emotional intelligence is a lifelong personal growth process. Start with building and expanding your own, since our academic achievements, which have allowed us to be higher education professionals, unfortunately do not say much about our emotional and social skills.

ACTIVITY 52: THE TEFI VALUES SURVEY

Samantha Bouwer, PhD[77]

DESCRIPTION

The TEFI (Tourism Education Futures Initiative) values are advocated as key value sets to be embedded into tourism curricula. Such inclusion (perhaps through the setting of values-based learning outcomes) suggests that "values internalisation" should be assessed, in addition to the traditional knowledge- and skills-based learning outcomes. However, the assessment of values-based learning outcomes is extremely challenging. The challenges generally pertain to assessor subjectivity, the lack of a viable hierarchical taxonomy and student social desirability reporting, among others (refer to Buissink-Smith et al., 2011; Gano-Phillips, 2009; Krathwohl et al., 1964).

However, it would be logical to assume that educational practitioners would still wish to understand the impact of a values-based curriculum, even if values-based learning outcomes are not being formally assessed as a necessity for graduation from a higher education tourism programme.

USAGE SUGGESTIONS

It is suggested that the survey first be administered with students upon enrolment to the tourism programme, and then later upon qualification/graduation. It allows the educational practitioner to understand (to some extent) the impact of values-based education as part of the tourism qualification. It may also allow the practitioner to identify cases that are worthy of further qualitative exploration (for example, if there is a major change with regard to a particular value).

THEORETICAL FOUNDATION

Values can be measured directly and indirectly, by participants either endorsing overt value statements or making selections which are indicative of their values, respectively (Mumford et al., 2002). Similarly, values measurement can employ a qualitative or a quantitative methodology. Values research has been dominated by the latter, with measurement instruments designed to elicit values directly by requiring participants to rank or rate values. Examples include the Rokeach Value Survey (RVS), List of Values (LOV) and the Schwartz Value Survey (SWS), to name a few (refer to Kahle, 1983; Rokeach, 1979; Schwartz, 1992).

However, direct values measurement has been criticised in regard to the challenging and time-consuming nature concerning the ranking of values (Weeden, 2011), particularly where there is a large number of value items. Mumford et al. (2002) also allude to direct values measurement being predicated on the assumption that people know what their values are, have clearly defined values preferences and can consciously articulate their values. Schwartz and colleagues (2001) also acknowledged these limitations and in response developed the Portrait Values Questionnaire (PVQ). In the PVQ, short verbal portraits of 40 different people are presented. Each portrait implies a value, and the participants have to indicate the extent to which the hypothetical person is like them, by means of a Likert scale. This allows for the capturing of an individual's values without the individual having to explicitly articulate their values. This approach is currently utilised in the European Social Survey (ESS-ERIC, n.d.).

DEVELOPMENT OF THE TEFI VALUES SURVEY

The indirect values measurement approach of the PVQ has been employed in the development of the TEFI Values Survey. Short verbal portraits of 50 people are presented in the survey that are indicative of the values within the five TEFI value sets. The portraits have been developed by reviewing the explication of the TEFI values sets in the *TEFI White Paper: A Values-based Framework for Tourism Education: Building the Capacity to Lead* (2010).

Each portrait represents either a "behaviour" or an "attitude" of a person. This is based on the assertion that values underpin attitudes and behaviours (Becker and Conner, 1983; Moscardo and Murphy, 2011). Each portrait indirectly implies a value (that is, the values are not explicit in the portraits). By means of a Likert scale, participants indicate the extent to which the hypothetical person is like them.

Important! It is important to recognise that the proposed TEFI Values Survey is not a measurement instrument that has been scientifically tested. It is essentially a simple tool that educational practitioners could use to ascertain any change in student values between entry to, and exit from, higher education tourism programmes. Some simple reliability measures have been considered, including statements that imply the opposite of a value (questions 30, 33 and 50), in addition to a number of portraits being repeated later in the survey but again, in the form of a statement implying the opposite of the value item (questions 2 and 18, 6 and 24, 7 and 11, 8 and 49, 35 and 47, 36 and 48).

FURTHER POINTS

- The survey can be amended to be gender-neutral. "They" is commonly accepted as a singular gender neutral pronoun
- It is recommended that the survey does not have the word "values" in the title
- The survey takes approximately 15 minutes to complete
- The survey could be administered online or in printed format
- The portraits can be adapted/expanded upon as the educational practitioner sees fit

Table 13.2   Tourism undergraduate/graduate survey

		Very much like me	Like me	Somewhat like me	A little like me	Not at all like me
1.	He has pride and confidence in himself	1	2	3	4	5
2.	He is self-governing; he can direct and manage himself independently	1	2	3	4	5
3.	He is open; he does not try to hide or conceal anything	1	2	3	4	5
4.	He strives for excellence	1	2	3	4	5
5.	He enjoys producing new ideas and findings solutions to problems	1	2	3	4	5
6.	He does not care what others think of him; he does not change his behaviour for the benefit of others	1	2	3	4	5
7.	He has a modest or low view of his own importance	1	2	3	4	5
8.	He accepts responsibility for his actions	1	2	3	4	5
9.	He examines and questions knowledge; he doesn't just accept it at face value	1	2	3	4	5
10.	He is truthful and sincere	1	2	3	4	5
11.	He sees himself as "better" than others	1	2	3	4	5
12.	He cares about the natural environment	1	2	3	4	5
13.	He enjoys leading a group of people to act towards achieving a common goal	1	2	3	4	5

		Very much like me	Like me	Somewhat like me	A little like me	Not at all like me
14.	He is consistently truthful	1	2	3	4	5
15.	He is self-aware and understands his own identity	1	2	3	4	5
16.	He believes that everyone should be empowered to take responsibility	1	2	3	4	5
17.	He accepts that everyone is unique; he acknowledges individual differences	1	2	3	4	5
18.	He likes to be told what to do	1	2	3	4	5
19.	He likes to find solutions to difficult or complex issues	1	2	3	4	5
20.	He consistently acts in ways which are considered by society as "good actions"	1	2	3	4	5
21.	He feels a responsibility towards the protection of the natural environment for future generations	1	2	3	4	5
22.	He is willing to allow the existence of opinions or behaviour that he does not necessarily agree with	1	2	3	4	5
23.	He enjoys "serving" others	1	2	3	4	5
24.	He cares what others think of him; he changes his behaviour for the benefit of others	1	2	3	4	5
25.	He "thinks outside of the box"; he looks at things from different angles	1	2	3	4	5
26.	He shows his true self and how he feels	1	2	3	4	5
27.	He seeks to understand and respect the beliefs, values and opinions of others	1	2	3	4	5
28.	He feels a responsibility towards local communities; service to the community is important to him	1	2	3	4	5
29.	He acts in a timely manner	1	2	3	4	5
30.	He thinks knowledge should be protected and not shared	1	2	3	4	5
31.	He always seeks to find solutions to conflicts	1	2	3	4	5
32.	He feels it's important to inspire others to strive for excellence	1	2	3	4	5
33.	He thinks it's important for individual achievements to be rewarded more so than collective (i.e., group) achievements	1	2	3	4	5
34.	He believes in partnership-building to achieve desired outcomes	1	2	3	4	5
35.	He believes it's important to work together as a team rather than as an individual	1	2	3	4	5
36.	He looks ahead, anticipating needs and identifying possible outcomes	1	2	3	4	5
37.	Changing things for the better is important to him	1	2	3	4	5
38.	He believes it's important to acknowledge different sociocultural values and quality-of-life aspirations	1	2	3	4	5
39.	He believes that learning is ongoing; it never stops	1	2	3	4	5
40.	He is practical; he is concerned with the actual doing or use of something rather than with theory and ideas	1	2	3	4	5
41.	He enjoys being able to apply and implement his creative ideas	1	2	3	4	5
42.	He recognises and acknowledges the existence of inequalities concerning ethnicity, gender, religion, etc.	1	2	3	4	5
43.	Having specialist knowledge to perform a task is important to him	1	2	3	4	5
44.	He believes that outputs (i.e., what is produced) should be current and appropriate	1	2	3	4	5

		Very much like me	Like me	Somewhat like me	A little like me	Not at all like me
45.	Creating and attaining a shared vision with others is important to him	1	2	3	4	5
46.	He perseveres until he has achieved success at the task in hand	1	2	3	4	5
47.	He believes that working individually is more important than working in a team	1	2	3	4	5
48.	He waits for problems to arise and responds to them rather than anticipating problems	1	2	3	4	5
49.	He blames others for his own failures	1	2	3	4	5
50.	He believes that tourism, in its current form, can last forever	1	2	3	4	5

Listed in the table above are descriptions of 50 different people. Please read each description and think about *how much this person is like you*. Rate your responses on a scale of 1–5, where "1" means "very much like me", and "5" implies "not at all like me". Circle the corresponding number.

Table 13.3   For educational practitioner use

		Knowledge	Mutuality	Ethics	Stewardship	Professionalism
1.	He has pride and confidence in himself. *(self-respect)*		✓			
2.	He is self-governing; he can direct and manage himself independently. *(autonomy)*					✓
3.	He is open; he does not try to hide or conceal anything. *(transparency)*			✓		
4.	He strives for excellence. *(commitment to excellence)*					✓
5.	He enjoys producing new ideas and findings solutions to problems. *(creativity)*	✓				
6.	He does not care what others think of him; he does not change his behaviour for the benefit of others. *(authentic self)*			✓		
7.	He has a modest or low view of his own importance. *(humility)*		✓			
8.	He accepts responsibility for his actions. *(responsibility)*				✓	✓
9.	He examines and questions knowledge; he doesn't just accept it at face value. *(critical thinking)*	✓				
10.	He is truthful and sincere. *(honesty)*			✓		
11.	He sees himself as "better" than others. *(humility)*		✓			
12.	He cares about the natural environment. *(sustainability)*				✓	
13.	He enjoys leading a group of people to act towards achieving a common goal. *(leadership)*			✓		✓
14.	He is consistently truthful. *(integrity)*			✓		
15.	He is self-aware and understands his own identity. *(reflexivity)*			✓		✓
16.	He believes that everyone should be empowered to take responsibility *(inclusion; sustainability)*		✓		✓	

		Knowledge	Mutuality	Ethics	Stewardship	Professionalism
17.	He accepts that everyone is unique; he acknowledges individual differences.*(diversity)*		✓			
18.	He likes to be told what to do. *(autonomy)*					✓
19.	He likes to find solutions to difficult or complex issues. *(problem-solving)*					✓
20.	He consistently acts in ways which are considered by society as "good actions". *(right conduct)*			✓		
21.	He feels a responsibility towards the protection of the natural environment for future generations. *(sustainability/responsibility)*				✓	
22.	He is willing to allow the existence of opinions or behaviour that he does not necessarily agree with. *(tolerance; open-mindedness)*		✓			
23.	He enjoys "serving" others. *(service to the community; services)*				✓	✓
24.	He cares what others think of him; he changes his behaviour for the benefit of others. *(authentic self)*			✓		
25.	He "thinks outside of the box"; he looks at things from different angles. *(critical thinking)*	✓				
26.	He shows his true self and how he feels. *(authentic self)*		✓			
27.	He seeks to understand and respect the beliefs, values and opinions of others. *(respect; tolerance)*		✓			
28.	He feels a responsibility towards local communities; service to the community is important to him. *(service to the community)*				✓	
29.	He acts in a timely manner. *(timeliness)*					✓
30.	He thinks knowledge should be protected and not shared. *(networking)*	✓				
31.	He always seeks to find solutions to conflicts. *(conflict resolution)*			✓		
32.	He feels it's important to inspire others to strive for excellence. *(leadership)*					✓
33.	Giving matters serious thought and reflection is important to him. *(reflection)*	✓				
34.	He believes in partnership-building to achieve desired outcomes. *(partnership-building)*					✓
35.	He believes it's important to work together as a team rather than as an individual. *(teamwork)*					✓
36.	He looks ahead, anticipating needs and identifying possible outcomes. *(proactivity)*					✓
37.	Changing things for the better is important to him. *(positive change agent)*		✓			
38.	He believes it's important to acknowledge different sociocultural values and quality-of-life aspirations. *(sustainability)*				✓	
39.	He believes that learning is ongoing; it never stops. *(lifelong learning)*		✓			✓
40.	He is practical; he is concerned with the actual doing or use of something rather than with theory and ideas. *(practicality)*					✓
41.	He enjoys being able to apply and implement his creative ideas. *(innovation)*	✓				
42.	He recognises and acknowledges the existence of inequalities concerning ethnicity, gender, religion, etc. *(equity)*		✓			
43.	Having specialist knowledge to perform a task is important to him. *(specialist knowledge)*					✓

		Knowledge	Mutuality	Ethics	Stewardship	Professionalism
44.	He believes that outputs (i.e., what is produced) should be current and appropriate. *(relevance)*					✓
45.	Creating and attaining a shared vision with others is important to him. *(leadership)*					✓
46.	He perseveres until he has achieved success at the task in hand. *(perseverance)*					✓
47.	He believes that working individually is more important than working in a team. *(teamwork)*					✓
48.	He waits for problems to arise and responds to them rather than anticipating problems. *(proactivity)*					✓
49.	He blames others for his own failures. *(responsibility)*				✓	✓
50.	He believes that tourism, in its current form, can last forever. *(sustainability)*				✓	

ACTIVITY 53: THE TOURISM GAME 2

Stephen Fairbrass, MA[78]

DESCRIPTION

A roleplaying exercise to explore the costs and benefits of the development of tourist enterprises in an emerging economy.

(This game was written by Stephen Fairbrass for Norfolk Education and Action for Developments' (NEAD's) "Just Business" project. The format is loosely based on NEAD's "Debt Game". The game has been slightly edited by Johan Edelheim.)

"The Tourism Game" is designed for use by diverse groups of students and tourism stakeholders. It requires no specialist knowledge to play, and may also be utilised in any curriculum areas, to explore values, citizenship issues and decision-making processes and to develop skills of discussion, critical thinking and persuasive argument.

The game is based in the hypothetical country of Latasica (derived from Latin America, Asia and Africa). It brings together a number of different issues connected with tourism.

The game requires approximately one hour of playing and debrief time for the initial session (or slightly longer if the preliminary exercise is used).

The game can stand alone, or it can be used as the basis for a variety of follow-up work. The game requires a minimum of 12 players to play all 12 roles, but by leaving out some roles it can be played with less participants too, plus a teacher/facilitator. It can be used with groups of up to 50.

The game requires no specialist equipment other than the role cards contained within the pack. It is useful to have a board or flip chart and marker pens to record important points at the debrief stage.

CONTENTS

PRELIMINARY EXERCISE (OPTIONAL)

"The Tourism Game" may be enhanced by encouraging participants to think "locally" in the first instance. This preliminary exercise, which can take from 5–15 minutes, helps set the scene for the subsequent game.

1. Divide the group into two equal halves
2. Ask members of half (a) to think of any ways they as individuals, their families, their friends or their community generally benefit or may benefit from tourism in their own town/city/region. Ask one person in the group to "scribe" this information for their group
3. Ask members of half (b) to think of any ways they as individuals, their families, their friends or their community are generally disadvantaged or may be disadvantaged by tourism in their own town/city/region. Ask one person in the group to scribe this information for their group
4. Bring the whole group back together. Ask each member of half (a) to give one "benefit" of tourism in turn, and write these on a board. Ask each member of half (b) to give one "cost" of tourism in turn, and write these on the board
5. Orally summarise the information on the board, and make the point that tourism has the potential to bring benefits to a community, but also has the potential to bring costs. The issue is whether the costs outweigh the benefits, or vice versa. This provides the lead into the game, which is about the potential costs and benefits arising from a tourism development proposal in an "emerging economy" country

Note: benefits identified may include the creation of local jobs, increased local incomes, improved infrastructure, development of local amenities, greater availability of goods and services, and so on. Costs may include pollution of various kinds (for example, litter, noise), traffic congestion, overcrowding on public transport and other local amenities, increased prices in local shops, erosion of footpaths, and so on.

INSTRUCTIONS FOR PLAYING THE GAME

1. Either read out, or distribute copies of, the background information sheet to participants. Deal with any questions arising. (3/4 minutes)
2. Divide the class into individuals (if playing with the minimum 12) or groups for each role. Allocate a seating area for each group. Distribute role cards and give participants time to read through them. Again, deal with any queries. (3/4 minutes)
3. Announce that there will be a public meeting in 20 minutes' time, at which the issues will be discussed, and following which the government will make an announcement about

whether or not it will support the proposed tourism development. In the meantime, participants should talk with other groups to find out what they think about the plans, try to form alliances, persuade others to support them, and so on. (20 minutes)

During this period, discussion can be stimulated by the facilitator circulating around the groups posing as a "journalist", and asking what is going on in Latasica, what are the issues, how do people feel, and so on. The "journalist" can also prompt different groups to talk to one another.

Note: when playing "The Tourism Game" in a virtual context, it is useful to ask participants (a) to rename themselves to their role/own name, and (b) what other roles their role would like to discuss issues with, so that breakout rooms can be assigned easily.

4. Call the public meeting. Get groups to sit in a circle and invite Airtravel representatives to outline why they believe their proposals would be good for the country. Then invite representative(s) of each interest group in turn to put forward their views and state whether or not they support the proposals. Finally, invite the government to state whether or not it will allow the development to go ahead, and the reasons for its decision. (20 minutes)
5. Ask everybody to stand up and move to another seat, and to come out of role. The Chair will now lead a discussion on what was learned from the exercise. Facilitators should use their own experience and judgement about how to encourage discussion of the issues at this stage. (12–14 minutes)

BACKGROUND INFORMATION

Latasica is a country in the Global South. It has a long warm summer and is blessed with wide, sandy, palm-fringed beaches leading down to a blue ocean. It also has extensive inland areas inhabited by exotic wildlife.

Latasica's population is relatively small. There are two key areas of employment. The first is the fishing industry, located mainly around the coastal town of Ambria. This produces output mainly for the domestic market. There is also arable farming (based further inland) producing some crops for domestic consumption, but primarily concentrating on production of coffee for export. The coffee crop is Latasica's main source of earnings of foreign currency, but world prices have been falling for some years. Much of the inland area is populated by groups of self-sufficient nomadic herders, who wander large areas in search of grazing land for their animals.

Latasica has a small-scale tourist industry, attracting a limited number of independent travellers from the Global North.

Airtravel, a large Europe-based holiday company, is now proposing to develop and market Latasica as a high-volume luxury tourist destination, for both beach and "safari" holidays, with the aim of increasing by up to ten times the number of visitors to the country. Airtravel is currently in negotiations with the government of Latasica regarding the proposed development.

Airtravel is willing to finance the building of two large luxury hotels in the previously quiet beachside town of Ambria. Airtravel would market Ambria as a luxury beach resort, with a variety of water sports activities, including sailing and windsurfing, waterskiing and scuba diving.

Airtravel is also willing to finance a third hotel, a "safari lodge", in an area of the country that it wants the government to designate as a game reserve. The rules of the reserve would encourage conservation of wild animals and forbid hunting. Human settlement, outside the safari lodge and associated environs, would be banned. Tourists would make guided excursions to view and photograph wildlife.

However, Airtravel requires some support from the government of Latasica before it finally proceeds with the project:

- Airtravel is asking that the government spends money to build a new airport within an hour's drive from Ambria and two hours from the game reserve, because research has shown that rich tourists are reluctant to undertake long road transfers
- It also requires the government to finance improvements in the infrastructure of roads, power and water supplies, and telecommunications
- Airtravel also requires tax concessions on its investment, and a guarantee from the government that it will enact legislation designed to limit the power of trade unions and allow wage levels to be determined by market forces (that is, no minimum wage)

The purpose of this exercise is to decide if the proposed developments should go ahead. You will take on the roles of various participants in the debate. Your job is to assess the costs and benefits of the development from the point of view of your role, and decide whether you think the project should proceed.

You should also discuss the development with other participants. You may wish to explain your point of view and try to convince others to support you. You should listen to other views and be prepared to negotiate a mutually satisfactory position.

The exercise will conclude with a public meeting at which all the affected parties will be able to express their opinions and the government will be invited to make a final decision on whether to approve the project.

ROLE CARDS

The Government

You are the government of Latasica. You have to decide whether to support the tourism development. You have to act in what you think are the best interests of your country and its people. You should consult with the people who live in your country and find out their opinions before you make your decision.

You should be aware of the following information. Your country is heavily in debt to Western governments and the International Monetary Fund (IMF), which is insisting that you repay the loans. Interest repayments each year take up about 40 per cent of your national income. In order to meet your debt obligations, it is essential that you earn foreign currency. The revenue you receive from coffee exports is insufficient for this end, and the debt is getting worse.

Tourism is often presented as one of the world's largest economic sectors, and (at least until the outbreak of COVID-19) one of the fastest growing ones. The tourism development would bring in foreign visitors who would spend yuan, dollars, pounds, euros, yen and other currencies.

However, some of this money would leave your country as profits to Airtravel, and to pay for imports of drinks, foodstuffs, and so on, that foreign tourists expect (for example, soft drinks and mineral water, Scotch whisky and the like). Capital equipment, fuel and other resources would also need to be imported. You have to consider the likely net effect on your balance-of-payments position.

If you decide to approve the project, you will have to spend large sums of money to build the airport, the associated infrastructure of roads, and so on. You have limited funds available to you, particularly because the IMF, as a condition of its loan to you, has insisted on a "structural adjustment programme" which involves cuts in government spending.

However, the IMF is very keen for you to encourage foreign investment, because it believes this will help your economy grow and you will then be able to afford to pay off your debts.

The infrastructure capital spending would create jobs in your economy (jobs will of course also be created by the hotels) and may represent a profitable long-term investment, with a positive multiplier effect.

However, you would have to cut current spending elsewhere, at least in the short term, perhaps on health care and education, in order to be able to afford it.

Airtravel plc

You are the Senior Management Team of Airtravel plc, the world's third biggest tourism company. The global tourism industry is dominated by a few large firms. You are keen to maintain your company's position as one of the market leaders.

Recent years have seen a number of mergers and takeovers in the industry, as firms compete for market share. There is a rumour that the largest company in the industry is planning a bid to buy Airtravel. You are fearful for your future careers if Airtravel is taken over because takeovers usually mean "rationalisation" at the top, and job losses among management. In order to survive as an independent operation, it is essential that Airtravel should grow.

Profit margins on each individual holiday in the mass market sector are normally small. High turnover is necessary to earn good returns on investments. The last few summer seasons have seen "price wars" between competitors, with weaker firms being taken over or simply going out of business. The survivors have been those companies that have been able to cross-subsidise loss-making parts of their business with revenues from the high-margin luxury market.

The luxury market in recent years has seen a steady expansion of demand, and in particular there seems to be a trend among better-off tourists towards more exotic destinations, outside Europe. This section of the market offers higher-than-average profit per holiday because demand is less price-sensitive than for cheaper packages.

Latasica seems just the sort of destination that the discerning tourist would seek. It is "unspoilt", there being no significant tourist industry. Furthermore, none of your rivals seems yet to have recognised its potential.

Your task is to convince the government and people of Latasica that the development you propose is in all of your best interests. You may find some resistance from people who are nervous of change.

Ambrian Business Community

You are the local business community in the town of Ambria. You have to decide whether the proposed development is in the interests of your businesses and your families, and then seek to influence the government to support your view. You might also wish to persuade other members of the population to support you.

You have worked hard to establish your business and have taken many risks. You have put in long hours. You are now making a good living compared to most Latasicans. You believe you deserve what you have earned. If others want to succeed all they have to do is work as hard as you. You believe the government has been too soft on people in the past, and it should encourage them to get off their backsides and work.

More tourists coming to your country would give you the opportunity to sell more goods, and to make larger profits. You will be able to sell goods and services directly to tourists, who will want souvenirs, local handicrafts, food and drink, and so on. Tourists will be willing and able to pay higher prices than the local population, and you can make large profits from them. You will also be able to supply the hotels with goods and services. You will be able to expand your business and be able to hire more workers. The tourism development has the potential to make you and your country rich.

The hotels, and the airport, will also be seeking to hire workers, and may be willing to offer higher wages than you are currently paying your staff.

This may persuade your staff to look for new jobs or you may have to pay more to keep them with you; this would increase your costs and eat into your profits. However, there are many unemployed people in your country, and migrants from the rural areas arrive in town every day looking for work; you would have no problem recruiting staff.

Your country is heavily in debt to Western governments, and it has many economic problems. The government says the tourism development could solve your country's economic problems. By earning foreign currency from rich tourists, the debts could be paid off. You are not sure if you trust the government; it has made promises of prosperity before, which have turned out to be false.

Perhaps you should talk to other Latasican people and try to find out what they think about these plans.

Coffee Farmers

You currently make a living by farming coffee on hilly land that your family have rented for several generations. You sell all your coffee through a government-run marketing scheme. It is a simple existence and times are sometimes hard, but you do make enough income to feed yourself and your family. While you will never be rich, you do value your independence.

You have hopes for the future. You want your children to receive a good education and make a better life than you have had. You are concerned about older members of your family. You have elderly relatives whose health is deteriorating and who may need medicines and hospital care in years to come. In recent years there have been some cuts in government spending on education and health care. This is due to the "structural adjustment programmes" that the government has been operating to try to get the country out of debt. You are having to pay for services that were once free, and prices seem to be rising. This trend concerns you, because there seems no prospect of any increase in the income you receive from selling coffee.

The government has let it be known that it is considering supporting tourism development in your country. It says there would be jobs created in constructing an airport, roads, and so on. In the longer term, jobs would be available in the hotels and other tourist-related businesses. Maybe members of your family could find new jobs. However, in order to raise finance to build an airport for tourists, the government says it would have to further cut spending on health and education.

There has already been some tourism in your country, and you are aware that tourists are willing to pay high prices for food, and for craft goods which they take home as souvenirs. This has meant that the better-quality goods have gone to the tourists, and you have been forced by this competition to pay more for lower-quality products. Tourists also tend to be noisy and disrespectful of local customs, and pollute the country with litter.

You must consider whether the tourism development is in your family's interests and decide whether to support it, or if you will argue against it.

Ambrian Fishing Community

For many generations your families have fished the waters off the coast, and you have sold your catch in local markets. Small numbers of tourists have been visiting your country for some time now. When you catch the types of fish they know, they are prepared to pay high prices for them, and you can earn a good income. However, you are concerned because you are having to travel further and further out to sea to locate these types of fish; it seems as if the numbers of fish are declining.

The government says that the proposed new tourism development would bring economic growth and help it out of the debt crisis that has so affected your country in recent years. It says it will make everybody better off, bringing new jobs and prosperity.

The new hotels will bring in many more tourists, but they will want the beaches to be clean, and want to sail and waterski, and so on, on the sea. You are concerned that divers may damage the coral reef, which could affect the fish population who feed there.

You have traditionally landed your catch on the beaches, and stretched out your nets there for drying. The government is now saying that if the tourist development goes ahead you will have to move your boats and nets elsewhere. Generally, you are worried that tourists will have no respect for old traditional ways of life, and everything will change. But perhaps things have to change if your country is to become better off.

There is potential for you to make a very good living in the short term, by selling fish to the rich tourists and to the hotels. They will pay much higher prices than local people. You might be able to earn enough in the short term to buy a bigger boat, or you might create a new way of life altogether.

You must decide if the proposed development is in your interests and try to persuade others to support you.

Arable Farmers

You grow a variety of crops on rented land in the rural area that lies inland of the coastal town of Ambria. Some of the crops you use to feed yourself and your family; the remainder you take each week to the market in Ambria to sell for cash, which you use to buy fertilisers and other goods you require. (Fertilisers have been increasing in price in recent years, because the value of your currency has been falling.) Life is sometimes difficult, especially if you have a bad growing season, but you always seem to be able to make ends meet.

There is a rumour that the government wants to buy the land you farm in order to build an airport, and that the landowner is willing to sell, and that you will be evicted. You are very worried about what will then happen to you and your family.

The government says that the new tourist industry will create many jobs in the economy, but farming is the only occupation you know, and you feel that you are too old to change your life now. In any case, you value the independence you have in working for yourself and your family, and you are not sure that you want to work for someone else who will order you around.

Even if you manage to remain in farming, there could be problems for you. Tourists demand plentiful freshwater supplies for showers, for swimming pools and for golf courses, and regularly washed and changed sheets and towels. However, at certain times of the year there are already water shortages in your country, and you fear there will not be enough water for your crops if the development goes ahead.

You should talk to other groups of people and find out what they think about the proposed development. Perhaps they know more than you do about what will happen, or perhaps they will have ideas about what can be done.

Shanty Town Dwellers

You live in the shanty town that lies to the west of Ambria, and you have no proper job. You came from the country looking for work, because since new technology came to the farms there was less for you to do, and no money. But there is no secure work in the town either for people like you.

You struggle to find enough money to survive.

You do odd jobs. You may get a few days on a building site sometimes, or somebody might pay you to carry some bags. You have to be alert to every opportunity.

You are not sure about the new tourism plan the government has. On the one hand it will bring wealthy people into your country who will spend money. Perhaps there will be jobs building the hotels, and afterwards perhaps other work serving the tourists. If there is no steady job, maybe casual work, shining shoes, guiding, that kind of thing. However, this work will only be seasonal, and what will you do for the rest of the year? And more people may be attracted to move from the rural areas to Ambria from the countryside in search of work, which may mean more competition for jobs.

The tourists that already come here already cause problems. Because they want only the best fish, the fishermen no longer catch the fish that you can afford to eat. They would rather sell to the tourists at high prices. This means you have to pay more for your food, and often it is only the poor-quality stuff that the tourists have not bought; maybe it is not so fresh either.

And fruit and vegetables too: the tourists get all the best, and you go without or pay high prices for rubbish.

Will things get better or worse with more tourists? You should discuss your hopes and fears with others. Maybe you can work out a solution.

Nomadic Herders

Since time began, your people have lived on this land. Long before the people who grow crops or who fish the sea arrived here, your forebears wandered the plains. Yours is a simple life. You search for land for your animals to graze, and water for them to drink. You also take the food you need from the land. You hunt the wild boar, and you kill the puma if it threatens your herds. You also harvest fruits and other nutritious plants that grow wild. When water and grass become scarce you move on, maybe travelling hundreds of miles, to find fresh areas. Life has always been this way. The land you leave will recover, and in time you will return again.

Recently people calling themselves the government have begun to interfere with your way of life. They have said that you must not trespass on some lands because the elephants graze there, and the elephants are an "endangered species". But your people have lived in harmony with the elephants for many years, and it is because so much of the land is now under cultivation that the elephants find it hard to find food. If the elephants stray near the plantations the farmers shoot at them with guns.

Now the government is saying that it will make a big area of land "reserved" for the wild animals, and you will be forbidden to wander there. It is because the animals are becoming extinct, it says, but again this is not your fault; it is because of the way that the land is used, by people with no sympathy for the ways of nature.

Who is this "government"? Who gave it the right to tell you what to do? You were here long before it and have no need for its rules and regulations.

For too long your people's rights have been neglected. You need to campaign to protect your traditional way of life. You need to make it very clear to the government, and to the outsiders, how you feel.

Elderly People

You are very concerned about the proposed tourism development.

Already you have seen the ancient values, traditions and customs of your country being eroded, and you believe that the influence of foreign cultures is largely to blame. The voice of the older generation was always respected, but young people today seem no longer to value experience and the wisdom of years.

You are worried that young people will move away from home, and from traditional occupations, to take up jobs in the new industry. This will lead to the breakdown of the extended family network, and you are worried about who will then care for you in your old age. There are no old-age pensions in your country. You need medicines, yet the government seems to be proposing to cut spending on health to finance building an airport.

Tourists are disrespectful. They flaunt dress codes, walking semi-naked on the beach and not covering their heads, arms and legs when entering temples. They ignore local customs of politeness. They want to see "traditional" ceremonies, but they fail to appreciate their true significance.

Already you have been dismayed to see old religious rites being turned into neatly packaged spectacles for tourists. Sacred events that happened once a year are now being recreated almost every week to amuse the visitors.

The government says that progress is essential, but you have seen stories about so-called "progress" in the rich countries, where families break down and there is crime and disorder. If this is "progress", you want no part of it. You must try to persuade other people to see things from your point of view.

Young People

You are excited by the proposed tourism development, because you can see the opportunity to get a more exciting job than your forebears, to earn more money and perhaps to be able to buy the kinds of clothes and luxury items that all the foreigners seem to have. You are excited by the chance to meet new people, and to learn about their customs and beliefs.

Nothing ever seems to change around here, old people are so set in their ways and nobody in your family ever seems to listen to what you have to say.

If you get a job in one of the new hotels, maybe you will be trained by Airtravel, and maybe there are chances of promotion, and even of jobs with it in other countries.

Even if there is no work in the hotels, tourists have lots of money and will pay to be guided to where the best sights are to be seen, the quietest beaches, and so on. You could make a living by walking along the beach and going up to tourists and offering to show them round.

You would have to leave school, but what use is school anyway – there are no jobs, or only picking coffee on the plantations, and who needs school for that? You could earn more money in a day selling your services to tourists than in a week on the plantation.

You need to try to persuade others that the tourism development is the best thing that could possibly happen to your country.

Worldcare

You are a northern hemisphere-based developmental and environmental organisation.

You are very concerned about the tourism development. You realise that the project might bring large potential benefits to Latasica, allowing the country to earn foreign currency to repay its debts, and also perhaps creating jobs and wealth for the population. You fear, however, that unless the project is carefully managed the costs could far exceed the benefits.

You believe that the government has not fully considered the environmental implications. You are aware of the depletion of fish stocks in the waters around Latasica, caused by over-fishing, which large-scale tourism will make worse.

Northern tourists expect luxuries such as baths and showers and swimming pools, yet Latasica has a problem with freshwater supplies. In the short term, this could pose problems for local farmers needing water for their crops, and for local people who may suffer shortages of clean water for bathing and drinking. In the longer term, there might be problems of deser-tification and soil erosion if too much water is taken from the land.

Tourists always pose problems of waste disposal; that is, rubbish and sewage. There are also potential risks to the habitats of local wildlife, plants and trees.

You have witnessed similar tourist developments in other countries. You have seen young people neglect their education because it is possible to make quick money selling souvenirs to tourists on the beach, acting as guides or even simply begging. You are also concerned about "sex tourism", and the possible growth of child prostitution that has happened in other poor countries.

You are also aware that tourists' tastes are fickle. Latasica may become next year's fashionable destination, but if too many people visit it may become "old hat", and people will move on to somewhere else. You are concerned that large-scale tourism may not be sustainable in the long term.

You are also acutely aware of global pandemics that have swept over the world in recent decades, each causing disruption to any free movement across borders, and thus a disaster to anybody trying to make their living from foreign travellers. Climate change is also playing on your mind, and you are realising that Latasica is getting more and more severe weather patterns with storms, droughts and flooding than ever before.

Your task is to make the government and people of Latasica aware of these concerns.

Animaltrust

You are a northern hemisphere-based organisation devoted to the protection of endangered species.

You have heard that the Latasican government is considering designating a large area of land as a game reserve. You are very excited by this prospect. You have been campaigning for many years to save Latasica's endangered populations of elephants, pumas and wild boar. The game reserve will guarantee their safety because nobody will be able to hunt them. Additionally, because the government and Airtravel will want people to come to the reserve, they may be willing to spend money supporting breeding programmes to increase wildlife numbers.

You are a little concerned about the building of the "safari lodge". The new roads and the building programme may disturb the animals' natural habitats. You are also concerned about the guided tours to see the animals. These creatures are shy, and the presence of tourists may disturb them, but this may be a price worth paying to conserve these wonderful creatures.

You need to encourage the government to go ahead with the project, but you want certain safeguards built into the scheme to ensure that the animals' welfare always comes first.

NEWSFLASHES

The "newsflashes" below may be used at any time by the facilitator to provoke more discussion. They can be selectively leaked to one or more groups, or revealed to everybody simultaneously as required. They are optional extras and need not be used if the facilitator is happy with the progress of the game.

Newsflash!

War has broken out in the Middle East. The world's supplies of oil and petroleum are being seriously disrupted. This is causing prices of fuel to increase dramatically making travel more expensive. Additionally, Western governments are advising their citizens that due to the instability it is inadvisable to travel except to well-established safe destinations.

Newsflash!

Due to continued good growing conditions worldwide, it is anticipated that there will be global overproduction of coffee this year. This is expected to drive prices down by 50 per cent. Coffee is Latasica's main export product, accounting for over 60 per cent of its earnings of foreign exchange.

This will have severe consequences for Latasica's economy, including its ability to repay its debts.

Newsflash!

A highly contagious virus is spreading in Latasica's neighbouring countries, and the government is closing borders to all non-essential travel. There is also a chance that Ambria will go into a hard lockdown in case the virus starts to spread in Latasica, with nothing but health facilities operating.

DEBRIEF

These notes for debriefing the game are for general guidance. It is anticipated that an experienced teacher/facilitator will have their own ideas about how to follow up the game and integrate it into a general scheme of work.

1. Ask students to come out of role. Has anybody any questions, comments, and so on, about the game that they would like to raise at this stage?
2. Ask for a show of hands: forgetting the role they played, how many students (a) think Latasica should go ahead with this development, (b) think Latasica should not go ahead with this development, (c) are unsure about whether Latasica should go ahead with the development
3. Ask one or more of those "in favour" to explain their reasons. Similarly, ask one or more of those "against" and one or more of the "undecided". Use these responses to stimulate discussion/debate. If you have used the preliminary exercise, it may be useful to refer back to it during this discussion
4. Make the point that the potential costs and benefits accruing from tourism depend on the activities of tourists. "Values conscious" tourists seek to behave in such a way as to maximise the benefits while minimising the costs to their hosts and the environment. Ask the group to get into pairs and ask each pair to come up with one or more ways in which they

could behave in a way respecting diverse values in their own tourism. Ask each pair in turn to give an idea to the group, and discuss these

Ideas might include buying "local" rather than imported foods, drinks, souvenirs, and so on, thus maximising the amount of foreign exchange the visited country receives from tourism. Similarly, use local transport, locally owned restaurants and shops.

Protect the environment by not littering, not picking flowers or stealing rocks and similar for souvenirs. Do not buy ivory, coral, fur or snakeskin products that contribute to the extinction of species.

Respect local customs regarding clothing, standards of politeness and public displays of affection, to name some examples. Make an effort to learn at least the basics of the local language (if only standard phrases such as "hello", "goodbye", "excuse me", "please" and "thank you"). This shows respect for your hosts and is much appreciated. It may even bring you benefits as the standard of service you receive may improve as a result!

NOTES

1. Senior Lecturer, Department of Service Management and Service Studies, Lund University, Sweden, elin.bommenel@ism.lu.se.
2. Associate Professor, Department of Geography, Media and Communication, Karlstad University, Sweden, Richard.ek@kau.se.
3. Doctoral student, Department of Service Management and Service Studies, Lund University, Sweden, stuart.reid@ism.lu.se.
4. Assistant Professor and Co-Director of Tourism RESET, Department of Retail, Hospitality & Tourism Management, University of Tennessee, USA, sbenjam1@utk.edu.
5. Programme Director, EMTM master programme, University of Girona, Spain, jaume.guia@udg.edu.
6. Professor, School of Hospitality, Food and Tourism Management, University of Guelph, Canada, mjoppe@uoguelph.ca.
7. Associate Professor, Department of Tourism, Sport and Hotel Management, Griffith University, Australia, a.coghlan@griffith.edu.au.
8. Social Animator, Educator and Impact Entrepreneur, Collaborative Transdisciplinary Practitioner, ripper.se@gmail.com.
9. Professor, Department of Recreation, Park and Tourism Sciences, Texas A&M University, tjamal@tamu.edu.
10. PhD student, Department of Ecology and Conservation Biology, Texas A&M University, mrp126@tamu.edu.
11. Lecturer, University of Caen-Normandy, France, xavier.michel@unicaen.fr.
12. Senior Lecturer in Tourism, Faculty of Business and Law, Anglia Ruskin University, UK, sudipta.sarkar@aru.ac.uk.
13. Former Professor, Center for Advanced Tourism Studies, Hokkaido University, Japan, yasuba@icloud.com.
14. Senior Lecturer, Department of Service Management and Service Studies, Lund University, Sweden, elin.bommenel@ism.lu.se.
15. Associate Professor, Department of Geography, Media and Communication, Karlstad University, Sweden, Richard.ek@kau.se.
16. Doctoral student, Department of Service Management and Service Studies, Lund University, Sweden, stuart.reid@ism.lu.se.
17. Associate Professor, Coordinator and Head of Research Network for Tourism, Aalborg University, Denmark, balslev@hum.aau.dk.
18. Senior Lecturer, School of Management, Swansea University, UK, maggie.miller@swansea.ac.uk.

19. Professor, Graduate School of International Media, Communication and Tourism Studies, Hokkaido University, Japan, johan.edelheim@imc.hokudai.ac.jp.
20. Professor, Graduate School of International Media, Communication and Tourism Studies, Hokkaido University, Japan, johan.edelheim@imc.hokudai.ac.jp.
21. Senior Lecturer, York Business School, York St John University, UK, B.Paddison@yorksj.ac.uk.
22. Senior Lecturer in Tourism, Faculty of Business and Law, Anglia Ruskin University, UK, sudipta. sarkar@aru.ac.uk.
23. Former Professor, Center for Advanced Tourism Studies, Hokkaido University, Japan, yasuba@ icloud.com.
24. Associate Professor, Department of Culture and Learning, Aalborg University, Denmark, msab@ hum.aau.dk.
25. Postdoctoral researcher, Multidimensional Tourism Institute, University of Lapland, Finland, emily.hockert@ulapland.fi.
26. Coordinator, Education and Development Services, University of Lapland, Finland, outi.kugapi@ ulapland.fi.
27. Senior Lecturer (Tourism Research), Multidimensional Tourism Institute, University of Lapland, Finland, monika.luthje@ulapland.fi.
28. Associate Professor, Centre for Innovation and Research in Culture and Living in the Arctic (CIRCLA), Aalborg University, Denmark, ren@hum.aau.dk.
29. The European Credit Transfer and Accumulation System (ECTS) is an important element of the Bologna Process, aimed at making degree programmes and student performance more transparent and comparable across all countries that are members of the European Higher Education Area (EHEA).
30. Postdoctoral Fellow, Department of Management, Università Ca' Foscari Venezia, Italy, and Faculty of Management, University of British Columbia, Canada, linda.armano@unive.it.
31. Associate Professor and Director of Graduate Programs, School of Hospitality and Tourism Management, Purdue University, USA, gjday@purdue.edu.
32. University Lecturer of Art Education, Faculty of Art and Design, University of Lapland, Finland, maria.huhmarniemi@ulapland.fi.
33. Coordinator, Education and Development Services, University of Lapland, Finland, outi.kugapi@ ulapland.fi.
34. Senior Lecturer, Faculty of Business and Law, University of Northampton, UK, Nick.Naumov@ northampton.ac.uk.
35. Professor, School of Hospitality and Tourism Management, George Brown College, Canada, jgellatl@georgebrown.ca.
36. Professor, School of Hospitality and Tourism Management, George Brown College, Canada, jgellatl@georgebrown.ca.
37. Lecturer in Management, UTS Business School, University of Technology Sydney, Australia, Ece. kaya@uts.edu.au.
38. Associate Professor, UTS Business School, University of Technology Sydney, Australia, Deborah. Edwards-1@uts.edu.au.
39. Senior Lecturer, Faculty of Business and Law, University of Northampton, UK, Nick.Naumov@ northampton.ac.uk.
40. Senior Lecturer, Faculty of Business and Law, University of Northampton, UK, Nick.Naumov@ northampton.ac.uk.
41. Professor, Graduate School of International Media, Communication and Tourism Studies, Hokkaido University, Japan, johan.edelheim@imc.hokudai.ac.jp.
42. Associate Professor Emerita, School of Hospitality, Food and Tourism Management, University of Guelph, Canada, jflahert@uoguelph.ca.
43. Associate Professor Emerita, School of Hospitality, Food and Tourism Management, University of Guelph, Canada, jflahert@uoguelph.ca.
44. Assistant Professor, School of Hospitality, Food and Tourism Management, University of Guelph, krodenbur@uoguelph.ca.
45. Associate Professor, Department of Recreation and Leisure Studies, University of Waterloo, Canada, kboluk@uwaterloo.ca.

46. Associate Professor, Department of Recreation and Leisure Studies, University of Waterloo, Canada, kboluk@uwaterloo.ca.
47. Professor, School of Hospitality, Food and Tourism Management, University of Guelph, Canada, mjoppe@uoguelph.ca.
48. Professor, School of Hospitality, Food and Tourism Management, University of Guelph, Canada, mjoppe@uoguelph.ca.
49. Associate Professor, Multidimensional Tourism Institute, Faculty of Social Sciences, University of Lapland, Finland, outi.rantala@ulapland.fi.
50. Associate Professor, Faculty of Humanities, Social Sciences and Education, UiT The Arctic University of Norway, Norway, brynhild.granas@uit.no.
51. Professor, Faculty of Life and Environmental Sciences, University of Iceland, Iceland, gtj@hi.is.
52. Senior Lecturer, Faculty of Science, University of Oulu, Finland, kaarina.tervo-kankare@oulu.fi.
53. For Indigenous peoples in particular, animals and landscape features should be recognised as equal to humans.
54. Professor, International Tourism Program, Business School, Universidad de Monterrey, Mexico, blanca.camargo@udem.edu.
55. Senior Lecturer, Multidimensional Tourism Institute, Lapland University of Applied Sciences, Rovaniemi, Finland, sisko.haikio@lapinamk.fi.
56. Senior Lecturer, Multidimensional Tourism Institute, Lapland University of Applied Sciences, Rovaniemi, Finland, minna.vayrynen@lapinamk.fi.
57. Assistant Professor, Faculty of Tourism, University of Maribor, Slovenia, tanja.lesnik@um.si.
58. Associate Professor, Faculty of Tourism, University of Maribor, Slovenia, maja.turnsek@um.si.
59. Lecturer, School of Arts, Murdoch University, Singapore, n.abubakar@murdoch.edu.au.
60. Associate Professor, Department of Recreation and Leisure Studies, University of Waterloo, Canada, kboluk@uwaterloo.ca.
61. Senior Lecturer, Department of Service Management and Service Studies, Lund University, Sweden, elin.bommenel@ism.lu.se.
62. Associate Professor, Department of Geography, Media and Communication, Karlstad University, Sweden, Richard.ek@kau.se.
63. Doctoral student, Department of Service Management and Service Studies, Lund University, Sweden, stuart.reid@ism.lu.se.
64. Associate Professor Emerita, School of Hospitality, Food and Tourism Management, University of Guelph, Canada, jflahert@uoguelph.ca.
65. Assistant Professor in Tourism Management & Innovation/Entrepreneurship, College of Business and Management, VinUniversity, Hanoi, Vietnam, giang.ptl@vinuni.edu.vn.
66. Associate Professor, Department of Geography, Environmental Studies & Tourism, University of the Western Cape, South Africa, brink@uwc.ac.za.
67. Associate Professor, Coordinator and Head of Research Network for Tourism, Aalborg University, Denmark, balslev@hum.aau.dk.
68. Senior Lecturer, School of Management, Swansea University, UK, maggie.miller@swansea.ac.uk.
69. JSPS Postdoctoral Fellow, Graduate School of International Media, Communication and Tourism Studies, Hokkaido University, Japan, emilie.crossley@elms.hokudai.ac.jp.
70. Associate Professor Emerita, School of Hospitality, Food and Tourism Management, University of Guelph, Canada, jflahert@uoguelph.ca.
71. Assistant Professor, School of Hospitality, Food and Tourism Management, University of Guelph, Canada, krodenbur@uoguelph.ca.
72. Senior Lecturer, Faculty of Science, University of Oulu, Finland, kaarina.tervo-kankare@oulu.fi.
73. Professor, Faculty of Life and Environmental Sciences, University of Iceland, Iceland, gtj@hi.is.
74. Associate Professor, Faculty of Humanities, Social Sciences and Education, UiT The Arctic University of Norway, Norway, brynhild.granas@uit.no.
75. Associate Professor, Multidimensional Tourism Institute, University of Lapland, Finland, outi.rantala@ulapland.fi.
76. Associate Professor, Faculty of Tourism, University of Maribor, Slovenia, maja.turnsek@um.si.
77. Lecturer, Department of Tourism Management, Tshwane University of Technology, South Africa, bouwers@tut.ac.za.
78. Park Ranger, Broads National Park, UK, stephen1956@btinternet.com.

References

Abernathy, W. J., and Clark, K. B. (1985). Innovation: Mapping the winds of creative destruction. *Research Policy*, *14*(1), 3–22.

Abrahams, J., and Brooks, R. (2019). Higher education students as political actors: Evidence from England and Ireland. *Journal of Youth Studies*, *22*(1), 108–123. https://doi.org/10.1080/13676261.2018.1484431.

Airbnb (2020). What are the quality standards for Airbnb Experiences? www.airbnb .com/help/article/1451/what-are-the-quality-standards-for-airbnb-experiences.

Allt, S. (2020). *The Finland Guidebook*. www.expat-finland.com/employment/unions.html.

Alvesson, M., and Sköldberg, K. (2009). *Reflexive Methodology: New Vistas for Qualitative Research* (2nd ed.). SAGE.

Ambrose, S. A., Bridges, M. W., Lovett, M. C., DiPietro, M., and Norman, M. K. (2010). *How Learning Works: 7 Research-Based Principles for Smart Teaching*. Jossey-Bass.

Anderson, B. (1991). *Imagined Communities* (Revised ed.). Verso.

Andersson, J. O. (2009, December). Basic income from an ecological perspective [Research note]. *Basic Income Studies: An International Journal of Basic Income Research*, *4*(2), 1–8. https://doi.org/10. 2202/1932-0183.1180.

Andersson, T., Ellingsen, T., and Persson, T. (2020). The Prize in Economic Sciences 2020. www. nobelprize.org/prizes/economic-sciences/2020/press-release/.

Anonymous (2021a, February 20). The pandemic made the world realise the importance of human contact. *The Economist*, *438*(9233), 50–51.

Anonymous (2021b, February 13). A tale of two colleges. *The Economist*, *438*(9232), 28–29.

Anstey, M., and Bull, G. (2018). *Foundations of Multiliteracies: Reading, Writing and Talking in the 21st Century*. Routledge.

Apel, K.-O. (1982). The Erklären–Verstehen controversy in the philosophy of the natural and human sciences. In G. Fløistad (Ed.), *La philosophie contemporaine/Contemporary Philosophy* (Vol. 2, pp. 19–49). International Institute of Philosophy/Institut International de Philosophie. https://doi.org/ 10.1007/978-94-010-9940-0_2.

Arasaratnam, L. A. (2016). Intercultural competence. In J. F. Nussbaum (Ed.), *Oxford Encyclopedia of Communication*. Oxford University Press. https://doi.org/10.1093/acrefore/9780190228613.013.68.

Armano, L. (2018). *DiaEthic: Map Value Transformations in Consumer Research: Sensory Experiences and Cultural Interpretation Shape Concepts of "Ethical Diamond" and "Mining Work Ethic" in a Global Interconnection*. Marie Skłodowska-Curie project: H2020-MSCA-IF-2018H2020-MSCA-I F-2018v.

Asante, M. K. (2020). Toward a transformative African curriculum for higher education. *International Journal of African Renaissance Studies – Multi-, Inter- and Transdisciplinarity*, *15*(1), 25–40. https:// doi.org/10.1080/18186874.2020.1740059.

Ashton, M. C., and Lee, K. (2007). Empirical, theoretical, and practical advantages of the HEXACO model of personality structure. *Personality and Social Psychology Review*, *11*(2), 150–166. https://doi. org/10.1177/1088868306294907.

Ateljevic, I., Pritchard, A., and Morgan, N. (2007). *The Critical Turn in Tourism Studies: Innovative Research Methods*. Elsevier.

Balotsky, E. A., and Steingard, D. (2006). How teaching business ethics makes a difference: Findings from an ethical learning model. *Journal of Business Ethics Education*, *3*, 5–34. https://doi.org/10. 5840/jbee200632.

Bangura, A. K. (2005). Ubuntugogy: An African educational paradigm that transcends pedagogy, andragogy, ergonagogy and heutagogy. *Journal of Third World Studies, 22*(2), 13–53.

Barber, E. (2011). Case study: Integrating TEFI (Tourism Education Futures Initiative) core values into the undergraduate curriculum. *Journal of Teaching in Travel & Tourism, 11*(1), 38–75. https://doi.org/10.1080/15313220.2011.548732.

Baregheh, A., Rowley, J., and Sambrook, S. (2009). Towards a multidisciplinary definition of innovation. *Management Decision, 47*(8), 1323–1339.

Barkathunnisha, A. B., Lee, D., Price, A., and Wilson, E. (2018). Towards a spirituality-based platform in tourism higher education. *Current Issues in Tourism, 22*(17), 2140–2156.

Baruchello, G. (2018). Good vs. bad tourism: Homo viator's responsibility in light of life-value onto-axiology. In M. Gren and E. H. Huijbens (Eds), *Tourism and the Anthropocene* (pp. 111–128). Routledge.

Bateman, T. S., and Crant, J. M. (1993). The proactive component of organizational behavior: A measure and correlates. *Journal of Organizational Behavior, 14*(2), 103–118.

Becken, S. (2015). *Tourism and Oil: Preparing for the Challenge*. Channel View Publications.

Becker, B. W., and Conner, P. E. (1983). A course on human values for the management curriculum. *Journal of Management Education, 8*(1), 10–16. https://doi.org/10.1177/105256298300800102.

Belhassen, Y., and Caton, K. (2009). Advancing understandings: A linguistic approach to tourism epistemology. *Annals of Tourism Research, 36*(2), 335–352. https://doi.org/10.1016/j.annals.2009.01.006.

Benjamin, S., and Kline, C. (2019). How to yes-and: Using improvisational games to improv(e) communication, listening, and collaboration techniques in tourism and hospitality education. *Journal of Hospitality, Leisure, Sport & Tourism Education, 24*, 130–142. https://doi.org/10.1016/j.jhlste.2019.02.002.

Bennett, J. M. (2008). Transformative training: Designing programs for culture learning. In M. A. Moodian (Ed.), *Contemporary Leadership and Intercultural Competence: Exploring the Cross-Cultural Dynamics Within Organizations* (pp. 95–110). SAGE.

Bennett, M. J. (1986). A developmental approach to training for intercultural sensitivity. *International Journal of Intercultural Relations, 10*(2), 179–196.

Bennis, W. G. (2009). *On Becoming a Leader*. Basic Books.

Berardo, K. (2012). Voices from the past. In K. Berardo and D. K. Deardorff (Eds), *Building Cultural Competence: Innovative Activities and Model* (pp. 143–147). Stylus Publishing.

Berkes, F., Feeny, D., McCay, B. J., and Acheson, J. M. (1989). The benefits of the commons. *Nature, 340*(7), 91–93.

Berque, A. (2010). *Milieu et identité humaine : Notes pour un dépassement de la modernité*. Editions donner lieu.

Biggs, J. (2003). *Teaching for Quality Learning* (2nd ed.). McGraw-Hill Education.

Biggs, J., and Tang, C. (2011). *Teaching for Quality Learning at University* (4th ed.). McGraw-Hill.

Boluk, K. A., and Carnicelli, S. (2019). Tourism for the emancipation of the oppressed: Towards a critical tourism education drawing on Freirean philosophy. *Annals of Tourism Research, 76*, 168–179. https://doi.org/10.1016/j.annals.2019.04.002.

Boluk, K. A., Cavaliere, C. T., and Duffy, L. N. (2019a). A pedagogical framework for the development of the critical tourism citizen. *Journal of Sustainable Tourism, 27*(7), 865–881. https://doi.org/10.1080/09669582.2019.1615928.

Boluk, K. A., Cavaliere, C. T., and Higgins-Desbiolles, F. (2019b). A critical framework for interrogating the United Nations Sustainable Development Goals 2030 Agenda in Tourism. *Journal of Sustainable Tourism, 27*(7), 847–864. https://doi.org/10.1080/09669582.2019.1619748.

Boluk, K. A., Muldoon, M. L., and Johnson, C. W. (2019c). Bringing a politics of hope to the tourism classroom: Exploring an integrated curriculum design through a creative and reflexive methodology. *Journal of Teaching in Travel & Tourism, 19*(1), 63–78. https://doi.org/10.1080/15313220.2018.1560532.

Bonnett, M., and Cuypers, S. (2003). Autonomy and authenticity in education. In N. Blake, P. Smeyers, R. Smith and P. Standish (Eds), *The Blackwell Guide to the Philosophy of Education* (pp. 326–340). Blackwell.

Boroditsky, L. (2011). How language shapes thought: The languages we speak affect our perceptions of the world. *Scientific American, 304*(2), 63–65.

Bowels, S., and Carlin, W. (2020). What students learn in economics 101: Time for a change. *Journal of Economic Literature, 58*(1), 176–214. https://doi.org/10.1257/jel.20191585.

Bowels, S., and Cohen, J. (2019). Everyday economists: Samuel Bowels interviewed by Joshua Cohen. *Economics after Neoliberalism, Boston Review Forum II, 44*(3), 112–123.

Braidotti, R. (2018). Foreword. In R. Braidotti, V. Bozalek, T. Shefer and M. Zembylas (Eds), *Socially Just Pedagogies: Posthumanist, Feminist and Materialist Perspectives in Higher Education* (pp. xiii–xxvii). Bloomsbury Academic.

Bratsberg, B., and Rogeberg, O. (2018). Flynn effect and its reversal are both environmentally caused. *Proceedings of the National Academy of Sciences, 115*(26), 6674–6678. https://doi.org/10.1073/pnas. 1718793115.

Bricker, K. S., Black, R., and Cottrell, S. (2013). *Sustainable Tourism & The Millennium Development Goals: Effecting Positive Change.* Jones & Bartlett Learning.

Brlek Slaček, A. S., and Turnšek, M. (2010). Utopia and its discontents: How young people are making sense of the public sphere. *International Journal of Learning and Media, 2*(1), 25–37.

Brooker, E., and Joppe, M. (2014). Developing a tourism innovation typology: Leveraging liminal insights. *Journal of Travel Research, 53*(4), 500–508. https://doi.org/10.1177/0047287513497839.

Brookfield, S. D. (1987). *Developing Critical Thinkers: Challenging Adults to Explore Alternative Ways of Thinking and Acting.* Jossey-Bass.

Brookfield, S. D. (2012). *Teaching for Critical Thinking: Tools and Techniques to Help Students Question Their Assumptions.* Jossey-Bass.

Broomfield, J. (1997). *Other Ways of Knowing: Recharting Our Future with Ageless Wisdom.* Inner Traditions International.

Brown, T. (2009). *Change by Design: How Design Thinking Transforms Organizations and Inspires Innovation.* Harper Business.

Buissink-Smith, N., Mann, S., and Shephard, K. (2011). How do we measure affective learning in higher education? *Journal of Education for Sustainable Development, 5*(1), 101–114.

Burns, T., Machado des Johansson, N., and Corte, U. (2015). The sociology of creativity: Part I – Theory: The social mechanisms of innovation and creative developments in selectivity environments. *Human Systems Management, 34*, 179–199. https://doi.org/10.3233/HSM-150839.

Cabinet Office Government of Japan (2020). Society 5.0: Science and Technology Policy. Council for Science, Technology and Innovation. www8.cao.go.jp/cstp/english/society5_0/index.html.

Canda, E. R., and Furman, L. D. (2010). *Spiritual Diversity in Social Work Practice* (2nd ed.). Oxford University Press.

Capable NZ. (2020). *Master of Professional Practice (MProfPrac) learner guide* [Unpublished document].

Capra, F. (1996). *The Web of Life: A New Scientific Understanding of Living Systems.* Random House.

Caprara, G. V., Vecchione, M., Capanna, C., and Mebane, M. (2009). Perceived political self-efficacy: Theory, assessment, and applications. *European Journal of Social Psychology, 39*(6), 1002–1020. https://doi.org/10.1002/ejsp.604.

Carney, M. (2020). *How We Get What We Value.* BBC. www.bbc.co.uk/sounds/brand/b00729d9.

Caton, K. (2012). Taking the moral turn in tourism studies. *Annals of Tourism Research, 39*, 1906–1928. https://doi.org/10.1016/j.annals.2012.05.021.

Caton, K. (2014). Underdisciplinarity: Where are the humanities in tourism education? *Journal of Hospitality, Leisure, Sport & Tourism Education, 15*, 24–33.

Caton, K. (2015). Growing on the go? Moral development and tourism. *Annals of Leisure Research, 18*(1). https://doi.org/10.1080/11745398.2015.1004253.

Chambers, D. P., and Buzinde, C. (2015). Tourism and decolonization: Locating research and self. *Annals of Tourism Research, 51*, 1–16.

Cheng, M., and Foley, C. (2019). Algorithmic management: The case of Airbnb. *International Journal of Hospitality Management, 83*, 33–36. https://doi.org/10.1016/j.ijhm.2019.04.009.

Cheng, S., and Wong, A. (2015). Professionalism: A contemporary interpretation in hospitality industry context. *International Journal of Hospitality Management, 50*, 122–133.

Chim-Miki, A. F., and Batista-Canino, R. M. (2017). The coopetition perspective applied to tourism destinations: A literature review. *Anatolia*, *28*(3), 381–393.

Christensen, J. (2012). Telling stories: Exploring research storytelling as a meaningful approach to knowledge mobilization with Indigenous research collaborators and diverse audiences in community-based participatory research. *Canadian Geographer/Le Géographe canadien*, *56*(2), 231–242. https://doi.org/10.1111/j.1541-0064.2012.00417.x.

Chua, P. K., and Mazmanian, M. (2020, October). Are you one of us? Current hiring practices suggest the potential for class biases in large tech companies. *Proceedings of the ACM on Human–Computer Interaction Conference*, *3*(143). https://doi.org/10.1145/3415214.

CIA-Factbook. (2018). List of countries by life expectancy. Available as a graph at https://en.wikipedia.org/wiki/List_of_countries_by_life_expectancy.

Clark, M. D. (2020). DRAG THEM: A brief etymology of so-called "cancel culture". *Communication and the Public*, *5*(3–4), 88–92. https://doi.org/10.1177/2057047320961562.

Clarkson, L., Morrissette, V., and Régallet, G. (1992). *Our Responsibility to the Seventh Generation: Indigenous Peoples and Sustainable Development*. International Institute for Sustainable Development.

Clausen, H. B., and Andersson, V. (2018). Problem-based learning, education and employability: A case study with master's students from Aalborg University, Denmark. *Journal of Teaching in Travel & Tourism*, *19*(2), 126–139.

Constanti, P., and Gibbs, P. (2004). Higher education teachers and emotional labour. *International Journal of Educational Management*, *18*(4), 243–249.

Coops, N. C., Marcus, J., Construt, I., Frank, E., Kellett, R., Mazzi, E., Munro, A., Nesbit, S., Riseman, A., Robinson, J., Schultz, A., and Sipos, Y. (2015). How an entry-level, interdisciplinary sustainability course revealed the benefits and challenges of a university-wide initiative for sustainability education. *International Journal of Sustainability in Higher Education*, *16*(5), 729–747.

Coulter, C., Michael, C., and Poynor, L. (2007). Storytelling as pedagogy: An unexpected outcome of narrative inquiry. *Curriculum Inquiry*, *37*(2), 103–122. https://doi.org/10.1111/j.1467-873X.2007.00375.x.

Covey, S. (1989). *The Seven Habits of Highly Effective People*. Simon & Shuster.

Coyle, T. R., Rindermann, H., and Hancock, D. (2016). Cognitive capitalism: Economic freedom moderates the effects of intellectual and average classes on economic productivity. *Psychological Reports*, *119*(2), 411–427. https://doi.org/10.1177/0033294116659854.

Crang, M. (1997). Picturing practices: Research through the tourist gaze [Review article]. *Progress in Human Geography*, *21*(3), 359–373. https://doi.org/10.1191/030913297669603510.

Cranton, P. (2000). *Planning Instruction for Adult Learners* (2nd ed.). Wall & Emerson.

Crossley, É. (2017). Criticality in tourism education. In P. J. Benckendorff and A. Zehrer (Eds), *Handbook of Teaching and Learning in Tourism* (pp. 427–438). Edward Elgar Publishing.

CTE (2015). Active learning activities. Centre for Teaching Excellence, University of Waterloo. https://uwaterloo.ca/centre-for-teaching-excellence/teaching-resources/teaching-tips/developing-assignments/assignment-design/active-learning-activities.

Cuffy, V. V., Airey, D., and Papageorgiou, G. C. (Eds) (2018). *Lifelong Learning for Tourism: Concepts, Policy and Implementation*. Routledge. https://doi.org/10.4324/9781315407821.

Czernek, K., and Czakon, W. (2016). Trust-building processes in tourist coopetition: The case of a Polish region. *Tourism Management*, *52*, 380–394.

Daniels, H. (2016). *Vygotsky and Pedagogy* (2nd ed.). Routledge.

Deniston-Trochta, G. (2003). The meaning of storytelling as pedagogy. *Visual Arts Research*, *29*(57), 103–108.

Denzin, N. K., and Lincoln, Y. S. (2011). *The SAGE Handbook of Qualitative Research* (4th ed.). SAGE.

Détroit, F., Mijares, A. S., Corny, J., Daver, G., Zanolli, C., Dizon, E., Robles, E., Grün, R., and Piper, P. J. (2019). A new species of *Homo* from the Late Pleistocene of the Philippines. *Nature*, *568*, 181–186. https://doi.org/10.1038/s41586-019-1067-9.

Dietrich, A. (2004). The cognitive neuroscience of creativity. *Psychonomic Bulletin & Review*, *11*(6), 1011–1026.

Dobson, H. (2006). Mister Sparkle meets the Yakuza: Depictions of Japan in *The Simpsons*. *Journal of Popular Culture*, *39*(1), 44–68.

Dredge, D. (2018). Rescuing policy in tourism network research. *Via – Tourism Review*, *13*. https://doi.org/10.4000/viatourism.2120.

Dredge, D., Benckendorff, P. J., Day, M., Gross, M., Walo, M., Weeks, P., and Whitelaw, P. A. (2012). The philosophic practitioner and the curriculum space. *Annals of Tourism Research*, *39*(4), 2154–2176.

Duxbury, N., and Richards, G. (2019). Towards a research agenda for creative tourism: A synthesis of suggested future research trajectories. In N. Duxbury and G. Richards (Eds), *A Research Agenda for Creative Tourism* (pp. 1–14). Edward Elgar Publishing.

Edelheim, J. (2005). Experience the "real" Australia: a liminal authentic cultural experience. In C. Ryan and M. Aicken (Eds), *Indigenous Tourism: The Commodification and Management of Culture* (pp. 247–260). Elsevier.

Edelheim, J. (2015). *Tourist Attractions: From Object to Narrative*. Channel View Publications.

Edelheim, J. (2017). Teaching–research nexus in tourism, hospitality and event studies. In P. J. Benckendorff and A. Zehrer (Eds), *Handbook of Teaching and Learning in Tourism* (pp. 467–483). Edward Elgar Publishing.

Edelheim, J. (2020). How should tourism education values be transformed after 2020? *Tourism Geographies*, *22*(3), 547–554. https://doi.org/10.1080/14616688.2020.1760927.

Edwards, R. B. (2010). *The Essentials of Formal Axiology*. University Press of America.

Ely, R. J., Meyerson, D., and Davidson, M. N. (2006). Rethinking political correctness. *Harvard Business Review*, *50*(9), 1–11. https://hbr.org/2006/09/rethinking-political-correctness.

Emdin, C. (2020). A ratchetdemic reality pedagogy and/as cultural freedom in urban education. *Educational Philosophy and Theory*, *52*(9), 947–960. https://doi.org/10.1080/00131857.2019.1669446.

ESS-ERIC. (n.d.). European Social Survey: Source Questionnaire. www.europeansocialsurvey.org/methodology/ess_methodology/source_questionnaire/.

Estanek, S. M. (2006). Redefining spirituality: A new discourse. *College Student Journal*, *40*(2), 270–281.

Evans, L. (2017, January 11). *Own Your Behaviours, Master Your Communication, Determine Your Success* [Video file]. TEDxGenova. www.youtube.com/watch?v=4BZuWrdC-9Q&list=PLbcsblFvydZPvaTR4hSPOFn9qXZRBnYF1&index=4.

Fairbrass, S. (n.d.). *The Tourism Game*. Norfolk Education and Action for Developments (NEAD). www.scottishfairtradeforum.org.uk/reports/schools/pdf/The%20Tourism%20Game.pdf.

Fennell, D. A. (2018). *Tourism Ethics* (2nd ed., Vol. 81). Channel View Publications.

Finkelstein, L. M., and Farrell, S. K. (2007). An expanded view of age bias in the workplace. In K. S. Shultz and G. A. Adams (Eds), *Aging and Work in the 21st Century* (pp. 73–108). Psychology Press.

Fisher, K. M. (2017). Look before you leap: Reconsidering contemplative pedagogy. *Teaching Theology & Religion*, *20*(1), 4–21.

Fisher, M. (2009). *Capitalist Realism: Is There No Alternative?* O Books.

Florida, R. (2002). *The Rise of the Creative Class: And How It's Transforming Work, Leisure, Community and Everyday Life*. Basic Books.

Flynn, J. R. (2013, September 26). *Why Our IQ Levels Are Higher Than Our Grandparents'* [Video file]. TEDx. www.youtube.com/watch?v=9vpqilhW9uI.

Fox, C. (2018). *I Still Find That Offensive*. Biteback Publishing.

Freire, P. (1970). *Pedagogy of the Oppressed*. Continuum.

FSDS (Foundation for Democracy and Sustainable Development) (2015). The Ecuadorian Constitution was the first national constitution to give rights to nature. FSDS. www.fdsd.org/ideas/ecuadorian-constitution-rights-to-nature/.

Fullagar, S., and Wilson, E. (2012). Critical pedagogies: A reflexive approach to knowledge creation in tourism and hospitality studies. *Journal of Hospitality and Tourism Management*, *19*(1), 1–6. https://doi.org/10.1017/jht.2012.3.

Funes, Y. (2018). The Colombian Amazon is now a "person", and you can thank actual people. *Gizmodo – Earther*, 9 April. Retrieved 3 November 2020, from https://earther.gizmodo.com/the-colombian-amazon-is-now-a-person-and-you-can-thank-1825059357.

Game, A., and Metcalfe, A. (2009). Dialogue and team teaching. *Higher Education Research & Development*, 28(1), 45–57.

Gano-Phillips, S. (2009). *Affective Learning in General Education*. Chinese University of Hong Kong. www.oge.cuhk.edu.hk/oge_media/rcge/Docs/Journal/Issue_06/01_SusanGanoPhilips.pdf.

Gardiner, K. (2021, 10 February). Stereotypes have fuelled a tourism boom in Europe's icy North. Can things change? *National Geographic*. www.nationalgeographic.com/travel/article/changing -indigneous-cultural-tourism-in-arctic-sapmi-region.

Gardiner, S. M., and Thompson, A. (2017). *The Oxford Handbook of Environmental Ethics*. Oxford University Press.

Gellatly, J. P. (2016). *A Global Tourism: Qualitative Descriptive Multiple Case Study of Consequences of Industry Defragmentation* (Doctoral dissertation, University of Phoenix).

Gentile, M. C. (2010). *Giving Voice to Values: How to Speak Your Mind When You Know What's Right*. Yale University Press.

Gentile, M. C. (2013). Giving voice to values. In S. O. Idowu, N. Capaldi, L. Zu and A. D. Gupta (Eds), *Encyclopedia of Corporate Social Responsibility*. Springer.

Gentile, M. C. (2017). Giving voice to values: A pedagogy for behavioural ethics. *Journal of Management Education*, 41(4), 469–479. https://doi.org/10.1177/1052562917700188.

Gibbs, G. (1988). *Learning by Doing: A Guide to Teaching and Learning Methods*. Oxford Further Education Unit.

Gilstrap, D. L., and Dupree, J. (2008). Assessing learning, critical reflection, and quality educational outcomes: The Critical Incident Questionnaire. *College & Research Libraries*, 69(5), 407–426.

Glassner, V., and Pochet, P. (2011). Why trade unions seek to coordinate wages and collective bargaining in the Eurozone: Past developments and future prospects. *SSRN Electronic Journal* (Economics, European Trade Union Institute (ETUI) Research Paper Series). https://doi.org/10.2139/SSRN. 2221845.

Glowacki-Dudka, M., and Barnett, N. (2007). Connecting critical reflection and group development in online adult education classrooms. *International Journal of Teaching and Learning in Higher Education*, 19(1), 43–52.

Gordon, T. (2001). *Leader Effectiveness Training*. Penguin.

Gordon, T. (2010). *Teacher Effectiveness Training*. Random House.

Gössling, S., Hanna, P., Higham, J., Cohen, S., and Hopkins, D. (2019). Can we fly less? Evaluating the "necessity" of air travel. *Journal of Air Transport Management*, 81(October), 101722. https://doi.org/ 10.1016/j.jairtraman.2019.101722.

Grandey, A. A. (2000). Emotion regulation in the workplace: A new way to conceptualize emotional labor. *Journal of Occupational Health Psychology*, 5(1), 95–110.

Greenleaf, R. K. (1977). *Servant Leadership: A Journey into the Nature of Legitimate Power and Greatness*. Paulist Press.

Gruenewald, D. A. (2003). The best of both worlds: A critical pedagogy of place. *Educational Researcher*, 32(4), 3–12.

Guia, J. (2021). Conceptualizing justice tourism and the promise of posthumanism. *Journal of Sustainable Tourism*, 29(2–3), 502–519. https://doi.org/10.1080/09669582.2020.1771347.

Guia, J., and Jamal, T. (2020). A (Deleuzian) posthumanist paradigm for tourism research [Research note]. *Annals of Tourism Research*, 84(September 102982). https://doi.org/10.1016/j.annals.2020. 102982.

Gulikers, J., Bastiaens, T., and Kirschner, P. (2004). A five-dimensional framework for authentic assessment. *Educational Technology Research and Development*, 52(3), 67–85.

Hall, R., and Smyth, K. (2016). Dismantling the curriculum in higher education. *Open Library of Humanities*, 2(1), 1–28. https://doi.org/10.16995/olh.66.

Halpern, D. F. (2014). *Critical Thinking across the Curriculum: A Brief Edition of Thought & Knowledge*. Routledge.

Halstead, J. M., and Taylor, M. J. (2000). Learning and teaching about values: A review of recent research. *Cambridge Journal of Education*, 30(2), 169–202. https://doi.org/10.1080/713657146.

Harari, Y. N. (2014). *Sapiens: A Brief History of Humankind*. Vintage.

Harari, Y. N. (2016). *Homo Deus: A Brief History of Tomorrow*. Harvill Secker.

Haraway, D. J. (2008). *When Species Meet*. University of Minnesota Press.

Haraway, D. J. (2016). *Staying with the Trouble: Making Kin in the Chthulucene*. Duke University Press. https://doi.org/10.1215/9780822373780.

Harman, G. (2018). *Object-Oriented Ontology: A New Theory of Everything*. Pelican Books.

Hart, T. (2014). Presence, resonance, transcendence: Education, spirituality and the contemplative mind. In J. Watson, M. d. Souza and A. Trousdale (Eds), *Global Perspectives on Spirituality in Education* (pp. 247–257). Routledge.

Hartman, R. S. (2019). *Five Lectures on Formal Axiology* [Book version of a series of lectures given in the late 1960s and early 1970s]. Izzard Ink.

Hase, S., and Kenyon, C. (Eds) (2013). *Self-Determined Learning: Heutagogy in Action*. Bloomsbury.

Healey, M. (2005). Linking research and teaching: Exploring disciplinary spaces and the role of inquiry-based learning. In R. Barnett (Ed.), *Reshaping the University: New Relationships Between Research, Scholarship and Teaching* (pp. 67–78). McGraw-Hill Education.

Helyer, R. (Ed.) (2016). *Facilitating Work-based Learning: A Handbook for Tutors*. Palgrave.

Herrington, J., Reeves, T., and Oliver, R. (2010). *A Guide to Authentic e-Learning*. Routledge.

Heuts, F., and Mol, A. (2013). What is a good tomato? A case of valuing in practice. *Valuation Studies*, *1*(2), 125–146. https://doi.org/10.3384/vs.2001-5992.1312125.

Higgins-Desbiolles, F., Carnicelli, S., Krolikowski, C., Wijesinghe, G., and Boluk, K. A. (2019). Degrowing tourism: Rethinking tourism. *Journal of Sustainable Tourism*, *27*(12), 1926–1944. https://doi.org/10.1080/09669582.2019.1601732.

Higgs, M., and Aitken, P. (2003). An exploration of the relationship between emotional intelligence and leadership potential. *Journal of Managerial Psychology*, *18*(8), 814–823.

Hill, M., and Varone, F. (2014). *The Public Policy Process* (6th ed.). Routledge.

Hillman, W., and Radel, K. (Eds) (2018). *Qualitative Methods in Tourism Research*. Channel View Publications.

Hinett, K. (2002). *Improving Learning through Reflection: Part Two*. Higher Education Academy. http://citeseerx.ist.psu.edu/viewdoc/download?doi=10.1.1.615.9998&rep=rep1&type=pdf.

Hobbs, R. (November 2010). *Digital and Media Literacy: A Plan of Action – A White Paper on the Digital and Media Literacy Recommendations of the Knight Commission on the Information Needs of Communities in a Democracy*. Aspen Institute. www.aspeninstitute.org/wp-content/uploads/2010/11/Digital_and_Media_Literacy.pdf.

Hochschild, A. R. (1979). Emotion work, feeling rules, and social structure. *American Journal of Sociology*, *85*(3), 551–575.

Hochschild, A. R. (1983/2003). *The Managed Heart: Commercialisation of Human Feeling*. University of California Press.

Höckert, E., Rantala, O., García-Rosell, J.-C., and Haanpää, M. (2020). Knowing with nature: The future of tourism education in the Anthropocene. *Journal of Teaching in Travel & Tourism*, *20*(3), 169–172. https://doi.org/10.1080/15313220.2020.1797613.

Holiday, I. (2020, January 12). Grizzly bear death prompts call for changes to Wildlife Act. CTV Vancouver Island. www.vancouverisland.ctvnews.ca/grizzly-bear-death-prompts-call-for-changes-to-wildlife-act-1.4764126.

Hollingsworth, J. (2020). This river in New Zealand is legally a person: Here's how it happened. CNN World. https://edition.cnn.com/2020/12/11/asia/whanganui-river-new-zealand-intl-hnk-dst/index.html.

Honey, M. (2008). *Ecotourism and Sustainable Development: Who Owns Paradise?* (2nd ed.). Island Press.

Humberstone, B., and Stan, I. (2012). Nature and well-being in outdoor learning: Authenticity or performativity. *Journal of Adventure Education and Outdoor Learning*, *12*(3), 183–197. https://doi.org/10.1080/14729679.2012.699803.

Hurst, C. E., Grimwood, B., S.R., Lemelin, R. H., and Stinson, M. J. (2020). Conceptualizing cultural sensitivity in tourism: A systematic literature review. *Tourism Recreation Research*, 1–16. https://doi.org/10.1080/02508281.2020.1816362.

International Union for Conservation of Nature and Natural Resources (1980). *World Conservation Strategy: Living Resource Conservation for Sustainable Development*. IUCN–UNEP–WWF.

Inui, Y., Wheeler, D., and Lankford, S. (2006). Rethinking tourism education: What should schools teach? *Journal of Hospitality, Leisure, Sport & Tourism Education*, 5(2). https://doi.org/10.3794/johlste.52.122.

Jafari, J. (1990). Research and scholarship: the basis of tourism education. *Journal of Tourism Studies*, 1(1), 33–41.

Jamal, T. (2019). *Justice and Ethics in Tourism*. Routledge.

Jamal, T., and Camargo, B. A. (2018). Tourism governance and policy: Whither justice? *Tourism Management Perspectives*, 25, 205–208. https://doi.org/10.1016/j.tmp.2017.11.009.

Jamal, T., Camargo, B. A., and Wilson, E. (2013). Critical omissions and new directions for sustainable tourism: A situated macro–micro approach. *Sustainability*, 5(11), 4594–4613.

Jamal, T., Kircher, J., and Donaldson, J. P. (2021). Re-visiting design thinking for learning and practice: Critical pedagogy, conative empathy. *Sustainability*, 13(2), 964. https://doi.org/10.3390/su13020964.

Jamal, T., Taillon, J., and Dredge, D. (2011). Sustainable tourism pedagogy and academic-community collaboration: A progressive service-learning approach. *Tourism and Hospitality Research*, 11, 133–147. https://doi.org/10.1057/thr.2011.3.

Jasper, M. (2013). *Beginning Reflective Practice* (2nd ed.). Cengage Learning.

Jenks, C. (1993). *Culture*. Routledge.

Jimura, T. (2019). *World Heritage Sites, Tourism, Local Communities and Conservation Activities*. CABI.

Jóhannesson, G. T. (2019). Looking down, staying with and moving along: Towards collaborative ways of knowing with nature in the Anthropocene. *Matkailututkimus – Journal of Finnish Tourism Research*, 15(2), 9–17.

Jóhannesson, G. T., Ren, C., and van der Duim, R. (Eds) (2015). *Tourism Encounters and Controversies: Ontological Politics of Tourism Development*. Ashgate.

Johnson, C. W. (2009). Writing ourselves at risk: Using self-narrative in working for social justice. *Leisure Sciences*, 31(5), 483–489. https://doi.org/10.1080/01490400903199815.

Kahle, L. R. (1983). *Social Values and Social Change: Adaption to Life in America*. Praeger Publishers.

Keefer, J. M. (2009). *The Critical Incident Questionnaire (CIQ): From Research to Practice and Back Again*. Adult Education Research Conference. http://newprairiepress.org/aerc/2009/papers/31.

Keiding, T. B., and Qvortrup, A. (2014, September 3). The didactics of higher education didactics. European Conference on Educational Research (ECER 2014) – The Past, the Present and Future of Educational Research in Europe, Porto.

Ker, G. R. (2017). *Degrees by Independent Learning: A Case Study of Practice at Otago Polytechnic, Dunedin, New Zealand*. Middlesex University Research Depository. https://eprints.mdx.ac.uk/id/eprint/22862.

Kershner, I. (2021, February 18). As Israel reopens, "Whoever does not get vaccinated will be left behind". *New York Times*. www.nytimes.com/2021/02/18/world/middleeast/israel-covid-vaccine-reopen.html?smid=url-share.

Kerstenetzky, C., and Punzo, L. F. (2008, June). *Sustainable Tourism: Basic Income for Poor Communities*. 12th BIEN (Basic Income Earth Network) Congress University College, Dublin, Ireland. http://citeseerx.ist.psu.edu/viewdoc/download?doi=10.1.1.549.3844&rep=rep1&type=pdf.

Khaira, H. G., and Yambo, D. (2005, June). The practicality of authentic assessment. First International Conference on Enhancing Teaching and Learning Through Assessment, Hong Kong Polytechnic University.

Kidder, R. M. (2009). *How Good People Make Tough Choices: Resolving the Dilemmas of Ethical Living*. Harper.

Killion, L., and Fisher, R. (2018). Ontology, epistemology: Paradigms and parameters for qualitative approaches in tourism research. In W. Hillman and K. Radel (Eds), *Qualitative Methods in Tourism Research: Theory and Practice* (pp. 1–28). Channel View Publications.

Kiwanuka, N. (2019, June 7). Irshad Manji: Rethinking life on the left. TVO. www.tvo.org/video/irshad-manji-rethinking-life-on-the-left.

Koch, A. J., D'Mello, S. D., and Sackett, P. R. (2015). A meta-analysis of gender stereotypes and bias in experimental simulations of employment decision making. *Journal of Applied Psychology*, 100(1), 128–161. https://doi.org/10.1037/a0036734.

Koch, T. (1998). Story telling: Is it really research? *Journal of Advanced Nursing, 28*(6), 1182–1190. https://doi.org/10.1046/j.1365-2648.1998.00853.x.

Kolb, A. Y., and Kolb, D. A. (2009). Experiential Learning Theory: A dynamic, holistic approach to management learning, education and development. In S. Armstrong and C. Fukami (Eds), *The SAGE Handbook of Management Learning, Education and Development* (pp. 42–68). SAGE.

Krathwohl, D. R., Bloom, B. S., and Masia, B. B. (1964). *Taxonomy of Educational Objectives: The Classification of Educational Goals, Handbook II: Affective Domain.* David McKay Company.

Kubota, R. (2020, October). Confronting eistemological racism, decolonizing scholarly knowledge: Race and gender in applied linguistics. *Applied Linguistics, 41*(5), 712–732. https://doi.org/10.1093/applin/amz033.

Kugapi, O. R., Huhmarniemi, M., and Laivamaa, L. (2020). A potential treasure for tourism: Crafts as employment and a cultural experience service in the Nordic North. In A. Walmsley, K. Åberg, P. Blinnikka and G. T. Jóhannesson (Eds), *Tourism Employment in Nordic Countries: Trends, Practices, and Opportunities* (pp. 77–99). Palgrave Macmillan. https://doi.org/10.1007/978-3-030-47813-1 030-47813-1.

Kuokkanen, R. (2007). *Reshaping the University: Responsibility, Indigenous Epistemes, and the Logic of the Gift.* UBC Press.

Landrum, R. E., Brakke, K., and McCarthy, M. A. (2019). The pedagogical power of storytelling. *Scholarship of Teaching and Learning in Psychology, 5*(3), 247–253. https://doi.org/10.1037/stl0000152.

Lange, E., and Young, S. (2019). Gender-based violence as difficult knowledge: Pedagogies for rebalancing the masculine and the feminine. *International Journal of Lifelong Education, 38*(3), 301–326. https://doi.org/10.1080/02601370.2019.1597932.

Lashley, C. (2018). Education for Hospitality Management. In J. Oskam, D. M. Dekker and K. Wiegerink (Eds), *Innovation in Hospitality Education: Anticipating the Educational Needs of a Changing Profession.* Springer Nature. https://doi.org/10.1007/978-3-319-61379-6.

Lawson, T. (2019). *The Nature of Social Reality: Issues in Social Ontology.* Routledge.

Lea, S. J., Stephenson, D., and Troy, J. (2003). Higher education students' attitudes to student-centred learning: Beyond educational bulimia? *Studies in Higher Education, 28*(3), 321–334. https://doi.org/10.1080/03075070309293.

Lee, J. J., and Ok, C. (2012). Reducing burnout and enhancing job satisfaction: Critical role of hotel employees' emotional intelligence and emotional labor. *International Journal of Hospitality Management, 31*(4), 1101–1112. https://doi.org/10.1016/j.ijhm.2012.01.007.

Lee, L., and Madera, J. M. (2019). A systematic literature review of emotional labor research from the hospitality and tourism literature. *International Journal of Contemporary Hospitality Management, 31*(7), 2808–2826. https://doi.org/10.1108/IJCHM-05-2018-0395.

Leiper, N. (2004). *Tourism Management* (3rd ed.). Pearson Education.

Leonard, K., and Yorton, T. (2015). *Yes, and: How Improvisation Reverses "No, but" Thinking and Improves Creativity and Collaboration.* Harper Business.

Lew, A. A. (2018). Why travel? Travel, tourism, and global consciousness. *Tourism Geographies, 20*(4), 742–749.

Liburd, J. J., Mihalič, T., and Guia, J. (2018). Values in tourism higher education: The European master in tourism management. *Journal of Hospitality, Leisure, Sport & Tourism Education, 22*, 100–104.

Lin, P. M. C., Kim, Y., Qiu, H., and Ren, L. (2017). Experiential learning in hospitality education through a service-learning project. *Journal of Hospitality & Tourism Education, 29*(2), 71–81.

Lindholm, J. A., and Astin, H. S. (2008). Spirituality and pedagogy: Faculty's spirituality and use of student-centered approaches to undergraduate teaching. *Review of Higher Education, 31*(2), 185–207. https://doi.org/10.1353/rhe.2007.0077.

Liobikienė, G., and Juknys, R. (2016). The role of values, environmental risk perception, awareness of consequences, and willingness to assume responsibility for environmentally-friendly behaviour: The Lithuanian case. *Journal of Cleaner Production, 112*(4), 3413–3422. https://doi.org/10.1016/j.jclepro.2015.10.049.

Löfgren, O. (2002). *On Holiday: A History of Vacationing.* University of California Press.

Longart, P., Wickens, E., Ocaña, W., and Llugsha, V. (2017). A stakeholder analysis of a service learning project for tourism development in an Ecuadorian rural community. *Journal of Hospitality, Leisure, Sport & Tourism Education, 20*, 87–100. https://doi.org/10.1016/j.jhlste.2017.04.002.

Macbeth, J. (2005). Towards an ethics platform of tourism. *Annals of Tourism Research, 32*(4), 962–984.

Mak, B., Lau, C., and Wong, A. (2017). Effects of experiential learning on students: An ecotourism service-learning course. *Journal of Teaching in Travel & Tourism, 17*(2), 85–100. https://doi.org/10.1080/15313220.2017.1285265.

Mäkinen, M., Rantala, O., and Tervo-Kankare, K. (2018). Väylänvarrella – Tieteidenvälisen dialogin soveltamisesta luontomatkailukohteiden suunnitteluun [Applying interdisciplinary dialogy in designing of nature-based tourism destination]. *Matkailututkimus – Journal of Finnish Tourism Research, 14*(1), 26–41.

Mazzei, P. (2021, February 18). Questions grow in Florida about vaccine favoritism for the wealthy. *New York Times*. www.nytimes.com/live/2021/02/18/world/covid-19-coronavirus/questions-grow-in-florida-about-vaccine-favoritism-for-the-wealthy.

Mazzucato, M. (2019, July). *What Is Economic Value, and Who Creates It?* [Video file]. TED. www.ted.com/talks/mariana_mazzucato_what_is_economic_value_and_who_creates_it.

McArthur, J., and Huxham, M. (2013). Feedback unbound: From master to usher. In S. Merry, M. Price, D. Carless and M. Taras (Eds), *Reconceptualising Feedback in Higher Education: Developing Dialogue with Students* (pp. 92–102). Routledge.

McDonald, H. P. (2004). *Radical Axiology: A First Philosophy of Values*. Rodopi.

McGehee, N. G. (2012). Oppression, emancipation, and volunteer tourism. *Annals of Tourism Research, 39*(1), 84–107.

McHarg, I. L. (1992). *Design with Nature*. John Wiley & Sons.

McKeachie, W. J., and Svinicki, M. (2013). *McKeachie's Teaching Tips: Strategies, Research, and Theory for College University Teachers*. Cengage Learning.

McMullin, B., Price, P., Jones, M. B., and McGeever, A. H. (2020). Assessing negative carbon dioxide emissions from the perspective of a national "fair share" of the remaining global carbon budget. *Mitigation and Adaptation Strategies for Global Change, 25*, 579–602. https://doi.org/10.1007/s11027-019-09881-6.

McMurtry, J. (2009–10). The Primary Axiom and the Life-Value Compass. In J. McMurty (Ed.), *Encyclopedia Life Support Systems (EOLSS)* (pp. 212–256), (Vol. 1). Developed under the Auspices of the UNESCO, EOLSS Publishers. www.eolss.net.

McMurtry, J. (2013). *The Cancer Stage of Capitalism: From Crisis to Cure* (2nd ed.). Pluto Press.

Merton, R. K., and Storer, N. W. (1973). *The Sociology of Science: Theoretical and Empirical Investigations*. University of Chicago Press.

Metcalfe, A., and Game, A. (2006). The teacher's enthusiasm. *Australian Educational Researcher, 33*(3), 91–106.

Meyer, E. (2014, August 14). What's your cultural profile? *Harvard Business Review*. https://hbr.org/web/assessment/2014/08/whats-your-cultural-profile.

Mihalič, T., Liburd, J. J., and Guia, J. (2015). Values in tourism. In P. J. Sheldon and C. H. C. Hsu (Eds), *Global Issues and Trends* (pp. 41–59). Emerald Group.

Miike, Y. (2019). Intercultural communication ethics: An Asiacentric perspective. *Journal of International Communication, 25*(2), 159–192. https://doi.org/10.1080/13216597.2019.1609542.

Miller, J. P. (2019). *The Holistic Curriculum* (3rd ed.). University of Toronto Press.

Minett-Smith, C., and Davis, C. L. (2020). Widening the discourse on team-teaching in higher education. *Teaching in Higher Education, 25*(5), 579–594.

Miyazaki, K. (2011). Encountering another dialogic pedagogy. *Journal of Russian & East European Psychology, 49*(2), 36–43. https://doi.org/10.2753/RPO1061-0405490205.

Moore, G. E. (1903). *Principia Ethica*. Cambridge University Press.

Morales, C. (2021, February 18). Black and Latino Americans confront many challenges to vaccinations. *New York Times*. www.nytimes.com/2021/02/18/world/us-coronavirus-vaccine-minorities.html.

Morgan, N. J., and Pritchard, A. (1998). *Tourism Promotion and Power: Creating Images, Creating Identities*. John Wiley & Sons.

Moscardo, G., and Murphy, L. (2011). Towards values education in tourism: The challenge of measuring the values. *Journal of Teaching in Travel & Tourism, 11*(1), 76–93. https://doi.org/10.1080/15313220.2011.548736.

Mottiar, Z., Boluk, K. A., and Kline, C. (2018). The roles of social entrepreneurs in rural destination development. *Annals of Tourism Research, 68*, 77–88.

Müller, D. K., Carson, D. A., de la Barre, S., Granås, B., Jóhannesson, G. T., Øyen, G., Rantala, O., Saarinen, J., Salmela, T., Tervo-Kankare, K., and Welling, J. (2020). *Arctic Tourism in Times of Change: Dimensions of Urban Tourism*. Nordic Council of Ministers, Nordic Council of Ministers Secretariat. http://norden.diva-portal.org/smash/record.jsf?pid=diva2%3A1471328&dswid=-2759.

Mumford, M. D., Connelly, M. S., Helton, W. B., Van Doorn, J. R., and Osburn, H. K. (2002). Alternative approaches for measuring values: Direct and indirect assessments in performance prediction. *Journal of Vocational Behavior, 61*(2), 348–373. https://doi.org/10.1006/jvbe.2001.1860.

Musikanski, L., Rogers, P., Smith, S., Koldowski, J., and Iriarte, L. (2019). Planet happiness: A proposition to address overtourism and guide responsible tourism, happiness, well-being and sustainability in world heritage sites and beyond. *International Journal of Community Well-being, 2*(3–4), 359–371.

Niemiec, R. M. (2017). *Character Strengths Interventions: A Field Guide for Practitioners*. Hogrefe Publishing.

NobelPrize.org. (2021). Alfred Nobel's will. Nobel Media AB. www.nobelprize.org/alfred-nobel/alfred-nobels-will/.

Nunn, P. D. (2018, October 18). The oldest true stories in the world. *Anthropology Magazine – Sapiens*. www.sapiens.org/language/oral-tradition/.

O'Boyle, T. (2020). 5 reasons why diversity is important in the 21st century. AMP Global Youth. https://ampglobalyouth.org/2020/06/20/5-reasons-diversity-important-21st-century/.

O'Sullivan, E. V., Morrell, A., and O'Connor, M. A. (Eds) (2002). *Expanding the Boundaries of Transformative Learning: Essays on Theory and Practice*. Palgrave Macmillan.

Olsen, K. O., Abildgaard, M. S., Brattland, C., Chimirri, D., de Bernardi, C., Edmonds, J., Grimwood, B., S.R., Hurst, C. E., Höckert, E., Jaeger, K., Kugapi, O. R., Lemelin, H., Lüthje, M., Mazzullo, N., Müller, D. K., Ren, C., Saari, R., Ugwuegbula, L., and Viken, A. (2019). *Looking at Arctic Tourism through the Lens of Cultural Sensitivity: ARCTISEN – A Transnational Baseline Report*. Multidimensional Tourism Institute. https://lauda.ulapland.fi/handle/10024/64069.

Ostrom, E. (1990). *Governing the Commons: The Evolution of Institutions for Collective Action*. Cambridge University Press.

Oyler, D. R., and Romanelli, F. (2014). The fact of ignorance: Revisiting the Socratic method as a tool for teaching critical thinking. *American Journal of Pharmaceutical Education, 78*(7), 1–9. https://doi.org/10.5688/ajpe787144.

Paavola, S., Lipponen, L., and Hakkarainen, K. (2004). Models of innovative knowledge communities and three metaphors of learning. *Review of Educational Research, 74*(4), 557–576.

Padurean, L., and Maggi, R. (2011). TEFI values in tourism education: A comparative analysis. *Journal of Teaching in Travel & Tourism, 11*(1), 24–37. https://doi.org/10.1080/15313220.2011.548729.

Palmer, C. A. (2018). *Being and Dwelling through Tourism: An Anthropological Perspective*. Routledge.

Palmer, P. J. (1998). *The Courage to Teach: Exploring the Inner Landscape of a Teacher's Life*. Jossey-Bass.

Palmer, P. J. (2007). *The Courage to Teach: Exploring the Inner Landscape of a Teacher's Life* (10th anniversary ed.). Jossey-Bass.

Palmer, P. J., Zajonc, A., and Scribner, M. (2010). *The Heart of Higher Education: A Call to Renewal – Transforming the Academy Through Collegial Conversations*. Jossey-Bass.

Paul, R., and Elder, L. (2006). *The Thinkers Guide to the Art of Socratic Questioning*. Foundation for Critical Thinking Press.

Paul, R., and Elder, L. (2008). *The Miniature Guide to Critical Thinking Concepts and Tools*. Foundation for Critical Thinking Press. www.criticalthinking.org/pages/defining-critical-thinking/766.

Paul, R. W., and Binker, A. J. A. (1990). *Critical Thinking: What Every Person Needs to Survive in a Rapidly Changing World*. Center for Critical Thinking and Moral Critique.

Pernecky, T. (2010). The being of tourism. *Journal of Tourism and Peace Research, 1*(1), 1–15.

Peterson, R. E. (2009). Teaching how to read the world and change it: Critical pedagogy in the intermediate grades. In A. Darder, M. Baltodano and R. Torres (Eds), *The Critical Pedagogy Reader* (pp. 305–324). Routledge.

Phan, L.-H. (2017). *Transnational Education Crossing "Asia" and "the West": Adjusted Desire, Transformative Mediocrity and Neo-colonial Disguise.* Routledge.

Pherson, K. H., and Pherson, R. H. (2020). *Critical Thinking for Strategic Intelligence* (3rd ed.). SAGE.

Pietschnig, J., and Voracek, M. (2015). One century of global IQ gains: A formal meta-analysis of the Flynn effect (1909–2013). *Perspectives on Psychological Science, 10*(3), 282–306. https://doi.org/10.1177/1745691615577701.

Pine, B. J. I., and Gilmore, J. H. (1999). *The Experience Economy.* Harvard Business School Press.

Pink, S. (2015). *Doing Sensory Ethnography* (2nd ed.). SAGE.

Pohls, M. (2016). *Viini, laulu ja taustajoukot.* Inokustannus.

Pritchard, A., Morgan, N., and Ateljevic, I. (2011). Hopeful tourism: A new transformative perspective. *Annals of Tourism Research, 38*(3), 941–963.

Project Implicit (n.d.). Implicit Association Test. Harvard University. https://implicit.harvard.edu/implicit/.

Raber, C. (2015). Design-based learning. Teaching With Design. www.teachwithdesign.com/dbl.

Rakic, T., and Chambers, D. P. (Eds) (2012). *An Introduction to Visual Research Methods in Tourism.* Routledge.

Ransfield, A. K., and Reichenberger, I. (2021). Māori Indigenous values and tourism business sustainability. *AlterNative: An International Journal of Indigenous Peoples.* https://doi.org/10.1177/11771801211994680.

Rantala, O., de la Barre, S., Granås, B., Jóhannesson, G. T., Müller, D. K., Saarinen, J., Tervo-Kankare, K., Maher, P. T., and Niskala, M. (2019). *Arctic Tourism in Times of Change: Seasonality.* Nordic Council of Ministers, Nordic Council of Ministers Secretariat. http://norden.diva-portal.org/smash/record.jsf?pid=diva2%3A1312957&dswid=7020.

Rasmussen, M., Guo, X., Wang, Y., Lohmueller, K. E., Rasmussen, S., Albrechtsen, A., and Willerslev, E. (2011). An Aboriginal Australian genome reveals separate human dispersals into Asia. *Science, 334*(6052), 94–98.

Rawls, J. (1971). *A Theory of Justice.* Harvard University Press.

Raworth, K. (2018, April). *A Healthy Economy Should Be Designed to Thrive, Not Grow.* TED Conferences. www.ted.com/talks/kate_raworth_a_healthy_economy_should_be_designed_to_thrive_not_grow/transcript.

Reeve, J. (2012). A self-determination theory perspective on student engagement. In S. L. Christenson, A. L. Reschly and C. Wylie (Eds), *Handbook of Research on Student Engagement* (pp. 149–172). Springer.

Regional Council of Lapland (2017). Tourism in Lapland. www.lappi.fi/lapinliitto/lapin-matkailu.

Reigeluth, C. M., and Keller, J. B. (2009). Understanding instruction. In C. M. Reigeluth and A. A. Carr-Chelman (Eds), *Instructional-Design Theories and Models, Vol. 3: Building a Common Knowledge Base* (pp. 27–39). Routledge.

Ren, C., Krogh Petersen, M., and Dredge, D. (2015). Guest editorial: Valuing tourism. *Valuation Studies, 3*(2), 85–96. https://doi.org/10.3384/VS.2001-5992.153285.

Ren, L., and Qiu, H. (2019). Developing a measurement scale for cultural values and norms of Chinese mass travellers. *Journal of Hospitality and Tourism Management, 38*, 168–175. https://doi.org/10.1016/j.jhtm.2018.04.006.

Rhodes, T. (2010). *Assessing Outcomes and Improving Achievement: Tips and Tools for Using Rubrics.* Association of American Colleges and Universities.

Richards, G. (2012). *Tourism, Creativity and Creative Industries.* Creativity and Creative Industries in Challenging Times Conference, NHTV University of Applied Sciences, Breda, NL.

Richards, G., and Wilson, J. (2006). Developing creativity in tourist experiences: A solution to the serial reproduction of culture? *Tourism Management, 27*(6), 1209–1223. https://doi.org/10.1016/j.tourman.2005.06.002.

Richardson, H. S. (1994). *Practical Reasoning about Final Ends.* Cambridge University Press.

Rodenburg, K. S. (2020). So much to learn, so many students, so little time. *Transformative Dialogues: Teaching and Learning Journal*, 13(1). https://journals.kpu.ca/index.php/td/article/view/363.

Rogers, C. R. (1961/2016). *On Becoming a Person*. Robinson.

Rokeach, M. (1979). *Understanding Human Values: Individual and Societal*. Free Press.

Rosenberg, M. (2015). *Nonviolent Communication: A Language of Life* (3rd ed.). Puddle Dancer Press.

Ruggeri, A. (2017). People have always whinged about young adults. Here's proof. *BBC Worklife*, October 3. www.bbc.com/worklife/article/20171003-proof-that-people-have-always-complained-about-young-adults.

Saari, R., Höckert, E., Lüthje, M., Kugapi, O. R., and Mazzullo, N. (2020). Cultural sensitivity in Sámi tourism: A systematic literature review in the Finnish context. *Finnish Journal of Tourism Research*, 16(1), 93–110. https://doi.org/10.33351/mt.88061.

Sacks, A. (2021). *Planning for the Recovery* [Video file]. Oxford Economics. www.youtube.com/watch?v=7puvzNyj5XE&feature=youtu.be.

Salmón, E. (2000). Kincentric ecology: Indigenous perceptions of the human–nature relationship. *Ecological Applications*, 10(5), 1327–1332.

Sapiro, G. (2015). Habitus: History of a concept. In J. D. Wright (Ed.), *International Encyclopedia of the Social & Behavioral Sciences* (2nd ed., Vol. 10, pp. 484–489). Elsevier.

Sarantou, M., Kugapi, O. R., and Huhmarniemi, M. (2021). Context mapping for creative tourism. *Annals of Tourism Research*, 86, 103064. https://doi.org/10.1016/j.annals.2020.103064.

Satterthwaite, D. (2011). How urban societies can adapt to resource shortage and climate change [Review]. *Philosophical Transactions of the Royal Society A*, 369, 1762–1783. https://doi.org/10.1098/rsta.2010.0350.

Scholz, U., Doña, B. G., Sud, S., and Schwarzer, R. (2002). Is general self-efficacy a universal construct? *European Journal of Psychological Assessment*, 18(3), 242–251.

Schumann, K., Zaki, J., and Dweck, C. S. (2014). Addressing the empathy deficit: Beliefs about the malleability of empathy predict effortful responses when empathy is challenging. *Journal of Personality and Social Psychology*, 107(3), 475–493. https://doi.org/10.1037/a0036738.

Schwartz, S. H. (1992). Universals in the content and structure of values: Theoretical advances and empirical tests in 20 countries. *Advances in Experimental Social Psychology*, 25, 1–65. https://doi.org/10.1016/S0065-2601(08)60281-6.

Schwartz, S. H., Melech, G., Lehmann, A., Burgess, S., Harris, M., and Owens, V. (2001). Extending the cross-cultural validity of the theory of basic human values with a different method of measurement. *Journal of Cross-cultural Psychology*, 32(5), 519–542. https://doi.org/10.1177/0022022101032005001.

Schwarzin, L. (2013). To act as though the future mattered. In I. Ateljevic, N. Morgan and A. Pritchard (Eds), *The Critical Turn in Tourism Studies: Creating an Academy of Hope* (pp. 135–148). Routledge.

Sfard, A. (1998). On two metaphors for learning and the dangers of choosing just one. *Educational Researcher*, 27(2), 4–13. https://doi.org/10.3102/0013189X027002004.

Shapiro, S. L., Brown, K. W., and Astin, J. A. (2011). Toward the integration of meditation into higher education: A review of research evidence. *Teachers College Record*, 113(3), 493–528.

Sheldon, P. J. (2020). Designing tourism experiences for inner transformation. *Annals of Tourism Research*, 83, 102935. https://doi.org/10.1016/j.annals.2020.102935.

Sheldon, P. J., and Daniele, R. (2017). *Social Entrepreneurship and Tourism*. Springer International.

Sheldon, P. J., Fesenmaier, D. R., and Tribe, J. (2011). The Tourism Education Futures Initiative (TEFI): Activating change in tourism education. *Journal of Teaching in Travel & Tourism*, 11(1), 2–23. https://doi.org/10.1080/15313220.2011.548728.

Shoyama, K., and Yamagata, Y. (2016). Local perception of ecosystem service bundles in the Kushiro watershed, Northern Japan: Application of a public participation GIS tool. *Ecosystem Services*, 22(A), 139–149. https://doi.org/10.1016/j.ecoser.2016.10.009.

Sigmar, L. S., Hynes, G. E., and Hill, K. L. (2012). Strategies for teaching social and emotional intelligence in business communication. *Business Communication Quarterly*, 75(3), 301–317.

Sigmon, R. L. (1994). *Serving to Learn, Learning to Serve: Linking Service with Learning*. Council for Independent Colleges.

Simmons, B. A. (2004). Saying the same old things: A contemporary travel discourse and the popular magazine text. In C. M. Hall and H. Tucker (Eds), *Tourism and Postcolonialism: Contested Discourses, Identities and Representations* (pp. 43–56). Routledge.

Simoska, M. (2017, 1 September). Kiistelty liikemies kaavailee Utsjoelle isoa investointia – paikalliset yrittäjät epäileväisiä: "Aivan järkyttävä tieto". *Ilta Sanomat.* www.iltalehti.fi/talous/201708312200364160_ta.shtml.

Sims, T., Koopmann-Holm, B., Young, H. R., Jiang, D., Fung, H., and Tsai, J. L. (2018). Asian Americans respond less favorably to excitement (vs. calm)-focused physicians compared to European Americans. *Cultural Diversity and Ethnic Minority Psychology, 24*(1), 1–14. https://doi.org/https://doi.org/10.1037/cdp0000171.

Skinner, G., and Clemence, M. (2019). *Global Trust in Professions: Who Do Global Citizens Trust?* www.ipsos.com/sites/default/files/ct/news/documents/2019-09/global-trust-in-professions-trust-worthiness-index-2019.pdf.

Smith, L., and Akagawa, N. (2009). *Intangible Heritage.* Routledge.

Smith, M., MacLeod, N. E., and Hart Robertson, M. (2010). *Key Concepts in Tourist Studies.* SAGE. https://doi.org/10.4135/9781446251027.

Spivak, G. C. (1988). Can the subaltern speak? In C. Nelson and L. Grossberg (Eds), *Marxism and the Interpretation of Culture* (pp. 271–313). University of Illinois.

Stern, N. (2009). *A Blueprint for a Safer Planet.* Bodley Head.

Steup, M., and Ram, N. (2020). Epistemology. In E. N. Zalta (Ed.), *The Stanford Encyclopedia of Philosophy.* https://plato.stanford.edu/archives/fall2020/entries/epistemology/.

Stoner, G., and Milner, M. (2008). Embedding generic employability skills in an accounting degree: Development and impediments. *Accounting Education, 19*(1–2), 123–138. https://doi.org/10.1080/09639280902888229.

Strømsø, H. I. (2016). Forskningsbasert undervisning. In H. I. Strømsø, K. H. Lycke and P. Lauvås (Eds), *Når læring er det viktigste: Undervisning i høyere utdanning* (pp. 40–53). Cappelen Akademisk forla.

Sung, Y. K., and Sakoi, J. (2017). Stories of the Ainu: The oldest Indigenous people in Japanese children's literature. *Bookbird: A Journal of International Children's Literature, 55*(1), 4–13. https://doi.org/10.1353/bkb.2017.0001.

Suopajärvi, L. (2001). *Vuotos- ja Ounasjoki-kamppailujen kentät ja merkitykset Lapissa.* University of Lapland, Rovaniemi. http://urn.fi/URN:NBN:fi:ula-20111131020.

Susskind, D. (2020). *A World Without Work: Technology, Automation and How We Should Respond.* Penguin.

TEFI (Tourism Education Futures Initiative) (2010). *TEFI White Paper: A Values-based Framework for Tourism Education: Building the Capacity to Lead.* http://tourismeducationfutures.org/tefi-values/.

Tollefson, J. (2018). IPCC says limiting global warming to 1.5°C will require drastic action. *Nature, 562,* 172–173. https://doi.org/10.1038/d41586-018-06876-2.

Topham, G. (2019, October 17). "Flight-shaming" could slow growth of airline industry, says Iata. *The Guardian.* www.theguardian.com/business/2019/oct/17/flight-shaming-could-slow-growth-of-airline-industry-says-iata.

Trahan, L. H., Stuebing, K. K., Fletcher, J. M., and Hiscock, M. (2014). The Flynn effect: A meta-analysis. *Psychological Bulletin, 140*(5), 1332–1360. https://doi.org/10.1037/a0037173.

Trevino, L. K., and Brown, M. E. (2004). Managing to be ethical: Debunking five business ethic myths. *Academy of Management Perspectives, 18*(2), 69–81. https://doi.org/10.5465/ame.2004.13837400.

Tribe, J., and Liburd, J. J. (2016). The tourism knowledge system. *Annals of Tourism Research, 57*(2), 44–61. https://doi.org/10.1016/j.annals.2015.11.011.

Trowler, P., and Cooper, A. (2002). Teaching and learning regimes: Implicit theories and recurrent practices in the enhancement of teaching and learning through educational development programmes. *Higher Education Research & Development, 21*(3), 221–240.

Tsaur, S.-H., and Tang, W.-H. (2013). The burden of esthetic labor on front-line employees in hospitality industry. *International Journal of Hospitality Management, 35*(12), 19–27.

Tschimmel, K. (2012, June 17–20). *Design Thinking as an Effective Toolkit for Innovation.* Proceedings of the XXIII ISPIM Conference, Action for Innovation: Innovating from Experience, Barcelona, Spain.

Tucker, H. (2018). *Destination Dynamics: On the Unintended, Unexpected and Indeterminate*. ATLAS Reflections 2018. http://web.natur.cuni.cz/ksgrrsek/geovoc/wp-content/uploads/2018/10/ATLAS-Reflections-2018.pdf.

Türkkahraman, M. (2014). Social values and value education. *Procedia – Social and Behavioral Sciences*, *116*, 633–638. https://doi.org/10.1016/j.sbspro.2014.01.270.

Twohey, M., Collins, K., and Thomas, K. (2020, December 20). Rich countries have first dibs on vaccines, while poor nations struggle to get enough. *New York Times*. www.nytimes.com/2020/12/15/world/rich-countries-have-first-dibs-on-vaccines-while-poor-nations-struggle-to-get-enough.html?smid=em-share.

Ulmer, J. B. (2017). Posthumanism as research methodology: Inquiry in the Anthropocene. *International Journal of Qualitative Studies in Education*, *30*(9), 832–848. https://doi.org/10.1080/09518398.2017.1336806.

UNESCO (2003). *Convention for the Safeguarding of the Intangible Cultural Heritage*. https://ich.unesco.org/doc/src/15164-EN.pdf.

UNWTO (United Nations World Tourism Organization) (2020). All countries: Domestic tourism – trips 1995–2019. Tourism Statistics, Issue 2.

UNWTO (United Nations World Tourism Organization) (2021). Tourist arrivals down 87% in January 2021 as UNWTO calls for stronger coordination to restart tourism. www.unwto.org/taxonomy/term/347.

Vande-Berg, M. (2014). *Identity: My Culturally Diverse Heritage*. Cultural awareness workshop, Purdue University.

Vella, J. (2000). A spirited epistemology: Honoring the adult learner as subject. *New Directions for Adult and Continuing Education*, *85*, 7–16. https://doi.org/https://doi.org/10.1002/ace.8501.

Viken, A., Höckert, E., and Grimwood, B., S.R. (2021). Cultural sensitivity: Engaging difference in tourism. *Annals of Tourism Research*, *89*, 103223.

Villarroel, V., Bloxham, S., Bruna, D., Bruna, C., and Herrera-Seda, C. (2018). Authentic assessment: Creating a blueprint for course design. *Assessment & Evaluation in Higher Education*, *43*(5), 840–854.

Wackernagel, M., and Beyers, B. (2019). *Ecological Footprint: Managing Our Biocapacity Budget*. New Society Publishers.

WCED (World Commission on Environment and Development) (1987). *Our Common Future: Report of the World Commission on Environment and Development*. United Nations. https://sustainabledevelopment.un.org/content/documents/5987our-common-future.pdf.

Weaver, G. R., and Agle, B. R. (2002). Religiosity and ethical behavior in organizations: A symbolic interactionist perspective. *Academy of Management Review*, *27*(1), 77–97. https://doi.org/10.5465/amr.2002.5922390.

Weeden, C. (2011). Responsible tourist motivation: How valuable is the Schwartz value survey? *Journal of Ecotourism*, *10*(3), 214–234. https://doi.org/10.1080/14724049.2011.617448.

Weimer, M. (2002). *Learner-centered Teaching: Five Key Changes to Practice*. Jossey-Bass.

Wenger, E. (1998). *Communities of Practice: Learning, Meaning and Identity*. Cambridge University Press.

Wiedmann, T., and Minx, J. (2008). A definition of "carbon footprint". In C. C. Pertsova (Ed.), *Ecological Economics Research Trends* (pp. 1–11). Nova Science Publishers.

Wikan, U. (1992). Beyond the words: The power of resonance. *American Ethnologist*, *19*(3), 460–482. https://doi.org/10.1525/ae.1992.19.3.02a00030.

Wilber, K. (2000). *A Theory of Everything*. Shambhala.

Williams, N. L., Wassler, P., and Ferdinand, N. (2020). Tourism and the COVID (mis)infodemic. *Journal of Travel Research*. Online first. https://doi.org/10.1177/0047287520981135.

Worrell, R., and Appleby, M. C. (2000). Stewardship of natural resources: Definition, ethical and practical aspects. *Journal of Agricultural and Environmental Ethics*, *12*(3), 263–277.

WTTC (World Travel & Tourism Council) (2020). Economic impact reports. https://wttc.org/Research/Economic-Impact.

WTTC (World Travel & Tourism Council) (2021). Travel Demand Recovery Dashboard. https://wttc.org/Research/Recovery-Dashboard.

Wyatt, W. (2016). The ethics of trigger warnings. *Teaching Ethics*, *16*(1), 17–35. https://doi.org/10. 5840/tej201632427.

Young, D. A., and Olutoye, O. A. (2015). *Handbook of Critical Incidents and Essential Topics in Pediatric Anesthesiology*. University Printing House.

Zhang, J. (2015). Landscape, tourism. In J. Jafari and H. Xiao (Eds), *Springer Encyclopedia of Tourism*. Springer. https://doi.org/10.1007/978-3-319-01669-6_119-1.

Ziegert, J. C., and Hanges, P. J. (2005). Employment discrimination: The role of implicit attitudes, motivation, and a climate for racial bias. *Journal of Applied Psychology*, *90*(3), 553–562.

Index

Printed and bound by CPI Group (UK) Ltd, Croydon, CR0 4YY

16/04/2025

14658495-0001